DEVELOPING AND MANAGING EXPERT SYSTEMS
Proven Techniques for Business and Industry

DAVID S. PRERAU

ADDISON-WESLEY PUBLISHING COMPANY

Reading, Massachusetts ■ Menlo Park, California ■ New York
Don Mills, Ontario ■ Wokingham, England ■ Amsterdam ■ Bonn
Sydney ■ Singapore ■ Tokyo ■ Madrid ■ San Juan

Many of the designations used by manufacturers and sellers to distinguish their products are claimed as trademarks. The publisher has made every attempt to supply trademark information about manufacturers and their products mentioned in this book.

Library of Congress Cataloging-in-Publication Data

Prerau, David S.
  Developing and managing expert systems : proven techniques for
business and industry / by David S. Prerau.
      p.   cm.
  Includes index.
  ISBN 0–201–13659–7
  1. Expert systems (Computer science)   I. Title.
QA76.76.E95P74   1990
006.3'3—dc20   89–6801
                                                                                    CIP

ABCDEFGHIJ-MA-89

This book presents proven, practical techniques for developing and managing expert systems in business and industry, based on extensive real-world experience.

Expert systems are advanced computer programs that can perform difficult tasks—at a high level of competence—by embodying the knowledge and experience of expert practitioners of the tasks. These programs are coming into widespread commercial use, and as this happens, there is a need for practical information related to their development. My primary purpose in writing this book is to provide some of that practical information based on my broad experience developing expert systems in industry. Therefore this book has a different focus (and, as shall be mentioned, a different organization) from most other books on expert systems.

The book provides a practical step-by-step approach to developing and managing expert systems in the business world. For each step, proven techniques are described and pragmatic advice offered for dealing with the technical and (often overlooked but very important) nontechnical problems that must be faced. These techniques are based on my knowledge and experience in developing expert systems—among which is my experience at GTE Laboratories leading the development of one of the largest industrial expert systems, GTE's *COMPASS*.

This book is organized in a unique manner, interweaving general information with concrete examples yet keeping them distinct. Every section of each chapter of the book (other than introductory material) consists of two parts. The first of these parts presents a complete, detailed discussion of the approach, techniques, and recommendations related to a step in expert system development. When appropriate, generic examples are used to illustrate points. The information in this part generally can be applied to any expert system development project, large or small, and for any application area. This is the information that readers can use—and, I hope, will use—to develop their own expert systems.

The second part of each section appears in a different, slightly smaller type style. It describes how the subject matter of the section was applied by the *COMPASS* project. My objective in recounting the pertinent real-world experiences we encountered in the development of *COMPASS* is fourfold. First, the *COMPASS* experience provides an example of the use of the technique examined in the first part of the section. This should contribute to a better understanding of the points and suggestions made, and thus should be beneficial even for those with no particular interest in *COMPASS* itself. Second, the description of the successful use of a technique or approach should give it added credibility. Third, the discussion of any problems we encountered in *COMPASS* related to the technique or approach might alert the reader to be wary and thus might help in avoiding similar problems. And fourth, for those who might be interested in some of the details of an industrial expert system development project, these parts of the book, taken as a whole, provide a great deal of in-depth, inside information of the development of *COMPASS*, often at a level of detail never before appearing in print about any expert system project.

This novel format should allow readers maximum flexibility in using the book in the way that would be most beneficial for their own particular purposes.

In addition to the section format, there is another feature in the book's organization that I hope will prove useful: At the end of each chapter, I have provided a detailed checklist, highlighting the major points of the chapter. The set of checklists taken together cover all of the steps in expert system development. I have found such checklists to be very useful during my work on *COMPASS* and other expert systems, and I hope they will prove valuable in other such projects. The checklists also provide a succinct summary of the important points of each chapter.

I have written this book to provide useful information to several types of readers. These include (but are not limited to):

■   Inexperienced expert systems developers, who can benefit from step-by-step guidance and practical advice as they proceed through their project.

■   Experienced expert systems developers, who would pick up many useful practical pointers.

■   Managers and technical leaders of expert system development projects, who would benefit especially from some of the nontechnical points discussed, such as on maneuvering through company politics.

■   Upper managers under whom expert systems are being or may be developed, who would learn what is reasonable to expect from this new and exciting (but often oversold) technology.

■ Professionals considering developing an expert system, who would find it valuable to see what goes into a serious expert system development.

■ People interested in learning about (and, possibly, entering) the expert systems field, who would learn a great deal about all aspects of real expert system development, including some aspects not often discussed.

■ Researchers and academics in fields related to expert systems, who would find out about some of the restraints and problems that affect expert system development in the business world.

■ Undergraduate and graduate students, who would learn about how artificial intelligence theory is applied in practical expert system development.

I hope that the unique information and organization of this book will allow these different types of readers to find the book a valuable resource.

I thank the many people who have made important contributions to this book. First I must express my great appreciation to the members of the *COMPASS* project team, every one of whom did an outstanding job—Alan Gunderson, Robert Reinke, Alan Lemmon, and Mark Adler of GTE Laboratories, the principal developers of *COMPASS*; W. (Rick) Johnson of GTE-Southwest, the *COMPASS* No. 2 EAX expert; Russ Sivey of GTE Laboratories, the *COMPASS* corporate interface; Charles Rich of MIT, the project consultant; and Ralph Worrest, Roland van der Meer, and Marie Goslin of GTE Laboratories and Scott Schipper of GTE Data Services, who contributed to specific phases of the development of *COMPASS*. Many of these people were coauthors with me of published and unpublished papers, reports, and documentation on *COMPASS*, several of which I have used as sources for this book. I am grateful to the personnel of GTE Data Services and the GTE telephone companies who contributed to the successful transfer, deployment, and operation of *COMPASS*. I also thank the management and staff of GTE Laboratories for providing an excellent working environment in which a project like *COMPASS* could thrive.

A number of people provided me with valuable advice and suggestions on the writing of this book. I especially want to acknowledge the extensive efforts of Mark Adler, Alvah Davis, Alan Gunderson, and Sam Levine of GTE Laboratories and the support of Robert Hoffman of Adelphi University.

Finally, I must give great thanks and much love to my family: to my parents, Lillian and Milton Prerau, who have been my lifelong advisers and supports, and, to the two people who sacrificed the most to allow me to write this book—Gail Prerau, my wife, and Michael Prerau, my son, who provided me with strong, loving support and encouragement and accepted a missing husband and father for much longer than we had expected to allow the completion of this book.

CONTENTS

1 INTRODUCTION 1

1.1 Artificial Intelligence 2
1.2 Expert Systems and Knowledge Engineering 3
1.3 Benefits of Applying Expert System Technology 3
1.4 Expert Systems and Experts 5
1.5 Roles of Expert Systems 6
1.6 Application Areas of Expert Systems 7
1.7 Special Capabilities and Features of Expert Systems 7
1.8 Limitations of Expert Systems 8
1.9 Developing an Expert System 9

2 BASIC CONCEPTS OF EXPERT SYSTEMS 11

2.1 Developing an Expert System 12
2.2 Knowledge Acquisition 12
2.3 Development of an Expert System Program 16
2.4 Structure of an Expert System 17
2.5 AI Knowledge Representation Paradigms 18
     2.5.1 Production Rules 18
     2.5.2 Frames, Inheritance, and Object-Oriented Programming 23

3 **PLANNING AND MANAGING THE DEVELOPMENT** 29

3.1   Initial Phases   **30**
    3.1.1 Project Start-up   **30**
    3.1.2 Selection of the Domain   **34**
    3.1.3 Selection of the Development Environment   **36**
3.2   Core Development Phases   **38**
    3.2.1 Development of a Feasibility Prototype System   **38**
    3.2.2 Development of a Full Prototype System   **42**
3.3   Final Development and Deployment Phases   **44**
    3.3.1 Development of a Production System   **45**
    3.3.2 System Deployment   **48**
    3.3.3 System Operation and Maintenance   **50**
Checklist   **51**

4 **FORMING THE TEAM** 55

4.1   Project Technical Leader   **56**
4.2   Project Manager   **58**
4.3   Domain Selector   **58**
4.4   Domain Expert   **59**
4.5   Consulting Domain Expert   **60**
4.6   Hardware and Software Selector   **60**
4.7   Knowledge Acquirer   **61**
4.8   Knowledge Representer   **62**
4.9   Knowledge Implementer   **63**
4.10   Systems Engineer   **64**
4.11   Project Tool Developer   **65**
4.12   Corporate/Client Interface   **65**
4.13   Technical Documenter/Writer   **67**
4.14   System Tester and Evaluator   **68**
4.15   System Deployer   **69**
4.16   Trainer   **70**
4.17   System Operator   **70**
4.18   System Maintainer   **71**
4.19   Consultant   **72**
4.20   End User   **73**
Checklist   **74**

5 SELECTING THE DOMAIN: THE PROCESS 77

5.1 Importance of Domain Selection **78**
5.2 A Method for Evaluating Application Domains **79**
Checklist **96**

6 SELECTING THE DOMAIN: DESIRED DOMAIN ATTRIBUTES 97

6.1 Basic Requirements **98**
    6.1.1 Need for the Expert System Approach **98**
    6.1.2 Existence of Experts **99**
    6.1.3 Need to Capture the Expertise **101**
    6.1.4 Limited Success Is Acceptable **102**
    6.1.5 Payoff **102**
    6.1.6 Risk versus Payoff **105**
6.2 Type of Problem **106**
    6.2.1 Use of Symbolic Reasoning **106**
    6.2.2 Use of Heuristics and Other Task Characteristics **107**
    6.2.3 Widespread Knowledge and Common Sense **107**
    6.2.4 Not Driven by a Particular Technology **108**
    6.2.5 Task Definition **110**
    6.2.6 Task Inputs **110**
    6.2.7 Task Outputs **111**
    6.2.8 Similarity to Successful System **112**
6.3 Expertise **112**
    6.3.1 Experts Are Better than Novices **113**
    6.3.2 Availability of Expertise **113**
    6.3.3 Utilizing a Single Expert **114**
6.4 Task Bounds **114**
    6.4.1 Bounds on Task Difficulty **114**
    6.4.2 Estimated Lower Bound on Task Knowledge **115**
    6.4.3 Estimated Upper Bound on Task Knowledge **115**
    6.4.4 Narrowness of Task **116**
6.5 Domain Area Personnel and Politics **116**
    6.5.1 Domain Personnel's Expectations of Success **116**
    6.5.2 Domain Leaders' Task Agreement and Continuing Involvement **117**
    6.5.3 Problem Previously Identified **118**
    6.5.4 Top-Level Support **118**

6.5.5 Users Want It   **118**
6.5.6 Introduction of the System   **119**
6.5.7 Cooperative User Group   **120**
6.5.8 Political Problems Related to System Control   **120**
6.5.9 Political Problems Related to System Results   **121**
6.5.10 Problems Related to the Sensitivity of the Knowledge   **121**
6.6 Development, Testing, and Deployment   **122**
6.6.1 Incomplete Coverage   **122**
6.6.2 Decomposability   **123**
6.6.3 Teachable Skill   **124**
6.6.4 Written Material   **124**
6.6.5 Availability of Test Cases   **125**
6.6.6 Real-Time and Performance Issues   **125**
6.6.7 User Interface   **126**
6.6.8 Long-Term System Need   **127**
6.6.9 No Alternative   **128**
6.6.10 Stability   **129**
6.6.11 Project Dependencies and Milestones   **129**
6.6.12 Tolerance to Incorrect Results   **130**
6.6.13 Measurable Payoff   **131**
6.6.14 Expert Agreement on Correctness   **132**
Checklist   **134**

7 **SELECTING THE HARDWARE AND THE SOFTWARE DEVELOPMENT TOOL** 139

7.1 A Process for Selecting the Development Environment   **141**
7.2 Criteria and Parameters for Comparing Software Tools or Hardware   **146**
7.3 Obtaining the System   **147**
7.3.1 Availability   **147**
7.3.2 Cost   **148**
7.3.3 Legal Arrangements   **148**
7.3.4 Integration into Environment   **149**
7.3.5 Uniformity with Others   **149**
7.4 Background and Prospects   **150**
7.4.1 Vendor Track Record and Prospects   **150**
7.4.2 System History   **151**
7.4.3 Stage of Development   **151**
7.4.4 System Upgrading   **152**
7.4.5 System Maintenance by the Vendor   **152**

7.5 Learning to Use the System **153**
    7.5.1 Training Materials **153**
    7.5.2 Training Courses **153**
7.6 System Usability and General Features **154**
    7.6.1 System Interface **154**
    7.6.2 Supportive Programming Environment **154**
    7.6.3 Efficiency of the Programming Environment **155**
    7.6.4 Software Engineering-Related Facilities **155**
    7.6.5 Documentation **155**
    7.6.6 Performance **156**
    7.6.7 Size **157**
    7.6.8 System Interfaces **157**
    7.6.9 Security **158**
    7.6.10 User Support and Consultants **158**
7.7 Special Features Related to Software **159**
    7.7.1 Building or Buying a Software Tool **159**
    7.7.2 Knowledge Representation Paradigms **160**
    7.7.3 Incorporation of a Computer Language **162**
    7.7.4 Match to Problem **162**
    7.7.5 Access to Source Code **163**
7.8 Special Features Related to Hardware **163**
    7.8.1 Computer Type **164**
    7.8.2 System Software and File System **164**
    7.8.3 Support for Multiple Tools **165**
7.9 Issues Related to Deployment **165**
    7.9.1 Use as Deployment Vehicle **165**
    7.9.2 Easy Transfer to Deployment Vehicle **166**
    7.9.3 Operation and Maintenance of the Deployed Expert System **167**
Checklist **169**

8 | SELECTING THE DOMAIN EXPERTS 173

8.1 Responsibility for Selecting the Experts **174**
8.2 Attributes of Good Domain Experts **175**
    8.2.1 Existence of Domain Expertise and Experience **175**
    8.2.2 Level of Expertise **175**
    8.2.3 Extensiveness of Experience **176**
    8.2.4 Reputation **176**
    8.2.5 Finding Experts with the Right Experience **177**

8.2.6 Communication Skills   **178**

8.2.7 Temperament   **179**

8.2.8 Cooperativeness   **180**

8.2.9 Working Relations   **181**

8.2.10 Availability   **181**

8.2.11 Management Support for Expert Involvement   **182**

8.2.12 Computer and AI Background   **183**

8.2.13 Experts as Domain Representatives   **184**

8.2.14 Expectations   **186**

8.3   The Process of Selecting Domain Experts   **186**

8.4   When No Experts Are Available   **190**

8.5   The Number of Domain Experts   **192**

8.5.1 Using a Single Expert   **192**

8.5.2 Using Multiple Experts   **194**

8.6   Consulting Domain Experts   **195**

Checklist   **197**

9 ACQUIRING THE KNOWLEDGE 199

9.1   Considering Knowledge Acquisition at the Project's Beginning   **201**

9.1.1 Selecting the Domain with a View toward Knowledge Acquisition   **201**

9.1.2 Selecting Experts with a View toward Knowledge Acquisition   **202**

9.2   Knowledge Acquisition Meetings   **203**

9.2.1 Maximizing Access to the Experts   **203**

9.2.2 Allowing the Experts to Demonstrate their Expertise   **204**

9.2.3 Minimizing Interruptions   **205**

9.2.4 Accessing the Implementation   **206**

9.2.5 Locating Meetings at the Project Team's Site   **207**

9.3   Beginning the Knowledge Acquisition   **208**

9.3.1 Meeting Atmosphere   **208**

9.3.2 Focusing the Knowledge Acquisition   **209**

9.3.3 Getting Background Domain Knowledge   **209**

9.3.4 Preparing a Tutorial Document   **210**

9.3.5 Giving the Domain Experts Some AI Background   **211**

9.3.6 Using Written Materials for Initial Knowledge   **211**

9.3.7 Initial Steps   **212**

9.4   Documenting the Knowledge   **213**

9.4.1 Using Quasi-English Knowledge Acquisition Rules   **213**

9.4.2 The Knowledge Document   **214**

9.4.3 Readability of the Knowledge Documentation   **216**

9.4.4 Terminology Used in the Knowledge Documentation   **216**

9.4.5 Devising Terminology for Documentation and Discussion   **217**

9.4.6 Identifying the Knowledge Acquisition Rules and Procedures   **219**

9.4.7 Organizing the Knowledge Acquisition Rules and Procedures   **220**

9.4.8 Utilizing an Explanatory Clause   **220**

9.4.9 Domain Description and Glossary   **221**

9.5   Acquiring the Knowledge   **221**

9.5.1 Basic Knowledge Acquisition Cycle before Implementation   **221**

9.5.2 Basic Knowledge Acquisition Cycle after Implementation Has Begun   **223**

9.5.3 Using Test Cases to Elicit Expert Knowledge   **225**

9.5.4 Using Acquired Knowledge to Guide Related Knowledge Acquisition   **226**

9.5.5 Using Knowledge Acquisition Formalisms Directly   **227**

9.5.6 Updating the Knowledge Documentation   **227**

9.5.7 Deferring Specification of Certain Details   **227**

9.5.8 Generating Test Cases from Test Cases   **228**

9.5.9 Establishing a Default for Close Decisions   **229**

9.5.10 Finding the Extent of Rules   **229**

9.6   Recording the Knowledge   **230**

9.6.1 Flexibility   **230**

9.6.2 Recording Reminders   **231**

9.6.3 Recording Benefits of the Expert System   **231**

Checklist   **233**

10   **REPRESENTING THE SYSTEM KNOWLEDGE**   237

10.1   Decomposing the Problem   **238**

10.2   Paradigm(s) for Representation   **248**

10.3   Frames, Inheritance, and Demons   **249**

10.4   Production Rules   **254**

10.5   Object-Oriented Programming   **257**

10.6   Programming Language Code   **258**

10.7   Representing and Rerepresenting   **259**

Checklist   **263**

11	**IMPLEMENTING THE SYSTEM** 265

11.1 Expert System Implementation Compared with the Implementation of Conventional Programs **266**

  11.1.1 Implementation without a Full Specification **266**

  11.1.2 Reimplementing the Implementation **269**

11.2 Some Techniques for Knowledge Implementation **277**

  11.2.1 Correspondence of Knowledge Acquisition Rules and Implementation Rules **277**

  11.2.2 Grouping Rules in Rulesets **278**

  11.2.3 Implementing and Debugging **279**

  11.2.4 Documentation **280**

11.3 Managing the Implementation and Promoting Maintainability **282**

  11.3.1 Software Modularity and Task Assignment **283**

  11.3.2 Uniformity of Style **284**

  11.3.3 Use of Paradigms that Promote Maintainability **286**

  11.3.4 Configuration Management and Control **288**

  11.3.5 Data Flow and Access **290**

  11.3.6 Control Flow **292**

  11.3.7 Input/Output **293**

Checklist **296**

12	**TESTING AND EVALUATING THE SYSTEM** 299

12.1 Validation and Verification during Expert System Development **300**

  12.1.1 Validation and Verification as Inherent Parts of Knowledge Acquisition **300**

  12.1.2 Validation Testing by Consulting Experts **302**

12.2 Validation of the Developed Expert System **303**

  12.2.1 Validating Absolutely **303**

  12.2.2 Validating against Expert Performance **306**

  12.2.3 Validation by Field Testing **307**

12.3 Verification of an Expert System Program **308**

12.4 Evaluation Effort and Standards **310**

Checklist **312**

13 TRANSFERRING AND DEPLOYING THE SYSTEM 315

13.1 Developing an Expert System with Technology Transfer and Deployment
in Mind **316**

    13.1.1 Issues Related to Domain Selection **316**

    13.1.2 Issues Related to Knowledge Representation and Implementation **318**

13.2 Technology Transfer **319**

13.3 Organizational Roles and Activities in Technology Transfer **321**

13.4 Transferring AI Expertise **324**

    13.4.1 General Training Requirements **324**

    13.4.2 AI Techniques, Tools, and Systems Training **325**

    13.4.3 Domain Training **326**

    13.4.4 Training on the Expert System Program **327**

    13.4.5 Knowledge Acquisition Training **328**

13.5 Deployment **328**

    13.5.1 Deployment Environment **328**

    13.5.2 Reliability, Maintainability, and Security **331**

    13.5.3 Integration of the Expert System **333**

13.6 Gaining User Acceptance of the Deployed Expert System **334**

    13.6.1 Educating the Users **334**

    13.6.2 Introducing the Expert System **336**

    13.6.3 Use of the Expert System **337**

Checklist **339**

14 EXPERT SYSTEM TRENDS AND DIRECTIONS 341

Glossary **347**

Index **353**

CHAPTER 1

Introduction

▬▬ What is artificial intelligence?

▬▬ What are expert systems?

▬▬ What is knowledge engineering?

▬▬ In what kinds of situations might an expert system be used?

▬▬ What benefits might be derived from an expert system?

▬▬ Can expert systems ever perform better than the best experts?

▬▬ What expert roles can an expert system fill?

▬▬ In what fields have expert systems been developed?

▬▬ What special features and capabilities do expert systems have that distinguish them from conventional programs?

▬▬ What are the limitations of current state-of-the-art expert systems?

Interest in and excitement about the use of artificial intelligence (AI) for applications in business and industry have been growing dramatically. Practical use of AI is still relatively new, but almost all major corporations and many smaller ones are involved in AI to some extent. Many commercial and government organizations have set up their own expert system development groups; others have purchased AI products.

Probably the primary area of commercial interest in AI is the field of expert systems. Expert systems technology offers great possibilities for solving difficult real-world problems—problems that might not be amenable to solution by any other technology. By utilizing expert systems, organizations have gained valuable benefits, such as lowered costs, improved quality of products and services, increased profitability, the development or expansion of competitive advantage, and the generation of new products and services.

This book describes and discusses proven techniques for developing expert systems. Let us begin the discussion of expert system development with some background on AI and expert systems.

1.1 ARTIFICIAL INTELLIGENCE

Although AI has burst onto the commercial scene relatively recently, it has been an active discipline in an academic environment for some years; the term *artificial intelligence* was first formally used in the mid-1950s. **Artificial intelligence** can be defined as the science of making machines behave in a way that would generally be accepted as requiring human intelligence. It attempts to provide ways for modeling and mechanizing intelligent processes that otherwise could not be automated. In addition to conventional computer approaches, work in AI is often based on symbolic, nonalgorithmic methods of problem solving and the uses of computers for reasoning with concepts rather than calculating with numbers.

AI is a field of computer science. Aspects of it are closely related to several other disciplines, such as psychology, cognitive science, computational linguistics, data processing, decision support systems, and computational modeling, and it draws from all of these disciplines.

There are several important subfields of AI, including robotics, computer vision, speech synthesis and recognition, automated reasoning and theorem proving, natural language processing, automatic programming, automated learning, neural networks—and expert systems. All of these subfields are under study in universities and certain industrial laboratories, but only some have reached the stage of commercial applicability. Of these, expert systems is the subfield of AI that has evoked the most interest in business and industry and has resulted in the greatest number of practical applications.

1.2   EXPERT SYSTEMS AND KNOWLEDGE ENGINEERING

An **expert system** is an advanced computer program that can, at a high level of competence, solve difficult problems requiring the use of expertise and experience; it accomplishes this by employing knowledge of the techniques, information, heuristics (rules of thumb), and problem-solving processes that human experts use to solve such problems. Expert systems thus provide a way to store human knowledge, expertise, and experience in computers—that is, a way to "clone" human experts (at least to some degree).

Heuristics are the basis of expert systems. They are the rules of thumb or strategies that aid experts in solving problems or making decisions. Heuristics cannot be proved formally, and they are not correct in all cases, but they provide an expert with a way to make a decision when stronger rules do not apply. Experts develop these heuristics through long periods of performance of a task. An example of a heuristic is: "If you drive no more than 5 miles per hour above the speed limit, you will not get a speeding ticket." Although this cannot be proved and may occasionally be wrong, many experienced drivers use it as a rule of driving.

Expert systems are often called **knowledge-based systems,** and sometimes **knowledge systems.** Some people make a distinction between these terms, but we will consider them synonymous. The terms emphasize different important aspects of the definition: the systems perform tasks at an expert level based on the knowledge that human experts use.

The process of developing an expert system is called **knowledge engineering,** and the people who develop expert systems are thus **knowledge engineers.** The term *knowledge engineering* is sometimes confined to the task of acquiring knowledge for an expert system from an expert, but we shall use the term broadly to indicate all of the technical aspects of developing an expert system.

1.3   BENEFITS OF APPLYING EXPERT SYSTEM TECHNOLOGY

Expert system technology might be considered for any situation where it is valuable to preserve expertise or to widen the distribution of and access to expertise. Expert systems may be appropriate (and in many cases may be the only technology that might be successful) in the following situations:

- To provide expertise when it is scarce.
- To provide expertise when obtaining expertise is expensive.

- To provide expertise at times when experts are not available.

- To provide expertise if experts are not available in all locations where they are needed.

- To speed up the time an expert analysis takes.

- To upgrade the performance of less experienced and less skilled personnel, especially when there is a wide range of skill levels for the desired task.

- To upgrade the performance of experienced and skilled personnel so that they perform closer to the level of a top expert.

- To apply expert analyses to situations for which specialists do not have time (such as analyzing large amounts of data or giving consideration to every possibility—even the most unlikely—before making a decision), thus upgrading the performance of even the best experts.

- To capture and preserve knowledge when expertise may be lost through reassignment, retirement, or other loss of personnel.

- To capture and preserve knowledge when experts, at the top of their expertise today, may lose some of their present skill in the future, such as through less concentrated work on the task.

- To provide access to expertise when human specialists are absent, such as due to illness or vacation.

- To provide access to expertise when human specialists may be at reduced performance levels.

- To minimize or eliminate a continuing need to train new people in a skill, such as when there is a continual turnover of personnel.

- To minimize or eliminate the clerical and other low-level errors made by task practitioners, even the best experts.

- To utilize automated expertise as a basis for automating other related tasks, thus allowing the complete automation of a large function.

- To ensure that expertise is applied uniformly, objectively, and consistently at all times, so that, for example, corporate policy is uniform.

- To free the time of the best experts for the most difficult problems or for other important tasks.

- To automate expertise that can be marketed as a product or service (or as part of a product or service).

Thus expert systems can provide the expert knowledge to improve performance and quality, increase productivity, promote uniformity, preserve vital knowledge, promote better use of personnel resources, and allow new or better products to be marketed.

1.4 EXPERT SYSTEMS AND EXPERTS

When we discuss the use of expert systems for capturing and distributing the knowledge of human experts, it must be clear what is meant by an expert. An **expert** here means any person who, through training and experience, can perform a task with a degree of skill that is beneficial to capture and distribute. The expert—an aspect of whose expertise we attempt to embody in an expert system—may be a Nobel Prize–winning physicist or a highly competent file clerk. (In fact, for many companies it might be much more valuable to capture and distribute the expertise of the latter.) Although we usually want to capture the knowledge of a top-level task performer, at times capturing and automating the judgment of even an average decision maker can be beneficial (such as to ensure uniform application of policies). In this case, such a person could be considered an expert for our purposes.

Can expert systems perform some tasks better than the best human experts? From one point of view, expert systems for complex tasks can never fully reach the level of proficiency of top human experts. Such systems are based on the expertise of human experts. For any reasonably complex application, it is unlikely that an expert system can ever contain every subtle aspect of a human's expertise and every fragment of memory based on long experience. Therefore it is unlikely that any expert system for a complex task will be able to duplicate completely the expertise of top experts. But since expert systems are computer programs, they can add to a human expert's skill all the power of a computer. They can perform analyses much faster; they can handle larger amounts of data much easier; they can handle very complex situations much better; they can have faster and better access to data sources; they can have much less likelihood of making clerical errors; they can perform ancillary calculations much faster; and so on.

Consequently expert systems can in many cases perform better on a task than the best expert. For example, even the best expert may not have enough time to perform every analysis or consider every possibility before making a decision. In fact, experts often develop heuristics (which we might call meta-heuristics) about which analyses and heuristics to consider and which ones are likely to be fruitless. Because an expert system can usually perform far faster than an expert, it often can dispense with these meta-heuristics and analyze every possibility, no matter how unlikely. Thus in cases where the unlikely possibility is actually the correct result, the expert system will be correct and the human expert will be incorrect.

Another way that an expert system can be better than a human expert is by combining the expertise of many experts, especially experts in different subdomains. Although combining the expertise of several experts in an expert system is not a simple task, if it is done successfully, the expert system may have an expertise that no one person has.

1.5   ROLES OF EXPERT SYSTEMS

An expert system can perform one or more of several possible expert roles:

- **Autonomous expert:** The expert system analyzes a situation, makes a decision, and then acts on it directly or commands a human action—all without human participation in or scrutiny of the decision. It reacts appropriately to unique or unusual circumstances. For example, in the role of an autonomous expert, an expert system might directly run a chemical process, reading sensors and making adjustments of controllable variables such as temperature and pressure. Or it might direct a low-level human technician to replace a machine part that the system has determined to be faulty.

- **Autonomous expert with human override:** The expert system acts as an autonomous expert but presents its decisions to a human expert, who can override or modify them. In this role, an expert system might formulate a complex design, which a human designer reviews before it is executed.

- **Expert consultant:** The expert system provides consulting at an expert level for a task practitioner in the manner similar to that of a human expert consultant: providing recommendations on particularly difficult or unusual situations. The expert system might improve the performance of average practitioners to be closer to the performance of experts. An example is an expert system that would recommend treatments for rare diseases to a general physician.

- **Colleague:** The expert system gives suggestions to a human peer. Although it might not have a higher skill level than the human, it may be able to apply itself to analyses that the human does not have the time to make, or it might explore many complex alternatives while the human pursues the most likely course of action. For example, a troubleshooting expert system might be able to investigate unlikely causes of faults that human troubleshooters do not pursue because the likelihood of finding one of these unlikely causes does not usually warrant the time needed for the analysis.

- **Intelligent assistant:** The expert system acts as an intelligent assistant to the practitioner. It might make a set of plausible suggestions or determine a list of items to consider when a certain circumstance occurs. It could monitor data, looking for certain combinations of variables that might be of interest to the practitioner. For example, in the role of an intelligent assistant, an expert system might monitor sensors in an operating industrial plant and indicate on a display panel when it determines some combination of sensor values that could be a problem.

■ **Low-level intelligent assistant:** The expert system performs relatively low-level, time-consuming tasks, freeing the practitioner to work on more difficult parts of the job. For instance, an expert system might perform the first step in a complex expert analysis by transforming large quantities of raw data into smaller amounts of partially processed data, which the human expert analyzes.

1.6 APPLICATION AREAS OF EXPERT SYSTEMS

The number of problem types in which expert systems have been and are being applied is continually growing as interest in the technology spreads. They include:

■ diagnosis

■ scheduling

■ planning

■ monitoring

■ process control

■ design

■ forecasting

■ signal interpretation

■ configuration

■ training

The number of industries and disciplines in which expert systems have been used is also growing. Figure 1.1 shows several fields for which expert systems have been developed.

1.7 SPECIAL CAPABILITIES AND FEATURES OF EXPERT SYSTEMS

Expert systems have several capabilities and features that distinguish them from conventional computer programs (although as these systems become more widely applied and more integrated with conventional software, the distinction between expert systems and conventional programs is becoming less well defined). The basic goal of an expert system is to capture and

Aerospace	Engineering	Medicine
Agriculture	Engineering design	Military science
Chemical engineering	Environmental sciences	Nuclear engineering
Chemistry	Finance	Publishing
Computer-aided design	Geology	Resource management
Construction	Government	Telecommunications
Electrical engineering and electronics	Insurance	Training
	Manufacturing	Transportation
Electrical utilities		

FIGURE 1.1 Some fields in which expert systems have been developed

distribute the heuristic expertise of human experts; the goal of a conventional program is to implement a set of algorithms.

Expert systems can be used in situations considered very difficult or impossible to be handled by conventional approaches. For example, expert system technology is able to deal with expert rules of thumb that occasionally give the wrong result. Also expert systems have the capability to handle situations where the information required is incomplete or the information available is inconsistent. Techniques within the technology of expert systems treat uncertain situations and uncertain data, and some expert systems can change their beliefs as new information becomes available. In addition, often an expert system can provide an explanation of its decisions or of why it is performing a certain operation or asking for certain information.

FIGURE 1.2 General distinctions between expert systems and conventional computer programs

Expert System	Conventional Program
Makes decisions	Calculates results
Based on heuristics	Based on algorithms
More flexible	Less flexible
Can handle uncertainty	Cannot handle uncertainty
Can work with partial information, inconsistencies, partial beliefs	Requires complete information
Can provide explanations of results	Gives results without explanation
Symbolic reasoning	Numeric calculations
Primarily declarative	Primarily procedural
Control and knowledge separated	Control and knowledge interlaced

Expert systems are based primarily on symbolic reasoning about concepts rather than numeric calculations. They usually are programmed using declarative rather than procedural approaches, and the programming techniques allow program control to be separated from domain knowledge to a large extent. The use of declarative knowledge separated from program control often makes expert systems more flexible and easier to revise and update than conventional programs.

All of these capabilities would be difficult to include in a conventional program, if they could be included at all. Figure 1.2 compares expert systems and conventional computer programs.

1.8 LIMITATIONS OF EXPERT SYSTEMS

Although expert systems can perform better than the best experts in some cases and although expert system technology can be used to solve problems that are extremely difficult (if not essentially impossible) to solve by conventional programming techniques, these systems should not be thought of as a general panacea. No technology can solve all problems, and therefore the limitations of expert systems should be recognized.

In any reasonably complex domain, it is unlikely that an expert system can ever contain the complete expertise and experience of a leading expert. And since expert systems are based on the knowledge of humans, it is unlikely that expert systems can solve problems that no human experts could solve (except problems where humans lack the time or access to resources that the computer has).

Furthermore there are limitations on what is possible under the present state of the expert system art. It is possible to develop an expert system only for a narrow and well-bounded domain—one that does not require much common sense or encyclopedic knowledge. Current expert systems often perform poorly at their boundaries, and many of these systems have difficulty determining if a situation is within their scope. Current commercial expert systems do not include significant learning capabilities, and few can make use of the basic first principles of a domain when heuristics fail (although there is research in both of these areas). We discuss at length in Chapters 5 and 6 methods of determining whether specific application domains are appropriate for expert system technology.

1.9 DEVELOPING AN EXPERT SYSTEM

This book describes all of the steps followed in developing an expert system. The development of expert systems for business and industrial applications is different in many ways from the development of conventional software, and is still a new field. It is not yet(?) a science: there are no immutable laws of expert system development, there are many situations where more than one approach might be used, and there are few standard techniques that work in all cases. Therefore for each step, this book focuses on proven techniques that have been successful in practice.

Chapter 2 defines some important terms and presents some of the basic concepts related to expert systems. The following chapters discuss in detail the steps in planning and staffing an expert system project, selecting a good application domain and development environment, acquiring the expert knowledge for the system, developing the expert system program, evaluating the expert system's performance, transferring the technology, and deploying the system. In almost every case, a specific example from the development of the *COMPASS* expert system follows the general discussion to show how the general point was put into practice.

CHAPTER 2

Basic Concepts of Expert Systems

- What steps go into developing an expert system?
- What is the structure of an expert system?
- What are the difficulties in acquiring knowledge from an expert?
- What are production rules, forward chaining, and backward chaining?
- What are frames and inheritance?
- What is object-oriented programming?

This chapter examines several of the basic concepts related to the development of expert systems, and it defines many terms used in later chapters. These concepts and terms form a foundation for the remainder of the book. Experienced expert system developers might skim this chapter or use it for a review.

2.1 DEVELOPING AN EXPERT SYSTEM

At its most basic, expert system development consists of four fundamental steps:

1. Domain selection: Selecting a domain (application area) for the expert system.

2. Selection of expert(s): Selecting one or more experts in that domain.

3. Knowledge acquisition: Determining the techniques, knowledge, and heuristics used by the expert(s) to perform tasks in the domain.

4. Program development: Designing and implementing a computer program that embodies those techniques, knowledge, and heuristics.

There are many technical and nontechnical considerations that should go into the first step, selection of an appropriate domain for an expert system, and we will discuss these in Chapter 5. Similarly, several factors should be taken into account in identifying a domain expert for an expert system development project, and we will examine these in Chapter 8.

The primary goal of expert system development is to acquire, from an expert in the selected domain, the knowledge that the expert has gained through experience in a domain task and then to implement that knowledge in an expert system program. The basic transfer of knowledge is shown in Figure 2.1. This chapter presents some of the basic concepts related to knowledge acquisition and to the development of an expert system program.

2.2 KNOWLEDGE ACQUISITION

The process of finding domain knowledge—facts, rules, heuristics, procedures—from experts during expert system development is called **knowledge acquisition.** Knowledge engineers developing an expert system try to determine from documents and directly from experts the manner in which experts solve the problem that the expert system is attempting to solve. The result of knowledge acquisition is a specification of the knowledge of the expert system.

Knowledge acquisition usually is accomplished by meetings between knowledge engineers and domain experts, at which the knowledge engineers attempt to elicit the experts' knowledge. A common approach is for

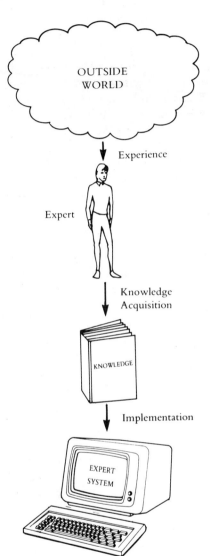

FIGURE 2.1 Transfer of knowledge in expert system development

knowledge engineers to interview a domain expert, asking questions about how the expert performs the domain task to try to determine the expert's procedures and heuristics. The knowledge engineers might present situations (for example, data from a real domain case) to the expert and attempt to elicit the heuristics used to make a decision in that situation. This is typically an iterative process. The knowledge engineers and the expert use test cases to compare the elicited domain knowledge against the expert's performance. Weaknesses in the system's knowledge are found, modified, and resubmitted to expert evaluation. This cycling continues until the expert system's knowledge is built up to the desired point.

The task of knowledge acquisition is often difficult. Most experts cannot easily describe their expertise or the way they make decisions. Many are not as articulate and communicative as would be desired. Furthermore experts frequently perform their tasks without being fully aware of the processes and heuristics they use and of how they make use of their experience. They may not realize all the different aspects of a situation that they actually considered when they made a decision. Because of factors such as these, the process of knowledge acquisition usually requires the knowledge engineers to have long periods of interaction with the domain experts in order to determine as well as possible complete and correct expert heuristics.

Box 2.1 provides a simple illustration of a typical knowledge acquisition process. It also exhibits some of the many difficulties that may occur during knowledge acquisition. Chapter 9 discusses knowledge acquisition in detail and describes several useful techniques for knowledge acquisition.

BOX 2.1
A SIMPLE EXAMPLE OF KNOWLEDGE ACQUISITION

As an illustration of a typical knowledge acquisition process (and to point out some of the difficulties), consider the following hypothetical example in an area of widespread expertise—a possible dialogue between a knowledge engineer and an expert in driving an automobile.

Knowledge engineer: Tell me about the techniques you use to drive a car.

Expert: . . . and when the car is stopped at a red light and the light turns green, I start the car moving forward by depressing the accelerator. Then I . . .

Knowledge engineer: Stop there. That sounds like an important heuristic. Let's record it. Could you say it again?

Expert: It's a very common situation. When the light turns green, I start the car moving forward by depressing the accelerator. It's just that simple.

Knowledge engineer: Okay. Let's formalize that into a heuristic rule:

> **MOVE-FORWARD-WHEN-LIGHT-TURNS-GREEN Rule**
> *If* the car is stopped at a red light,
>   *and* the light turns green,
> *Then* move the car forward by depressing the accelerator.

[Note that expert heuristics are often written in *if-then* rule form.]

> **Expert:** That's it. I told you I use very simple rules. We should be finished very soon.

Later in the knowledge acquisition:

> **Knowledge engineer:** Now consider this scenario: You are driving down South Street, and you are stopped at a red light. Then the light turns green. What do you do?
> **Expert:** I push down on the accelerator and start the car moving forward.
> **Knowledge engineer:** Using the set of rules we've collected so far, our system would make the same decision. When it got to that point, the MOVE-FORWARD-WHEN-LIGHT-TURNS-GREEN Rule would be invoked. So far, so good.

The heuristic may seem correct. However, later the knowledge engineer might ask:

> **Knowledge engineer:** Now consider this situation: You are stopped at a red light, and the car is facing a "Do Not Enter" sign. What do you do when the light turns green?
> **Expert:** I can't go forward then. I have to turn left or right.
> **Knowledge engineer:** But that contradicts the MOVE-FORWARD-WHEN-LIGHT-TURNS-GREEN Rule that we previously found.
> **Expert:** That's right. Sorry. I forgot to tell you that I would only move forward if there was no "Do Not Enter" sign.
> **Knowledge engineer:** Okay. We'd better expand the MOVE-FOR-WARD-WHEN-LIGHT-TURNS-GREEN Rule to:

> **MOVE-FORWARD-WHEN-LIGHT-TURNS-GREEN Rule**
> *If* the car is stopped at a red light,
>   *and* the light turns green,
>   *and* there is no "Do Not Enter" sign directly ahead,
> *Then* move the car forward by depressing the accelerator.

Then, later on:

> **Knowledge engineer:** What do you do if someone is walking across the street in front of the car against the light?

Expert: Didn't I mention that before? I certainly check to see if there is anyone walking in front of the car before I start driving forward. I go forward only if there isn't anyone there.

Knowledge engineer: I understand. Let's expand the MOVE-FOR-WARD-WHEN-LIGHT-TURNS-GREEN Rule again. It now reads:

MOVE-FORWARD-WHEN-LIGHT-TURNS-GREEN Rule
If the car is stopped at a red light,
    and the light turns green,
    and there is no "Do Not Enter" sign directly ahead,
    and there is nobody in front of the car,
Then move the car forward by depressing the accelerator.

Knowledge engineer (at various later times): What do you do if there is a big pothole is front of the car? [or] What do you do if you hear a siren coming from down a side street?

And so on. An important point is that experts really do check for "Do Not Enter" signs, sirens, and so on, but these checks may be so inherent in their performances that, when asked, they will not state that that is what they are doing. Seemingly simple heuristics may be much more complicated than originally thought. The talent of the knowledge engineer is to elicit each heuristic—and the full heuristic—from the expert.

2.3   DEVELOPMENT OF AN EXPERT SYSTEM PROGRAM

There are five basic elements in developing an expert system program to embody the expert knowledge found during knowledge acquisition:

1. Selection of the software tool
2. Selection of the hardware
3. Knowledge representation
4. Knowledge implementation
5. Testing and evaluation of the program

Most expert systems are developed using a **software tool** or **shell,** which is a software package that provides facilities to aid in expert system development. Expert system developers should determine if such a package is to be used (as opposed to programming directly in a computer language), and if so they must select one. They also must determine on which computer hardware the expert system will be developed. We discuss the process of selecting the software tool and hardware, which together will be called the development **environment,** in Chapter 7.

Knowledge representation is the process of taking the domain knowledge found during knowledge acquisition and defining the approach that will be used to represent that knowledge in the expert system program. The expert knowledge can be represented in the computer using a programming language, but it is usually represented by making use of one or more **AI paradigms,** such as production rules, frames, or object-oriented programming. These paradigms will be defined and described in the following sections. With these paradigms (usually provided by the software tool), expert system developers determine a representation scheme for the expert knowledge. We discuss knowledge representation in Chapter 10.

Knowledge implementation is the process of taking the knowledge found during knowledge acquisition and translating it into an operational expert system program by employing the structures and paradigms that comprise the knowledge representation. Knowledge implementation is addressed in Chapter 11.

During development and also before final transfer or deployment, the expert system program should be tested and evaluated. Some aspects of expert system programs make their testing and evaluation somewhat different from the testing and evaluation of conventional computer programs, as we discuss in Chapter 12.

2.4   STRUCTURE OF AN EXPERT SYSTEM

A typical simple expert system "program" (for example, a set of rules) describes what to do in particular circumstances but does not specify a definite set of steps (that is, an algorithm) to follow. The program control and the knowledge used to reach a conclusion are separate. Changes can be made to the knowledge without affecting the control part of the expert system at all.

This basic architecture of a simple expert system consists of three parts: the knowledge base, the inference engine, and the working memory (Figure 2.2).

The **knowledge base** stores the facts and heuristics of domain experts (as obtained, usually, by knowledge engineers). It also includes expert techniques on how and when to use these facts and heuristics. As opposed to conventional computer programs, each nugget of knowledge in the knowledge base is essentially independent. The sequence in which the facts and heuristics are stored does not in general affect the way they are used.

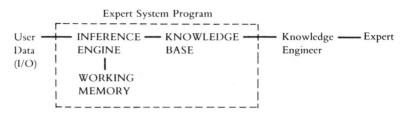

FIGURE 2.2 Basic expert system architecture

The **working memory** contains the information the system has received about the problem at hand. In addition, any information the expert system derives about the problem is stored in the working memory.

The **inference engine** provides the system control. It applies the expert domain knowledge (which is in the knowledge base) to what is known about the present situation (which is the information in the working memory) to determine new information about the domain. This process will lead, it is hoped, to the solution of the problem. The inference engine often also contains the expert system's interfaces to data sources and to the user.

The information that is in the knowledge base and the working memory and that is manipulated by the inference engine is, in general, made up of symbols that stand for concepts and is only occasionally numbers.

2.5   AI KNOWLEDGE REPRESENTATION PARADIGMS

Techniques of knowledge representation are used to store the acquired domain knowledge in the expert system program.

Expert system knowledge may be represented by use of a programming language. Some expert systems are implemented in conventional programming languages, but often specialized AI computer languages are used. The two most common of these are Lisp and Prolog. Such specialized languages provide mechanisms and structures that facilitate symbolic reasoning. However, the knowledge in an expert system is usually represented by making use of one or more recognized AI representational techniques, which we will call **AI paradigms** or **knowledge representational paradigms.** The most commonly utilized AI paradigms are production rules, frames, and object-oriented programming.

2.5.1 PRODUCTION RULES

The knowledge representational paradigm used most often in expert systems is **production rules** or *if-then* rules. Such rules have the basic form:

If **A** and **B** and **C,**
then **D** and **E.**

A sample of one such rule is that discussed in Box 2.1:

MOVE-FORWARD-WHEN-LIGHT-TURNS-GREEN Rule
  If the car is stopped at a red light,
    and the light turns green,
    and there is no "Do Not Enter" sign directly ahead,
    and there is nobody in front of the car,
  Then move the car forward by depressing the accelerator.

In an expert system, a production rule represents a single nugget of knowledge. Production rules are characterized by two clauses: the **antecedent** or *if* clause, and the **consequent** or *then* clause. A production rule such as "*If A, then B*" can be read in several slightly different ways:

- If **A** occurs, then do **B.**
- If **A** is true, then **B** is always true as well.
- If **A** is found, then conclude **B.**
- One way to prove **B** is to prove **A.**

Therefore the production rule formalism is a flexible mechanism, providing modularity and standardization of representation. It can be used to represent several types of knowledge, as the following examples show:

Situation/action: *If* it is raining, *then* close the window.
Premise/conclusion: *If* it is raining, *then* the roof becomes wet.
Sufficiency: *If* it is raining, *then* it is precipitating.
Definition: *If* it is raining, *then* water droplets are falling from the sky.

Expert systems often deal with knowledge that is not certain. We may want to represent a rule of thumb that works most of the time or a fact that is somewhat in doubt. Many production rule systems have ways to represent uncertainty. A common approach is to make use of **certainty factors:** a number attached to a rule or fact that denotes the degree of certainty we assign to it—for example,

- It will rain today, with certainty 0.5.
- *If* it is raining, *then* the sky is dark, with certainty 0.75.
- *If* it will rain today with certainty > 0.3, *then* carry an umbrella.

A set of production rules can embody a large collection of expert knowledge. To reproduce part of an expert's reasoning processes, we can use sequences of rules by **chaining.** In **forward chaining,** we use the available set of known facts (that is, data about the situation of interest that are in working memory) to trigger, or **fire,** applicable rules. The consequents of these fired rules are newly derived facts about the situation, and they are added to working memory. From the total set of facts now in working memory, additional rules may be triggered, asserting still more derived facts. This process continues until we discover all that can be found from the initial data. Because forward chaining is triggered by the known facts or specific events that occur, it is called **data driven** or **event driven.** An example of forward chaining is shown in Box 2.2.

In **backward chaining,** we start out with the goal of proving a possible conjecture, say *C.* We look for a rule that might prove it—a rule such as "*If A* and *B, then C*" that has the conjecture in its consequent. If *A* and *B* are known to be true, then we have established *C.* If not, we try to establish the rule by setting up the subgoals of trying to prove the rule's antecedents (that is, trying to prove both *A* and *B*). Each of these subgoals is worked on in the same way, thus trying to prove *A* by finding a rule with *A* in its consequent and establishing that rule's antecedents as new subgoals. The chaining continues backward through rules, from consequents back to antecedents, until antecedents are reached that are given data or can be confirmed externally (such as by asking the system's user), or we fail because we get to antecedents that we cannot prove or are known to be false. Because backward chaining starts with possible hypotheses or goals, it is called **hypothesis driven,** or **goal driven.** An example of backward chaining is shown in Box 2.2.

BOX 2.2
FORWARD CHAINING AND BACKWARD CHAINING

Assume the following expert rules of baseball strategy are established:

Rule I:
   If the game is in the late innings,
      and **X** is the batter,
      and **X** is a weak hitter,
   Then replace **X** with a pinch hitter.

Rule II:
   If the game is in the late innings,
      and **X** is playing in the field,
      and **X** is a poor fielder,
   Then put in a substitute fielder for **X**.

Rule III:
   If the batting average of **X** is less than .250,
      and **X** is not a power hitter,
   Then **X** is a weak hitter.

Rule IV:
> *If* the inning is the eighth,
>   *or* the inning is the ninth,
> *Then* the game is in the late innings.

Here are the facts that are known about the present situation, which are in working memory:

Fact 1: The inning is the ninth.
Fact 2: Prerau is the batter.
Fact 3: Prerau is a poor fielder.
Fact 4: The batting average of Prerau is .187.
Fact 5: Prerau is not a power hitter.

FORWARD CHAINING

In a forward-chaining system, the system takes all of the given facts and sees what can be determined from them. The following occurs:

Fact 4 and Fact 5 trigger Rule III, which asserts:
   Fact 6: Prerau is a weak hitter.
Fact 1 triggers Rule IV, which asserts:
   Fact 7: The game is in the late innings.
Fact 2 and derived Facts 6 and 7 trigger Rule I, which asserts:
   Fact 8: Replace Prerau with a pinch hitter.

No other rule can fire, so the forward chaining ends. Thus we have found three new facts—all that can be discovered from the given data using the four established rules. The last of the derived facts is an action item that the system recommends. Note that not all facts and rules may be utilized in a particular situation. Also note that initally both Rule III and Rule IV could have fired. The system utilized the simple conflict-resolution rule of choosing the first rule in the list that could fire.

BACKWARD CHAINING

In a backward-chaining system, the system would start with a conjecture: "Replace Prerau with a pinch hitter" is a *possible* action. Does the expert system consider it to be a *correct* action?

The following would occur:

Goal: Prove "Replace Prerau with a pinch hitter" is correct.
The only rule that might prove this is Rule I. The system can establish Rule I if it can prove all of its three antecedent statements, which are set up as Subgoals 1, 2, and 3:

Subgoal 1: Prove "The game is in the late innings" is correct.

The only rule that might prove this is Rule IV. The system can establish Rule IV if it can prove either one of its two antecedent statements, which are set up as Subgoals 1.1 and 1.2:

Subgoal 1.1: Prove "The inning is the eighth" is correct.

The system has no way to prove this, so Subgoal 1.1 fails.

Subgoal 1.2: Prove "The inning is the ninth" is correct.

This statement is given (Fact 1), so Subgoal 1.2 succeeds.

Therefore Subgoal 1 succeeds.

Subgoal 2: Prove "Prerau is the batter" is correct.

This statement is given (Fact 2), so Subgoal 2 succeeds.

Subgoal 3: Prove "Prerau is a weak hitter" is correct.

The only rule that might prove this is Rule III. The system can establish Rule III if it can prove both of its two antecedent statements, which are set up as Subgoals 3.1 and 3.2:

Subgoal 3.1: Prove "The batting average of Prerau is less than .250" is correct.

This statement is true from the given (Fact 4), so Subgoal 3.1 succeeds.

Subgoal 3.2: Prove "Prerau is not a power hitter" is correct.

This statement is given (Fact 5), so Subgoal 3.2 succeeds.

Therefore Subgoal 3 succeeds.

Therefore the primary goal succeeds.

The conjecture has been established, and the backward chaining ends.

In both forward and backward chaining, usually two or more rules are applicable at the same time. This set of applicable rules is called the **conflict set.** When there is more than one rule in the conflict set, **conflict-resolution** techniques are utilized to determine which rule should fire. An example of a simple conflict-resolution technique would be to choose the rule that appears earliest in the knowledge base's list of rules. Two more sophisticated techniques are:

1. Select the rule of the conflict set that is the most specific to the situation (thus preferring a more customized rule to a more general rule).

2. Select the rule that is most related to the result of the rule just used (thus encouraging following of a line of reasoning to its conclusion before trying another line of reasoning).

Forward chaining is used to determine what can be found from a set of data. Backward chaining is used when we have a set of conjectures and want to establish which one(s) are correct. Sometimes it is beneficial to use both inference techniques in different parts of the same problems. This approach is sometimes called **mixed chaining.**

2.5.2 FRAMES, INHERITANCE, AND OBJECT-ORIENTED PROGRAMMING

An important way to represent knowledge in an expert system is by utilizing frames. A **frame** is a structure containing information about a single entity—a concept, item, or class. It consists primarily of a set of slots, each of which contains information about the entity. A **slot** is component of a frame that refers to a specific attribute of the frame entity and contains the value of that attribute (if the value is known). For example, to represent information including Facts 2–5 of Box 2.2, we might establish a frame for the "Prerau" entity. The PRERAU frame would have slots for "Batting Average" and the other attributes of Prerau that we want to represent. This frame might look as shown in Figure 2.3.

A slot can contain different types of information: information that is fixed (such as FULL–NAME), information that is probably static for the problem at hand (FIELDING–ABILITY), and information that can vary during a program run (PRESENT–STATUS–IN–GAME). It can also act as a placeholder for information that is currently unknown (IS–WEAK–HITTER?) and might be filled in during the processing of the program. In some frame systems, slots can contain multiple values.

Each slot can have a set of **facets,** which contain additional information related to the slot. One facet that a slot might have is RANGE, which

FIGURE 2.3 A frame

FRAME–NAME: Prerau	
Attribute	*Value*
BATTING–AVERAGE	.187
COLOR–OF–UNIFORM	[unknown]
FIELDING–ABILITY	Poor
FULL–NAME	David Stewart Prerau
OWNS–BASEBALL–GLOVE?	[unknown]
IS–POWER–HITTER?	No
IS–WEAK–HITTER?	[unknown]
PRESENT–STATUS–IN–GAME	Batter

would contain the set of possible values for the slot. (A frame system with this feature would issue an error message if a value outside the range is inserted in the slot.) For example, the BATTING-AVERAGE slot should have RANGE = *0* to *1.000,* while the IS-POWER-HITTER? slot might have RANGE = *"Yes"* or *"No"*. Other common facets are DEFAULT VALUE, COMMENT, and the slot's VALUE itself.

A slot might have an associated **demon,** a program that is triggered when a particular action related to the slot occurs, such as when the slot value is initially inserted, when it is changed, or when it is retrieved. For example, it is possible to defer calculation of a slot value until the program actually needs that value by using an if-needed demon. The slot value is *"unknown"* until the program needs the value of that attribute and tries to retrieve it. When that happens, the demon is triggered, and the program is run to calculate the value and fill it in the slot. Thus, instead of calculating and storing Prerau's BATTING-AVERAGE, the PRERAU frame could store his OFFICIAL-TIMES-AT-BAT and TOTAL-HITS. If and when Prerau's batting average is needed and the program tries to retrieve the value of the BATTING-AVERAGE slot, this action would trigger a demon, which would run a procedure, *Get-Batting-Average.* This procedure would calculate

$$BattingAverage = TotalHits / OfficialTimesAtBat$$

by retrieving the TOTAL-HITS slot value, dividing it by the OFFICIAL-TIMES-AT-BAT slot value, and returning the result as the value of the BATTING-AVERAGE slot. If Prerau's batting average is never needed during a particular program run, the calculation never need be performed.

A set of frames can be arranged in a frame structure, relating certain frames to other frames. The most basic relation between frames is the parent-child relation. Here, one frame (the parent) represents a class of items, and a set of (child) frames represents either the class's subclasses or the specific members (or "instances") of the class. For example, there could be a generic frame called BASEBALL-PLAYER representing the class of baseball players and containing information common to or generally considered true for all baseball players (for example, that they are good athletes, that they own a baseball glove, and so on). Each subclass of the class of baseball players, such as the set of players for a specific team (e.g., the Blue Sox), would be represented by a frame that is a child of the BASEBALL-PLAYER frame. Thus a generic BLUE SOX-PLAYER frame would be a child of BASEBALL-PLAYER and would contain information generally true for every Blue Sox player (such as the name of their manager, the color of their uniform, and so on). Frames representing specific instances of that subclass, that is particular players on the team (such as Prerau), would be children of the BLUE SOX-PLAYER frame. This hierarchical situation can be represented by a structural chart (Figure 2.4). A large frame hierarchy is shown in Figure 10.10.

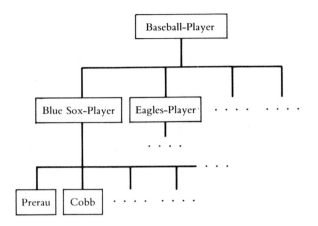

FIGURE 2.4 A simple frame structure

There are many possible relations between frames in addition to the subclass and instance relations. For example, one frame could represent A-PART-OF what is represented by another frame (thus the INFIELD frame has the A-PART-OF relation with the BASEBALL-FIELD frame). While A-PART-OF is a standard type of relationship, it is often possible to define frame relationships specifically for the situation at hand. Thus the frame representing the Blue Sox team's manager and the frame representing Prerau would be related by the IS-MANAGER-OF relation.

A major benefit of utilizing a frame structure is to make use of **inheritance.** When an entity is known to be a member of a class, generally a great deal can be assumed about it (generally baseballs are white, baseball bats are long and thin, baseball games are nine innings long, members of the Blue Sox have a certain manager, and so on). Inheritance allows all the information known about class members in general to be considered true for each individual member of the class, unless we know expressly to the contrary. This inherited information therefore does not have to be entered specifically for each member. A generic class frame is set to contain attribute values that usually or always apply to the members of the class. Then the frame system's inheritance mechanism causes each class member's frame to inherit these values automatically from the class frame. If we know specific information about the class member that contradicts an inherited value, this information is entered directly in the appropriate slot in the class-member frame, and it overrides any inherited value. For example, if it is known that the color of the uniform of Blue Sox players is royal blue, then that information does not have to be specified for each individual player. We would insert the value "Royal-Blue" in the COLOR-OF-UNIFORM slot in the generic BLUE SOX-PLAYER frame. The value would be automatically inherited by all the child frames, including the PRERAU frame (Figure 2.5). Thus if at some point the expert system program wanted to retrieve the value of COLOR-OF-UNIFORM from the PRERAU frame,

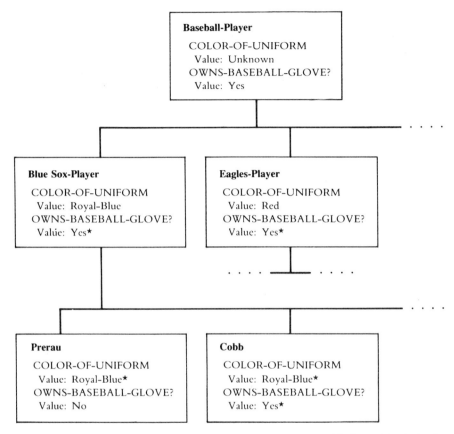

FIGURE 2.5 Inheritance of slot values

it would get the value "Royal-Blue" even though that value had never been specifically entered in the frame.

Values can be inherited through more than one level of the frame structure. Thus if we assume every baseball player owns a baseball glove, we can set the OWNS-BASEBALL-GLOVE? slot in the generic BASE-BALL-PLAYER frame to the value "Yes". That value would be inherited by the generic BLUE SOX-PLAYER frame and, through it, by the PRERAU frame and similarly every other frame representing a specific baseball player. Inherited values can be overridden when specific counter information is known. If we know that Prerau does not own a baseball glove, we would set the value of OWNS-BASEBALL-GLOVE? in the PRERAU frame to "No", as shown in Figure 2.5. This value would take precedence over the value that would otherwise have been inherited.

In some frame systems, the same frame can be a child of (and thus inherit from) more than one parent frame. This **multiple inheritance** can be used to give an individual that is a member of more than one class the attributes of each of the classes. It can also be a way to create a frame from a set of feature frames by "mixing in" those features that pertain to the created frame. If Prerau is also a knowledge engineer, then the PRERAU frame will be a child of both the BLUE SOX-PLAYER and the KNOWL-EDGE-ENGINEER generic frames, as shown in Figure 2.6., and it will have slots and slot values inherited from both.

If two parent frames of the same child frame have the same slot (and thus potentially two different values to inherit), then a technique for determining the inheritance must be specified. Thus the value in one particular parent frame might always be inherited, or the sum of the two values, or the average of the two values, or the higher of the two, and so forth. For example, if there were standard salaries for Blue Sox players and for knowledge engineers, the SALARY slot of the PRERAU frame would be set up to sum the values of the SALARY slots of its parent frames.

Object-oriented programming is a set of techniques that allows programs to be built using objects as the basic data item and using actions on objects as the active mechanism. An **object** here is a data structure that contains all information related to a particular entity, and thus it might be considered a frame with some additional features. The primary additional features are the ability to contain and invoke methods and the ability to send and receive messages. Objects can be related to other objects by subclass, instance, and other relations, just as frames can.

Methods are procedures related to an object. They are distinguished from standard procedures in that they are stored in (or inherited by) an object's data structure and are invoked when the object receives a **message** from another object. The message contains information for the receiving object on which method to invoke. It also might contain parameters for the method. Different objects may have different methods with the same name, thus allowing the same message to invoke a distinct procedure in each object. When a method runs, it may compute and return some result,

FIGURE 2.6 Multiple inheritance

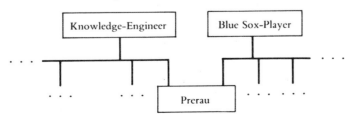

make changes to its own internal data, and/or send messages to other objects (thus invoking methods in those objects).

For example, a PRERAU object might have a *Compute-My-Batting-Average* method. This method computes batting average in a way similar to the demon. When any object needs to know Prerau's batting average, it would send the message *"What-is-your-batting-average?"*, to the PRERAU object. This object would be set up such that when it receives the *"What-is-your-batting-average?"* message, it runs the *Compute-My-Batting-Average* method and returns the result.

Objects in a parent–child relation can inherit not only attribute values but also methods. Thus rather than writing a *Compute-My-Batting-Average* method for each baseball player's object, we can put that method in the generic BASEBALL PLAYER object. It would then automatically be inherited to every baseball player instance (such as PRERAU).

CHAPTER 3

Planning and Managing the Development

- What are the major phases of an expert system project?
- What steps should be taken to start an expert system development project?
- How should each development phase be planned and managed?
- How should the final deployment phase be handled?
- What types of resources are needed for each phase?

There are several major phases to an expert system development project. Each requires certain resources and requires personnel with certain skills (which may differ from the skills required for other phases). No two projects are alike, and there are several ways to plan and manage an expert system project. Nevertheless a reasonable plan for an expert system development project will probably include the phases similar to those shown in Figure 3.1. This chapter defines each phase, discusses how to plan for and manage them, and takes up issues related to the initiating and managing of an expert system project. Subsequent chapters delve into each of the major areas of expert system development in detail.

3.1 INITIAL PHASES

In the initial phases of the project, management approval is obtained for the project, and the original project team is formed. The team investigates possible domains for the expert system and selects one. In addition, project personnel survey available computers and knowledge engineering software tools and then choose the development environment for the project.

3.1.1 PROJECT START-UP

At the start of an expert system development project, the objectives should be clearly defined. The objectives may depend on such factors as the extent of previous company experience in expert system development, the expertise of available staff, and the level in the hierarchy and the purview of the person who initiates the project. Some possible project goals are:

■ To "do something in artificial intelligence"; to "show that we're in AI."

■ To learn about the expert systems field to "see what it can do for us."

FIGURE 3.1 Phases of an expert system development

```
INITIAL PHASES
    ■  Project start-up
    ■  Selection of the domain
    ■  Selection of the development environment
CORE DEVELOPMENT PHASES
    ■  Development of a feasibility prototype system
    ■  Development of a full prototype system
FINAL DEVELOPMENT AND DEPLOYMENT PHASES
    ■  Development of a production system
    ■  System deployment
    ■  System operation and maintenance
```

- To educate the staff about expert systems technology.

- To encourage the spread of AI technology around the corporation.

- To build a flashy demonstration system to try to ensure additional funding.

- To build a small system for a small but real application with a payoff to the company.

- To develop a major expert system for a real application with a large payoff, either for use internally or as a product to sell.

- To study or discover expert system development techniques.

- To perform theoretical AI research.

Some projects have more than one objective. The vital point is that the objective(s) should be clear and understood by all concerned. It is important from the beginning of the project to avoid unreasonable expectations.

The project should not, in most cases, simultaneously attempt both to develop a real expert system for actual use and to make major advances in the state of the art of expert system technology. It is a formidable task to try to make a major advance in the state of the art of expert systems. It is equally formidable to try to develop a major expert system for a practical application and to overcome all the technical, economic, and political obstacles to its success. Attempting to do both simultaneously is laudable but much more difficult than doing either alone. This is not to say that a project developing an application expert system cannot generate new expert system concepts. It might be that the only way to attack a problem is to try new approaches. In fact sometimes a real problem might reveal a previously unknown weakness in a standard technique, or it might reveal that no known technique fits. In either case the development project might have to research new areas and may formulate new concepts or principles. On the other hand, a more research-oriented project might use a real-world application as a test case and might in the process develop an expert system usable to solve a real problem.

It is the goal of the project that should be clear. The project decisions should be made based on whether the project is investigating a particular expert system technology (using those applications, real world or "toy", that are the most helpful for testing ideas in the technology) or whether it is developing a particular expert system application (using those expert system technologies, new or established, that are the most helpful to developing the best possible system).

Once the project objectives are determined and before the technical parts of the project can begin, there are several additional start-up steps to be taken:

1. Leaders: Determine managerial and technical leadership for the project (discussed in detail in Chapter 4).

2. Management approval: Obtain approval of upper management for the project, or at least for its first phases. Sometimes management is eager to support the project (they may have initiated it). Other times, they must be sold on the project.

3. Resources: Estimate project staffing and resource requirements. Expert system projects usually are more successful if the staff is not very large and is well qualified. About three to five people is ideal for a larger project, and smaller projects can often be handled by a single knowledge engineer. The part-time participation of one or more domain experts should be provided for, as well as appropriate computer facilities.

4. Funding: Obtain internal approval for funding for the project—or at least the first phase—or solicit it externally and then obtain the grant or contract.

5. Schedule: Set up a project schedule. The development of expert systems in business and industry is relatively new and frequently technologically risky, and therefore it is often difficult to be sure that the project will succeed at all, no less to determine a precise schedule for it. Furthermore estimating the amount of work needed may be significantly more difficult than estimating the schedule of a standard software project.

If the expert system's domain has been determined, then in addition to the problems inherent in standard software scheduling, expert system schedulers have to attempt to estimate in advance the amount of the knowledge an expert uses to perform a task. They also have to estimate how subtle the knowledge is (and therefore how difficult it will be to acquire it). Such estimates are very difficult and are often in error. If, as recommended herein, domain selection is part of the project and not predetermined, it is even more difficult to forecast accurately the time these tasks will take. Schedulers can make an estimate based on the time similar projects have taken, set a tentative schedule and then wait until more is known about the domain before a more solid schedule is set up, or set up a fixed schedule and resource level for the project, based on a best effort by project staff. In the latter case, project personnel would attempt to select an application for which the allotted time and effort is likely to allow production of an acceptable system. Later in the project, if it becomes clear that a full-functionality expert system for the domain could not be expected to be developed in the time allotted, then a decision could be made on what should be done—extending the schedule, adding personnel, limiting the expected functionality of the expert system, or limiting the coverage of the system to a subdomain. Also after a domain is selected, a minimum functionality for the expert system and a set of additional desirable features or coverages might be defined. Within the fixed schedule, project personnel would attempt to develop the minimum-functionality system and add as many more features as is possible.

With such difficulty inherent in project scheduling, it is advisable to be conservative in setting project milestones within the limits set by the need to obtain project approval or to meet a narrow window of opportunity. Experience has shown that it it is always much better to set conservative milestones and finish ahead of them than to set optimistic milestones and not be able to meet them.

6. Team members: Identify initial members of the project team and arrange for them to be assigned to the project. Project leadership should consider whether these initial project personnel—and any others expected to be made available to the project—have the appropriate skills, qualifications, and training to perform all the functions required. Projects developing large expert systems for complex applications require well-trained, highly experienced personnel. Projects undertaking smaller and simpler applications can utilize staff with lower qualifications. (Expert system project functions and the desired qualifications of the people who will perform them are discussed in Chapter 4.)

If qualified personnel are not or will not be available to the project to perform one or more of the required functions, an important task is to plan how such functions will be handled. It may be possible to find and to hire people with the appropriate credentials; however, this approach may be difficult due to the limited pool of qualified people, and it may be ruled out entirely by staffing or funding constraints. The other possibility is to train available staff. Depending on what skills are lacking and on the size and complexity of the system under development, the training may require extensive university instruction, one or more short courses, some intensive self-study, some brush-up, or (for smaller, simpler systems) possibly just some introductory reading or hands-on training. (Training is discussed further in Chapters 4 and 13.)

All of these steps are highly dependent on the organization and the specific situation.

> The project that produced the *COMPASS* expert system was called the Knowledge-based Systems Applications Development Project. The project was initiated in the Knowledge-Based Systems Department of GTE Laboratories' Computer and Intelligent Systems Laboratory. I was selected to be the leader of the project, with the title Principal Investigator.
>
> The objectives of the project were:
>
> ■   To encourage the use of AI within the GTE Corporation.
>
> ■   To do this by developing a major expert system to solve a significant problem for the GTE telephone companies.
>
> ■   To develop general techniques for building expert systems.
>
> ■   To transfer expert system technology to other GTE business units.

After the objectives of our project were decided upon, we produced a project proposal outlining the approach that would be used to meed the goals. The project was approved through the standard approval mechanism at GTE Laboratories, with initial funding for a staffing level of three full-time members of the technical staff. The project actually started with two part-time people (including myself). Eventually, in the full prototype phase, the staffing grew to four full-time staff members. We also required the support of a domain expert at one-quarter time (plus travel expenses) and the availability of four development computers and four copies of a knowledge engineering software tool.

The project staff had excellent training and experience in AI. Of the five staff members who made major contributions to the development phases of *COMPASS*, three had doctorates, one had a master's degree, and one a bachelor's degree, all in AI or computer science. One project member came directly out of a top AI school with a degree in AI. The others had three to sixteen years of industrial experience, including two to ten years in industrial AI.

The original schedule called for a limited feasibility demonstration within one year of the project's inception and a full prototype system within a year and a quarter after that. Although the expert knowledge in the domain turned out to be significantly more complex than expected, the desired capabilities of the system were greatly expanded, and a major additional task was added (the originally unplanned transfer and deployment of the first version of *COMPASS*), the project was able to produce the two systems within about two months of the originally scheduled dates.

3.1.2 SELECTION OF THE DOMAIN

After project start-up, the first major phase of an expert system development project is the selection of the domain—the application area—of the system. In this phase, project personnel search for possible applications or investigate management-suggested or management assigned applications. Their goal is to select the one domain best suited for the project, based on a combination of technical and nontechnical considerations.

The domain should not be determined before the project begins if at all possible. The selection of an appropriate domain may have more to do with the ultimate success of the effort than any other decision made. Therefore it should be planned as an important phase of the project, and time and resources should be allocated for the selection process. If the project is preassigned a domain, however, an investigation of the appropriateness of the domain should be planned as an early part of the project. The larger, more important, more visible, and more costly a project is, the more effort should be invested in selecting the base available domain.

In certain circumstances (such as while finishing up some other project), it might be advisable to start investigating possible domains for a new project on a part-time basis. If domain selection requires making contacts with many people, interfacing with different and unfamiliar organizations, or traveling to several remote locations, there may be significant waiting between steps in the investigation. When domain selection is not a full-time process, the remaining time might be used to finish up another project, to allow the project team to augment their AI background, or to start the project's hardware and software selection phase.

As the project team gets closer to selecting an application, they should spend more time on domain investigation. This effort will not be wasted. A significant part of the work will be spent investigating the domain that eventually will be chosen. All of that work may be considered the beginning of the system development phase, since one part of that phase consists of getting background information on the domain. Even the time spent investigating other nonchosen domains often proves valuable. The next time this or another associated group begins an expert system project, they can consider the domains that were rated almost as highly as the selected domain to be good candidates for reinvestigation by the new project and can use any information and contacts made during the original investigation.

Although one person can pursue domain selection, a team of two or more is preferable for a larger project. Speaking to people in disciplines often far removed from one's own is difficult. It is easy to miss a major point or later to realize that a point that seemed evident while speaking to the domain person was not clear. Therefore it is very helpful for a domain selection person to have others to talk with to help clarify some of these problems and to pursue ideas. Moreover weighing the possible applications is a highly judgmental process, and it is useful to have more than one opinion on many of the issues. For this reason, using the same team of people to investigate all major candidate domains is recommended, if at all possible. (We consider techniques for selecting the domain in Chapter 5.)

The importance of domain selection was clearly demonstrated in the *COMPASS* project. We devoted a large effort to exploring possible application areas before we selected the *COMPASS* application: the maintenance of a large telephone switching system, GTE's No. 2 EAX. (The *COMPASS* domain is described in detail in Chapter 5.)

At many points during the *COMPASS* development I thought to myself, "Had we selected domain *X* [one of several others we had considered] for this project, we would probably be having problem *Y* at this point in the development. But, we are not having that problem because of the selection of the *COMPASS* domain."

Management had assigned our project a particular part of the corporation in which to explore applications—the GTE telephone companies—but we were not given any constraints beyond that. I worked with another member of the AI group at GTE Laboratories investigating possible applications. We started on a part-time basis—initially about one-quarter time—while working on another project. The time I spent on domain analysis increased to about one-half time (with the other half of my time spent working on other parts of the project, primarily the surveying and evaluating of knowledge engineering tools.) Included was the significant amount of time I spent researching, considering, and compiling a set of criteria for selecting a domain (which form the basis of the set of attributes of a good expert system domain that is presented in Chapter 6). Assisting the two project domain selectors on an as-needed basis was a member of the GTE Laboratories' staff whose job was to act as an interface between the Laboratories and the rest of the corporation.

Based on contacts found initially through the interface person and later from leads found during earlier meetings, we visited several corporate locations and met with over fifty corporate managers and experts. We considered over thirty extremely diverse possible expert system applications areas and eventually selected the *COMPASS* application area. (Chapter 5 describes domain selection in more detail.)

We did not (and we do not) consider almost any of the time expended on domain selection to have been wasted. The *COMPASS* area proved to be an excellent domain for an expert system application. The time spent studying it directly benefited the subsequent phases of the project. The other results of the domain search—the identification of several other potentially good domains for an expert system (as well as information and contact persons related to those domains)—became a starting point for our follow-on projects to *COMPASS,* as well as being used by other groups in GTE considering the development of an expert system.

3.1.3 SELECTION OF THE DEVELOPMENT ENVIRONMENT

Another early phase of an expert system development project is the selection of the project's development environment—the computers to be used and the knowledge engineering software tool or computer language to be used for the development. In this project phase, available computers suitable for expert system development and available knowledge engineering tools should be surveyed to find the hardware and software pairing best suited for the project, based on both technical and nontechnical factors.

As with domain selection, this task should be considered part of the project and not something determined before the project begins. Since the choices for expert system hardware and software are rapidly changing and since projects often have unique requirements, each project should expend the time and resources necessary to make the optimal selections. This selection effort should be in reasonable proportion to the size of the project and should make use of any similar efforts done previously. There are several criteria to consider in making the selection, such as cost, capability, ease of use, and suitability for deployment. (We look further into the selection process in Chapter 7.)

Some projects are allowed little or no choice for their development environments, such as when the software and hardware have already been purchased and upper management will not allow any additional money to be spent. It is reasonable to give strong consideration to hardware and software already in house, especially if major expenditures have been made. However, project leaders should make it clear to upper management that new and significantly modified hardware and software products are continually coming on the market, and thus many decisions made in the past are no longer optimal. Moreover each project is unique: project personnel have certain skills; the particular application has certain requirements. Decisions made for other projects thus are often not best for this project, and it may be false economy to force an unsuitable environment on a project.

Ideally the environment selection should be performed after the domain selection because certain requirements of the domain affect the choice of the best environment. (For example, if the selected domain task requires a real-time response, hardware and software performance becomes a critical issue.) However, it is possible to work on both phases concurrently. The initial surveying of hardware and software choices can certainly be done before the domain is known. As the set of possible domains is narrowed, those remaining should be investigated to see if any have requirements that might affect environment selection. If none do or if the remaining candidate domains at least do not have conflicting requirements, then the domain and environment selection phases can proceed in parallel.

> Just prior to the beginning of the COMPASS project, our GTE Laboratories department made a study of possible computers for AI projects, and Xerox Lisp machines were selected and purchased. By the time the hardware for the COMPASS project was to be selected, nothing significant had changed to indicate that we should make a different decision, even if we could have convinced management to buy additional machines. Therefore we spent little time deciding on hardware and utilized the department machines.

> Because as we were the first at GTE Laboratories (and in the entire corporation) to attempt to build a major expert system, no one at the Laboratories had yet used a knowledge engineering software package. Therefore the decision as to whether to use such a tool—and, if so, the choice of that tool—was important, strongly influencing the knowledge representation and the success of the implementation. Thus we made this decision a major phase of the project.

> We started work on tool selection about a month after the domain selection process began. I worked on both phases of the project in parallel, slowly phasing out other work. A recently graduated engineer assigned to the project temporarily worked with me on the survey, and later an experienced member of our AI group joined the project and participated in the final evaluation. Using the techniques and considerations detailed in Chapter 7, we selected IntelliCorp's KEE knowledge engineering tool, finishing this phase of the project about the same time as the domain selection phase was completed.

3.2   CORE DEVELOPMENT PHASES

The actual development of the expert system program can be thought of as occurring in three major phases, although there can be more or fewer. The first two of these are the core development phases, when the expertise and experience of a domain expert is put into the system. First, a small feasibility prototype system is produced relatively rapidly to show the feasibility of the application. Then a full prototype is produced having all of the knowledge and scope of the final system. In the third phase, the production system is built, as will be discussed in section 3.3.1. In a smaller project, two or all three of these phases might be combined.

Each core development phase has three major aspects (discussed at length in Chapters 9–11):

1. Knowledge acquisition: Members of the project team meet with domain experts to find the expert knowledge used to perform the task of interest.

2. Knowledge representation: Members of the project team try to determine the best way to represent the elements and the structure of the expert knowledge, using the facilities and paradigms available in the development environment.

3. Knowledge implementation: The project programmers use the development environment to implement the acquired knowledge into a computer program based on the knowledge representation developed.

3.2.1 DEVELOPMENT OF A FEASIBILITY PROTOTYPE SYSTEM

Once a domain has been selected, the project can begin developing a feasibility prototype system. This is a rapid prototype expert system that implements a subset of the problem being tackled by the complete system. When completed, a feasibility prototype system should, as the name implies, give evidence of the feasibility of using expert system technology for the application. Another primary use of the system is as a demonstration to management, outside experts, and potential users. If support of the project has been weak or if funding needs to be renewed, flashy features can be added to the feasibility system to impress the funding and support sources.

The domain knowledge found for the feasibility prototype is valuable and likely to be the foundation of the knowledge for the final system. However, one approach to implementing the knowledge for a feasibility prototype system is to perform the implementation as rapidly as possible, with the goal being just make it work. Using this approach, the implementation ideally is done with the understanding that large portions (or possibly all) of the program may be completely rewritten when the work on the full prototype system or the final production system begins. (Thus the corresponding acquired knowledge would be reimplemented.) With this understanding, the implementation of the feasibility prototype can be significantly speeded. There need be little consideration made of efficiency, readability, uniformity, maintainability, and so on.

In addition to a rapid implementation, the feasibility prototype might use makeshift input and output communications. It might make do with fabricated input. It might have big holes in the system that are faked or programmed around. Finally it might not approach the skill level required in the final system. Since the feasibility system is by design limited in scope and performance, these limitations should be made clear to all interested parties, especially management and potential users, so that expectations are at the appropriate levels.

A feasibility prototype system can serve a number of important purposes, both technically and politically:

■   It allows the project developers to get a good idea of whether it is feasible to attempt to tackle the full application using expert system technology.

■   It provides a vehicle through which to study the effectiveness of the knowledge representation.

■   It provides a vehicle through which to study the effectiveness of the knowledge implementation.

■   It may disclose important gaps or important problems in the proposed final system.

■   It yields a tangible product of the project at an early stage.

■   It gives an opportunity to impress management or system funders with a flashy system demonstration, helping to retain or increase support of the project.

■   It gives an idea of what the final system will do and will look like to outside experts and potential users.

■   It allows the possibility of an early midcourse correction of the project direction based on feedback from management, consulting experts, and potential users.

■   It provides a first system that can be field-tested—yielding experience in using and testing the system and, if the tests are successful, credibility that the eventual final system will perform its desired function well.

■   It might provide a system with enough utility that, although it is not a final product, it may be put in the field on an extended basis. This early deployment of a limited system yields some domain benefits, gives experience to system deployers, system operators, and system maintainers, and might identify potential problems in those areas.

The feasibility prototype development phase requires staffing by the best people available, especially in knowledge acquisition and knowledge representation. In those two areas, project personnel will make initial decisions in this phase that may well determine the basic structures and methodologies utilized for the remainder of the project.

We developed a feasibility prototype system for *COMPASS* in about seven months. The staff started at two full-time people and soon added two half-time people. We selected a domain expert, who averaged about one week per month working on the project. Besides actually developing the system, during this period we spent a significant amount of time familiarizing ourselves with the KEE system.

Two "major" outputs of our work on this initial development phase were the selection of a name for the expert system and the design of a project logo. We spent a long time considering various names, constrained by the realization that almost all names related to telecommunications systems are acronyms. We wanted the name to convey what the system does for a telephone company: accept a central office switching system's maintenance printout data, perform an analysis of the data, and produce a set of prioritized suggestions for maintenance actions. (Box 5.1 discusses the *COMPASS* application in detail.) Finally our expert proved his importance to the project by suggesting the name *COMPASS* ("to point the way toward better maintenance"), which is an acronym for the Central Office Maintenance Printout Analysis and Suggestion System. Based on this new name, I developed a project logo (Figure 3.2). Such devices as a satisfying project name and logo added a little extra spirit to the project.

FIGURE 3.2 *COMPASS* logo

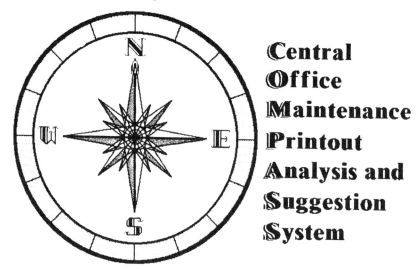

Central Office Maintenance Printout Analysis and Suggestion System

We called the feasibility prototype system *COMPASS-I* or *COMPASS-X*, the *X* standing for "experimental." Although the No. 2 EAX telephone switching system produces several types of maintenance messages, we restricted the system's scope to one type of No. 2 EAX maintenance message, the Network Recovery 20 (NR20), the most important No. 2 EAX maintenance message type. The system was developed as a rapid prototype.

We tried to make the *COMPASS-I* knowledge acquisition solid since we planned to use the knowledge that was found in any final system. The knowledge representation was the best we could do based on our fragmentary understanding of the domain at the time. However, the implementation was done as fast as possible, without a great deal of concern about uniformity, readability, maintainability, efficiency, and so on. From the beginning, the plan was to revise the knowledge representation completely and to rewrite the implementation of the feasibility prototype when the development of the full prototype began.

We ran carefully controlled field tests on *COMPASS-I*. The test results were excellent, exceeding our expectations. This gave us impetus and support to continue the development of the system to the full prototype stage.

We demonstrated the system to peer experts of the project's No. 2 EAX expert from three of GTE's telephone companies. We also went through much of the recorded knowledge in *COMPASS-I* with them, showing many examples *COMPASS*'s reasoning process, and used their strong approval to give backing to our decision to build the full prototype system. We solicited from them comments on how to proceed, getting their answers to questions such as, "What existing parts of *COMPASS-I* should be strengthened?" "What additional coverage is needed?" "Is it more important to strengthen the existing parts or to expand coverage?" "What features should be added to *COMPASS-I?*" "What should the output look like?" For the most part, we followed their advice in planning subsequent objectives.

We demonstrated *COMPASS-I* to GTE Laboratories' management and representatives of GTE telephone company management. They seemed favorably impressed by the demonstration, enough at least to give continued support for the project.

In all official documents, we called the *COMPASS-I* feasibility prototype a "limited feasibility demonstration." By using three weakening words—*limited, feasibility*, and *demonstration*—and by calling the system *COMPASS-X* for "experimental," we tried to make clear that this was not a final production-quality expert system—that the design might be weak, that the implementation had been done rapidly. These statements were true. But our attempts to keep the limited *COMPASS-I* in the laboratory met with limited success. Representatives of the telephone companies thought *COMPASS-I*, restricted in scope as it was, was a valuable system and wanted to get it into the field as soon as possible. Therefore although it was not originally designed for field use, we transferred *COMPASS-I* to GTE Data Services (GTEDS), GTE telephone operations' internal software organization. After a lot of work by our group at the Laboratories and the group at GTEDS, *COMPASS-I* was fielded. It was

used for over a year on a daily basis for about 20 different No. 2 EAXs (usually twelve at one time, rotating its use) in three GTE telephone companies.
Results and comments from users were encouraging.

3.2.2 DEVELOPMENT OF A FULL PROTOTYPE SYSTEM

Based on the results of in-house tests and field tests of the feasibility prototype system and the feedback from outside experts and managers, potential users and others, the leaders and management of the expert system
project must decide whether to continue development of the expert system.
If the results and feedback are positive enough for the project to continue,
it is time to begin the development of the full prototype system. The goal
of this phase is to acquire and implement all of the knowledge desired in
the final system. The full prototype is an upgrade and expansion of the
feasibility system to the complete coverage and capabilities desired, but
does not necessarily meet all other specifications (such as reliability and
speed) that may be required in a fielded product.

The final expert system can be produced directly from a feasibility
prototype by combining the full prototype and the production system
phases, but there are different concerns within each of these phases. Thus
it is probably better, especially for the development of larger expert systems, to keep these phases separated—at least to the extent of developing
the full functionality before concentrating on deployment concerns. However, since a deployable system is the ultimate goal of a real development
effort, deployment issues should be kept in mind during the development
of the full prototype.

The knowledge acquisition process for the full prototype phase should
make use of all the knowledge found during the feasibility prototype phase
and go on from there. That knowledge may need to be refined further,
and additional knowledge will, of course, be needed to expand the scope
from the limited scope of the feasibility prototype.

The knowledge representation devised for the feasibility prototype system should be completely reexamined, and then it should be revised where
needed or possibly a completely new representation developed. The major
decisions in determining the feasibility prototype's knowledge representation were made earlier in the project, when the team's understanding of
the domain and the structure and elements that need to be represented was
not as good as it is when the full prototype development begins. Thus at
the beginning of the full prototype phase, it may be possible to fashion a
knowledge representation significantly superior to that used previously.

As with knowledge representers, the project programmers know much
more at the beginning of the full prototype phase about what needs to be
implemented than they did when they generated the code for the feasibility

prototype. They likely can devise a much better, cleaner, and more efficient program organization. Since much or all of the code implemented for the full prototype might be part of the final fielded system, it is imperative to try to make the implementation efficient, maintainable, readable, and of uniform style. These were not major goals of the feasibility prototype implementation, where the primary goal was speed of implementation. Thus at the beginning of the full prototype phase, consideration should be given to reimplementing major parts of the implementation or possibly to rewriting the entire feasibility prototype implementation. Consider saving only the parts of the old implementation that were developed with final implementation in mind or will not form part of the final production system anyway (such as some utilities or any communications programs that will be rewritten based on deployment decisions not yet made). If it seems too extreme to rewrite the entire feasibility prototype implementation, the project should budget more time for the feasibility prototype development phase in order to produce code that can be carried through to final production.

If at this point the possibility exists of rewriting the program in large measure, the project might reconsider its hardware and software choices. It may not be worthwhile to make a detailed analysis, but based on the original project survey of hardware and software and the additional knowledge garnered during the feasibility prototype phase, the project team can consider whether a change might be warranted. Even easier to do, and often beneficial, is to change to a new release of the software or to a new upgrade or new system software release of the hardware.

When the full prototype nears completion or, if the program parts are separable into functional units, when a major part of the program is completed, field tests and a review by outside experts might be arranged. Favorable results give credibility to the system, as it goes into the deployment phases.

Producing the full prototype system requires project staffing to do the work required in knowledge acquisition, knowledge representation, and knowledge implementation, as well as in testing and evaluating the system.

> The development of the full *COMPASS* prototype system, *COMPASS-II*, took about one year. The staff started at three full-time people (and the quarter-time domain expert) and grew with the addition of one full-time person at about the midpoint of the year. We spent a great deal of time first instructing and then aiding GTE Data Services personnel in their deployment of *COMPASS-I*. Later GTEDS participated in some aspects of the development of *COMPASS-II*, including one GTEDS staff member who attended and contributed to all of the later knowledge acquisition sessions. Because of the great interest in AI and because the *COMPASS-I* demonstration was visual and impressive and the *COMPASS* field trials had excellent results, *COMPASS* became a standard stop on every visitor's tour of GTE Laboratories. Preparing for and giving these demonstrations took a good deal of time.

We began the development of *COMPASS-II* by deciding in what areas the knowledge of *COMPASS-I* should be expanded. Based on outside experts' recommendations and the opinions of the *COMPASS* domain expert, it was decided to expand *COMPASS* to cover all maintenance messages that require any analysis by the user. (Many maintenance messages clearly define a particular problem and thus require no analysis by a maintenance person, just a standard maintenance response.) This decision resulted in a desired *COMPASS* expansion from the capability to analyze one message type, the NR20, to the capability to analyze a total of 10 types. Also we decided that *COMPASS-I*'s analysis of NR20 messages was more than satisfactory, and therefore it did not seem worthwhile to invest effort in attempting to improve it. (The analysis of NR20s did improve as we developed *COMPASS-II* because we came upon some small modifications that could be made in the NR20 analyses while discussing the analyses of other maintenance messages.)

Thus the *COMPASS-II* knowledge acquisition began by using the NR20 knowledge intact from *COMPASS-I*. The knowledge acquisition techniques that proved successful in *COMPASS-I* were used for the remaining nine maintenance message-types. We decided that the basic *COMPASS-I* knowledge representation was good and should be kept, although many modifications were needed to allow for multiple message types, to allow for the different types of analysis techniques that might be required, and to include more modularity for ease of implementation by multiple programmers.

We decided to rewrite the *COMPASS-I* implementation completely. *COMPASS-I* had been implemented rapidly, with little consideration for uniformity of style, maintainability, readability, efficiency, comments, documentation, and so forth. In addition, a new and more powerful version of KEE became available just as work began on *COMPASS-II*. We utilized the new release of KEE and redesigned and completely reimplemented the NR20 program of *COMPASS-I*, this time with understanding that much of the program would be part of the final, deployed system. We put a great deal of effort into increasing the maintainability of the system, used a much more uniform style and more comments, and tried to eliminate all obscure code.

At the end of the *COMPASS-II* development, we ran carefully controlled field tests that yielded excellent field test results, giving us confidence that a deployed *COMPASS* would work well. We demonstrated *COMPASS-II* to peer experts of our *COMPASS* No. 2 EAX expert from three GTE telephone companies. Paralleling the procedure from the *COMPASS-I* development, we went through *COMPASS-II*'s recorded knowledge with them, showing many examples of its reasoning processes. Once again we obtained their strong approval of *COMPASS* and also their support for its deployment.

3.3   FINAL DEVELOPMENT AND DEPLOYMENT PHASES

In the final phases of an expert system development, the final production system is built and the system is deployed. For as long after deployment as the final system is in production operation, the program is in a maintenance phase, with program and knowledge bugs fixed and possibly new information and features continually added.

3.3.1 DEVELOPMENT OF A PRODUCTION SYSTEM

The decision as to whether to develop a production-quality version of the expert system from the full prototype system is based on several factors: the results of field tests of the prototype system; feedback from outside experts, potential users, and management; and estimates of the cost versus benefits or potential sales of the final system. If the decision is made to proceed, the development of the production system is initiated. In this phase, the full prototype is "productized"—made into a program that is robust, reliable, and can be fielded. Then the system is deployed and put into long-term operation. To produce the deployment system, several issues should be explored:

- **Possible rerepresentation and reimplementation:** As there were several potential benefits to redesigning the knowledge representation and reimplementing the feasibility prototype program when beginning the full prototype phase, there often are benefits in doing a redesign and reimplementation when beginning work on the deployment system. However, the full prototype program is usually much larger than the feasibility prototype program, and, since generally it is based on a later knowledge representation and implementation, it is usually in much better shape. Therefore relative to the full prototype phase, the benefits of developing for the final product a new representation and implementation over and above the costs expended in money, effort, and elapsed time may not be as great. Nevertheless it may be advantageous to do so. For example, when it is decided that the final production system should be completely rewritten to allow it to be run on new hardware or with a new software tool, the additional cost of redesigning the representation and the implementation would be significantly lower.

- **Deployment hardware:** The deployment hardware does not necessarily have to be the same as the development hardware, although often the hardware for development was selected with eventual deployment in mind. If the two are not the same, the porting of the system from one to the other should have been considered and planned. However, if the choice of deployment hardware has not yet been made, the system deployers should select the deployment computer based on what is best for the fielded situation.

The costs of porting the program from the development computer to another computer should be considered. Porting may require a significant amount of labor and may allow the introduction of errors, or it may be relatively simple and straightforward. The costs of porting should be balanced against the potential gains of using a computer different from the development computer: lowering the hardware cost (especially important if the system is to be deployed at many sites), making program operation and program maintenance easier, allowing the expert system to integrate better with other related systems or databases, using a hardware vendor that provides better support, using hardware that is standard in the application area, and putting the expert system on hardware that can be (or is being) used for other purposes as well.

■ **Deployment software:** At the same time the deployment hardware is being chosen, the deployment software—the knowledge engineering tool or the base language—should be selected. The deployment software tool does not necessarily have to be the same as the development software tool. As with hardware, the use of the same base software for both development and deployment may have been decided earlier in the project. Otherwise system deployers should consider the possibility of reimplementing the expert system program based on what is best for the fielded situation.

The cost of converting the program is an important factor. Conversion frequently requires a significant amount of labor and may allow the introduction of errors in the program, although in some cases it may be relatively simple and straightforward. The cost of conversion should be balanced against the potential benefits: lowering the software licensing or purchase cost (especially if the system is to be deployed at many sites), lowering the size requirements of the program by using a stripped-down deployment version of the knowledge engineering tool or by using a smaller tool, increasing the speed of program runs, making operation and program maintenance easier, adding better software facilities for dealing with program input/output and communications, integrating the expert system with other programs or into another program, using a software vendor providing better support, and using a software package that is already being used for other purposes by the system operators or maintainers (thus minimizing training and possibly purchase costs).

■ **Communications:** The full prototype system's communications routines and interfaces to databases and other data sources may not be optimized for efficiency in the deployment environment and mode of operation. As part of the building of the production system, they should be reconsidered and might need to be completely rewritten.

■ **Input/output formats and mechanisms:** The formats and mechanisms used to get user inputs and to deliver output to users may have to be reconsidered. Comments from the users involved in the field tests and from domain experts may aid in the design of good input/output formats. The production system's mode of operation may determine the input/output mechanisms needed.

■ **Testing:** The production system should be tested and evaluated. Validation tests should determine that the system effectively solves the problem for which it was built, at an acceptable level of expertise. Verification tests should ensure that the expert knowledge acquired has been correctly implemented, that the system is operating accurately to the extent required and is, as far as possible, free of programming errors, and that the operation is smooth and reliable. The extent of evaluation depends on the requirements of the task, but in many cases an extensive set of in-house tests and field trials should be performed.

The testing procedure should attempt to test the production system throughly. If possible, every part of the system should be exercised, in all expected modes of operation. The system should be run on a large selection of feasible input data, covering as many cases as possible.

The field tests should test the system in samples of all of the environments in which it will be used or at least in several typical environments. The duration of the tests should be long enough to allow to happen many or most of the types of situations that might reasonably occur during system use. Testing should also be long enough to allow users to become familiar with the system and to begin to adapt their work mode to take advantage of it. If the production system must meet certain service constraints, such as continual service with a prescribed maximum downtime or real-time response within a given time duration, tests should ascertain whether it can work within the required bounds in a real situation. (We discuss testing and evaluation procedures in Chapter 12.)

■   **Documentation:** The documentation that will accompany the system must be designed and written. It might consist of printed manuals, on-line documentation, or both. There may be levels of documentation for system maintainers, system operators, and system users.

The skills needed for the development and deployment of a production system differ to a degree from those needed to develop system prototypes. There is less need for great experience and knowledge of AI and much more need for experience and knowledge in areas related to the production of efficient, reliable software products.

GTE Laboratories' corporate function within the GTE Corporation includes the development of systems such as *COMPASS-II*, but not their operation or long-term maintenance. Thus it was expected from the beginning of the project that *COMPASS* would be transferred to another GTE organization for operation and maintenance.

Since GTEDS was running *COMPASS-I*, it was decided that *COMPASS-II* would be initially transferred to GTEDS. GTEDS ran *COMPASS* in limited production use for the GTE telephone companies while final *COMPASS* deployment decisions were being made. GTE Laboratories acted as consultants to GTEDS and slowly phased out direct involvement. The same GTEDS group responsible for the running of *COMPASS-I* was responsible for *COMPASS-II*. Much of what they did and learned with *COMPASS-I* was directly applicable to *COMPASS-II*. They tested the *COMPASS* software and phased over their production runs from *COMPASS-I* to *COMPASS-II* as parts of the latter passed the tests. They also developed some input/output packages and techniques that aided their use of *COMPASS*.

The GTE Laboratories *COMPASS* staff prepared a large amount of documentation: four volumes detailing the *COMPASS* knowledge, one volume on field-testing techniques, three volumes detailing the *COMPASS*'s knowledge bases, and one volume on *COMPASS*'s knowledge engineering tools.

3.3.2 SYSTEM DEPLOYMENT

When the production system is completed and fully tested, the system can be deployed. There are several factors to be assayed related to the deployment.

■   **Mode of deployment:** The deployment mode (or modes) of the production system must be selected. There are many options. The final system could be delivered to users as a turnkey stand-alone system; it could be operated as a separate entity but integrated into the user's environment; it could be imbedded into another system; or it could be run as a service, with the user's requests and data remotely accessed and the results delivered to the user.

The users of the expert system may be responsible for operating it, they may have responsibility for both operating and maintaining it, or they may just utilize the system as a service. The system could be available on a demand, scheduled, or continual basis. It could be available 24 hours a day or during selected hours and could be run interactively or in batch mode. A single system could service one user, many users in one site, or many users in many sites. There may be one level of service provided or a set of service levels, depending on the user or the price.

■   **Pricing:** If the system is to be sold outside the company or if there are to be internal payments made for its use within the company, price is an important deployment issue. To set the price, it might be necessary to perform an analysis to estimate the cost of operating and maintaining the system in production mode and other associated costs, such as marketing and training. A marketing study might determine the needs of users and the potential benefits of the system to them. Consideration should be given to the benefits to the developing company of getting into the AI market, being associated with a relatively new high-tech field, and so forth.

■   **Marketing:** If the user group is in-house and receiving the system without cost, marketing the system may not be important. However, users who must pay for the system, whether in-house or external, must be made aware of the system's availability (if they are not already aware of it) and will have to be sold on the benefits of using it. A major marketing effort may be called for.

■ **System introduction:** If the user group has been clearly identified and involved throughout the development, introducing the system into the working environment may not pose many problems. Users to whom the system is new might have to be convinced to change their present mode of operation. Introduction of a new system will change the status quo and may arouse the fears associated with automation. Beyond these standard problems, expert systems have an additional aspect that may cause problems in system introduction but that is inherent to the technology: expert systems sometimes make mistakes. Since the performance of expert systems is based on (and usually not as good as) the performance of human experts and since human experts in most fields occasionally make mistakes, expert systems occasionally (and sometimes frequently) are incorrect. Often users can accept incorrect results more easily from a human expert than from a computer program, and therefore there may be problems getting users to trust the system.

■ **User training:** The methods to be used for training system operators, maintainers, and users must be decided. Training may include formal courses, training manuals, and/or on-line tutorials.

■ **Documentation:** Any documentation for system operators, maintainers, or users not already written should be developed.

Although these areas are directly related to deployment, many can be examined and the choices decided on while the production system is being developed and tested or even earlier in the project. The project should have a deployment plan specifying the selected deployment mode, hardware, software, pricing, and so forth. It should specify the sequence and timing of events that will be followed to bring about the initial system deployment.

> While GTEDS continued limited *COMPASS-II* production runs, corporate management considered final deployment options for *COMPASS*. This decision took some time because several corporate organizations were involved (GTE Laboratories, GTEDS, GTE corporate headquarters, and the different GTE telephone companies) and because several possible options were considered. The decision made was that the final *COMPASS* deployment mode would be to have *COMPASS* sited in telephone companies and have it run directly by telephone company staff, without long-term involvement of either GTE Laboratories or GTEDS.

> Corporate management asked GTE Laboratories to perform the transfer of *COMPASS* to the telephone companies. We developed the final *COMPASS* deployment package (including additional software), provided training and documentation to telephone company personnel, and aided in the initial installation and runs of *COMPASS* at telephone company sites.

> The benefits of porting *COMPASS* to new hardware and software were outweighed by the costs in time and effort, and therefore *COMPASS* was deployed using KEE on Xerox Lisp machines. To offload communications from

the main *COMPASS* processing, an Apple Macintosh computer was used as a front-end and back-end for *COMPASS*. To deploy *COMPASS,* none of the core expert system parts of *COMPASS-II* was changed, although project staff developed additional input, output, and communications software. A comprehensive *COMPASS* operator's manual was written and delivered, and a training course for operators and maintainers was developed and provided to telephone company personnel. GTE Laboratories personnel spent time at telephone company sites installing *COMPASS* and then working with the telephone company people operating it. The deployment-related tasks were performed primarily by one of the original *COMPASS* developers, with the assistance of a technical writer. (More information on the deployment of *COMPASS* may be found in Chapter 13.)

COMPASS is deployed for use at 46 No. 2 EAX sites in GTE. These sites serve about half a million GTE customers.

Only minor training was necessary for users of the *COMPASS* output to understand what the system offers because the output is in the language of the users, the switching personnel. *COMPASS* has performed very well in the field. Its users have been highly enthusiastic.

3.3.3 SYSTEM OPERATION AND MAINTENANCE

As part of the deployment, several decisions should be made concerning the long-term use of the deployed system. Groups or individuals should be designated and trained (if necessary) to perform several functions.

■   **System operation:** If the expert system is to be delivered as a service, a system operations group (or several groups if there are several sites) should be formed and trained. If the system is to be a product run by users, an operator training group may need to be formed, and consideration should be given to providing help for user–operators with problems. Complete operator documentation should be provided. If the system is imbedded into another system, the operators of the other system should be trained in any new operating procedures required.

■   **System maintenance:** A long-term maintenance group (or groups) should be designated or formed and, if necessary, trained. Maintenance encompasses not only fixing problems found during system operation but also revising internal data and knowledge that has changed over time. Since maintenance will surely require not just changes to the implementation of knowledge but also changes to the knowledge itself, it is almost mandatory that a domain expert be involved in the maintenance process—at least on a consulting basis. A decision must be made whether to have centralized maintenance, with program patches and new releases coming from a single source, or a more distributed maintenance. The latter results in many nonstandard versions of the system and thus may not be preferred; however, it does allow complete customization of the system to the different circumstances of each site (a major advantage if such differences are important).

If the expert system is imbedded in another system, some thought should be given to whether one maintenance group will be used for the overall system or whether the expert system will be maintained separately. If separate maintenance is chosen, procedures for coordinating the two maintenance groups should be found.

■ **System expansion:** It may be desirable, during the years that the expert system operates, to make major changes to the system—perhaps expanding coverage, adding major new features and capabilities, or developing other expert systems or conventional systems that will integrate with or communicate with the original system. System revision can be done by the system maintenance people, but if the expansion is large enough, it may be preferable to use an independent group.

The skills needed for operating and maintaining the expert system differ from those needed to develop the prototype systems and from those needed to develop the production system. AI or software development expertise is not required to a high degree, especially for system operators. People with less experience and background can be utilized to run the system and to maintain it. Of course, if large revisions or expansions of the system are to be done, personnel with greater expertise usually will be needed.

> The decision was made for the GTE telephone companies to operate and maintain *COMPASS*, with GTE Laboratories to provide consulting as needed. Our role is planned to phase out, leaving *COMPASS* fully operated and maintained by telephone company staff. Decisions on whether there will be any future expansion of *COMPASS* and, if so, who would develop the expanded *COMPASS* have not yet been made.

CHECKLIST FOR PLANNING AND MANAGING THE DEVELOPMENT

☐ Set well-defined project objectives, and make sure all people concerned understand them.

☐ Use a relatively small but well-qualified staff.

☐ In projecting milestones and making promises, be as conservative as possible without losing support.

☐ View the selection of the expert system domain as an important phase of the project, not something determined before the project begins.

☐ View the selection of the development environment (the hardware and the knowledge engineering software tool) as an important phase of the project, not something determined before the project begins. Let the availability of already-owned hardware and software be a major factor, but not the only one, in selection.

☐ Plan to develop, relatively rapidly, a feasibility demonstration system with limited scope. It can give evidence of the feasibility of using an expert system for the application, provide an early demonstration of the system to management, outside experts, and potential users, and fulfill several other technically and politically important purposes.

☐ Make clear to all concerned the limitations of the feasibility prototype system in scope and performance to keep expectations at the appropriate level.

☐ Develop a full prototype system with complete functionality and scope, based on what was learned from the feasibility prototype development and feedback from demonstrations of the feasibility prototype system.

☐ For the full prototype, keep the knowledge found for the feasibility prototype, but consider completely revising the knowledge representation of the feasibility prototype and rewriting its implementation.

☐ Test and evaluate the full prototype and demonstrate it to management, experts, and potential users to determine whether to produce a production system for deployment.

☐ For the production system, explore the possibility of changing the system hardware and the system software tool with a view toward what is best for the deployed system. Upgrade the communication and input/output mechanisms, if needed, and throughly test the system before deployment.

☐ Determine the documentation needed for the operators, maintainers, and users of the expert system and produce it.

▭ Determine the mode of deployment (e.g., as a service or as a product).

▭ If the deployed system is to be used externally, adopt marketing procedures and set a price for the system.

▭ Find methods for smoothing the introduction of the system into the work environment.

▭ Set up a means of training users.

▭ Set up or designate a system maintenance group. Remember that since the knowledge as well as the program must be maintained, the maintenance group must contain or have access to a domain expert.

▭ Consider having a different group from the developers operate and maintain the final system. That group can be less experienced in software development.

Prerau, Developing and Managing Expert Systems (Addison-Wesley)

CHAPTER 4

Forming the Team

- What functions must be performed as part of an expert system development?
- What types of personnel are needed to perform these functions?
- What background, training, and skills are needed for each function?

Forming the team that will develop and implement (i.e., engineer) a major expert system requires putting together a group of people with many different kinds of expertise to perform the many different types of tasks required. Some tasks are related to the initiation of the project, such as the selection of the domain; some are part of the actual development of the system, such as acquiring knowledge from project experts and implementing the knowledge in a computer program; some occur toward the end of development, such as testing and deploying the system; and some relate to the nontechnical parts of the project, such as the political tasks of corporate interfacing and the provision of project leadership and management. In addition to the working members of the development team, there are additional people involved in the expert system, from those who give the system its first upper management support to those who operate the final system.

This chapter identifies the functions performed as part of the development of a typical expert system (see Figure 4.1) and discusses each in some detail. With such a large number of functions required, it can be expected that members of the project team will act in multiple capacities; however, it is certainly not necessary that every team member have every skill and participate in every part of the project. If no team member has a skill required, someone will need to be trained or people with such skills will need to be hired.

There is a limited pool of qualified, experienced expert system developers. It is obviously desirable to start a knowledge engineering group by finding and hiring either experienced AI people or university graduating students that are AI trained. If appropriate people with the right experience and qualifications cannot be found or if funding or staffing constraints prevent their hiring, the best approach is to train staff members. To train people unfamiliar with expert systems to the point where they can successfully perform some of the specialized functions discussed in this chapter may not be easy. If the goal is to develop small, simple expert systems, it may be possible to start with a small amount of training and background. But vendor claims to the contrary, the developing and maintaining of a large, complex commercial expert system is significantly different from other software-related tasks and is very difficult. Although tools for developing expert systems are improving, it still may take a good deal of time and expense to train someone, especially someone with no AI background, to be a highly competent knowledge engineer or AI systems engineer. Training is further explored in Chapter 13.

4.1 PROJECT TECHNICAL LEADER

The project technical leader needs a wide variety of skills to lead the expert system development from its infancy as an initial search for a domain, through all the steps of the development of the system, to the introduction of a successful production system. The leader specifies the types of skills needed by the project at each of its stages and works with the project manager to assemble the development team.

The project leader guides the team members in all the technical aspects

- Project technical leader
- Project manager
- Domain selector
- Domain expert
- Consulting domain expert
- Hardware/software selector
- Knowledge acquirer
- Knowledge representer
- Knowledge implementer
- Systems engineer
- Project tool developer
- Corporate/client interface
- Technical documenter/writer
- System tester and evaluator
- System deployer
- Trainer
- System operator
- System maintainer
- Consultant
- End user

FIGURE 4.1 Functions performed in an expert system development

of the project and thus needs a firm grasp of AI and expert systems. The leader controls and gives technical direction to AI people, some of whom may be used to the technical freedom historically available to those developing AI systems (for example, few restrictions on programming style or structure).

At the same time, the project leader leads the nontechnical parts of the project, keeping management happy and avoiding political problems. AI has been oversold in some of the technical and nontechnical literature, and many upper managers may expect expert systems to solve all of their problems. Others may see little promise for expert systems in the corporation. The project leader steers management, sometimes especially his own direct management, toward having realistic expectations of the project.

The project leader interfaces with people of all levels and of many disciplines: project staff, corporate management, the domain experts, potential system users, and so on. An important skill for the leader is the ability to foresee potential problems in the development process—political or technical—and to take early steps to avoid them or to minimize their impact.

I was the project technical leader of the COMPASS development. I came to the project with over ten years' experience in the technical management of projects in large organizations, a doctorate in computer science, and a diverse technical background. I had worked for several years directly in expert systems and in fields related to AI.

4.2   PROJECT MANAGER

The project manager performs all the typical management tasks but with a realistic perspective of the present state of expert system technology.

The manager selects or confirms the project leader and, perhaps with the assistance or the concurrence of the project leader, hires or assembles the personnel for the project. The manager motivates the project staff to perform well on the project.

The manager fights for upper management approval and funding for the project. The manager sets (or proposes to upper management) project schedules and monitors milestones, being careful not to overpromise what the project can do or to set overly ambitious milestones.

The manager is often the main political interface to other interested organizations, such as potential system operators and end users, and keeps the communications lines open to these groups. It is important to make sure that, as the project evolves, these groups' expectations match the present project status and the project's expected future directions. If the user or operating group does not have the personnel or the skills needed to assume their task, the manager attempts to encourage, guide, and assist their management toward making the correct decisions and expending the appropriate resources to ensure the ultimate success of the expert system.

Like the project leader, the project manager should have the ability to foresee potential problems in the development process—political or technical—and to take early steps to avoid them or minimize their impact.

The manager of the department that included the *COMPASS* project had been at GTE Laboratories for several years. Prior to *COMPASS* he had not worked with the GTE telephone companies.

4.3   DOMAIN SELECTOR

Domain selection is the process of meeting with corporate managers, experts, operating personnel, and potential expert system users to survey possible application areas for the expert system project and ultimately to select the project domain. In addition, the domain selection process should result in obtaining the political and financial backing necessary to begin the development phase of the project.

Domain selectors explain to the people with whom they meet (who are often not knowledgeable about AI and expert systems) what expert systems are and what types of applications are suitable. The domain selectors should be able to learn, in a short time, enough about an application domain with which they are unfamiliar that they can ask appropriate questions to determine whether the application is suitable for an expert system development. They need the interpersonal communications skills and tact necessary to elicit information from people whose jobs may be threatened or at least strongly affected by an expert system or who may have political reasons to push for or against particular applications. The domain selectors might be directed by management to consider only one particular application or to give special consideration to some pet application. They must be able tactfully to say "No" to management (or, at least, strongly advise "No") if the application domain is unsuitable.

The domain selectors attempt to keep expectations for the expert system project at an optimal level from the project's viewpoint—high enough to get management backing and sufficient resources for the project yet low enough that miracles are not expected.

Domain selectors need a good appreciation for the technical and nontechnical attributes that make a good expert system application. Thus they should have a good background in expert system technology, as well as a realistic insight into the political workings of the corporation. Using techniques such as those discussed in Chapters 5 and 6 as a starting point, they analyze possible application areas, pinpoint the good and bad points of each, weigh these points, and select the best application domain.

There is no specified training for the skills needed for the domain selection task beyond technical familiarity with expert systems; however, good domain selectors would optimally have good interpersonal communication skills, tact, a broad background, the ability to deal with areas outside their own background, and a familiarity with the corporate political process.

> A coworker and I were the domain selectors for *COMPASS*. We started with little knowledge of the GTE telephone companies, since both of us had worked previously at GTE Laboratories only on projects related to the nontelephone company parts of GTE. My coworker had been at GTE Laboratories for over five years and had some familiarity with the corporate political process though not any directly related to the telephone companies. We both had good communications skills and broad backgrounds.

4.4   DOMAIN EXPERT

Domain experts are the source of domain information for the expert system. They have a high degree of expertise in their field and the ability to impart the information to the knowledge acquirers and work well with the knowledge acquirers and the rest of the project personnel. (Chapter 8 discusses in depth the selection of domain experts for the project.)

> The *COMPASS* expert was a top expert in the telephone switch maintenance domain. He met to a large degree all of our other criteria for an expert system project expert.

4.5   CONSULTING DOMAIN EXPERT

Consulting domain experts can advise the project's primary expert(s) during the project, participate in major reviews of the system, evaluate the correctness of the final expert system program, and act as spokespersons for the ultimate users of the system. They are peer experts of the project's primary expert(s), with the expertise to discuss domain-related concerns with a primary expert (since the AI and computer people on the project team usually have little or no domain knowledge). They should be available on an occasional basis for such discussions.

A team of consulting experts can provide broad background and experience. They should be selected, if possible, from parts of the corporation or user community far removed from that of the primary expert(s) and possibly from subdomains different from that of the primary expert(s).

Consulting experts may also assist in the testing and evaluation part of the project. They can confirm that program output and the internal reasoning behind it are valid.

Clearly the consulting experts should have a high degree of expertise in their field. Although they should be able to impart the information to the knowledge acquirers, this requirement is not as important as for a primary project domain expert, since the consulting experts will usually be dealing with the primary expert and can use standard domain jargon. These close contacts, however, imply that they should be able to work well with a primary expert. They should not have any jealousy for that expert, should not feel threatened by the expert system, and should not have any other reason to be negative toward the project. They should be interested or excited by their association with the expert system project and feel that they are members of the project team, not outside critics. (Chapter 8 addresses the use of consulting experts in more detail.)

> The COMPASS project used three consulting domain experts, chosen as the top domain experts from three different GTE telephone companies. They met with the COMPASS project team on an occasional basis and worked well with the COMPASS primary expert.

4.6   HARDWARE AND SOFTWARE SELECTOR

The hardware and software selectors choose the project's knowledge engineering software tool or development language and the hardware. They survey literature, attend demonstrations of the leading products, perhaps arrange to do some work on units of the hardware candidates or use copies of the leading software candidates, sometimes run benchmarks or other tests to compare products, and eventually choose the best products for the project.

They should be able to make a reasonable trade-off between high performance and low cost. They should understand enough about the project domain (or of possible project domains, if one has not yet been selected) to give consideration to how the domain affects the selection of hardware and software (such as the effect on the hardware and software selection if real-time response is required, if fast access to external databases is required, and so on). They must understand enough about the project's deployment options to give consideration to how these options may affect the selection of hardware and software (for example, if the deployment is required to be on a certain computer).

A hardware selector ideally should be an experienced AI programmer with background on one or more of the major AI platforms. The ideal software selector should be an experienced AI programmer with good knowledge of expert system development paradigms and experience using one or more of the major tools. (We discuss a great deal more about selecting the system hardware and software in Chapter 7.)

> Our department had performed a study of available hardware for AI projects not long before the initiation of the *COMPASS* project. It was expected from the beginning that the project would use the machines selected by the department study and purchased by the department, and therefore the *COMPASS* project did not have a formal hardware selection team. However, we had a team of two, and later three, project members looking into the selection of a knowledge engineering software tool for the project. The initial two (including myself) started with little experience in AI software tools but learned a great deal. The third person had a large amount of experience with AI software although little with commercial tools. We were assisted in the selection process by the *COMPASS* project consultant.

4.7 KNOWLEDGE ACQUIRER

Expert system knowledge acquirers find the fundamental heuristics, facts, rules, and procedures used to solve the problem at hand. The knowledge is acquired primarily through a series of meetings with domain experts. (Chapter 9 examines techniques for knowledge acquisition.)

Typically, knowledge acquirers do not have expert status or prior experience in the application domain and often know little or nothing about the domain concepts or terminology. They should be able to deal easily with a person (an expert) who often has a completely different background and perhaps a completely different social and educational level. They should be able to learn quickly some of the important concepts of the expert's field and to pick up quickly and use (and feel comfortable with) the terminology and jargon of the project domain.

Knowledge acquisition is a difficult task. Knowledge acquirers should be able to understand an expert's often incomplete explanations and be able to structure and categorize the expert's knowledge. They should have the ability to specify and document the acquired domain knowledge based on a good knowledge of AI paradigms and the possible knowledge representations that may be used. Their experience with expert system implementation should allow them to consider feasibility of implementation whenever possible in making knowledge specification decisions, although their concern with implementation details should not be great.

The *COMPASS* knowledge acquisition, which I led, usually consisted of myself and one or two other project people meeting with the *COMPASS* No. 2 EAX expert. The knowledge acquirers were generally people with extensive training or long experience in AI. In addition to my AI background and experience, my lengthy experience in dealing with experts from fields other than my own proved to be useful background for the knowledge acquisition task.

4.8   KNOWLEDGE REPRESENTER

Knowledge representers develop the expert system's knowledge representation, defining the paradigms and structures that will be used to represent the knowledge in the implementation. Early in the project, knowledge representers may contribute to the selection of a suitable development environment. They will be most interested in the selection of the software tool and the paradigms that the tool will make available. If the selection is done before the project application has been defined or before much knowledge acquisition has taken place, the knowledge representers should have the ability to foresee the representation structures and paradigms most likely to be needed by the project and then select a development tool that makes the necessary paradigms available. If the development tool selection is made after a large amount of knowledge acquisition has occurred, they should be able to analyze the knowledge representation and select the best available system accordingly.

A knowledge representer should be able to develop quickly a good understanding of the expert system domain and the knowledge acquired during the first phases of knowledge acquisition. Based on an understanding of the AI paradigms available and the domain knowledge that must be represented, project knowledge representers select, define, and structure the knowledge representation (as we shall discuss in Chapter 10). Once the knowledge representation has been defined, the knowledge representers may decide how to partition the program implementation to the knowledge implementers. Furthermore since the knowledge acquired will continue to grow as the implementation continues, they monitor the acquired knowledge and alter the representation and the partitioning of the knowledge implementation accordingly. At one or more points in the development process, there may be a major redesign of the implementation, starting with a complete rethinking of the knowledge representation by the knowledge representers.

Knowledge representers for the development of large, complex expert systems should have extensive AI background and be familiar with potential AI paradigms for knowledge representation, such as forward and backward chaining production rules, frames and inheritance, and object-oriented programming. They should understand the strengths and weaknesses of each paradigm and be familiar with techniques for utilizing multiple paradigms in one system. For the development of simpler expert systems using lower-level tools or a subset of a larger tool, the available paradigms are usually restricted and the concepts to be represented simpler. For such projects, knowledge representers with less experience and skill can be utilized.

One to two other members of the *COMPASS* staff worked with me on the original *COMPASS* knowledge representation and subsequent revisions. Each had an excellent background in AI and was familiar with AI knowledge representational paradigms.

4.9 KNOWLEDGE IMPLEMENTER

Knowledge implementers develop the expert system program. They use the knowledge representational structures and paradigms defined by the knowledge representers to implement the expert system's domain knowledge as found by the knowledge acquirers. Knowledge implementers are the most skilled AI programmers of the development team. They design the detailed implementation structures of the program and implement their designs. As they implement portions of the program, they test these parts and find and repair program bugs. (We will discuss knowledge implementation in Chapter 11.)

Competent knowledge implementers should have a solid understanding of AI principles, as well as a high level of skill relative to the use and operation of AI tools and languages and relative to the running of AI computers and workstations. For example, they should be skilled at programming in the computer language chosen, using the project's expert system development tool (if one is used), and working in the environment of the project's hardware. Knowledge implementers should be able to learn quickly to use new languages, tools, and hardware.

The competency required by the knowledge implementers should have come about through extensive programming and expert system implementation experience. If personnel with this experience are not available, the competency required can be gained only by first obtaining tool-oriented, language-oriented, and machine-oriented training and then gaining practical experience with the target technology environment. As with other aspects of expert system development, if the goal is to develop a smaller, simpler expert system, knowledge implementers need not be as well trained or experienced.

The knowledge implementers participate in the selection of a suitable development environment for the project. They should be proficient or be able to learn quickly to be proficient in using the selected development tool to best implement the acquired knowledge.

> The *COMPASS* knowledge implementers had already developed the *COMPASS* knowledge representation. Each was an excellent, experienced AI programmer. None had any knowledge of KEE before starting on the project, but all had an excellent understanding of the AI paradigms provided by KEE and were able to learn KEE rapidly.

4.10 SYSTEMS ENGINEER

Systems engineering activities in the expert system development are directed at establishing and maintaining the knowledge implementation technology environment. The role of an AI systems engineer is similar to that of a traditional systems programmer.

Project systems engineers install and maintain the current versions of system development tools and languages on the project hardware and maintain an operational network environment if required. They develop the interfacing and communications between the expert system and the conventional software systems and databases that will be used by the expert system for input or output. This task often requires people who can learn rapidly the details of systems and database interfaces and have enough communications knowledge to develop the communications between those systems and the expert system.

Systems engineers may participate in the selection of special input or output systems, if needed, such as graphics displays, and they will likely be involved in programming them. They assist in the expert system debugging process by determining if a system software error is present and fixing such a problem if it is found.

An AI systems engineer should have an in-depth knowledge of AI software and machine internals but needs only a general understanding of AI principles and representation paradigms. The systems engineering aspect of expert system development has been largely ignored by the vendors of commercial expert system development tools. Consequently there is little formal training in this area offered by the vendor community. A good systems programmer with experience using the base language of the hardware and experience in computer communications and other related skills can make a good AI systems engineer.

One *COMPASS* staff member spent most of his time acting as the project's systems engineer. He had several years' prior experience in industrial AI programming.

4.11 PROJECT TOOL DEVELOPER

An expert system project's tool developers may fill the gaps in commercially available expert system tools to provide needed facilities for project knowledge implementers or may develop and provide a custom knowledge engineering tool for the project. If an available knowledge engineering tool (such as a commercial tool) is used by the expert system project, the tool developer should be able to develop needed utilities and software engineering facilities to augment it. Even the best available expert system development tools usually lack important facilities needed for real-world expert system development (see Chapter 7). At the beginning of the implementation and as the project proceeds, project knowledge implementers are likely to find important facilities that are needed by the project but that are missing or inconvenient to use in the expert system development tool being used. The trade-off between trying to work around these problems using the tool's existing capabilities and having the tool developer design and build a custom tool should be considered.

If the project requires a new knowledge engineering tool—customized or general purpose—the project's tool developers develop it. The development of a new knowledge engineering tool is a large task and in most cases should be a separate project.

A project tool developer should have a good deal of knowledge and experience in AI programming and machine internals and should be familiar or be able to become familiar rapidly with the inner workings of the software tool being used. The tool developer also needs to understand the project's implementation and should have a good working knowledge of possible tool features and representational paradigms. This knowledge will allow the identification of potential added facilities.

The *COMPASS* systems programmer also functioned as the tool developer. He developed several utility programs and other useful add-ons to the commercial software tool we used.

4.12 CORPORATE/CLIENT INTERFACE

A corporate/client interface person for an expert system development provides project personnel with information about and contacts within the operational parts of the corporation related to the expert system domain or with potential customers of the system. The development staff personnel are often unfamiliar with the application domain of the system and with the corresponding operational units in the corporation or the user community. Therefore, they often need assistance in finding information about a domain or in contacting the correct people to ask questions. This situation frequently occurs at the first stages of an expert system project, when the domain selection process is beginning, and may continue to a degree throughout the project.

When an expert system is being developed in a large company, a person unfamiliar with the corporate organizational structure may have difficulty tracking down the correct people to meet with or answer questions. This problem often results in a large expenditure of time and many unproductive searches. A good interface person can identify the correct people quickly and might know which of several people with the same title or in similar positions is the best one to approach. If the expert system project has little corporate clout, an interface person can help project people gain entree to and credibility with others in the organization who would otherwise be less likely to assist the project. When potential domains are considered, interface people should be able to point out potential political problems and turf battles related to particular domains, aiding in the selection process.

If the system users are external to the company, a client interface person may be able to arrange meetings with potential customers or with people familiar with potential customers. Such meetings can be used to gather information on the needs for the expert system, the potential customer base, possible revenues, and any technical or nontechnical obstacles to success. Client interface people might provide some of this information from their own knowledge of the client base.

When the project is selecting domain experts and consulting experts, an interface person's contacts can help identify the best domain experts and aid in arranging for the participation of the experts selected.

Relating to technology transfer, interface personnel might aid in the selection of the technology transfer receiving group and help obtain their participation. They can assist and guide the technology transfer and try to smooth any points of contention.

Corporate/client interface people should have a thorough knowledge of the workings of the corporation or customer base—at least the parts of it that are potential expert system domains. They should have a good understanding of the political as well as operational processes that make those parts work and should be able to speak the language of the domain personnel. On the other hand, they should understand or be able to learn enough about AI and expert systems to allow them to explain the expert system development project and make presentations about it to domain personnel.

COMPASS project members had little knowledge of the operations and organizational structure of the telephone companies that were to use the system. Therefore, from almost the beginning of the project, we had a corporate interface person working with us. He was a member of a GTE Laboratories group whose function was to provide liaison between the Laboratories and the rest of the corporation. Because he had worked in GTE telephone companies for several years, he understood their organizational structure and their needs and could speak the jargon of telephone company personnel. His participation proved very helpful to the project. His contribution was especially important during domain selection (see Chapter 5) and later during the technology transfer.

4.13 TECHNICAL DOCUMENTER/WRITER

Technical documenters and writers organize, record, and document important information for the expert system project. They write project-related reports, papers, and other documentation and perform project librarian and publications coordinator functions.

The most important information documented during the development phases of an expert system project is the knowledge elicited from domain experts during knowledge acquisition. It should be carefully and completely recorded during the knowledge acquisition sessions and then documented in a form usable by future knowledge acquisition sessions, by knowledge implementers, and by others—such as consulting domain experts—who may need to examine the knowledge. The state of the knowledge will change rapidly at times, and therefore maintenance of the document is very important.

Another type of knowledge important to document is intermediate information on the project. The tasks here may include keeping track of decisions made, suggestions to be remembered, standards set, and results found.

Project documenters and writers participate in producing the internal reports on the project that may be required and any external papers and reports. They may assume project librarian functions—organizing, cataloging, and storing the written documents of the project. Also they may act as publications coordinators, interacting with publishers or with a company publications department.

As the expert system passes from development to deployment, complete sets of documentation and manuals are usually required for system end users, operators, and maintainers. End users may need a users' manual to explain what the expert system can do, detail the options available, and describe how to direct the system to do what they require. Operators of the system (who may or may not be the end users) need manuals to describe all aspects of the system operation. System maintainers need full and detailed documentation of the expert system program and the expert knowledge contained in it. Furthermore when an expert system is deployed, there may be a need for promotional or sales material related to the expert system.

Project documenters should be good organizers and good writers. To document expert domain knowledge requires more than just recording rules and procedures from the knowledge acquisition. Much of the knowledge defined at knowledge acquisition sessions may seem complete at the time, but it is agreed upon in a particular context and often with some tacit assumptions. A good documenter should be able to understand and take into account this assumed information when putting together the final knowledge documentation. To do so, documenters of the domain knowledge should have some understanding of AI formalisms and should be able to understand the domain concepts used.

On the other hand, the development of more standard documentation—operators' manuals, users' manuals, external papers and reports, and so on—may require the skills of professional technical writers. Such people need to know just a little about AI and expert systems but should learn enough about the domain to understand what the expert system does and to utilize domain terminology and jargon. They may need to know about the publication process to act as publication coordinators.

> All of the *COMPASS* staff participated in knowledge documentation, but one (myself at first and later another project member) acted as the primary knowledge documenter. The two of us who filled this role had relatively good writing and information-organizing skills, as well as a good understanding of the domain knowledge being acquired.
>
> Documentation of the *COMPASS* program was handled by the implementers of each program part. It was compiled and integrated by a professional technical writer, who worked a short time with the project. A second professional technical writer developed a detailed *COMPASS* operator's manual. She had an advanced degree in technical and professional writing and several years' experience. She also participated in operator training and developed training material.

4.14 SYSTEM TESTER AND EVALUATOR

System testers evaluate the expert system program. Validation tests ascertain whether the system is appropriately producing expert results at an acceptable level of accuracy, and verification tests determine if the program implements the acquired knowledge and operates correctly.

In expert system development, these kinds of tests go on constantly. During development, the implemented system is continually compared against the expert on test cases. Differences between them usually mean that either the system knowledge is incorrect and should be corrected or that there is a bug in the implementation. System testers perform more formal tests on the expert system. They may evaluate the system's results by comparison against the project expert's results or against the results of an outside expert or panel of experts. Testers may design and run a real-world field trial. Other tests include standard ones done for any production software, such as line-by-line testing of the code. Testers may perform testing of knowledge structures. (Chapter 12 addresses in depth the techniques of testing and evaluating expert systems.)

System testers should be able to organize a testing situation, operate the system, quickly fix small bugs in the system, and compile, analyze, and interpret test results. They should have access to (or should themselves be) the knowledge implementers in case major troubles appear that might otherwise invalidate the tests. Furthermore system testers should be good coders, familiar with the system's software development tool and base language. They should understand the techniques of formal software testing.

> The entire GTE Laboratories project team participated as system testers and evaluators, running tests against the *COMPASS* expert and other experts, and running several field trials. GTE Data Services personnel performed several tests on the program as well and also ran their own field trials.

4.15 SYSTEM DEPLOYER

Expert system deployers prepare the expert system for production use and deploy it.

Deployment personnel consider many issues: determining the method of delivery (e.g., as a service or as a product), selecting the delivery hardware, porting to new hardware if necessary, selecting the delivery software shell, porting to a new software shell if necessary, designing and developing the final user interface, optimizing the obtaining of the system inputs and the generating of the system outputs, and optimizing communications with any conventional software systems and external databases. They should be involved in performing reimplementation if necessary, optimizing the code, determining methods to attract users, determining operational procedures, determining maintenance procedures, integrating the system into the users' working environment, and selecting a pricing structure. (We discuss deployment in Chapter 13.)

The deployment staff thus needs to understand the software tool and language of the program. They need knowledge of hardware and software deployment options and the skills to port the system to the selected options. They need knowledge of databases and communications. The deployment staff needs to include someone with skills in marketing and interfacing with potential users.

> The final deployment of *COMPASS* was performed by GTE Laboratories *COMPASS* project members and GTE telephone company personnel. The telephone company people were trained on *COMPASS* by GTE Laboratories.

4.16 TRAINER

Training staff provide training related to the operation and use of the expert system. As part of the original deployment effort and possibly continuing for the life of the expert system, there is a need for training. Depending on the transparency of the expert system interface and output, end users may need training on how to get the system to provide the information they require and on how to make use of its results. System operators may need to be trained on the operation of the system. System maintainers may need training, beyond documentation, on the inner working of the expert system program. Both operators and maintainers may need training on the expert system domain so that they can understand the knowledge in the system and the inputs and outputs of the system. Training may consist of formal classes, training in the field, or both.

Some expert systems may require the use of professional trainers, with experience in the education field. Other projects may be able to utilize project technical personnel or technical writers. Trainers should be good communicators so they can convey the concepts of the expert system. They should be as technically proficient as the trainees require in the domain, in AI and expert systems, and in knowledge of the expert system. For example, training maintainers about a complex expert system program requires great expertise in expert systems and the particular expert system program; training users of an expert system with a clearly designed output may require little technical skill. Trainers should be able to understand the problems met by the people being trained.

> The training of the telephone company personnel during *COMPASS* deployment was done by two members of the *COMPASS* project team: one of the developers of *COMPASS* and a technical writer. Training consisted of somewhat formal courses held at GTE Laboratories plus on-the-job training at telephone company sites. The developer provided excellent and detailed technical knowledge of *COMPASS*. The technical writer was able to put the training in terms more understandable to the trainees, relate to the problems the trainees had, and work with the trainees to overcome their training problems. She had previous training experience.

4.17 SYSTEM OPERATOR

System operators run the expert system program. They may operate it from a central location (as when the expert system is run as a service) or run it at the end users' site. If operation is simple enough or if the user group is sophisticated, the operators may be the system users.

System operators do not have to know a great deal about the internals of the system or about AI and expert systems in general. They should be able to learn how to get the expert system running (and how first to get the computer running, if the system is on a stand-alone computer), how to make the system perform under its various options, what procedures to take if there are system problems during the run, how to deal with direct complaints from users, what the system security procedures are, how to keep records of runs and outputs, and all the other details involved with running the system.

Thus, if not an end user, an operator often can be a relatively junior or lower-ranked person. However, if the system uses specialized AI hardware (e.g., Lisp machines), the operator should have a good knowledge of how to operate these specialized machines.

> GTE telephone company personnel operate *COMPASS* in its deployment at their companies. They began with little or no background in AI and expert systems, although some had background in computers, and others had experience working with the No. 2 EAX.

4.18 SYSTEM MAINTAINER

System maintainers perform maintenance on the expert system program. They find or are notified of bugs in the operating expert system, analyze the problem information and the system code, and find and fix the problems. Maintainers modify the expert system program as situations change and, if needed, make major alterations and extensions.

There may be more than one level of system maintainers. For example, there could be site-level maintainers who make quick local fixes for simple program bugs and also make customizing alterations. There could be centralized maintainers who make official bug fixes, maintain and update documentation, issue new releases of the code, and so on. A higher level of maintainers might make surface-level modifications to the program as new situations occur, such as changing data tables or parameter values. Finally, there could be a still higher level of maintainers who make major alterations and extensions to the program, including the acquisition of additional expert knowledge.

Maintainers should have good skills relative to the use and operation of AI tools and languages and the running of AI systems. In particular, they need skill and experience on the software and hardware utilized by the expert system. If people with such experience are not available, experienced programmers may be able to pick up these skills on the job, with some training, or by examining the expert system program in detail and learning from the knowledge implementers. Higher-level maintainers need more in-depth knowledge and experience in AI tools and knowledge representations, as well as knowledge of knowledge acquisition techniques.

> GTE telephone company personnel are maintaining *COMPASS* in consultation with GTE Laboratories. They are programmers with varied knowledge of expert system programs. Through training and detailed examination of the *COMPASS* program and documentation, they are learning how to maintain the program. The role of GTE Laboratories personnel is planned to phase out.

4.19 CONSULTANT

Consultants can be used to aid the expert system development team in any or all phases of the project. They can supply experience in expert system development to supplement that of the team. They might bring a broad background in AI, an academic view of expert system development, a knowledge of the latest techniques in the field of expert systems, expertise in developing expert systems in industry, or several of these.

A well-known consultant can provide technical credibility to the project effort—especially useful for internally justifying project decisions. Often management accepts the views of an external consultant when they would question the same views if they came from an employee. Consultants can give external visibility and credibility to an expert system project if they have a big name, are related to a well-known expert system development, or are associated with a university or other organization with a good reputation in AI.

Occasional regular meetings with a consultant can provide a focus for a status review for the project. These reviews can be used to discuss and decide on the next set of major decisions for the project. The consultant can be used as a sounding board for new ideas related to the project. The consultant should aid in steering the project on the correct course and in avoiding possible bad decisions or fruitless searches.

A consultant for the overall project should have established a good reputation in AI and expert system by having completed important research related to expert system and/or having been involved with one or more important expert system developments. The consultant should be familiar with all aspects of expert system development, including domain selection, knowledge acquisition, knowledge representation, use of AI software and hardware, and coding.

> The *COMPASS* project utilized one consultant, an MIT researcher with broad knowledge of AI and expert systems. He provided useful advice in most aspects of the project, especially in software tool selection, knowledge representation, and knowledge implementation. He also provided some initial technical credibility to the project until it established its own credibility.

4.20 END USER

End users utilize the output of the expert system in some manner to aid in performing their jobs. They do not need to know a great deal about AI, expert systems, or how this particular expert system works (unless they are fulfilling other of the functions mentioned in this chapter). They should, however, have training or knowledge in two areas. First, they should understand or be trained to understand how to interpret the results of the expert system and how to incorporate them into their job performance. Second, they should understand or be taught the limitations of the expert system. They should know what they can reasonably expect from the system and what they cannot. They should be made to understand that, like an expert, an expert system can and will make mistakes and that these errors cannot be corrected by fixing program bugs. Most end users, if they are familiar with computers at all, will be used to conventional programs that are always correct except for occasional bugs. Thus it may be difficult at first for them to understand that expert systems are a different class of system.

> End users of *COMPASS* are the No. 2 EAX maintenance personnel. They have found *COMPASS*'s output easy to understand and utilize. They required no formal training—usually no more than an explanation of its output form and a discussion on how to use it. Since *COMPASS* users were familiar with performing No. 2 EAX maintenance procedures that were often unsuccessful in fixing the problem at hand, they did not expect COMPASS to be infallible.

Cｈｅｃｋｌｉｓｔ ｆｏｒ ｆｏｒｍｉｎｇ ｔｈｅ ｔｅａｍ

☐ When forming the project team, consider who will perform each of the functions needed for the expert system development. Each project member normally performs several of these functions.

☐ The project leader needs a wide variety of skills, including the abilities to lead both the technical and nontechnical parts of the project and to work with management and domain personnel.

☐ The project manager performs managerial and political interface tasks based on a realistic perspective of the present state of expert system technology.

☐ Domain selectors should have good communications skills and a broad background to allow them to understand and evaluate domains with which they have no previous familiarity.

☐ Project domain experts should have great domain expertise and the ability to communicate well.

☐ Consulting domain experts should have great domain expertise and the ability to work with and advise a project primary expert.

☐ Project hardware and software selectors should be experienced AI programmers with broad background and knowledge of possible platforms and of knowledge engineering software development tools.

☐ Expert system knowledge acquirers should be able to deal easily with and to elicit information from an expert in an unfamiliar domain. They should be able to learn detailed information about that domain quickly and should understand the AI paradigms that will be used to implement to expert knowledge.

☐ Project knowledge representers should have extensive knowledge of AI paradigms. They should be able to use early knowledge about the domain to plan a knowledge representation.

☐ Expert system knowledge implementers should be excellent AI programmers.

☐ AI systems engineers need the skills of conventional systems programmers and an in-depth knowledge of AI software and machine internals.

☐ Project tool developers should have experience in AI programming and the ability to learn quickly and in depth the inner workings of a knowledge engineering software development tool.

☐ Project documenters should be good organizers and good writers, should have some understanding of AI formalisms, and should be able to understand the domain concepts used.

☐ Corporate/client interface people should have a thorough knowledge of the corporation in which the expert system will be used or of the clients for the system. They should have a good understanding of the operational and political processes pertinent to the project.

☐ Expert system test and evaluation personnel should understand techniques for testing expert systems and software in general and be able to organize and run formal tests on the expert system program.

☐ System deployers should know software, hardware, and operational options for the deployed system, how to optimize or reimplement the system, and how to integrate the system into the working environment.

☐ System operators need to know how to get the system to run and perform its several options, how to take corrective action when there are system problems during a run, and how to perform clerical tasks related to the system.

☐ System maintainers should be good expert system programmers. There may be several levels of maintainers—from those who make small fixes to those who make major changes, upgrades, and extensions of the program.

☐ Project consultants can aid project personnel in any or all of the expert system development tasks and provide technical credibility to the project.

☐ End users should understand or be taught the limitations of the expert system and how to interpret and utilize the outputs of the system.

Prerau, Developing and Managing Expert Systems (Addison-Wesley)

CHAPTER 5

Selecting the Domain: The Process

- Why is the selection of domain the most important project decision?

- Why is it undesirable for management to assign a specific domain?

- How can potential expert system applications be identified?

- What process can be used to evaluate the possible application domains, rank them, and select the best one?

The first major activity on the expert system project is the identification and evaluation of possible application domains and the selection of the best of them to be the domain of the project. This chapter discusses some methods for the identification, evaluation, and selection of the application domain.

5.1 IMPORTANCE OF DOMAIN SELECTION

The selection of an appropriate domain for the project may have more to do with the ultimate success of the effort than any other decision. It is a formidable task to develop an expert system for a suitable domain; a project attempting to develop an expert system for a poorly-chosen domain is likely to encounter many additional problems—making development more difficult and possibly causing the project to fail.

Since the choice of domain is so critical, a significant amount of effort should go into it, even for a small project. Selection should be a full phase of the project, not something determined before the project begins. Any time and money savings gained by short-circuiting the domain selection process will probably be more than eliminated by the problems caused by not selecting the best available domain.

To select the expert system domain, members of the expert system project team are chosen to investigate potential application areas. For larger projects, it is beneficial if at least two project members are involved. Their goal is to choose the one application best meeting the technical and non-technical requirements of the project. The flexibility they have in this decision depends on the circumstances.

Often in a corporate environment there is a very specific application—chosen by management—for which an expert system is to be developed. If those who selected the application area had little technical knowledge of AI or expert systems—the likely case—then the project team should evaluate the domain to determine whether the selected application is a good one. Frequently an application selected by someone unfamiliar with expert systems is not best suited to solution by present expert system technology. It may be best handled by non-AI technologies, such as database techniques, operations research, statistical methods, or differential equation modeling. Or it may be an application beyond the state of the art of expert system technology and for which there currently exists no expert system methodology likely to succeed (beyond converting the expert system development project into an advanced research project). If the problem can best be solved using a different technology, if the application is beyond the state of the art, or if there is any other major reason that the domain may not be suitable to expert system development, then the project team should act to try to change the domain.

Under another typical scenario, the project team may be asked to choose the best of several preselected corporate problems. Again the people selecting the list of applications may not understand expert system technology, and so the project team should evaluate each application for suitability to present expert system technology. In addition, they must rank the potential domains and select the best available application.

Under a third possible scenario, the domain selectors may be given large latitude. They may be asked to survey corporate or customer concerns within wide bounds to find a good application of expert system technology. Here they must find and identify potential expert system applications. Then they should decide which applications are suited to present expert system technology, ranking the potential domains and selecting the best available application.

To evaluate the potential of a possible application, it has proved useful to have a set of the attributes desired in a good expert system domain. In this chapter, we discuss a method for selecting a good expert system domain based on such a set of attributes. Chapter 6 describes an attribute set that can be used.

The experience of the *COMPASS* project clearly demonstrated the importance of domain selection. Throughout the *COMPASS* development, we saw situations where a major problem might have occurred had another domain been selected.

5.2   A METHOD FOR EVALUATING APPLICATION DOMAINS

Let us assume that the project has the charter to select any domain (or any domain within wide boundaries). An effective method for the domain selectors to identify potential domains, evaluate them, rank them, and select the best one is:

1. Get initial leads. To get some initial candidate domains to investigate, the domain selectors identify areas of high impact or major problems to the corporation or potential customers. In addition, management may give some guidance or suggestions as to desirable areas to consider. For all the identified areas, the selectors get names of people in those areas and use them as initial leads.

2. Set up meetings with domain personnel. The domain selectors meet with and interview managers, experts, and/or journeyman practitioners involved in each candidate application area. They should try to visit the locations where the domain tasks are performed, especially if there is a special environment or if special equipment is used. In a more limited project, a series of telephone calls or brief interviews might suffice.

3. Introduce expert systems. During these interactions with domain personnel, the first task is to introduce AI and expert systems to people who have never heard of them or, more frequently, have some vague (often erroneous) idea of what they entail. The goal is to introduce the people at these meetings quickly to the little they need to know about expert systems for the purposes of the meeting. One good way of accomplishing this is to discuss the set of attributes of a good expert system domain (or its highlights). This process brings up the pertinent issues without getting into unnecessary technical detail. Another useful practice is to describe some examples of successful expert systems. Certainly there is no reason to delve into such concepts as backward chaining or multiple inheritance.

4. Find domain concerns. Once the participants from the domain understand something about expert systems, they might be asked to describe problems and concerns in their domain that they think could be amenable to solution by an expert system. They should consider likely concerns in the future, as well as pressing problems of the present.

Many of the suggested application areas will be obviously unsuitable to expert systems technology. Some may be clearly unrealistic and far beyond the state of the art (especially if the meeting participants have been exposed to AI hyperbole); others may seem to the project team to be easily (or at least more easily) solvable by conventional programming approaches. This is not surprising since certain domain personnel may regard AI as magic that can solve any problem, and others may use the discussion to state their gripes and problems to someone who will listen.

5. Analyze reasonable candidates. Any of the suggested application areas that seem to have some promise as an expert system domain should be analyzed in more detail. Here is a prime use of the list of desirable domain attributes appearing in Chapter 6. A discussion of these attributes, point by point, for each suggested application will necessarily focus on many of the most important issues related to the potential success of a future expert system for the application. Some issues may emerge that require future study or consultation with other people. Even for a small project with limited resources for domain investigation, each attribute on the list should be considered, even if briefly for each possible domain. Otherwise the one weak attribute of the domain that could cause the project problems in the future might be overlooked.

Frequently major potential negative points for an application surface. They may immediately eliminate a potential application (for example, if it is found that the problem will no longer exist at the time when the expert system is expected to be available). More often, they provide incentives to try to rework the problem statement to find a related problem that is more feasible.

6. Get further leads. During and especially at the end of a meeting with or call to domain personnel, it is wise for the project team to ask the participants to suggest any other people who might be knowledgeable about other application areas that appear to have potential for expert system development. After the discussions the domain personnel have just had, they should have a much better idea of what is being sought than they did before the discussions began.

7. Further investigate possibilities. After several discussions with domain personnel, the domain selectors should review all the reasonable candidate domains, compile a list of prime candidates, and, if necessary, investigate them further. If time and resources are available, it may be valuable to meet with additional domain personnel and get more information, ask additional questions of the people originally interviewed, or observe domain operations, especially expert task performance.

8. Evaluate and eliminate. When the domain selectors believe they have enough information, when they have realistically depleted the reasonably available sources of domain information, or when they have reached some project limit on the time or resources available for investigation, they make the final evaluation of the candidate domains. Based on the attributes described in Chapter 6, the major pros and cons of each potential domain should be considered. Thought should be given to the possibilities of amplifying each positive point and minimizing or eliminating each negative one. For example, if the scarcity of available experts in a domain is a negative point, consideration should be given to determining if there might be some way to overcome this (such as devoting a larger–than–planned part of the budget to paying for an expert's time). Then some global evaluation of the domains should be made. This step is difficult since it inevitably means weighing the various attributes. The decision process is far from being well formulated enough to allow simple, numerical weights, but surely some issues will be more important than others. Exactly which attributes are most important depends almost entirely on the particular circumstances of the project. For example, in some situations certain political issues (such as "Will top management like the system?") will be of overwhelming importance, whereas for others these same issues may be relatively unimportant, while payoff, degree of risk, or some other issue may be paramount.

Based on the evaluations, the candidate domains should be put into some rank order, or at least put into ordered categories such as "good possibility," "has major negatives," and so on. If there is one obvious best candidate domain, then the search is over (Congratulations!). Otherwise the domains in the top category (or categories) might be more deeply investigated if time and resources are available, iterating the previous step and this one until one winner emerges.

When the best domain is chosen, the set of attributes discussed in Chapter 6 can be used to justify the selection. The attribute set might also play a useful role by providing a justification for the rejection of politically favored candidate domains.

The method described is for the situation where the domain selectors are given a wide choice as to application area. It can also be used if a set of possible domains has been preselected, but in this case the search for leads to new areas must confined to subdomains of the given domains.

Even if a single domain has been assigned to the project by management, it is still important to investigate and analyze that domain using all of the steps that are pertinent. Meetings similar to those described, in conjunction with an analysis of the given application using the attributes discussed in Chapter 6, might allow the reformulation of the problem to make it more amenable to the expert system approach.

In the project that ultimately became *COMPASS*, we were given a broad charter by management to select the best expert system domain available that would benefit the GTE telephone companies. We were given no constraints beyond that.

The GTE telephone companies form the largest part of the GTE Corporation. They provide local telephone service in all or part of 30 U.S. states. Each company covers a distinct geographic area—for example, GTE-Southwest covers parts of Arkansas, New Mexico, Oklahoma, and Texas. In addition, GTE has telephone company subsidiaries in Canada and elsewhere. Each GTE telephone company is a large company in its own right; together they have had in recent years total annual revenues of over $10 billion.

To start looking for a good expert system application area, another project member and I met with people familiar with GTE telephone company problems and tried to get some initial suggestions for possible domains. We were aided a great deal by a GTE Laboratories employee who acted as an interface between the Laboratories and the GTE telephone companies. A former GTE telephone company employee, he was familiar with the organizational structure of the telephone companies and with many of their problems.

We identified some possible expert system application areas and asked our liaison person to arrange meetings for us with telephone company people related to these areas. He helped us through the maze of complex—at least to us who were unfamiliar—telephone company organization structures, finding the correct contacts, setting up the meetings, and aiding us in understanding some of the telephony concepts we were not clear about.

The meetings, held at the telephone company sites around the country, were sometimes attended by higher-level managers and sometimes by working-level telephone personnel. There were times when only one person from the application area attended and other times when the room was filled.

I usually began each meeting by defining terms like *artificial intelligence* and *expert systems*. I gave a brief background and discussed some well-known expert systems. Then I would discuss briefly each point on our list of the attributes of a good expert system domain. The presentation proved to be an effective way to give the attendees a general idea about expert systems while serving our specific purpose of introducing the attributes we were looking for in an expert system domain without getting overly technical.

Then we described any applications in their area that had been suggested to us and tried to get more information to see if any of these seemed to be a potential expert system candidate. Also we asked those present to discuss problems they were having or expected to have that they thought might be suitable for an expert system. Victims of AI hyperbole suggested grandiose applications, far beyond the state of the art. Others treated us as someone—anyone!—to tell their troubles to. We were outsiders from a distant corporate organization, and maybe we could help them. Some of their problems appeared solvable only by decisions of upper management or by organizational changes that they favored. Still other attendees suggested problems that seemed (at least on first examination) to require only the standard application of some well-known computer technology—not the advanced and powerful expert system technology we were offering. Others suggested problems that appeared to require no more than simple procedural changes, like a better filing system for paper records. We gave suggestions as to how these problems might be solved but did not, of course, choose any of these to be our application.

We used the list of desired expert system domain attributes to examine in greater detail any of the suggested application areas that seemed promising. We often handed out a copy of the list to each of the meeting attendees. I used a new copy for myself for each application we examined and made notes next to each printed point about how that point related to the application.

Often the examination of a potential application uncovered important difficulties that might occur. For example, some suggested applications were related to immediate, important problems but would have little payoff by the time the expert system might be available in the field. (Thus we were asked to develop an expert system to deal with a transition that had to be made due to a change in the telecommunications law. It was clear to us that by the time we developed such a system, the telephone companies would have gone through the transition.) Also many suggested applications involved tasks for which no expert existed or was available. Using the attribute list was a good methodical way to examine each candidate application fully and to ask all the necessary questions. By making use of the list, there were few times when we forgot to investigate any of the important issues about a domain.

During the course of the domain selection process, we visited nine corporate locations, in eight widely separated parts of the country. We met with over

50 corporate managers and experts. We considered over 30 extremely diverse possible expert system applications areas, using our list of attributes as guide, including applications in areas such as maintenance, planning, marketing, design, and customer relations. The task experts for these applications ranged from a junior clerk to an economist with a doctorate. Some of these applications could be eliminated after brief consideration. Others needed to be examined in more detail.

Eventually the list of candidate applications was narrowed to eight major possibilities. These were further analyzed, sometimes necessitating more information-gathering trips. As we learned more details about each application, we were able to develop a better idea of each application's strengths and potential problems as an expert system domain. Two primary candidate areas emerged. After studying them in even greater detail, we selected what we considered to be the better of these: the maintenance of telephone switches, which became the *COMPASS* application area. The specific *COMPASS* application, the maintenance of the No. 2 EAX (a large telephone switching system), is described in Box 5.1.

BOX 5.1

THE *COMPASS* APPLICATION
Maintenance of the No. 2 EAX

COMPASS (Central Office Maintenance Printout Analysis and Suggestion System) accepts maintenance printout data from a telephone company central office switch, analyzes the data, and produces a set of prioritized suggestions for maintenance actions—all at the level of a top telephone company switching expert.

A central office telephone "switch" is an extremely complex switching system that connects several thousand or tens of thousands of telephone lines to each other or to external trunks (which carry calls out of the local area). *COMPASS* captures the knowledge used by a top telephone switching expert in performing maintenance on such a central office switch, GTE's No. 2 EAX (Electronic Automatic Exchange).

A No. 2 EAX is made of several million components, such as relays and circuit boards, and miles of wires. It is physically very large, often filling an entire floor of a warehouse-sized building. Since the No. 2 EAX is so large and has so many components, a number of components can be expected to (and do) fail or work marginally every day. The reliability requirements of central office telephone switches are very high, however. Therefore the No. 2 EAX is designed to be self-testing to allow it to identify situations where a component is faulty, and it is designed with redundant circuitry to allow it to deal with such situations. Maintenance of the No. 2 EAX is performed continually, with faulty components being found and replaced while the switch remains in operation. The continuous maintenance of the switch is a complex task because of the size of the No. 2 EAX, and it is a very important task because of the high level of its reliability requirements.

When a telephone call is being connected, the No. 2 EAX sets up an electrical path through the switch to connect the telephone lines of the two parties. As the switch goes though the steps required to complete the call, it performs several tests to see if there are any problems in the path: open circuits, short circuits, or devices not operating within the required amount of time. If the switch detects a problem, it prints a particular maintenance message. A typical No. 2 EAX switch produces thousands of maintenance messages daily. If an identified problem is severe, the switch aborts the call. (The redundant circuitry of the No. 2 EAX ensures that when the originator of an aborted call tries the call again, a different path can be used to complete it.) Two goals of switch maintenance are to minimize the number of aborted calls and to ensure that switch faults are repaired quickly enough so that every pair of lines always has some of its redundant paths available. More than one available path is desired because parts of a path may be in use at any time for other calls.

In GTE telephone companies, a GTE software system, Remote Monitor and Control System (RMCS), monitors the output maintenance messages of several telephone switches, which are usually at geographically remote locations. It collects messages of selected types on a real-time basis, stores them, and prints them in reformatted form upon request. Maintenance personnel access the RMCS from switch sites to obtain a maintenance printout for a particular switch (Figure 5.1). The switch personnel analyze the maintenance printout to determine the actions that should be taken to maintain the switch. It is this process—as performed by a top expert—that *COMPASS* automates. The automated process is shown in Figure 5.2.

The analysis of the RMCS printouts and the determination of the appropriate maintenance procedures to be performed require expertise and experience. There is wide range of expertise among switching personnel; those with less expertise take longer and perform the job less well than those with greater expertise. When less expert telephone company people cannot solve a problem, they confer with (up to four levels of) internal consultants who have more expertise. The expertise involves judgment based on heuristics accumulated over many years.

A small portion of a typical RMCS output for a No. 2 EAX is shown in Figure 5.3. An average switch produces many pages such as this. Each printed line is an RMCS-reformatted version of a No. 2 EAX maintenance message. Each maintenance message describes a problem that occurred during he telephone call-processing operation of the switch. There are several maintenance message types, falling into two classes: network recoveries (NRs) and system maintenance analyses (SMAs). Some messages are status reports,

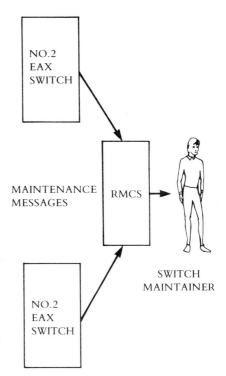

FIGURE 5.1 Manual analysis
of No. 2 EAX maintenance
messages

requiring no action. Others call for a clearly defined action and therefore
require no analysis. However, many important maintenance message types
require extensive analysis of large numbers of messages. These message types
occur frequently—often over a thousand per day are put out by a single
switch.

A typical cause of such a maintenance message is the following situation:

The switch software attempted to complete a connection path
through the switch between two switch terminals (which were, in
turn, connected to the telephone lines of the two parties to the call).
The path was created by setting relays on several circuit cards. At a
point in this process before the two parties were connected, the
switch performed an electrical test on the path and found a short
circuit to some (unspecified) part of the path. Because of this finding,
the switch stopped the connection process and aborted the call.
Finally the switch printed a maintenance message describing the
entire electrical path that the switch had attempted to complete.

A No. 2 EAX maintenance message indicates that a problem exists somewhere in a particular electrical path going through the switch; that is, some

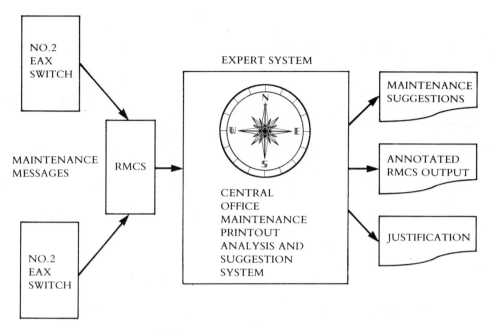

FIGURE 5.2 *COMPASS* block diagram

component part of the electrical path is faulty. But the message gives no indication as to which component of the path is faulty or where along the path the problem is located. The problem could be in any of the path's components: in any one of several relays, in the circuitry on any of several circuit cards, or in any of the many wires connecting the cards. Therefore from a single maintenance message, even the best expert cannot identify the cause of a problem.

The specific causes of switch problems can be identified only by collecting a series of messages over a period of time and utilizing expertise to analyze these data. Let us examine the simplest example. Among all the faulty paths identified by maintenance messages in the RMCS printout, suppose that several paths can be found that all go through the same particular relay but that differ in all other aspects, as shown in Figure 5.4. From this information, we might conclude that that relay probably was the cause of the problems in all of those paths. A switchperson would look for such commonalities to give clues to the causes of the maintenance problems. But even in this simple situation, the analysis is not without complications. It is also possible that each path had its own individual problem and the fact that all of the paths included the same relay was coincidental. Ambiguity in path commonalities is just one of many reasons that the analysis of No. 2 EAX maintenance messages requires significant expertise and that experts can perform much

Page 2

```
•SOR• SORT TALLY REPORT  06/14     3:37:34
FLT NU  PM              IM              FM              FRM  ICNF       TIM
(HISTOGRAPH SCALING: • • 001)
```

FLT	NU	PM	IM	FM	FRM	ICNF	TIM		
01	8	0,3,1,3,0,2,0,1	3,0,1,1,3,3,0	1,3,0,0,3,0,3	2.0	NUC8.0 ,PC1	13/.19:43:52	1	•
0E	0	0,1,1,3,2,2,3,0	1,3,0,1,3,2,2	0,2,2,3,1,0,2	1.0	NUC0.1 ,PC0	14/.11:04:46	1	•
0E	3	2,1,1,3,3,1,2,1	1,2,1,1,3,1,2	1,1,2,2,1,0,2	1.2	NUC3.1 ,PC1	14/.09:00:10	1	•
0E	3	3,1,3,3,3,2,3,1	1,3,1,3,3,0,0	1,0,0,3,1,3,3	1.3	NUC3.0 ,PC1	14/.11:02:54	1	•
0E	3	3,3,2,2,3,3,0,1	3,0,1,2,2,0,0	1,0,0,0,3,2,0	1.3	NUC3.0 ,PC1	14/.09:00:10	1	•
0E	3	3,3,3,3,1,2,0,0	3,0,0,3,3,3,1	0,3,1,0,3,1,2	1.3	NUC3.0 ,PC0	13/.23:10:13	1	•
12	0	0,1,0,3,0,3,0,3	1,0,3,0,3,1,0	3,1,0,0,1,3,2	2.0	NUC0.0 ,PC0	13/.23:42:05	1	•
12	0	0,1,1,0,1,3,3,3	1,3,3,1,0,1,3	3,1,3,3,1,1,1	2.0	NUC0.0 ,PC1	13/.19:27:17	1	•
20	10	0,0,0,3,3,1,0,0	0,0,0,3,0,2,0	0,0,2,0,0,1,0	0.0	NUC10.0,PC1	14/.11:46:25	1	•
20	10	0,1,1,0,0,0,2,2	1,2,2,1,0,0,3	2,0,3,2,1,2,2	0.0	NUC10.0,PC1	13/.21:09:24	1	•
20	11	0,1,2,2,0,1,1,3	1,1,3,2,2,0,3	3,0,3,1,1,0,1	0.0	NUC11.0,PC1	14/.13:30:49	1	•
20	11	0,3,0,2,2,1,2,2	3,2,2,0,2,3,1	2,3,1,2,3,2,2	0.0	NUC11.1,PC0	13/.14:45:56	1	•
20	11	0,3,0,3,0,0,2,3	3,2,3,0,3,0,3	3,0,3,2,3,0,1	0.0	NUC11.0,PC0	13/.17:16:24	1	•
20	12	3,1,1,0,2,1,0,0	1,0,0,1,0,1,3	0,1,3,0,1,0,1	0.0	NUC12.0,PC0	14/.09:05:25	1	•
20	12	3,1,1,0,3,2,0,0	1,0,0,1,0,1,2	0,1,2,0,1,1,2	0.0	NUC12.0,PC0	13/.19:35:46	1	•
20	13	0,1,3,3,1,0,1	1,0,1,3,3,3,2	1,3,2,0,1,3,3	0.0	NUC13.0,PC1	14/.11:04:19	1	•
20	13	1,1,3,0,0,0,1,1	1,1,1,3,0,1,0	1,1,0,1,1,3,2	0.0	NUC13.1,PC1	14/.10:38:47	1	•
20	13	2,1,1,2,1,2,1,1	1,1,1,1,2,1,3	1,1,3,1,1,1,0	0.0	NUC13.0,PC1	14/.12:42:27	1	•
20	13	2,2,0,1,0,1,0,2	2,0,2,0,1,1,0	2,1,0,0,2,1,0	0.0	NUC13.1,PC1	14/.11:04:22	1	•
20	14	0,2,1,1,2,0,1,2	2,1,2,1,1,3,1	2,3,1,1,2,1,1	0.0	NUC14.0,PC1	14/.13:34:44	1	•
20	16	0,2,0,1,3,0,1,1	2,1,1,0,1,2,2	1,2,2,1,2,1,2	0.0	NUC16.1,PC1	14/.11:17:50	1	•
20	16	0,2,3,1,3,3,3,1	2,3,1,3,1,2,2	1,2,2,3,2,1,2	0.0	NUC16.0,PC0	13/.17:51:50	1	•
20	16	0,3,3,1,0,1,2,1	3,2,1,3,1,2,2	1,2,2,2,3,1,2	0.0	NUC16.1,PC0	13/.17:39:41	1	•
20	16	1,0,0,1,2,1,3,1	0,3,1,0,1,3,2	1,3,2,3,0,1,2	0.0	NUC16.1,PC1	14/.10:05:39	1	•
20	16	1,0,3,2,3,0,1,1	0,1,1,3,2,0,0	1,0,0,1,0,2,1	0.0	NUC16.1,PC1	14/.09:40:53	1	•
20	16	1,0,3,2,3,0,1,1	0,1,1,3,2,2,0	1,2,0,1,0,2,0	0.0	NUC16.0,PC1	14/.09:40:55	1	•
20	16	1,0,3,2,3,0,1,2	0,1,2,3,2,0,1	2,0,1,1,0,3,3	0.0	NUC16.0,PC1	14/.09:40:51	1	•
20	16	1,0,3,2,3,2,1,2	0,1,2,3,2,0,1	2,0,1,1,0,3,2	0.0	NUC16.1,PC1	13/.16:37:47	1	•
20	16	1,3,1,2,2,1,2,1	3,2,1,1,2,3,2	1,3,2,2,3,1,2	0.0	NUC16.0,PC1	14/.10:16:08	1	•
20	16	2,1,2,2,3,1,1,2	1,1,2,2,2,0,1	2,0,1,1,1,3,3	0.0	NUC16.0,PC1	14/.12:10:35	1	•
20	17	0,0,3,3,1,0,2,0	0,2,0,3,3,3,2	0,3,2,0,1,0,0	0.0	NUC17.1,PC0	14/.03:15:26	1	•
20	18	0,1,0,2,2,0,2,0	1,2,0,0,2,3,3	0,3,3,2,1,0,1	0.0	NUC18.1,PC0	13/.21:24:26	1	•
20	19	0,0,0,1,3,2,3,1	0,3,1,0,1,2,3	1,2,3,3,0,2,3	0.0	NUC19.0,PC1	14/.12:28:47	1	•
20	19	0,0,2,1,3,2,3,1	0,3,1,0,1,3,2	1,3,2,3,0,1,0	0.0	NUC19.1,PC0	14/.12:27:01	1	•
20	20	0,2,2,1,0,2,2,0	2,2,0,2,1,2,0	0,2,0,2,2,2,3	0.0	NUC20.0,PC1	13/.15:58:58	1	•
20	5	0,1,0,2,1,1,2,0	1,2,0,0,2,3,0	0,3,0,2,1,3,3	0.0	NUC5.1 ,PC0	13/.16:53:39	1	•
20	5	0,2,3,0,3,1,2,0	2,2,0,3,0,3,0	0,3,0,2,2,3,3	0.0	NUC5.0 ,PC0	14/.10:07:33	1	•
20	5	1,3,0,3,0,1,0,0	3,0,0,0,3,3,0	0,3,0,0,3,3,3	0.0	NUC5.0 ,PC0	13/.16:14:12	1	•
20	5	2,2,0,1,2,0,1,0	2,1,0,0,1,3,0	0,3,0,1,2,3,3	0.0	NUC5.0 ,PC0	13/.16:54:04	1	•
20	5	2,2,3,3,0,0,3,3	2,3,3,3,3,3,3	3,3,3,3,2,3,2	0.0	NUC5.1 ,PC0	14/.01:25:50	1	•
20	5	3,0,2,1,2,0,0,0	0,0,2,1,3,0,0	0,3,0,0,3,3,3	0.0	NUC5.1 ,PC0	14/.10:04:53	1	•
20	5	3,2,1,2,0,0,2,2	2,2,2,1,2,2,1	2,2,1,2,2,1,0	0.0	NUC5.0 ,PC0	14/.01:25:50	1	•
20	5	3,2,1,2,0,0,2,3	2,2,3,1,2,2,0	3,2,0,2,2,0,3	0.0	NUC5.0 ,PC0	14/.01:25:55	1	•
20	5	3,2,1,2,0,0,3,0	2,3,0,1,2,1,0	0,1,0,3,2,2,2	0.0	NUC5.1 ,PC0	14/.01:25:57	1	•
20	5	3,2,1,2,0,0,3,1	2,3,1,1,2,0,1	1,0,1,3,2,3,2	0.0	NUC5.0 ,PC0	14/.01:25:59	1	•
20	7	1,2,2,3,3,0,3,1	2,3,1,2,3,1,3	1,1,3,3,2,2,3	0.0	NUC7.0 ,PC1	14/.12:40:31	1	•
20	8	0,0,3,2,0,3,0,2	0,0,2,3,2,2,1	2,2,1,0,0,2,0	0.0	NUC8.1 ,PC1	13/.14:13:15	1	•
21	1	0,1,0,0,3,3,3,3	1,3,3,0,0,3,0	3,3,0,3,1,3,3	0.0	NUC1.1 ,PC1	14/.03:15:26	1	•
21	10	0,3,0,1,0,3,1,0	3,1,0,0,1,3,1	0,3,1,1,3,2,0	0.0	NUC10.0,PC0	13/.16:22:58	1	•
21	2	0,1,1,1,1,0,1,3	1,1,3,1,1,1,2	3,1,2,1,1,3,1	0.0	NUC2.0 ,PC1	14/.11:04:21	1	•
21	2	0,1,1,1,1,0,1,3	1,1,3,1,1,2,0	3,2,0,1,1,2,0	0.0	NUC2.1 ,PC1	14/.11:03:54	1	•
21	2	0,2,0,1,1,0,1,2	2,1,2,0,1,2,2	2,2,2,1,2,1,2	0.0	NUC2.0 ,PC0	13/.23:19:04	1	•
21	2	0,2,3,1,0,3,0,2	2,0,2,3,1,3,1	2,3,1,0,2,3,0	0.0	NUC2.0 ,PC0	13/.23:19:04	1	•

FIGURE 5.3 COMPASS input: A page of RMCS output

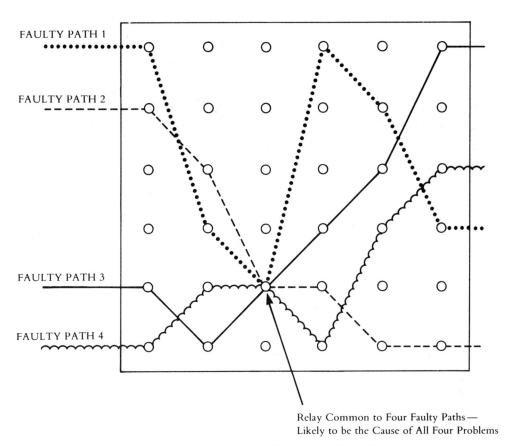

FAULTY PATH 1

FAULTY PATH 2

FAULTY PATH 3

FAULTY PATH 4

Relay Common to Four Faulty Paths —
Likely to be the Cause of All Four Problems

FIGURE 5.4 Fault identification by the use of path commonalities (simplest case)

better than less knowledgeable personnel. Figure 5.5 shows some paths from Figure 5.3 that an expert would pick out as having a significant commonality.

The analysis of No. 2 EAX maintenance printouts and the determination and prioritization of maintenance actions to be performed can be broken into five basic stages (Figure 5.6). Figure 5.7 shows some of the important results determined in these stages, starting from the maintenance messages and finally producing the prioritized ordered list of suggested actions. The five stages are:

1. **Input:** A request is sent to the RMCS to gather the desired maintenance data (for example, all maintenance messages for the last 24 hours for a particular switch). These data are used as the input to the analysis process.

```
*SOR* SORT TALLY REPORT   06/14      3:37:34
FLT NU  PM                IM           FM            FRM   ICNF        TIM
(HISTOGRAPH SCALING: * = 001)

01   8   0.3,1.3,0,2.0,1   3.0,1.1,3,3.0   1,3,0,0.3,0.3   2.0   NUC8.0 ,PC1   13/,19:43:52   1 *
0E   0   0,1,1.3,2,2.3.0   1,3,0,1.3,2.2   0,2,2,3.1,0.2   1.0   NUC0.1 ,PC0   14/,11:04:46   1 *
0E   3   2,1,1,3.3.1,2.1   1.2,1.1,3.1,2   1,1,2,2.1,0.2   1.2   NUC3.1 ,PC1   14/,09:00:10   1 *
0E   3   3.1,3.3.3.2.3.1   1.3,1.3.3.0.0   1,0,0,3.1,3.3   1.3   NUC3.0 ,PC1   14/,11:02:54   1 *
0E   3   3.3,2.2,3.3,0.1   3.0,1.2.2.0.0   1,0,0,0.3,2.0   1.3   NUC3.0 ,PC1   14/,09:00:10   1 *
0E   3   3.3,3.3.1,2,0.0   3.0,0.3.3.3.1   0.3,1.0.3.1,2   1.3   NUC3.0 ,PC0   13/,23:10:13   1 *
12   0   0,1,0,3.0,3.0.3   1.0,3.0,3.1.0   3,1.0,0,1.3.2   2.0   NUC0.0 ,PC1   13/,23:42:05   1 *
12   0   0.1,1.0,1.3.3.3   1.3,3,1.0,1.3   3,1,3,3,1,1.1   2.0   NUC0.0 ,PC1   13/,19:27:17   1 *
20  10   0.0,0.3.3.1.0.0   0.0,0.0,3.0.2   0.0,2.0,0.1.0   0.0   NUC10.0,PC1   14/,11:46:25   1 *
20  10   0,1,1.0,0.0.2.2   1.2.2,1.0,0.3   2,0.3,2.1,2.2   0.0   NUC10.0,PC1   13/,21:09:24   1 *
20  11   0,1,2,2.0,1.1.3   1,1,3.2,2.0.3   3,0,3.1.1.0.1   0.0   NUC11.0,PC1   14/,13:30:49   1 *
20  11   0.3,0,2.2.1,2.2   3.2,2.0,2.3.1   2.3,1.2.3.2.2   0.0   NUC11.1,PC0   14/,14:45:56   1 *
20  11   0.3,0.3.0,0.2.3   3.2,3.0.3.0.3   3.0,3.2,3.0.1   0.0   NUC11.0,PC0   13/,17:16:24   1 *
20  12   3,1,1.0,2.1.0.0   1.0,0,1.0.0.3   0.1,3.0.1.0.1   0.0   NUC12.0,PC0   14/,09:05:25   1 *
20  12   3,1,1.0,3.2.0.0   1.0,0,1.0.1.2   0.1,2.0.1.1.2   0.0   NUC12.0,PC0   13/,19:35:46   1 *
20  13   0,1,3,3.3.1,0.1   1.0,1.3.3.3.2   1.3,2.0,1.3.3   0.0   NUC13.0,PC1   14/,11:04:19   1 *
20  13   1,1,3,0.0,0.1.1   1.1,1.3,0.1.0   1.1,0,1.1.3.2   0.0   NUC13.1,PC1   14/,10:38:47   1 *
20  13   2,1,1.2,1.2.1.1   1.1,1.1.2.1.3   1,1,3,1.1.1.0   0.0   NUC13.0,PC1   14/,12:42:27   1 *
20  13   2.2,0.1,0.1.0.2   2.0,2.0.1.1.0   2.1,0,0.2.1.0   0.0   NUC13.1,PC1   14/,11:04:22   1 *
20  14   0,2,1.1,2.0,1.2   2.1,2.1.1.3.1   2.3,1.1.2.1.1   0.0   NUC14.0,PC1   14/,13:34:44   1 *
20  16   0,2,0,1.3,0.1.1   2.1,1.0.1.2.2   1,2.2,1.2.1.2   0.0   NUC16.1,PC1   14/,11:17:50   1 *
20  16   0.2,3.1,3.3.3.1   2.3,1.3.1.2.2   1,2.2,3.2.1.2   0.0   NUC16.0,PC0   13/,17:51:50   1 *
20  16   0.3,1.0,1.2.1.1   3.2,1.3.1.2.2   1.2,2,2.3.1.0   0.0   NUC16.0,PC1   13/,17:39:41   1 *
20  16   1.0,0.1,2.1.3.1   0.3,1.0.1.3.2   1.3,2.3.0.1.2   0.0   NUC16.1,PC1   14/,10:05:39   1 *
┌─────────────────────────────────────────────────────────────────────────────────────────┐
│20  16   1.0,3.2,3.0.1.1   0.1,1.3.2.0.0   1.0,0,1.0.2.1   0.0   NUC16.1,PC1   14/,09:40:53   1 *│
│20  16   1.0,3.2.3.0.1.1   0.1,1.3.2.2.0   1.2,0,1.0.2.0   0.0   NUC16.0,PC1   14/,09:40:55   1 *│
│20  16   1.0,3.2,3.0.1.2   0.1,2.3.2.2.0   2.0,1.1.0.3.3   0.0   NUC16.0,PC1   14/,09:40:51   1 *│
│20  16   1.0,3.2,3.2.1.2   0.1,2.3.2.0.1   2.0,1.1.0.3.2   0.0   NUC16.0,PC1   13/,16:37:47   1 *│
└─────────────────────────────────────────────────────────────────────────────────────────┘
20  16   1.3,1.2,2.1.2.1   3.2,1.1.2.3.2   1.3,2.2.3.1.2   0.0   NUC16.0,PC1   14/,10:16:08   1 *
20  16   2.1,2.2.3.3.1.2   1.1,2.2.2.0.1   2.0,1.1.1.3.3   0.0   NUC16.0,PC1   14/,12:10:35   1 *
20  17   0.0,3.3.1,0.2.0   0.2,0.3.3.3.2   0.3,2.2.0.1.0   0.0   NUC17.1,PC0   14/,03:15:26   1 *
20  18   0,1,0.2,2.0,2.0   1.2,0.0.2.3.3   0.3,3.2.1.0.1   0.0   NUC18.1,PC0   13/,21:24:26   1 *
20  19   0.0,0.1,3.2,3.1   0.3,1.0.1.2.3   1.2,3.3.0.2.3   0.0   NUC19.0,PC1   14/,12:28:47   1 *
20  19   0.0,0.1,3.2,3.1   0.3,1.0.1.3.2   1.3,2.3.0.1.0   0.0   NUC19.1,PC1   14/,12:27:01   1 *
20  20   0.2,2.1,0.2,2.0   2.2,0.2.1.2.0   0.2,0.2.2.2.3   0.0   NUC20.0,PC1   13/,15:58:58   1 *
20   5   0,1,0.2,1.1,2.0   1.2,0.0.2.3.0   0.3,0.2.1.3.3   0.0   NUC5.1 ,PC0   13/,16:53:39   1 *
20   5   0.2,3.0.3.1,2.0   2.2,0.3.0.3.0   0.3,0.2.2.3.3   0.0   NUC5.0 ,PC1   14/,10:07:33   1 *
20   5   1.3,0,3.0.1,0.0   3.0,0.0.3.3.0   0.3,0.0.3.3.3   0.0   NUC5.0 ,PC0   13/,16:14:12   1 *
20   5   2.2,0.1,2.0.1,0   2.1,0.0.1.3.0   0.3,0.1.2.3.3   0.0   NUC5.0 ,PC0   13/,16:54:04   1 *
20   5   2.2,3.3.0.0,3.3   2.3,3.3.3.3.3   3.3,3.3.2.3.2   0.0   NUC5.1 ,PC0   14/,01:25:50   1 *
20   5   3.0,2.1,2.0,0.0   0.0,0.2.1.3.0   0.3,0.0.0.3.3   0.0   NUC5.1 ,PC1   14/,10:04:53   1 *
20   5   3.2,1.2,0.0,2.2   2.2,2.1.2.2.1   2.2,1.2.2.1.0   0.0   NUC5.0 ,PC0   14/,01:25:50   1 *
20   5   3.2,1.2,0.0.2.3   2.2,3.1.2.2.0   3.2,0.2.2.0.3   0.0   NUC5.0 ,PC0   14/,01:25:55   1 *
20   5   3.2,1.2,0.0.3.0   2.3,0.1.2.1.0   0.1,0.3.2.2.2   0.0   NUC5.1 ,PC0   14/,01:25:57   1 *
20   5   3.2,1.2.0,0.3.1   2.3,1.1.2.0.1   1.0,1.3.2.3.2   0.0   NUC5.0 ,PC0   14/,01:25:59   1 *
20   7   1.2,2,3.3.0.3.1   2.3,1.2.3.1.3   1.1,3.3.2.2.3   0.0   NUC7.0 ,PC1   14/,12:40:31   1 *
20   8   0.0,3.2.0,3.0.2   0.0,2.3.2.2.1   2.2,1.0.0.2.0   0.0   NUC8.1 ,PC1   13/,14:13:15   1 *
21   1   0,1,0.0,3.3.3.3   1.3,3.0.0.3.0   3.3,0.3.1.3.3   0.0   NUC1.1 ,PC1   14/,03:15:26   1 *
21  10   0,1,0.0,1.0.3.1.0 3.1,0.0.1.3.1   0.3,1.1.3.2.0   0.0   NUC10.0,PC1   13/,16:22:58   1 *
21   2   0,1,1.1.1,0,1.3   1.1,3.1.1.1.2   3.1,2.1.1.3.1   0.0   NUC2.0 ,PC1   14/,11:04:21   1 *
21   2   0.1,1.1.1,0,1.3   1.1,3.1.1.2.0   3.2,0.1.1.2.0   0.0   NUC2.1 ,PC1   14/,11:03:54   1 *
21   2   0.2,0.1.1,0.1.2   2.1,2.0.1.2.2   2.2,2.1.2.1.2   0.0   NUC2.0 ,PC0   13/,23:19:04   1 *
21   2   0,2,3.1,0,3.0.2   2.0,2.3.1.3.1   2.3,1.0.2.3.0   0.0   NUC2.0 ,PC0   13/,23:19:04   1 *
```

FIGURE 5.5 Commonality in *COMPASS* data

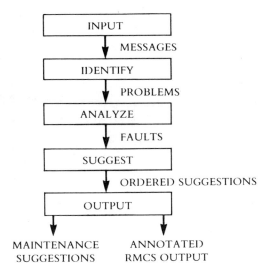

FIGURE 5.6 The five stages of *COMPASS*

2. Identify: Groups of messages are identified such that all members of a group are likely (in the analyst's judgment) to be caused by the same switch problem. For example, Figure 5.5 shows that an expert would identify the messages on lines 25–28 of Figure 5.3 as being such a group of messages. Thus each identifed switch problem corresponds to a group of maintenance messages, as shown in Figure 5.7. A common procedure is for the analyst to draw (as in Figure 5.5) a box around the group of messages. (The messages in a group sometimes but not always occur together in the sorted RMCS output.)

3. Analyze: The messages in each identified group are analyzed to determine the specific faults in the switch that could be causing the switch problem—that is, producing those maintenance messages (for example, a specific circuit card thought to be faulty). Although sometimes a single fault may be determined to be the cause of the problem, it is usually impossible, due to the ambiguity inherent in the data, for even for the best expert to determine that a single particular fault is definitely the cause of the group of messages. Thus, as shown in Figure 5.7, often two or more possible faults are associated with each problem. Estimates are made of the relative likelihood of occurrence of the possible faults.

4. Suggest: Maintenance actions are determined that might enable a switchperson to remedy these faults. There are often two or more possible maintenance actions for a single fault, as shown in Figure 5.7 (for example, one could run a diagnostic test on a potentially bad relay or replace the circuit card that the relay is on). The list of suggested actions is put in priority

| MAINTENANCE MESSAGES | SWITCH PROBLEMS | POSSIBLE SWITCH FAULTS | SUGGESTED MAINTENANCE ACTIONS | ORDERED SUGGESTION LIST | MERGED ORDERED SUGGESTION LIST |

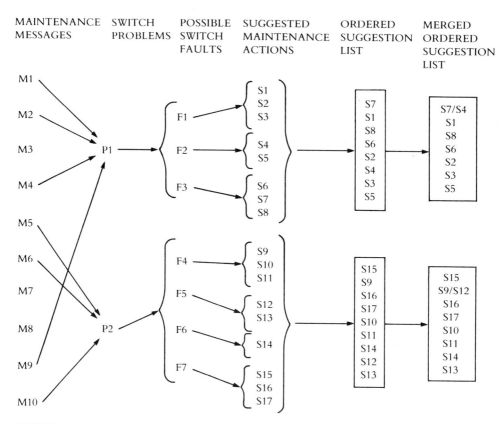

FIGURE 5.7 No. 2 EAX maintenance analysis: input, intermediate results, and output

order, taking into account the relative likelihood of occurrence of the possible faults, the ease of performing the actions, and the possible risk involved in performing the actions. Occasionally two suggested actions on the prioritized list can be performed as one merged action. If so, these two actions are merged, and a final prioritized suggested action list is produced (Figure 5.7).

5. Output: The system's maintenance suggestions are made known to the system user in a user-friendly way.

Each stage, especially the middle three, requires extensive domain expertise. *COMPASS* includes all of these different areas of expertise. (A detailed description of the *COMPASS* analysis is provided in Chapter 10.)

As shown in Figure 5.2, *COMPASS* produces two outputs. *COMPASS*'s primary output consists of an ordered list of suggested maintenance actions for each problem. Suggested actions are output in the form and language most familiar to the maintenance personnel. Frequently performed or simple suggestions are output succinctly. Detailed instructions are given for uncommon or difficult maintenance tasks. To facilitate field use, the format of the output provides areas where switch personnel can record the date and time a particular *COMPASS* recommended action is performed and, when there are multiple maintainers, the initials of the switchperson performing the action.

A sample page of the *COMPASS* primary output is shown in Figure 5.8. In this example, *COMPASS* has analyzed 24 hours of type NR20–22 maintenance messages for the TXRK switch. Among the switch problems that *COMPASS* identified was a problem that No. 2 EAX maintainers would call a "BC.NR20.6.1.1.1.2.1.x.x" problem. The output shows *COMPASS*'s maintenance recommendations to correct that problem, in priority order. The first suggested action,

DIAG NP6.2.1.2.1.x.x.1.1.x.x.x.x.

uses standard switch parlance to recommend the running of a particular switch diagnostic test. If the diagnostic test finds the problem, the rest of *COMPASS*'s suggested actions can be skipped. But due to the often transient nature of problems in the No. 2 EAX, switch diagnostics frequently do not find the problem cause. If the diagnostic does not succeed, the maintainer would go to *COMPASS*'s second suggestion:

Replace IGA6.1.1.1

which recommends replacing a particular circuit card. The best way to determine if this type of action succeeds is to wait to see if the problem reoccurs, so *COMPASS* requests waiting until the next *COMPASS* run before proceeding to the next maintenance action for this problem.

If the circuit card change did not correct the problem, the maintainer would perform *COMPASS*'s succeeding suggestions in order. Note that *COMPASS* knows that certain maintenance actions, such as No. 6, are risky and should be performed only during the low telephone traffic part of the day (usually the middle of the night).

Although *COMPASS* has proved very effective, we do not claim that it will find a correct fix for every conceivable situation. Therefore if all of *COMPASS*'s recommendations fail, the last suggestion on every *COMPASS* list is to request help from the local support group. This suggestion is almost never reached.

In addition to its primary output of maintenance suggestions, *COMPASS* outputs a copy of the RMCS output (which was the original input to *COMPASS*) with annotations grouping the messages and cross-referencing messages to the message groups found. A sample is shown in Figure 5.9. The *COMPASS* annotations are similar to the annotations an expert would write on an RMCS printout while doing the analysis. Therefore expert users can use this familiar output to check *COMPASS*'s internal analyses and its results.

```
TXRK  03/14     NR 20-22
COMPASS MAINTENANCE SUGGESTIONS

         /-----------------------------------------\
         |  Problem B:  BC.NR20.6.1.1.1.2.1.x.x  |
         \-----------------------------------------/
           Number of messages: 2

         The Suggestion Order is:
```

COMPLETED:

DATE TIME INIT

```
---- ---- ----   1.  DIAG NP6.2.1.2.1.x.x.1.1.x.x.x.x

---- ---- ----   2.  Replace IGA6.1.1.1

                     Wait for next COMPASS run before proceeding to next suggestion.
                     ----------------------------------------------------------------

---- ---- ----   3.  DIAG NP6.0.1.2.1.x.x.1.1.x.x.x.x

---- ---- ----   4.  DIAG NP6.3.1.2.1.x.x.1.1.x.x.x.x

---- ---- ----   5.  DIAG NP6.1.1.2.1.x.x.1.1.x.x.x.x

---- ---- ----   6.  WARNING: Wait for Low Traffic, then:

                     A possible backplane fault has been identified. Manually
                     test all connectors and wiring associated with the
                     following network areas:

                     PMXF 6.x.1.2.1.x.x.1.1
                     IMXF 6.1.1.1.2.1.x.x

---- ---- ----   7.  WARNING: Wait for Low Traffic, then:

                     Replace PGA6.2.1.2.1

                     Wait for next COMPASS run before proceeding to next suggestion.
                     ----------------------------------------------------------------

---- ---- ----   8.  WARNING: Wait for Low Traffic, then:

                     Replace PGA6.0.1.2.1

                     Wait for next COMPASS run before proceeding to next suggestion.
                     ----------------------------------------------------------------

---- ---- ----   9.  WARNING: Wait for Low Traffic, then:

                     Replace PGA6.3.1.2.1

                     Wait for next COMPASS run before proceeding to next suggestion.
                     ----------------------------------------------------------------

---- ---- ----  10.  WARNING: Wait for Low Traffic, then:

                     Replace PGA6.1.1.2.1

                     Wait for next COMPASS run before proceeding to next suggestion.
                     ----------------------------------------------------------------

---- ---- ----  11.  Request HELP

                     If all previously listed maintenance actions have been performed,
                     contact your technical support group for assistance.
```

FIGURE 5.8 Typical page of *COMPASS*'s primary output

ANNOTATED RMCS OUTPUT
PM SORT

SYN	NU	PM X M Q G S V S V	A B	IM M Q G S V S V	C D	FM M Q G S V S V	E F	NUC INIT	PC FINL	I F	TIME	#	MSGN	GROUPS
022	0	0.2.0.2.1.0.2.3		2.2.3.0.2.3.3		3.3.3.2.2.3.1		0.1	0.0	0 0	13.19:17:47	1	#007	
022	0	3.2.1.2.0.1.3.0		2.3.0.1.2.2.2		0.2.2.3.2.3.1		0.0	0.1	0 0	13.21:41:06	1	#011	
020	3	0.3.3.2.3.2.0.0		3.0.0.3.2.1.0		0.1.0.0.3.0.2		3.0	3.1	1 1	13.19:37:36	1	#010	
020	4	0.3.2.1.0.1.1.2		3.1.2.2.1.0.3		2.0.3.1.3.2.3		4.0	4.1	0 0	13.13:02:53	1	#001	
021	6	0.1.2.1.1.0.1.1		1.1.1.2.1.3.1		1.3.1.1.1.3.3		6.0	6.0	1 1	13.18:54:10	1	#006	

```
/-----------------------------------------------------------------------------------------\
|   NIT.NR21-22.6.0.1.2.1.1.1.x.x                                                          |
|                                                                                         |
| 021  6  0.1.2.1.1.1.1.1  1.1.1.2.1.0.0  1.0.0.1.1.2.1   6.0  6.0 1 1 13.19:21:34 1 #009 C|
| 021  6  0.1.2.1.1.1.1.1  1.1.1.2.1.3.2  1.3.2.1.1.1.0   6.0  6.0 1 1 13.19:21:30 1 #008 C|
\-----------------------------------------------------------------------------------------/
/-----------------------------------------------------------------------------------------\
|   BC.NR20.6.1.1.1.2.1.x.x                                                                |
|                                                                                         |
| 020  6  0.1.2.1.1.1.1.1  1.1.1.2.1.2.2  1.2.2.1.1.0.2   6.1  6.0 1 1 13.18:48:01 1 #004 B|
| 020  6  2.1.2.1.3.3.1.1  1.1.1.2.1.1.2  1.1.2.1.1.1.2   6.0  6.0 1 1 13.18:48:12 1 #005 B|
\-----------------------------------------------------------------------------------------/
/-----------------------------------------------------------------------------------------\
|   AB.NR20.10.0.2.1.0.2.0.0.x                                                             |
|                                                                                         |
| 020 10  0.2.1.0.2.0.0.2  2.0.2.1.0.3.0  2.3.0.0.2.2.3  10.1 10.0 1 1 13.13:20:00 1 #002 A|
| 020 10  0.2.1.0.2.0.0.3  2.0.3.1.0.3.1  3.3.1.0.2.2.1  10.1 10.0 1 1 13.15:06:12 1 #003 A|
\-----------------------------------------------------------------------------------------/
```

FIGURE 5.9 Typical page of *COMPASS*'s annotated RMCS output

Use of the annotated output helps No. 2 EAX experts build confidence in *COMPASS*'s expertise.

COMPASS also has some capability to explain and justify its decisions. It can generate a detailed output describing its reasoning and provides the option of on-line examination of operation. Problem analyses can be traced with graphs of rule and fact relationships. The explanation and justification options are designed for use by domain experts and system maintainers who are examining or validating *COMPASS*.

C HECKLIST FOR SELECTING THE DOMAIN: THE PROCESS

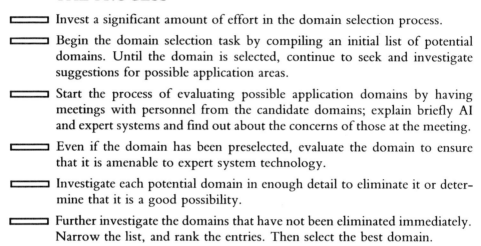 Invest a significant amount of effort in the domain selection process.

Begin the domain selection task by compiling an initial list of potential domains. Until the domain is selected, continue to seek and investigate suggestions for possible application areas.

Start the process of evaluating possible application domains by having meetings with personnel from the candidate domains; explain briefly AI and expert systems and find out about the concerns of those at the meeting.

Even if the domain has been preselected, evaluate the domain to ensure that it is amenable to expert system technology.

Investigate each potential domain in enough detail to eliminate it or determine that it is a good possibility.

Further investigate the domains that have not been eliminated immediately. Narrow the list, and rank the entries. Then select the best domain.

Prerau, Developing and Managing Expert Systems (Addison-Wesley)

CHAPTER 6

Selecting the Domain: Desired Domain Attributes

- What important technical criteria should be considered when selecting the domain for an expert system? ·
- What are the nontechnical issues that should be considered when selecting a domain, and why are these just as critical as the technical issues?

The process of selecting an expert system application domain discussed in the preceding chapter is based on the use of a set of desired domain attributes to evaluate each potential application area. This chapter describes such a set of desired attributes—both technical attributes and attributes related to nontechnical issues. Nontechnical strategic and political issues are usually at least as important as—and are often more important than—technical issues in influencing the choice of the expert system domain.

The attribute set was developed from the perspective of providing working expert systems to solve internal or customer problems for business and industry using state-of-the-art expert system techniques. However, most of the attributes apply as well to academic and other environments. The discovery of new or better methods for expert system development was not an objective—in fact, a domain that requires a major breakthrough in expert system methodology is probably not a good one to choose if the goal is to maximize the likelihood of success. Yet any project that is among the first to attack a particular domain is likely to find some unique properties of the domain, which may require new approaches.

Very few of these desired attributes are absolute. It is unlikely that any domain will meet all of the listed attributes completely, and a good domain may lack many of them. However, a missing attribute often identifies a major weakness of the domain. Knowing this potential weakness from the beginning of the expert system development may allow project personnel to attempt to minimize or eliminate the weakness or at least to monitor it carefully.

In each situation, the weighing of the factors is different. For example, a potential political problem may be merely bothersome in one situation while a similar political problem may spell certain failure in another situation. Also for each specific circumstance some additional unique factors may apply. The set of attributes described does provide, however, a fairly extensive list of aspects to consider in domain selection.

6.1 BASIC REQUIREMENTS

Some of the most basic and most important attributes to look for in a domain relate to the need for the use of expert system technology, the existence of experts, and the potential payoff of the system.

6.1.1 NEED FOR THE EXPERT SYSTEM APPROACH

Consider the use of expert system technology when conventional programming (algorithmic) approaches to the task are not satisfactory. If a conventional technique clearly will work well, there is often less technical risk to using it rather than an expert system approach.

Although the number of expert systems in use for practical applications is growing rapidly, there is still a great deal more experience in business and industry in developing, debugging, deploying, and maintaining conventional algorithmic programs. Therefore it is generally more conservative to use conventional programming in situations where both conventional and expert system techniques may be applicable. However, expert system technology is coming to be considered a standard computer technology. Furthermore an expert system may offer some advantages over a conventional program that justifies its development even when standard approaches are available. For example, expert system knowledge acquisition techniques may be the best way for the knowledge needed in the program to be found, and expert system paradigms and implementation techniques may be the best ways to represent and implement the knowledge.

> In our domain investigations (which eventually led to the *COMPASS* domain), applications were frequently suggested for which it was apparent to us that conventional programming techniques could be successful. For example, we considered a system to aid in determining the optimal locations for placing relief devices (which allow a cable's effective transmission capacity to be increased) in the cable networks that go from a telephone central office to the telephone subscriber premises. The placement of the devices is based on the predicted geographic area service demands. This type of problem was amenable to solution using operations research techniques and therefore did not seem to be one where there would be a big payoff to the use of expert systems.

> Some of the suggested expert system tasks seemed solvable by use of some fairly conventional database approaches, and therefore more powerful expert system technology was unnecessary. For example, one group designing certain telephone circuits sometimes devoted significant effort to designing a circuit and later found that a previous design would have been usable (possibly with slight modification). They asked for an expert system solution to this problem. We thought that the problem could be solved by a database that stored circuit data in a way that allowed the designers to find out easily if there were previously designed circuits that might be similar to the new circuit.

> On the other hand, the *COMPASS* task did not appear to have an obvious conventional solution. To the contrary, the domain initially seemed (and later turned out) to be very complex and to have many of the attributes discussed in this chapter that make an excellent domain for an expert system. We later found that there had been at least one attempt to produce a conventional program to aid the analysis of No. 2 EAX maintenance messages. This effort had not succeeded.

6.1.2 EXISTENCE OF EXPERTS

The domain should be established to the extent that domain expertise and experience exist. There should be recognized experts in the domain who will be the source of expertise for the system. Primary sources of the experts' abilities should be their special knowledge, judgment, and experience.

If an area is too new, there may be no real domain experts—that is, no one with the amount of task performance experience needed to be able to develop the insights that result in expert heuristics. Therefore there will be no source of expertise for the system. Similarly if a domain is quickly changing, no expert may exist whose heuristics (which were developed under previous situations) are still applicable. Frequently domains that are new or quickly changing are where major unsolved problems exist, and so these domains are often proposed for expert systems by people not familiar with the technology. But that is not the primary function of expert systems. Thus unless the project's objective is to take a technological risk or to do research, the domain should be one with real experts.

The project's goal should be to acquire the knowledge of a top-level expert or experts in a domain and put that into an expert system. If the project can succeed in doing that and if the domain is correctly chosen, the project will have accomplished something very useful.

> The analysis of maintenance messages of the No. 2 EAX is a task where domain expertise and experience exist. There are several levels of expertise—the better experts have developed heuristics based on years of experience analyzing No. 2 EAX maintenance problems.

> Several other domains suggested during the domain investigations were related to new or quickly changing areas, with new or changing technologies, procedures, equipment, or regulations. That these types of applications were suggested was not surprising. When one hears of a new methodology that might be capable of solving any problem and is asked to suggest an application, it is reasonable to suggest attacking a problem related to a new or quickly changing area for which good techniques have not yet been found. However, in these types of applications there may not exist any real experts. For example, GTE's GTD-5 is an all-digital switch newer than the No. 2 EAX, and its use is growing throughout the GTE telephone companies. Some switching domain people suggested that our project might develop an expert system to aid in the maintenance of the GTD-5. One of the primary reasons we rejected that possibility was that the GTD-5 was relatively new, and new hardware and software releases were coming out frequently. Thus someone working with GTD-5 maintenance at that time might just have started to develop rules of thumb based on one release when another would come out and invalidate many of the rules. From the standpoint of expert system development, there did not exist any real experts.

> For each domain suggestion, we asked the proposers if they could name someone (independent of availability) who had lengthy experience in the domain and could act as an expert. If they could not, it was an indication of the likelihood that there might not exist any real experts. In contrast, when we asked that question regarding the maintenance of the No. 2 EAX, people familiar with the domain had no trouble naming one or two top experts.

6.1.3 NEED TO CAPTURE THE EXPERTISE

There should be a need to capture the expertise from an expert and put it into an expert system. If the expertise is easily available and inexpensive, there may be no need to develop an expert system for the application. If, however, the expertise is not or will not be available on a reliable, continuing, and widespread basis, there is a need to capture it. For example, the expertise may be scarce. Perhaps only one or a few experts can perform the task at a high level. Equivalently (as far as the expert system is concerned) there may be a strong dependence on overworked experts for performance of the task. Another reason to want to capture an expert's knowledge is that the expertise is expensive. Experts may be available to hire or contract for their services, but the cost may make their widespread utilization prohibitive.

It is beneficial to capture expertise in a situation where the expertise available today will be unavailable or less available in the future. If the need for expertise will maintain its present level or grow but the availability of experts will decline or, at least, grow more slowly than the need, there is a good reason to capture the expertise now. This is even more vital in a circumstance where the expertise may completely disappear—for example, the only expert or experts who have certain valuable knowledge are retiring.

> In investigating the *COMPASS* domain, we found that top-level No. 2 EAX maintenance personnel were scarce. There were only a few in the GTE Corporation and probably no more than one or two in each of the GTE telephone companies—but there were hundreds of people who must analyze No. 2 EAX maintenance messages.
>
> Possibly even more important was the likelihood of a diminishing of the No. 2 EAX experts available within the corporation in the future. Although there were (and are) many No. 2 EAXs in the telephone companies, that switch is slowly being replaced by fully digital switches, primarily GTE's GTD-5. The better maintenance people usually want to learn about and work with the latest and best technology, especially when it appears to be a growth area. Some of these analysts had already moved to work on the GTD-5, and it seemed likely that this trend would continue and possibly accelerate. Corporate expertise in No. 2 EAX maintenance was consequently being lost. It seemed probable that while the number of No. 2 EAX in the corporation was slowly decreasing, the number of top- and mid-level No. 2 EAX experts would decrease at a faster rate. Accordingly there was a need to capture and preserve No. 2 EAX expertise to prepare for future scarcity. In *COMPASS*, we captured the expertise of a top No. 2 EAX expert while he was available and at peak performance.
>
> As another potential application, we looked into the possibility of developing an expert system to design certain special access circuits to the telephone network, which a telephone company provides for a fee upon the request of telephone subscribers. The design of these circuits appeared to be an excellent application from many respects. There were experts who performed the task based on years of experience, and the domain met most of the other

criteria for a good expert system application. The task, however, was in the process of becoming highly standardized in one of the GTE telephone companies (with the likelihood of this standardization spreading to other telephone companies), and the standardization was minimizing the amount of expertise required for the task. Rather than requiring a designer using long experience to make certain decisions from among a wide number of choices, the new design process standardized and limited the choices that had to be made. Thus there was a question as to whether there was a great need to automate the best designers' expertise and experience.

6.1.4 LIMITED SUCCESS IS ACCEPTABLE

If the project is successful in developing an expert system in the domain, the expert system produced will probably be no better than a limited version of an expert in a well-bounded subarea of the domain. That must be enough. Just like a human expert, the system will probably not produce optimal or correct results all the time. This kind of performance can be accepted from a human, but there are often higher expectations for computer programs.

Beyond that, the expert system produced will probably exhibit some or all of the weaknesses of present-day expert systems. It is not possible (and will not be possible in the near future) to produce an expert system for a complex application that will be as good as a top domain expert in all aspects of performance. The expert system will not have all of the history, all of the knowledge, and all of the subtlety of the human expert in all situations and will not be able to employ the basic first principles of the domain as a human expert would. Also the system will be more limited in scope than a human expert would be—confined to a narrow application area and probably not performing well at the application's boundaries. Domain selectors should consider whether the project would be considered successful in the domain selected if the final system has some or all of these weaknesses.

In the analysis of No. 2 EAX maintenance messages, the top experts make mistakes in pinpointing the faults causing switch problems, but they make many fewer mistakes than journeymen switch analysts and so find the faults and correct the problems much more quickly. We found that no one expected a No. 2 EAX maintenance expert system to be perfect. As long as its recommended actions were successful a reasonably high percentage of the time— which could be lower than the percentage of a top expert—that would be acceptable.

6.1.5 PAYOFF

Developing an expert system requires an investment by the company in staff and resources. The payoff of the completed system should justify this investment.

The expected payoff may consist of several different components, each bringing some benefit. Payoffs can be direct, such as when the system makes money for the company or saves company expenses, or indirect, such as when the system yields increased product quality, improved corporate image, higher levels of customer loyalty, and so on. In addition, payoff can be a result of the development of the system itself, such as the introduction of AI technology into the corporation.

Since the development of a major expert system requires a large investment, the expected return on investment should be large to justify the project. But even for a smaller system with a more modest goal, the payoff, although it can be smaller, still should warrant the effort. Managers, planners, and other authoritative personnel of the domain areas benefitting from the expert system should agree that the system's potential payoff justifies a business case for the development of the system. To evaluate the potential payoff, a cost/benefit analysis—formal or informal—might be produced; if so, key domain personnel should be involved in the study if possible.

During domain selection, we projected several different types of payoffs that might accrue to the corporation from the *COMPASS* project: some were direct, tangible benefits; others were indirect or less tangible but still very important benefits. Some of these potential benefits applied to the overall corporation and were among the major goals of the project:

- The promotion of the introduction and use of AI and expert systems in the GTE Corporation.

- The development of general techniques for developing expert systems that could then be used in GTE Laboratories and other parts of the GTE Corporation.

- The transfer of expert system technology to other GTE business units.

Based on an analysis of the *COMPASS* domain using the criteria of this chapter, we felt that the *COMPASS* project would have a good chance to meet these goals—and it turned out the *COMPASS* project generally was very successful in doing so.

In addition to these overall benefits, we identified, at the time we were selecting the domain, several direct payoffs and benefits that a No. 2 EAX maintenance expert system could provide:

- Increased No. 2 EAX maintenance productivity through automation of the No. 2 EAX maintenance message analysis process.

- Increased No. 2 EAX maintenance productivity by minimizing the number of fruitless maintenance actions.

- Increased No. 2 EAX quality of service by lowering the average number of uncorrected faults in a No. 2 EAX.

- New sales revenue for the corporation through the sale of the system (as a product or service) to other telephone companies.

■   The capturing of expert No. 2 EAX knowledge that will be scarcer—and perhaps unavailable—in the future.

■   Increased flexibility in management of staffing by allowing switchpeople primarily trained on other switches to work more easily on No. 2 EAX maintenance.

■   Increased ability to use less experienced or less trained personnel by minimizing the analyses that switchpeople needed to perform.

■   Provision of expert-level analyses whenever and wherever needed—every day, all times of day, any location, and without vacations, sick days, or days of lower performance.

We considered in the domain selection process that if we selected the No. 2 EAX domain, these payoffs and benefits would likely result, and the deployed *COMPASS* system is indeed realizing almost all of these operational benefits (although it has not been sold externally thus far, and so no sales revenue has been realized.) During domain selection, we did not know enough about the No. 2 EAX maintenance domain (and the No. 2 EAX people we spoke with did not know enough about expert systems) to be able to identify some additional benefits of *COMPASS,* such as its ability to perform some maintenance analyses that even the best human experts do not do. We recognized these added benefits as we learned more about the domain during lengthy discussions with the *COMPASS* expert. The GTE Corporation's decision to award the personnel of the *COMPASS* project with its highest corporate technical achievement awards indicates the importance GTE places on the benefits of the project to the corporation.

Considerations of payoff led us to downgrade some other candidate domains. During our search for applications, we found some areas that were good expert system domains in all other aspects but did not seem to have the potential to produce a high enough payoff to justify their selection. For example, we investigated the possibility of developing an expert system to perform some tasks of certain telephone company data transmission experts. These experts had significant expertise acquired over many years (satisfying one major criterion), and it was unlikely that any conventional program could capture this expertise (satisfying another important criterion). Moreover the domain met most of our other criteria (as described in this chapter) well. However, we found indications that the payoff of an expert system in this domain would not be great. First, each telephone company had only a few of these experts, so the potential direct payoff of replacing the experts would not be large. Second, the present human experts were having no trouble providing the expertise to the telephone company people who needed it within the time required, and thus the potential payoff for additional distribution of the knowledge did not appear to be great. Third, the need was expected to decrease in the future. Therefore, although there were experts with a useful expertise, the payoff of an expert system capturing their expertise did not seem large enough for us to pursue this application area.

6.1.6 RISK VERSUS PAYOFF

The domain selected should be the one that best meets overall project goals regarding the trade-off between expected net project payoff and likelihood of project success. An anticipated high payoff may not warrant work on an expert system project where there is a large chance of failure—that is, a large chance that the final system may not be able to perform at the level required for commercial use. It is likely that the final expert system will be able to "do something." However, in actual usage, the system will be a failure if it cannot perform at the level required by users of the system. Some examples of projects that risk failure are a project with a real-time response requirement that may not be able to be met by the use of state-of-the-art expert system technology, a project attempting to perform a task requiring such a wide breadth of knowledge that it appears unlikely that all the knowledge can be captured within the scope of the project effort, and a project handling a problem that seems likely to disappear or change significantly by the time the project is finished. Use of the list of attributes in this chapter will identify weaknesses in a domain that might lead to failure.

Since each attempt to develop an expert system entails some risk of failure, a project's domain selectors should determine how technologically conservative to be in their selection process. They should weigh the payoff gained by a successful project against the investment lost if the project does not succeed. These measures clearly depend on the particular circumstances of the project.

A conservative approach is to select for development the system that meets some minimum criterion for expected payoff and that appears to offer the best chance of successful development. (This approach is often desirable when the project to is develop a company's first expert system. If the first expert system project fails, there may not be a second, at least not for a long time.) A project that can afford to take more risk might select the domain that offers the highest payoff, as long as there is some reasonable chance of success. Other projects will accept a moderate risk to achieve a moderately high payoff or make other trade-offs.

For example, a small project with limited investment, under the conservative approach, would select the domain for which an expert system is the most likely to succeed technologically. For such a small project, however, it might be possible to consider a higher technological risk (especially if the project is not the company's first expert system project) since the loss of investment would not be great in case of failure.

> Among the main objectives of the COMPASS project was the production of a successful expert system so as to demonstrate the utility of this technology to the operational people in the corporation. Thus it was very important—be-

yond the direct payoff of the system—for the system to perform its task successfully. In this circumstance, it was important to be fairly conservative in domain selection.

In fact, we knew of a domain similar to the *COMPASS* domain that we judged to be much less complex than *COMPASS* and that we estimated might have a higher long-term payoff to the corporation—a *COMPASS*-like system to aid the analysis of maintenance messages for the GTD-5 switch. However, the GTD-5 was then in a rapidly changing state, in both its hardware and software, and there did not appear to be any real GTD-5 experts with developed heuristics. These were valid reasons to lower the expectations for the success of pursuing a GTD-5 project at that time, and therefore we chose the *COMPASS* domain. Looking back, we are fairly confident that the expected problems would have occurred had we selected the GTD-5 project. (Note, however, that when the GTD-5 hardware and software became more stable, it was possible for a GTE business unit to initiate a project developing a "*COMPASS*" for the GTD-5.)

6.2   TYPE OF PROBLEM

Some attributes related to the type of problem to be solved—such as the use of heuristics, the lack of reliance on common sense, and the availability of required input data—are important to the choice of domain.

6.2.1 USE OF SYMBOLIC REASONING

The task should primarily require symbolic reasoning—reasoning about things and concepts. It should not primarily involve numerical calculations. AI techniques are designed for reasoning about things represented as symbols. Although numerical calculations can be handled by expert systems, if the task of interest primarily involves computation, consideration should be given to using other programming approaches designed and optimized for these kinds of calculations.

The *COMPASS* analysis is based on data represented in numbers, but there is very little calculation in it. Although the data are numeric, the numbers represent the names of the parts of the No. 2 EAX. The *COMPASS* analysis would be exactly the same if each 0, 1, 2, and 3 in the maintenance messages were represented as, say, A, B, C, and D.

The potential application concerning placement of relief devices in cable networks (Section 6.1.1) seemed manageable by numerical operations research techniques. It did not appear to require symbolic reasoning.

6.2.2 USE OF HEURISTICS AND OTHER TASK CHARACTERISTICS

The task should require the use of heuristics—that is, problem-solving rules of thumb and strategies. Expert systems do not so much compute an answer as they find or build one. The system's heuristics enables it to do this.

A strength of expert systems is their ability to handle heuristics. Although it is possible to use expert system representation and implementation techniques on nonheuristic knowledge such as algorithmic reasoning, it is the ability to handle heuristics that allows expert systems to tackle problems that cannot be attacked by conventional techniques. Moreover domains where experts make substantial use of capabilities such as motor skills rather than relying on heuristic knowledge are also not best to attempt by expert system technology. Thus in most cases, to ensure the best use of limited expert system development resources, a domain should be chosen that involves heuristic decision making.

There may be some benefit to selecting an expert system task that requires consideration of an extremely large number of possibilities or that requires decisions to be based on incomplete or uncertain information. Problems with very large numbers of possibilities or with incomplete or uncertain information are difficult to attack by conventional approaches but may be amenable to expert system methodologies. Thus selecting such a problem domain might enable expert system technology to make a major impact in an area where conventional computer systems would not be applicable.

> Experts in the analysis of No. 2 EAX maintenance messages use heuristics in several parts of their task. For example, when deciding which of several applicable maintenance actions should be done first, an expert uses rules of thumb to weigh the possible actions. In another application we looked at, certain design procedures that formerly had required experienced engineers to make complex choices from wide-ranging possibilities had been simplified—the range of choices had been reduced significantly and a set of uniform criteria for decision making had been determined. Thus a fixed algorithm rather than a set of design heuristics was being used by practitioners to perform the task, and automation of this task did not appear to require an expert system.

6.2.3 WIDESPREAD KNOWLEDGE AND COMMON SENSE

The knowledge required for the expert system should be within clear bounds. The task should not require knowledge from a large number of areas, and it should not make major use of commonsense reasoning. If a task expert utilizes very widespread knowledge or general knowledge to perform the task being considered, it is likely that the amount of knowledge needed for the expert system is larger than the amount that a state-of-the-art expert system can practically contain. Furthermore great difficulties can be encountered in trying to combine highly heterogeneous knowledge into a single system.

Common sense can be thought of as a large accumulation of little bits of knowledge from a large number of areas. Utilizing common sense in AI systems is a topic of current research. However, for an expert system of today, it is not realistic to consider a domain where the use of common sense plays a major role because the system would require too much knowledge to be feasible.

> The knowledge required for the analysis of No. 2 EAX maintenance messages is well defined and relatively narrow. Only knowledge pertaining to the No. 2 EAX structure, its problem manifestations, the faults that cause its problems, and the maintenance actions that can fix its faults is pertinent. There is no use of general knowledge or common sense.

> We did look into possible application areas where widespread knowledge, general knowledge, and/or common sense were utilized by experts. For example, in one application involving forecasting telephone service expansion, we found that experts used widespread sources of data, a large amount of general knowledge, and some commonsense reasoning to aid their forecasting. An expert might read that Congress may be passing a larger-than-expected highway funding bill. From that, he might expect that a highway in a particular region may be funded. He might reason that new highways usually lead to new business and home construction and that new business and home construction leads to new demands for telephone service. Thus the expert might adjust upward his forecast of telephone service demand in the region.

> The reasoning process here is not difficult and could easily be produced by chaining rules in an expert system. But it would be difficult for an expert system to have all the knowledge needed to allow it to interpret a wide variety of such kinds of information. For just this one bit of reasoning, the system might need knowledge about the ways highways are funded, the mechanisms of bills passing in Congress, the effects of specific proposed congressional legislation on the region, the general effect of new highways on home and business construction and how this may be modified in the region of interest, and the expected effect of home and business construction on the demand for telephone service. For a system to be able to interpret a wide variety of such information at an expert level seemed to require such a large amount of widespread knowledge and common sense as to make the system unlikely to be successful using available techniques.

6.2.4 NOT DRIVEN BY A PARTICULAR TECHNOLOGY

The domain should be selected without concern about matching it to a particular expert system development technology. The goal of the project should be to develop an expert system for actual use or to make major advances in the state of the art of expert system technology. The focus in this book is on projects with the former goal. In such a project, as long as some expert system development technology seems applicable, the domain selectors should not give great consideration to the particular technology that might be used. The domain should drive the technology utilized, and the specific choices of technologies should be deferred until system development. In contrast, in a research-oriented project, the technology to be explored normally is selected first, and then a domain where the technology seemed applicable might be chosen as a testbed; that is, the technology drives the domain selection.

This is not to say that a project developing an expert system for a real application cannot and will not generate new expert system concepts. Sometimes the only way to attack a problem is to try new approaches. Also work on a new problem might reveal a previously unknown weakness in a standard technique or might determine that no known technique fits a particular situation. In either case, the development project may have to research new areas and formulate new concepts or principles. These activities, however, should be driven by the needs of the domain and should not be the primary reason for selecting the domain.

> We decided from the beginning that our goal was to produce an expert system to solve a real corporate problem, not to explore a specific expert system technology. Therefore we did not give any more or less priority to a domain based on which expert system techniques we thought we might use.

> Other projects at our laboratories were designed to research specific areas of expert system technology, such as a project on distributed AI. To aid their investigation of this technology, personnel on this project tried to find applications where they felt the technology would apply. Thus they selected a domain to explore only after and because they selected their particular technology to investigate.

> Our goal was not to develop new techniques as long as available techniques would suffice. However, the project encountered several situations where we could find no standard techniques or methodologies, and therefore we had to develop our own techniques out of necessity. Some of these were of general enough interest to warrant technical papers on the subjects. To cite an instance, the subject of this chapter and the preceding one—selecting an appropriate domain for an expert system—was not treated in any detail in any literature that I could find when we were investigating domains for the project. There was little discussion on the technical attributes of a good domain and no mention of the nontechnical issues in the business and industrial worlds. Therefore I started to formulate a process for domain selection and to compile a set of the attributes I thought would make a good application domain. This work grew and eventually became a fairly general methodology, which I formalized in a technical paper. However, I did not set out with the goal of developing a particular expert system methodology; it was a by-product of the goal of producing a real expert system application.

6.2.5 TASK DEFINITION

The task that is to be done by the expert system should be defined as clearly as possible. At the project outset, there should be a definition of the expected inputs of the system and the system outputs to be developed.

A clear definition is a good attribute of any task, and the more precise the definition, the better. The task definition, however, is not fixed. As the system evolves and as situations change, it should be possible to change the task definition accordingly. Often a general domain is chosen and then, only after the knowledge engineers get more familiar with the domain, the specific task is selected.

> In the *COMPASS* domain, we knew we were dealing with the analysis of No. 2 EAX maintenance messages. We knew the input would be some subset of these maintenance messages in some format and that the output would be advice on maintaining the switch, made available in some form to the maintenance personnel. This was enough to get us started. After a few meetings with the No. 2 EAX expert, we defined more specifically the task of the initial *COMPASS* system: the analysis of No. 2 EAX NR20 maintenance messages, based on the data in printouts available to maintenance people. The output would be a list of maintenance procedures to be done, in priority order. The exact format of the output was decided much later, near the end of the initial development.

6.2.6 TASK INPUTS

It should be established that the inputs needed to perform the domain task are available or can be made available to the expert system. Any required input that is not documented and is unlikely to be documented or is in any other way not available in computer form may cause a big problem for the expert system. For an expert system to make as good (or at least almost as good) decisions as an expert, it must have available the same information that the expert has.

In some applications, an expert uses a good deal of "local knowledge" He may know things that are not and will never be documented (no less computerized). He may know information for which the sources of data are so diverse and randomly encountered that it is infeasible to consider continuously updating the data, even if they were somehow computerized. (Note that this point is somewhat different from the problem of needing data from widespread fields. In that case, a huge knowledge base might eventually have enough knowledge in it to cover all the areas of interest. Here we are considering information that may not ever get into any knowledge base.) For example, an expert might get serendipitous information, such as that Gail had casually mentioned to him over coffee that she had seen something out of the ordinary last week. The expert might have observed something useful to his decisions, such as that it rained last Tuesday or that Milt seemed upset yesterday and so that anything he worked on yesterday might need to be rechecked. The expert may remember something historical and undocumented that helps him, such as that only for the last three years have new customers had a certain financial check made on them, or that in 1980 a change was made in the definition of what was "acceptable." He might have made some judgments that he utilizes when needed, such as that although Lillian is the responsible party, Mike is the one to call to get details of a certain process (although he now works in a completely different department). If these types of information are required for expert-level results and they are not likely to be available to the expert system, this finding should be considered a strong argument against the potential domain. If these types of information make only a minor impact, the domain might still be considered.

Sometimes there are important data that are available to an expert in some form, but it may appear difficult or impossible for those data to be made available to the expert system. The expert may look up needed information in a large handwritten or typed document that is never expected to be computerized or would require a great deal of interpretation even if computerized. The expert may look at hand-drawn schematics, sketches, or photographs. The expert may make a visual inspection for a crack, wait until something has turned a certain color, listen for a sound, smell a particular scent, feel a certain vibration, touch an object to test its roughness, and so on. The expert system needs to have these data as well. The domain selectors should consider whether and how obtaining these data for the expert system could be done, whether it practical for the project to try to do it, and, if it is not done, whether the system could perform acceptably well. In certain applications (such as process control), the existence and availability of sensors, the possibilities of constructing needed new sensors, and the associated sensor costs are often extremely important factors.

> In the *COMPASS* domain, we knew that the only input to an analyst was the set of No. 2 EAX maintenance messages. This input was available to the analyst as a computer printout, and the data were available in a computer. Therefore we did not think there would be any problem getting these data to the system. We were told (and later we found it to be true) that the analyst used little local knowledge.

> In some other applications we examined, experts used a good deal of undocumented and probably undocumentable knowledge, such as the anecdotal history of local problems. We downgraded these domains.

6.2.7 TASK OUTPUTS

It should be established that desired outputs for the domain task can reasonably be produced in the manner desired and delivered to the location desired. If the output is required in a form that is difficult or impossible (with the present state of the art) for a computer system to produce, this problem should be considered when investigating the domain. Also important is whether the expense of producing the output (the need for expensive devices, the need for large amounts of data communications, etc.) is too large to be feasible.

> We expected the output of *COMPASS* would be some computer-generated description of the maintenance procedures to be done. Although there seemed to be some options as to how the output might be accomplished (such as a printed description or a graphic representation), there did not appear to be (and were not) any major technical problems to overcome.

6.2.8 SIMILARITY TO SUCCESSFUL SYSTEM

It is a positive indication of the likelihood of project success (although no guarantee) if the task is similar to that of a successful existing expert system.

If the project objective is to develop an expert system to do something completely different from anything that has ever been done by an expert system, there is more of a chance that the project will encounter some major obstacles that may prove difficult to overcome. But if the domain is similar to a known expert system, then it increases confidence that solutions can be found to the problems the project will meet.

> There was no existing expert system related to telephone switching when we selected the domain, and thus we knew that our expert system would be the first in that area if we selected the No.2 EAX maintenance domain. Hence we knew that we would be the first to encounter any special problems related to this class of domains. On the other hand, the more general areas of troubleshooting and diagnosis were among the more investigated areas of expert system development. Taking both points into account, we did not think that these considerations were either very positive or very negative toward the selection of the No. 2 EAX maintenance domain.

> For some other domains we investigated, the similarity to existing systems had more effect on our evaluation. We looked into one domain related to telephone equipment configuration. Our feeling that this domain had some things in common with Digital Equipment Corporation's well-known XCON expert system for configuring computer systems was a positive factor in our consideration of it.

6.3   EXPERTISE

Some aspects of the experts and the expertise in a domain are important in determining if it is appropriate for an expert system, such as the availability of experts and the possibility of utilizing a single domain expert.

6.3.1 EXPERTS ARE BETTER THAN NOVICES

One necessary condition for the proposed task to require expertise is that experts are significantly better than amateurs in performing the task. If a novice can perform at or close to the level of an expert, there may not be enough expertise required in the task to make development of an expert system worthwhile.

> In No. 2 EAX maintenance, there is a spectrum of expertise levels and clearly a vast difference between the expertise of a novice and a top expert. This difference is apparent by performance measures and organizational structure. In examining performance, we were told (and later saw) that a top expert, such as the expert we eventually picked to work on *COMPASS*, could analyze in 5 to 15 minutes a set of data that might take a novice No. 2 EAX maintenance person 2 hours—and the expert would produce a better analysis. Organizationally a structural hierarchy exists in the telephone companies for maintaining a switch like the No. 2 EAX. When first-level maintenance people cannot analyze a problem correctly, they call second-level people. If these second level-people fail to find the problem, they call third-level people who, if they cannot solve it, call the top experts. We had no doubt that top No. 2 EAX experts had a large amount of expertise not easily acquired by newer people.

6.3.2 AVAILABILITY OF EXPERTISE

For the domain selected, it should be likely that domain experts, preferably some of the best experts, will be available to the project and that they will commit a substantial amount of time to the development of the system.

It is of no help to the project that domain expertise exists unless the expertise is available to the project. But that is not enough. The availability should be for at least the amount of time necessary for the project to have a good chance at success. There should be strong managerial support from the domain area, especially regarding the large commitment of time by an expert and the possible travel or temporary relocation. These issues should all be agreed upon early in the project.

Furthermore project experts should be leading experts in the domain. If a large amount of time, effort, and resources are to be expended on the development, the use of the knowledge of top experts will maximize the benefits of this investment. The availability of such domain experts is often a problem. The best experts, in the most important corporate areas, are usually the ones who can be least spared from their usual positions.

> In investigating the No. 2 EAX maintenance domain, we found that the GTE telephone companies generally had three or four levels of No. 2 EAX experts, and each had one or two experts at the highest level. We thought we could get a top expert for the project. We estimated that we would need his commitment for about one week per month for a year or more. After we selected

the *COMPASS* domain, we used the process detailed in Chapter 8 to select a leading No. 2 EAX expert and obtained the commitment of his time at the necessary level of effort for the duration of the project.

Another application we explored was a system to aid a market researcher. Although the application appeared to have many good attributes for expert system development, we were not sure that any of the very few top experts in the corporation would be available to us for necessary the amount of time. Thus we downgraded this possibility.

6.3.3 UTILIZING A SINGLE EXPERT

It is generally advantageous for the project to select a domain where it will be possible to acquire the expertise for the system (or at least for each subdomain area) principally from a single expert. A project using a single expert avoids the problems inherent in dealing with multiple experts. Experts in the same domain or subdomain may disagree on their conclusions—to a greater or lesser extent depending on the domain. Even experts who generally agree on their conclusions usually utilize somewhat different problem-solving techniques. Hence it is difficult to develop a consistent body of knowledge on a specific area of expertise by acquiring the knowledge partially from one expert and partially from another or several others.

Nevertheless in some situations there are advantages to using multiple experts that might outweigh the disadvantages. Multiple experts might provide strength of authority and political backing for the system or might provide a breadth of expertise not available in a single expert. (We examine the issue of single versus multiple experts at greater length in Chapter 8.)

We felt that we would be able to utilize a single primary expert to get knowledge on No. 2 EAX maintenance, and it seemed reasonably likely that we could get an expert's commitment for at least a year. It turned out that we did utilize just one primary expert for *COMPASS*. He was able to supply all of the knowledge needed, and we were able to maintain his commitment to the project for the entire length of *COMPASS* development—over two years.

6.4   TASK BOUNDS

The bounds that can be set on the expert system's task should be considered when selecting the domain. It the expert system task is too large or too small, too difficult or too easy, it may not be suitable.

6.4.1 BOUNDS ON TASK DIFFICULTY

The domain task selected should not be too easy or the development of the system may not warrant the effort. On the other hand, the task selected should not be too difficult or complex. If it is, the amount of knowledge needed by the expert system might be beyond the state of the art in knowledge base size. Work on developing such a system might never finish or might result in a program too large or too slow to be put into practical use.

One way to make a gross estimate of the difficulty of a task is to consider the time a human expert takes to perform the task. A task taking a human expert less than a few minutes might be too easy to consider; a task requiring more than a few hours might be too difficult. Another way to make an estimate is to consider how much time a novice needs to learn to perform the task. A task requiring a few hours to learn might be too easy, while a task requiring a graduate degree and twenty years' broad experience is generally too difficult.

> Depending on the size of the data input set, the analysis of NR20 mainte-
> nance messages (the task of the initial *COMPASS-I* system) took an expert
> about 5–15 minutes (a novice took much longer). We felt this was a reasona-
> ble level of task difficulty. We did not worry about this issue when we began
> developing the expanded *COMPASS-II;* our experience with *COMPASS-I* gave
> us a much better idea of the expected size of the *COMPASS-II* knowledge
> base than we could get from considering the expert's time.

6.4.2 ESTIMATED LOWER BOUND ON TASK KNOWLEDGE

The amount of knowledge required by the task should be large enough to make the knowledge base developed interesting and nontrivial; otherwise the task may be more amenable to another approach. For example, if all the knowledge that is needed to perform the task of interest can be repre-sented in a simple decision tree, there is usually no gain in utilizing expert system technology.

> It was difficult to estimate the amount of knowledge required by the *COM-*
> *PASS* task. But since there were at least four levels of No. 2 EAX maintenance
> people, it appeared that there was depth enough in the domain for the anal-
> ysis to be nontrivial. Our eventual compilation of 200 pages of concise
> English-language knowledge certainly confirmed this.

6.4.3 ESTIMATED UPPER BOUND ON TASK KNOWLEDGE

The number of important concepts (for example, rules) required by the task should be bounded to several hundred or a few thousand—a reason-able maximum for an expert system in the current state of the art. The number is hard to estimate, and especially so before knowledge acquisition has begun. One possibility is to develop a small, quick prototype of a very narrow domain area to use as a sample.

> We had no good estimate of the number of concepts in No. 2 EAX mainte-
> nance before selecting *COMPASS*. However, the subject matter related to the
> No. 2 EAX maintenance task seemed to be (and was) well bounded.

6.4.4 NARROWNESS OF TASK

The expert system task should be sufficiently narrow and self-contained. The aim should be not for a system that is expert in the entire domain but for one that is expert in a limited task within the domain. With these constraints, the task is more tightly bound, which should help keep the size of knowledge base bounded.

> When we began *COMPASS* development, we tried to be technologically conservative by not attempting to develop an expert system that would do switch maintenance in general or even one that would handle all No. 2 EAX maintenance tasks. Instead we initially chose to try to develop an expert system that would analyze one specific class of No. 2 EAX maintenance messages, the NR20s, and eventually expanded that to cover all classes of maintenance messages that required analysis.

> Had the initial task proved to be less difficult, we would have increased the scope or features of the final *COMPASS* or decreased our development time. Conversely had the initial task proved to be even more difficult than it was, we would have considered decreasing the scope of the final system—if that was satisfactory to the potential users. Otherwise we would have had to increase the time and/or staffing devoted to developing the final system.

6.5 DOMAIN AREA PERSONNEL AND POLITICS

Some important nontechnical attributes of a good domain for expert system development pertain to the domain area personnel and to the company politics surrounding the expert system.

6.5.1 DOMAIN PERSONNEL'S EXPECTATIONS OF SUCCESS

Personnel in the domain area—the expected recipients, users, and beneficiaries of the expert system—should be realistic. They should understand the potential of an expert system for their domain, but also realize that many expert system development projects have not resulted in production programs with commercial payoff. They should be neither very optimistic nor very pessimistic.

Domain personnel who believe the AI hyperbole they have heard (some of which may have come from the project team) and are overly optimistic about the project may put excessive demands on the system or have excessive expectations. Then they may be disappointed with the resulting system, no matter how well the system development went. Moreover they may expect the program to be available much sooner than it realistically can be produced. They may make plans based on these unrealistic schedules and then face large problems when the schedules are not met. They may assume that there is no chance that the project will fail to produce a system that performs at a certain acceptable level, and thus base their plans on the certainty of success. Again they might then have large problems if the project has technical problems in development and, as is certainly possible, cannot produce a system that performs at the required level.

On the other hand, if the domain personnel think that the project is promising more than it can produce or do not believe that some of the expertise derived from years of experience can actually be put into a computer program, they may be overly pessimistic. They might have less incentive to provide backing for the project, to provide a domain expert for the project, to act as consulting experts, to provide access to pertinent data and documents, to participate in field trials, and so on. They will generally be of less help to the project than they otherwise might have been.

In either case, the project team may have to educate domain personnel to understand what are reasonable expectations. The domain selectors should consider the likelihood of success in performing this educating and also how the project could be affected by unrealistic expectations if the education process is not wholly successful.

> During our investigations, I was careful not to raise false expectations with domain personnel. I always stated clearly that expert system development in industry is relatively new and there was a reasonable chance that any expert system we tried to develop might not perform at a high enough level of expertise to warrant use. (I was not sure, however, if listeners who believed the expert system hyperbole were persuaded to lower their expectations.)
>
> Many expert system developers are not in a position to be as honest as I was able to be. My project was supported by our corporate laboratory. Thus although the money came indirectly from the corporate profit centers, I was not asking anyone I met to spend their money to pay directly for the project (except to support an expert's participation). A project may not be able to downplay the possibility of success if it is asking for direct support.
>
> Since we came from the corporate laboratory and talked about high-tech possibilities as was expected, we saw little pessimistic reaction when describing system possibilities. This was especially true since we were offering to produce a system that otherwise would never have been developed.

6.5.2 DOMAIN LEADERS' TASK AGREEMENT AND CONTINUING INVOLVEMENT

The specific task within the domain should be jointly agreed upon by system developers and domain area personnel. Managers, planners, or others with domain responsibility should agree on the business need for the expert system. Their agreement on the task helps ensure that the system, if successful, will be useful and will be used. If domain representatives are not included in task selection, the system developed may not be what the potential users want or need.

Furthermore, the early participation of leading domain personnel makes more likely the participation of such people throughout the project. The continuing involvement of domain leaders is another valuable safeguard that a useful and utilized expert system will be developed.

> Within the general area of switch maintenance, most domain personnel we spoke to at all levels recommended our working on the maintenance of the No. 2 EAX. They realized that the GTD-5 was the up-and-coming switch but knew it was still new and understood our concern about the lack of existing expertise. The No. 2 EAX was widespread in the corporation and stable. In addition, expertise was beginning to be lost as some No. 2 EAX experts started to migrate to work on the GTD-5.

6.5.3 PROBLEM PREVIOUSLY IDENTIFIED

Managers in the domain area should have previously identified the need to solve the problem that the system addresses. This is strong evidence that the system is needed and makes managerial support more likely. However, since expert systems can attack problems beyond those handled by conventional programs, domain managers may not have identified a possible expert system problem because they may not even consider the possibility that a computer program could apply to the problem.

> Some switching managers had identified the problems involved with migration of expertise from the No. 2 EAX, and they mentioned this to us. Not surprisingly, no one we spoke to had identified the need to develop a computer program that could capture the expertise of a leading No. 2 EAX expert since none had considered that a possibility.

6.5.4 TOP-LEVEL SUPPORT

The project should be strongly supported by a senior manager. This high-level champion might provide entree to certain people for project personnel, and more importantly, might help the project win necessary support and provide political protection for the project.

> The switch maintenance domain was suggested by a vice president at GTE-Southwest. Although he did not follow the project actively, his name and word of his support was useful at the early stages of the project when we wanted to speak to domain people in GTESW and later when we needed an expert from GTESW to work with us.

> No single senior manager was our champion throughout the project beyond our own line managers. There were several times when a senior manager champion of our cause would have been helpful.

6.5.5 USERS WANT IT

Potential users might not want the system. They might feel their jobs are threatened. They might feel their jobs will be trivialized, with the program doing the more interesting work. They might feel that the system will disrupt their comfortable methods of doing things. They might be afraid of computers.

If potential users do not welcome the completed system, it might never be used. The project team should try to gauge how the potential user community might feel about the expert system through discussions with the project's primary and consulting experts, domain area managers, and potential users. Reactions of domain personnel to system tests and field trials should provide additional information. When project personnel have some idea of how the system might be received, they should consider ways to make the system unthreatening to users and welcomed by them. If it appears that these efforts may not succeed, the potential rejection (and possibly even intentional misuse or sabotage) of the system by users is an important negative for domain selection.

> When we selected the *COMPASS* domain, we realized that the eventual expert system developed could not directly replace a maintenance person since it could only recommend but not perform the maintenance tasks. Also it would free maintenance personnel, who usually like to work with their hands, from a paper-and-pencil analysis task that they may not enjoy. Nevertheless we also realized (and considered it a major benefit of the expert system) that a successful system would allow fewer people to be required to maintain a No. 2 EAX. From the users' standpoint, this eventuality could be viewed as a threat to some of their jobs.

> We were told that the better No. 2 EAX people generally recognized that their career would be enhanced if they could work with the newest central office switches, whose use was expanding in GTE. Therefore they could be expected to be happy if they could decrease their work on the No. 2 EAXs and increase their work on these other switches. But there still was the possibility of negative feeling from people comfortable with their work on the No. 2 EAX who would feel a threat to their working situation or even their jobs. We could not do anything to ameliorate the latter but did recognize the situation and tried to minimize the former; for example, one simple method was to call *COMPASS*'s recommended actions suggestions rather than demands or orders to try to avoid making the users feel that the system had taken control of their jobs. We have as yet heard of no domain personnel who are hostile (at least openly) to *COMPASS*.

6.5.6 INTRODUCTION OF THE SYSTEM

It is desirable that the domain selected is such that the expert system can be introduced into the working environment with minimal disturbance of the current practice. Users are more likely to accept a system that does not make a major impact on their work routine. If the introduction of the system brings about a radical change in the way work is done, there is more potential for problems.

We expected that an expert system that analyzed No. 2 EAX maintenance messages would make some change in the work practices at a switch site but not a radical one. The switchpeople would no longer have to analyze maintenance message data to find problems, and they would, if *COMPASS* had the expertise of a top expert, find the solutions to switch problems more quickly. But a large part of their job would not change much. For example, they still would replace circuit cards and still would work in the switch backplane tracking down faults (with *COMPASS* telling them which circuit cards to change and where in the backplane to look for the faults).

6.5.7 COOPERATIVE USER GROUP

The potential user group for the expert system should be cooperative and patient. Although at the project's beginning, the developers may not deal very much with the user community as a whole, the users will become more important later on, possibly as consulting experts, by involvement with a field trial, or by supplying some information. And, of course, they eventually will use the final system. If they are likely to be uncooperative or impatient with the project or the deployment of the system, that may be a potential problem to consider.

The users of the *COMPASS* system were known from the beginning to be the No. 2 EAX switch maintenance personnel. We did not expect anything but cooperation, except possibly for problems related to job security or disturbance of the working environment.

6.5.8 POLITICAL PROBLEMS RELATED TO SYSTEM CONTROL

The introduction of the expert system into use should not be politically sensitive or controversial. Company political problems related to control of the system could damage the possibilities for system success and therefore should be considered in advance.

Two typical problems are that the control or use of the system goes across existing organizational boundaries and that the system does not clearly fall under any existing organizational structure. In either event, the political infighting that might occur to determine which part of the organization has control of the system might make political enemies for the system itself. Some group or powerful individual might prefer that no one have the system if they cannot have control of it.

We did not foresee this as a problem for *COMPASS*, but it turned out to be one. Several organizations within GTE had interest in *COMPASS*: GTE Laboratories, the developers; GTE Data Services, to which it was transferred initially; GTE corporate management, representing the GTE telephone companies as a whole; and the individual telephone companies, the prospective users (especially GTE-Southwest, which had supplied the primary expert). Once GTE Laboratories finished with development and relinquished full control, each of the different organizations had its own ideas for and degrees of interest in *COMPASS* deployment. This led to a less defined course for *COMPASS* than might have occurred had there been a single group in full control, thus slowing deployment.

6.5.9 POLITICAL PROBLEMS RELATED TO SYSTEM RESULTS

The expert system's results should not be politically sensitive or controversial. Domain selectors should be concerned if the system's results might be challenged for reasons of company politics. It probably will be hard enough to get the system's recommendations accepted technically. If some individuals or groups have political motivation to resist the system, that would be an additional burden for system acceptance. An example is an expert system designed to decide the appropriation of funds within corporate groups. The "losers," that is, groups that the system decides should get low appropriations, will likely challenge not only the results but also the entire system's credibility.

> *COMPASS*'s output of prioritized maintenance actions surely makes no political enemies, and therefore this point was not a concern. We did look into some other possible expert system tasks that related to determining resource allocations. We considered the possibility of the system making political enemies to be negative factors for those domains.

6.5.10 PROBLEMS RELATED TO THE SENSITIVITY OF THE KNOWLEDGE

The knowledge contained by the system should not be sensitive or controversial. Some knowledge used by domain experts could cause problems if recorded. But if the project is to develop an expert system that performs at an expert level, the project must acquire this knowledge from the experts, record it, and eventually implement it. Anyone with access to the documentation of the knowledge, to the program, or to the program's documentation has access to this sensitive knowledge. If such sensitive knowledge does exist, consideration should be to given to how this knowledge will be handled before the domain is selected. It might be easier to leave this knowledge out of the expert system. If that is the case, the effect of the missing knowledge on the performance of the system should be ascertained.

What kinds of sensitive knowledge are we talking about? There may be certain practices or opinions, embodied in expert heuristics, that may prove embarrassing if written down. For example, a practice under which particular customers are given preferential treatment, a practice that ignores standard corporate procedures or goes around certain organizational structures, or expert opinion on the strengths and weaknesses of certain individuals. In addition, there may be some practices bordering on illegality that are part of an expert's techniques but that the company would not like to document. There may be closely guarded trade secrets that experts use in making decisions but would be risky to write down. Any of these kinds of situations that exist should be carefully investigated before the domain is selected.

> No sensitive or controversial knowledge was related to No. 2 EAX maintenance, so these concerns were not pertinent. While we were investigating domains, however, we did come across an area in which we felt some sensitive information was used as part of the expert's decision process. We downgraded that domain.

6.6   DEVELOPMENT, TESTING, AND DEPLOYMENT

Several of the attributes of a good expert system domain are related to the development, testing, and deployment of the expert system, including issues of coverage, availability of test cases, performance, stability, payoff, and others.

6.6.1 INCOMPLETE COVERAGE

It is desirable that the expert system need not perform the domain task completely in order for the system to be useful. If some percentage of incomplete coverage can be tolerated, at least initially, the system can be phased into use. An initial version of the expert system covering a small, closed subset of the complete task can be developed using relatively rapid prototyping techniques and then the system can be expanded to the complete task.

In this circumstance, it is important that the determination of whether a subproblem is covered by the available system should not be very difficult. Otherwise it may be hard to utilize effectively a system that has incomplete coverage, even if such a system were available.

If the expert system does not have to do everything in order to do something, it can be put in place much sooner. The more difficult subtasks can be tackled later, if at all. Moreover this situation allows the project to be broken into two or more major phases. In each of these major phases, the project can concentrate on one or a few subtasks rather than the entire task.

An initial system could be built for a limited subtask, which would be useful by itself. This small but useful system might justify early deployment or at least early system field trials. Either of these could provide important feedback to the development of the remainder of the system. But if the task must be accomplished in its entirety before the system can do something useful, any deployment or meaningful use of the system must be deferred until the entire development is completed.

> In the *COMPASS* domain, it became evident almost immediately that the task of analyzing maintenance messages could be split into subtasks, each one analyzing one class of maintenance message. Our expert indicated that he performed his analysis maintenance message class by maintenance message class and that the analyses of classes were independent of each other. Thus we had a natural way to break up the project: have each major project phase attack the analysis of one or more maintenance message classes.

> There was never any difficulty determining which classes of problems a particular version of the system could handle. The system could (or at least should) be able to handle those and only those problems related to the maintenance message classes covered by the system. (This partitioning also made obvious which input data a particular system version required—only the maintenance messages of the classes covered.)

> To prove feasibility, it seemed necessary to cover one maintenance message class. We chose the most important and most complex message class, the Network Recovery 20 (NR20) messages. This choice allowed our initial *COMPASS-I* system to do something useful, though its scope was limited, and although we did not plan to deploy this system, corporate personnel thought it useful enough to want it deployed.

> Once we chose to cover only one maintenance message class in *COMPASS-I*, our knowledge acquisition sessions did not even consider the analysis of any of the other message types. Subsequent expansion of *COMPASS* has added the capability of handling nine additional maintenance message classes— every other No. 2 EAX message type that requires detailed expert analysis.

6.6.2 DECOMPOSABILITY

The task, and preferably every subtask, should be decomposable into a series of steps to facilitate development. If the task or subtask is decomposable, the knowledge acquisition process can be focused on one step of the task at a time rather than on the entire task at once. Combined with the incomplete coverage feature, this means that the project can be directed, at any one time, to one subtask for one subdomain. Furthermore decomposability allows the implementation to be modularized in a meaningful and convenient form. Each step can be the basis of a separate module of the program (as discussed in Chapter 11).

The decomposability of a task may be obvious. For example, in a chemical process control task, there may be a set of steps performed in sequence to produce the final result (such as: Produce Mixture X; Add Heat; Add Chemical Y; Cool; etc.). For some other tasks, the decomposition may not be obvious to a nonexpert but will be clear to an expert. If either of these kinds of tasks is identified, the domain can be given some positive weight in the selection process. However, there are many tasks for which experts do not realize until long into knowledge acquisition that there is a reasonable decomposition. Unless there is some indication that the domain task being evaluated is such a task, there does not seem to be a way to take this possibility into account.

> In COMPASS, we (including our expert) did not know at first that the task of analyzing a single No. 2 EAX maintenance message was decomposable into a series of steps. Therefore we started knowledge acquisition by finding rules and procedures for the entire initial task (analysis of NR20 messages) and began knowledge implementation without a meaningful approach to modularization. Only after some knowledge acquisition did it become clear that the task could be decomposed into five major stages: input, identify, analyze, suggest, and output. After that, we concentrated knowledge acquisition at any one time on one particular stage of the COMPASS process. We used these stages as the basis for our modularization of the implementation. As we proceeded, we found that the five COMPASS stages could be broken further into nine substages or steps (as discussed in Chapter 10). This finding yielded even better focus for the knowledge acquisition and an even more modular program.

6.6.3 TEACHABLE SKILL

If the skill required by the task is normally taught to novices, it means that there is some experience teaching the domain knowledge to neophytes such as the project team—and ultimately the expert system. Furthermore it usually means that there is an organization to the knowledge that can prove useful (at least initially) in building the system.

> The maintenance of the No. 2 EAX is taught to new switch maintenance people in training courses and then by on-the-job training; however, the intricacies of the analysis of the maintenance messages are not formally taught.

> The meanings of the maintenance messages are available in reference manuals, but the heuristics No. 2 EAX experts use to analyze these messages are not formally passed from the experts to novices, though some can be gleaned from on-the-job training. Most experts could not teach these heuristics since they have not formalized them. (One possible use of the COMPASS knowledge documentation, not yet done, would be to use the extracted heuristics contained in it as a tutorial document).

6.6.4 WRITTEN MATERIAL

It is helpful to choose a domain with books, manuals, and other written materials available. In writing a book or manual, an expert has already extracted and organized some of the domain expertise. This organized knowledge might prove useful (at least initially) in building the system.

Note, however, that one benefit of capturing an expert's domain knowledge might be to take a step toward formalizing a domain that has not been treated formally.

> We were not able to find any No. 2 EAX documentation or tutorial that was useful enough to form the basis of *COMPASS* knowledge. However, some of the No. 2 EAX documentation was helpful when we were familiarizing ourselves with the domain at the beginning of our knowledge acquisition activities.

6.6.5 AVAILABILITY OF TEST CASES

The development of the expert system is made much easier if test cases for the task are available. A test case should be a complete example of the problem the expert system is trying to solve, containing all the inputs on which human experts would base their analysis in a form that could be made computer accessible. If possible, the test case can include all of the outputs that an expert produced.

The use of a large number of test cases facilitates knowledge acquisition. Later test cases can be used in program testing and evaluation. In some domains test cases abound; in others they do not. If it is difficult or impossible to obtain test cases, then this could have a strong negative impact on system development.

> No. 2 EAXs continually produce maintenance messages. The *COMPASS* analysis is based solely on several hours' or a day's maintenance messages from a particular No. 2 EAX. The maintenance message data are available in computer form and so are easy to collect and store, on site or remotely.

> Within GTE there are many No. 2 EAXs. Access to just one would provide a new *COMPASS* test case at least every day. Furthermore the analysis is changed when some messages are added and others deleted and thus it is possible for testing purposes to, say, get the last 24 hours of data every 12 hours. Although about half the messages for two successive sets of messages will be the same, the analyses would usually be different enough to be treated as different test cases.

> In another project, we looked into developing an expert system for a chemical engineering process. The process was performed in large batches, no more than once a day, and in only one location. Thus not many test cases were available. The data needed for test cases seemed hard to collect and store, being available in different forms and not online. We considered the difficulty of obtaining test cases a negative aspect of the domain.

6.6.6 REAL-TIME AND PERFORMANCE ISSUES

It is preferable that any requirement that the expert system meet certain performance standards in order to be successfully utilized (such as a strong real-time response requirement) should not necessitate extensive effort.

It is certainly possible to develop an expert system for a problem with strong performance requirements. If the payoff is substantial, such a domain may be the best one to select. Yet if a great deal of effort must be put into fulfilling these requirements, the considerations involved may divert effort from the primary development tasks: knowledge acquisition and knowledge implementation. For a project with limited resources or limited time, it is not prudent to choose a domain that requires the investment of large amounts of resources and time in nonprimary tasks, assuming there are other domains without such requirements that meet the other criteria for a good domain equally well. If such a domain is to be considered, it is advisable to attempt to get additional resources and time for the project so as not to shortchange the knowledge engineering of the system.

Furthermore the selection of a domain with time constraints adds a binary factor to the judgment of the success of the expert system. In most cases, the evaluation of an expert system results is not all or nothing; there is a range of successful operation of the expert system, from marginally acceptable through perfect, depending primarily on the degree to which the expert system matches domain experts. However, if the expert system must meet a time constraint, say a one second response time, the system will be considered a failure if it does not meet this constraint, even if its answers meet or surpass those of the best experts.

> The manual analysis of No. 2 EAX maintenance messages is done on a background basis by domain personnel—generally once per shift. It is usually based on data obtained over one day. We felt that an expert system performing the same task would have no response time constraint that would be severe enough to require major additional effort. It turned out that we could run *COMPASS* offline. As long as the results were ready in time for a maintenance person to use its results, the maintenance person did not care whether a *COMPASS* run took one minute or a few hours. Of course, run speed was still a concern since the more *COMPASS* runs that could be made daily on one machine, the lower the number of machines that would be needed to service a group of No. 2 EAXs. However, the point here is that *COMPASS* did not have to meet a critical response time threshold below which the system would be useless.

6.6.7 USER INTERFACE

It is desirable that any requirement for an elaborate user interface for the expert system does not necessitate a large undertaking.

As with the response requirements, an excessive diversion of effort to produce a user interface takes the focus of the development away from where it should be—on the knowledge acquisition and the knowledge implementation. Certainly a good user interface makes the system easier to use. Furthermore a flashy user interface is often the best salesman for the system. Therefore a reasonable amount of work on the interface can be rewarding (as well as, usually, lots of fun). However, what we are discussing here is an expert system task where the amount of work needed on the interface is a significant part of the total project work. Such a system may have large payoff and be useful, but if there is limited time and labor available, the work on the interface may come at the expense of the rest of the expert system development. In most cases, the goal is not an expert system with a great interface and little expertise. Therefore it is reasonable to select a domain without a big interface requirement or to attempt to obtain additional time or personnel to build the interface.

> No. 2 EAX maintainers are used to dealing with terse and obscure outputs from the switch and from associated computer systems. As exemplified in Figure 5.3, these outputs generally consist of strings of numbers and have few frills or explanatory features. Knowing the capabilities of the machines we would be working with and the level of capability of the system implementers, we were confident when we started *COMPASS* that any outputs we produced for the system could be more readable and in better format than the usual printouts that the maintenance people used. We were confident that we could make any interaction required at a terminal superior to the machine interfaces the users were used to. We were fairly sure that these output facilities could be accomplished with a small portion of the project effort.

6.6.8 LONG-TERM SYSTEM NEED

The need for the task should be projected to continue enough beyond the time of initial deployment of the expert system to generate an acceptable payoff. A problem that is important today may no longer exist in a year or two; it may be a transient problem or a long-term one whose importance is diminishing. In either case, there is little benefit to developing an expert system that will not be needed at the time it is completed or soon after. The effects of changes that will significantly alter the definition of the task should be foreseen and taken into account when evaluating the domain. If the structure, operation, goals, needs, and so forth of the corporation or of the potential customers or users of the expert system can be predicted to change and if these changes might affect the utility of the system by the time of deployment, the effects of these changes should be considered when estimating the potential payoff of the system.

> While considering the *COMPASS* domain, we explored the question of how long the task of No. 2 EAX maintenance would continue to exist. Although GTE plans eventually to replace its No. 2 EAXs with all-digital switches, it was estimated that this phasing out would take no fewer than 10 years and that there would be several No. 2 EAXs in the corporation well beyond that time. Thus at the time we projected *COMPASS* to become available, we expected that there would be many No. 2 EAXs in the corporation and that a signifi-

cant number of them would continue to be in operation for several more years.

Two additional factors added to our belief that the need for *COMPASS* would exist well beyond the completion of the project. First, we expected that the per-switch benefit of *COMPASS* would increase as the number of corporate switches went down. It was likely that the availability of top No. 2 EAX experts would decrease faster than the number of switches because the better maintenance people would move to work on the newer switches. Second, when GTE replaces a No. 2 EAX switch, the old switch is usually sold to another telephone company. The need for No. 2 EAX maintenance by these telephone companies (and thus the potential for sales of *COMPASS* to these companies) will be increasing as No. 2 EAX use in GTE decreases.

Some of the domains suggested during the domain survey were rejected because we felt that the need for the expert system would have diminished or disappeared before the system could be developed. For example, some major problems that telephone company personnel were worried about were related to certain equipment conversions that they were mandated by law to make. As we investigated these problems, we found that the conversions would probably be completed by the time any expert system could be developed and deployed and therefore rejected those domains.

6.6.9 NO ALTERNATIVE

It is good to select a domain where, as far as can be determined, no alternative solution to the problem is being pursued or is expected to be pursued. This situation clearly maximizes the chances for the expert system to be put into use and to provide an important payoff. If there is another effort—ongoing or expected—to solve the problem, its success would minimize the benefits that otherwise would have accrued from the expert system. If the problem is solved before the expert system is finished, the entire effort may have been for naught. (If a goal of the project is to compare expert system technology to other technologies, however, then the choice of a problem for which a conventional solution is being attempted may be just what is desired.)

We were fairly certain when we selected the *COMPASS* domain that if we did not develop a No. 2 EAX maintenance expert system, the process of maintaining No. 2 EAXs would continue as it had been for the preceding several years, with no major changes. It appeared highly unlikely that any effort would be made to automate or simplify the No. 2 EAX maintenance task further. We did find other potential applications where a corresponding situation did not exist. Upon investigating one of our leading possibilities, we found that there was an effort underway in GTE to accomplish the same goal by a conventional computer program. We did not know if this undertaking would be successful or the extent to which the program that would be developed might diminish the payoff of our system. Nevertheless it seemed reasonable to try to find a domain for which there was no prospect of such an alternative effort.

6.6.10 STABILITY

The domain should be fairly stable or at least slowly changing. Expected changes should be such that they utilize the strengths of expert systems (such as the ease of updating or revising specific rules in a knowledge base) or otherwise can be handled well (such as changes to the domain that would require additions to or deletions from the program of whole modules). It is not desirable to select a domain where changes are expected that will require major modifications in reasoning processes.

If an expert system is developed for a nonstable domain, expert knowledge and heuristics that are sound when acquired from an expert may not be applicable later. Thus the circumstance may occur where a large number of previously developed knowledge structures (such as rules) are no longer valid but cannot easily be changed without redoing a large part of the system development process. Such significant revisions might be accomplished in major new phases of an expert system development, but it is difficult to handle a situation where the heuristics change frequently during the time the system is being developed. It may not be evident which knowledge structures should be modified or replaced to make the changes. Even if it were, it may not be obvious that related parts of the knowledge might have been found in conjunction with the modified knowledge and thus may need to be modified as well.

> The No. 2 EAX domain was very stable. The No. 2 EAX was a well-established switch, and it was likely that no major changes to its hardware, architecture, control software, or maintenance procedures would occur. Moreover it was unlikely that even minor changes that could affect *COMPASS* would occur. Our expectations proved to be the case. From the time we started developing *COMPASS*, no rule had to be changed because of a change in the No. 2 EAX.
>
> Such a statement would not have been true for the newer GTD-5. At the time we chose our domain, modifications to the GTD-5 were occurring regularly. Experts heuristics developed to solve a certain problem in a certain situation became outdated rapidly; a new hardware or software release might solve the problem or significantly modify the situation in which the problem had to be solved. Hence an expert system developed based on those original heuristics would become invalid and would have to be modified repeatedly.

6.6.11 PROJECT DEPENDENCIES AND MILESTONES

If possible, the expert system project should not be on the critical path of any other project, development, or planned change of procedure. Ideally there should be loose milestones for completion of the project or broad, modifiable goals for the expert system.

The use of expert system technology for practical applications is still relatively new, so any development project has some risk of failure, no matter how conservatively the domain is selected. Therefore the less dependent other activities are on the successful completion of the expert system project, the better.

Since it is almost impossible in most cases to judge precisely how much knowledge a particular domain contains and how swiftly knowledge acquisition and the other project phases will proceed, it is difficult to guarantee tight milestones for the delivery of an expert system, especially a large one. However, if it is important to deliver an expert system development at a certain date, then the project should have flexibility in meeting at least some system goals, such as amount of coverage or degree of accuracy, or have the possibility of increasing staff size, if needed. Such flexibility can be used to compensate for unexpected difficulties and delays.

The dependence of others on the timeliness of the expert system project or on the full achievement of its goals multiplies the downside risk of the project and significantly increases the pressure on project leadership and project members. If the project completion is delayed or the final system does not fully meet some of its specific goals (on such items as coverage, response time, operating cost, or degree of agreement with an expert), the expert system developed may still be very useful and have a high payoff. Yet the overall judgment of the project may be negative if its delay or its failure to meet a specific goal causes a significant adverse impact on other projects dependent on the expert system.

If the development of the expert system is on the critical path for some other projects or changes of procedure, this situation might take away a great deal of the project's flexibility of direction. Since expert systems generally evolve their specifications as they are developed rather than have specifications detailed in advance, it is likely that the project may be able to move in certain directions not anticipated at the project's beginning. If other projects are tied to the expert system, the latitude for such alterations of direction may be significantly diminished.

> No developments or changes related to No. 2 EAX maintenance were dependent on the successful, full, or timely completion of *COMPASS*. If *COMPASS* was unable to perform at a high enough level of expertise, if its coverage was too small to be useful, or if it was significantly delayed in completion, there would be no impact on anyone other than the direct impact of *COMPASS*'s unavailability. Maintenance of No. 2 EAXs would continue to be performed as it had been for the last few years.

6.6.12 TOLERANCE TO INCORRECT RESULTS

The task should not be all or nothing. Users should be able to tolerate some percentage of incorrect or nonoptimal results. The more toleration users have for incorrect results, the faster the system can be deployed and the easier it will be to win system acceptance. For example, in a domain where even the best experts are often wrong, system users usually are not upset by an incorrect result from the expert system. If an average practitioner is correct 50 percent of the time on a task and a typical expert is correct 90 percent of the time on the task, an expert system that is correct 70 percent of the time would probably be very useful. This system could be deployed and used as is while efforts are underway to raise its performance closer to expert level. However, if only experts perform a task and they have a very good success rate, a system that performs below their level may never be used. If an expert system were used to provide directory assistance information, a 70 percent correct system would be well below present practice and would never be used. In this case, the system would have to be refined continually until its performance reached present standards before any consideration could be given to its deployment.

One or a few major incorrect results may destroy the credibility of the system. It appears that users often can accept a mistake from a human expert more easily than the same mistake from a computer program. This situation may change as the concept of fallible expert systems becomes more well known. Until then it is wise to be wary of a domain where a few mistakes by the system (even mistakes that experts would make) might result in the abandonment of the system.

In some situations, incorrect results produced by an expert system may have important ramifications in the area of legal liability. For example, if a user gets incorrect medical advice from an expert system, the expert system developer may be open to the possibility of a lawsuit. Therefore if a domain is such that the expert system's results might be used in a way that could make the developing company legally liable, that possibility should be thoroughly investigated before the domain is chosen.

> The best experts at No. 2 EAX maintenance make a large percentage of mistakes attempting to identify the faults causing maintenance messages. In most cases, there is not enough information in the maintenance messages to identify the proper fault, even if the best expert were given unlimited time for the task. The best an expert can do is to come up with a list of possible faults in some priority order. Even then, a good deal of the time the first choice of the expert will be wrong. Thus journeyman switch personnel consulting an expert are not surprised when the expert's advice is incorrect. For example, an expert may recommend replacing a circuit card and that circuit card may be in perfect condition. With this situation in No. 2 EAX maintenance, we did not expect any major problems if *COMPASS* made mistakes—as long as on the whole it performed at a reasonable level.

6.6.13 MEASURABLE PAYOFF

The task's payoff should be measurable. If it cannot be measured or if doing so is difficult and inexact, it is harder to demonstrate the success of the expert system to potential users and to skeptics.

Some applications have goals whose achievement is difficult or impossible to measure, while for other applications, there are simple measures that everyone can accept to determine the extent to which the goals were achieved. For example, it may not be too difficult to measure the success of a project whose goal is to agree with a certain leading expert 80 percent of the time, whose goal is to enable a standard task to be performed with half the personnel, whose goal is to reduce certain malfunctions by 20 percent, or whose goal is to produce more widgets per hour with the same production line. It is much more difficult to measure the success of a project whose goal is to enhance corporate image, to make 25-year forecasts, or to help humanity.

The measures of success for some expert system applications may be easily identified and monitored, but it may be difficult to isolate the effect of the expert system from other influences. A project whose goal is to increase sales may have difficulty proving that a realized sales increase should be attributed to the expert system and not to general economic conditions, changes in the product, new advertising, steps by the competition, or other possible causes.

> In the *COMPASS* domain, it was well known that the average No. 2 EAX maintenance person performed at a level significantly below that of a top expert. Our primary domain-related goal was to upgrade the expertise at all No. 2 EAX sites to be close to that of a top expert. The degree of closeness could be measured by comparisons of *COMPASS*'s recommendations with those of a top expert. Another way *COMPASS* results could be measured was to determine the percentage of time that *COMPASS* actually found and repaired (that is, recommended an effective repair for) switch problems.

> In the domain selection process, an application was suggested whose primary goal was to increase the goodwill of the company. It seemed difficult to measure corporate goodwill with any accuracy—a negative factor for selecting this application. Furthermore even if there were some accurate measures, it was plain that many factors would affect goodwill other than the expert system, and so it seemed unlikely that the impact of the expert system could have been determined accurately.

6.6.14 EXPERT AGREEMENT ON CORRECTNESS

When the expert system performs its function, domain experts should be able to agree on whether the system's results are correct. In situations where there is no single correct answer, domain experts should be able to agree on whether the system's results are good, reasonable, or, at least, acceptable.

If experts cannot agree on whether the system produces correct (or good) results, the results are open to challenge, even if the system accurately embodies a leading expert's knowledge. It is incumbent upon the system developers to try to foresee any attacks on the system and to try to avoid them.

> We were told when we investigated *COMPASS* that No. 2 EAX experts agree most of the time as to what maintenance procedures should be done. Disagreements are usually confined to the order of performing tasks and to procedures in unusual cases. Even when they disagreed, they usually would not consider that another expert's results were wrong—just that they were non-optimal. From our later meetings with experts other than the *COMPASS* primary expert, we found that this description seemed to be true.

> When we looked into an application involving economic planning, we found a domain where experts could radically disagree and downgraded the domain as a possibility.

CHECKLIST FOR SELECTING THE DOMAIN: DESIRED DOMAIN ATTRIBUTES

- [ ] Use expert system technology for domains where conventional programming is not likely to be effective or where the knowledge acquisition, representation, or implementation techniques of expert systems offer advantages over conventional approaches.

- [ ] There should be recognized experts who solve the problem.

- [ ] There should be a need to capture the expertise. For example, the expertise will not be available on a reliable, continuing, widespread, and inexpensive basis.

- [ ] The project goal should be a system with the capability of a limited version of an expert in a well-bounded subdomain. The domain should be such that a system meeting this goal would be considered a great success.

- [ ] It should be expected that, just as a human expert, the system may not produce optimal or correct results 100 percent of the time.

- [ ] The completed system should be expected to have a significant payoff to justify its development.

- [ ] Among possible application domains, select the domain that best meets overall project goals regarding project payoff versus risk of failure. For example, a conservative approach would be to attempt to develop a system that would meet some minimum criterion for payoff if successful and that seems to offer the best chance of success.

- [ ] The task should primarily require symbolic reasoning. For a task that primarily involves numerical computation, consideration should be given to other programming approaches.

- [ ] The task should require the use of heuristics, that is, rules-of-thumb, strategies, and so forth. It may require consideration of an extremely large number of possibilities; it may require decisions to be based on incomplete or uncertain information.

- [ ] The task should not require knowledge from a very large number of areas.

- [ ] The task should not require significant use of commonsense reasoning.

- [ ] The project should not have as its goal both the development of a real expert system and major advances in the state of the art of expert system technology.

- [ ] The task should be defined clearly. At the project outset, the inputs and outputs of the system should be defined as well as possible.

- [ ] All the inputs utilized by experts to allow them to perform the task should be available to the expert system, or it should seem likely that they could be made available. Examples of inputs that may not be available are paper data that cannot be obtained in computer form, undocumented local knowledge, and data for which available sensors cannot duplicate a human expert's perceptions.

- It should seem likely that the outputs required of the expert system could be produced in the manner desired and could be delivered to the location(s) desired.

- If possible, the task should be similar to that of a successful expert system.

- The experts should be significantly better than novices in performing the task.

- It should be probable that domain experts, preferably some of the best experts, will be available to the project and will commit a substantial amount of time to the development of the system.

- It should be possible to acquire the expertise for the system, at least that pertaining to one particular subdomain, primarily from one expert. The use of a single expert for a specific area of knowledge avoids the problems inherent in dealing with multiple experts whose conclusions or problem-solving techniques may not agree. There are, however, some advantages to using multiple experts, such as strength of authority and breadth of expertise in subdomains.

- The task should be neither too easy (for example, taking a human expert less than a few minutes) nor too difficult (requiring more than a few hours for an expert).

- The amount of knowledge required by the task should be large enough to make the knowledge base developed nontrivial. If it is too small, the task may be more amenable to another approach, such as a decision tree.

- It should appear that the number of important concepts (e.g., rules) required does not exceed the order of several hundreds or a few thousand— a reasonable size for a large expert system.

- The task should be sufficiently narrow and self-contained. The aim should not be for a system that is expert in an entire domain but for a system that can perform a limited task at expert level.

- Personnel in the domain area should have realistic expectations, understanding the potential of an expert system for their domain but also realizing that many expert system development projects have not resulted in production programs with industrial payoff.

- The specific task of the expert system should be jointly agreed upon by the system developers and the domain area personnel.

- Managers in the domain area should have previously identified the need to solve the problem the system attacks.

- The project should be strongly supported by a senior manager, for protection and follow-up.

- It should be probable that potential users would welcome the completed system.

- It should be possible to introduce the system into operation with minimal disturbance of current practices.

- The user group should be cooperative and patient.

- The introduction of the expert system into use should not be politically sensitive or controversial, such as when the control or use of the system goes across existing organizational boundaries.

- The system's results should not be politically sensitive or controversial. If some parties will challenge the system if its results do not favor them politically (such as on appropriation of funds), it will be much harder to gain system acceptance.

- The knowledge contained by the system should not be sensitive or controversial, such as when certain practices, embodied in heuristics, might prove embarrassing if written down (for example, how certain customers are treated relative to other customers).

- The expert system should not have to perform the entire task to be useful; some degree of incomplete coverage should be tolerable, at least initially.

- The task should be decomposable, allowing relatively rapid prototyping for a closed small subset of the complete task and then slow expansion to the complete task.

- The skill required by the task should be one that is taught to novices.

- There should be books or other written materials discussing the domain.

- Test cases should be readily available.

- Any performance requirements that might divert effort from the primary tasks of system development should be carefully consistent.

- The user interface should not require extensive effort that might divert effort from the primary tasks of system development.

- The need for the task should be projected to continue for several years.

- The effects of changes that will significantly alter the potential payoff of the task should be foreseeable and taken into account.

- No alternative solution to the problem should be presently being pursued or expected to be pursued.

- The domain should be fairly stable. The situation should not occur where a large amount of previously acquired knowledge is found to be no longer valid but cannot easily be changed without redoing a major part of the development process.

☐ The project should not be on the critical path for any other development. The less dependent other activities are on the successful completion of the expert system, the better.

☐ The project should not have rigid milestones for completion unless there is some flexibility in goals (such as degree of accuracy or amount of coverage) or in staffing level.

☐ The task should not be all-or-nothing; some percentage of incorrect or nonoptimal results should be tolerable.

☐ The task's payoff should be measurable.

☐ It should be likely that domain experts would agree as to whether the system's results are correct. In situations where there is no correct answer, domain experts should agree that the system's results are acceptable.

Prerau, Developing and Managing Expert Systems (Addison-Wesley)

CHAPTER 7

Selecting the Hardware and the Software Development Tool

■ What process can be used to select the hardware and the software tool for an expert system development project?

■ What are the criteria, technical and nontechnical, for selecting a computer for the expert system project?

■ What are the criteria, technical and nontechnical, for selecting an expert system development tool?

■ How should cost and other factors related to obtaining a development environment be considered?

■ How important is vendor and system history?

■ What issues related to training should be considered?

■ What critical elements related to the usability of a hardware or software system should be examined?

■ How should considerations related to deployment be taken into account?

Another important early step in the expert system development process is the selection of the project's development environment—the computer and the software to be used. This project phase can be separated into two interrelated tasks: investigating available computers suitable for expert system development to determine the best for the project and investigating available knowledge engineering software tools (and also the "no tool" option of developing directly in a computer language) to determine what should be used by the project. Although the two tasks can be separated to some degree, they cannot be completely divorced from each other since each software tool is limited to running on certain hardware (and, equivalently, each computer can run only certain software tools). The project's overall goal is to select the hardware and software combination best suited for the expert system development.

Let us consider terminology. For ease of reference, in this chapter the terms *knowledge engineering tool* and *software tool* will be used broadly to refer to a software system in which an expert system can be developed. This includes full shell systems, knowledge engineering aids, rule systems, AI programming languages such as Lisp or Prolog, conventional programming languages in which expert system might be developed, or some combination of these. *Hardware* and *computer* will be used synonymously. The term *development environment* will refer to the combination of a software tool and a computer, the combination on which the expert system will be developed. Finally the unmodified word *system* will be used to mean either the software tool or the hardware.

The selection of the hardware and software for an expert system development should be, ideally, an integral part of the project and not something determined before the project begins. The spectrum of available computers and software tools for developing expert system is extremely dynamic. New expert system development tools and newly improved versions of old tools are announced frequently. The same is true for expert system hardware. New computer models, new options and extensions for older hardware, and new possibilities for platforms for expert systems (conventional computers—from PCs to mainframes—as well as specialized AI workstations) regularly come on the market. Yet all computers and expert system building tools are not equally applicable to every problem and every situation. The best environment for one project may be poorly suited to another project. For example, some software tools are specialized to a certain type of problem (e.g., diagnosis), while others can be used for several classes of problems. Some computers may be too expensive or too nonstandard to consider. Some hardware-software combinations may be too slow or too small to be adequate for a particular expert system application.

Often management gives the project team little or no opportunity to select its development environment. If the project has available to it computers and/or software tools that have previously been bought by the company, management may demand or assume that these will be used by the project and will allocate no funding for new hardware or software. Project leaders should make it clear to upper management that each project has a unique application and that often effort has been wasted on expert system projects in the attempt to squeeze problems into unsuitable development environments. Also each project (usually) has a unique complement of personnel with particular experience and strengths. Therefore the selection of a development environment made at another time for another project may possibly be unsuitable for the present project.

The selectors of hardware and software should consider both technical factors and (sometimes of equal or greater importance) nontechnical factors. This chapter will first address some issues related to the process of selecting the expert system development environment.

Then, as for domain selection, several criteria, technical and nontechnical, for selecting a development environment will be presented. These criteria can help the project team focus on the good and bad points of a possible hardware/software choice.

7.1 A PROCESS FOR SELECTING THE DEVELOPMENT ENVIRONMENT

The following is a reasonable process for selecting the project's hardware and software (assuming the project has that option).

1. **Beginning the selection process.** The process of selecting the expert system development environment should begin early in the project. Ideally this phase can be started somewhat after the domain selection process begins and can proceed in parallel. But even if the process is started early, the final selection of the project's development environment should not be made prematurely.

Starting the selection process early should allow the final selections to be made with enough time for the development system to be available when needed. The time when the knowledge acquisition team has begun acquiring some knowledge that can be implemented is too late to begin looking for the project's development environment. Time should be allowed for the selection process and for all the other steps that must happen before the development system can be used by the project.

If the hardware or software system chosen is new to the company, then after the selection is made, there will usually be a significant wait until the system is available. Approvals must be obtained, and the paperwork for ordering the system must be processed. Following that there is frequently a lengthy waiting period until the system is delivered. Finally the system must be installed and integrated into the overall company environment. Project members may need to be trained (or train themselves) on the system. It may be necessary or desirable for project members to take training courses from the vendor. The total training could take a considerable amount of time, depending on the complexity, novelty, and transparency of the system and the experience and skill level of the project members.

Sometimes it is useful to start implementing the development environment as soon as the first chunk of domain knowledge is acquired from an expert. Certainly the system should be available and the implementers trained by the time a large enough amount of knowledge has been acquired to make machine simulation of the acquired knowledge preferable to hand simulation of paper rules. On the other hand, it is desirable that the problem domain be defined, or at least a set of candidate domains be known, before the final decision on the project's hardware and software is made. Domain requirements can have a major impact on the relative importance of the various attributes of the development environment. Indeed certain environments may be completely useless for developing certain applications. Thus a premature selection of development hardware and software might yield major problems.

Work on the environment selection phase and on the domain selection phase can go on concurrently. An initial surveying of hardware and software choices can certainly be done before the domain is known. As the domain possibilities are narrowed, if none of the remaining candidate applications have requirements that have a major effect on environment selection, or if they at least do not have conflicting requirements, the domain and environment selection phases can proceed in parallel. Otherwise it might be preferable to delay the final environment selection decision until the domain selection is made.

2. **Surveying possible systems.** A survey should be made of potentially usable hardware and software systems. A large expert system development project might be able to devote a significant effort to such a survey; a small project might attempt to gather whatever information can be found in a limited amount of time.

The set of available systems is dynamic. Many AI publications and newsletters periodically list (and sometimes evaluate) the leading hardware and software systems. Another source for possible systems is the ads that fill many AI publications and that fill the mailbox of anyone who is enough involved with AI to get on some mailing lists. Papers in technical journals may discuss successful (or, occasionally, unsuccessful) uses of particular hardware or software systems. These journals are also a good source for initial information on university-developed systems that may be available. The exhibits section of the major AI or expert system conferences and trade shows are other good sources of information.

It may be possible to eliminate immediately large classes of systems, such as those that are too expensive. For the remaining systems, the project's environment selection team should collect as much information as it can, such as:

■   sales literature

■   technical papers discussing the structure or use of a system

■   reviews and rankings in independent publications evaluating AI hardware and software, such as in application-oriented AI magazines and newsletters

■   results of any independent (e.g., university-run) benchmark tests

■   information garnered by meetings with the vendor's sales and technical people

■   system users' reviews of the systems. (Vendors can provide lists of satisfied users. More desirable are reviews from users from whom an honest evaluation could be expected, such as fellow employees or personal acquaintances.)

3. **System demonstrations.** For any system that seems a good possibility, the next step might be to arrange a system demonstration. Vendors are usually happy (usually *more* than happy) to arrange demonstrations of their systems for serious potential buyers. Although these demonstrations can be useful, beware of generalizing from them. Vendor demonstrations are designed to show the system in a good light and often to encourage the viewer to infer that the system has more power or features than it actually has. Ask good questions, using the points discussed in this chapter to help cover the most important areas.

4. **System use prior to purchase.** If it can be done, it is very valuable to arrange for project personnel to use potential systems before they are purchased to allow an in-depth analysis of the systems. Sometimes this system use is easy to arrange—for example, if a group in the same company already has the system in-house and will allow project personnel to work on it.

If no simple arrangement can be made, it may be possible to get vendors to agree to lend potential systems to the project for a limited time. Vendors are often less happy to do this, giving users freedom to examine all aspects of the system, than they are to arrange demonstrations, where they have primary control. However, if the vendor allows in-house use or if the project or corporation has enough leverage to demand it, possibly the one or two systems that seem the most likely to be chosen can be obtained on loan for a trial period.

In order for the project to benefit from use of a system prior to purchase, some project personnel (the system evaluators) must be able to put the system to use in an extensive and knowledgeable enough way to enable some conclusions about the system to be made from the test. This means that either the system should be so easy to learn to use that no extensive training is required (the ease of learning to use the system, of course, may be one of the important pieces of information found from the in-house test), or there should be some project personnel with enough experience and knowledge about hardware or software that they are able to learn to use a new system quickly.

When they are proficient, the system evaluators might formulate some benchmarks to compare different systems. A full comparative evaluation of systems is a very large and difficult task—a major project in itself. More likely the expert system developers will want to restrict the evaluation to the items that are of most importance to the project and to some restricted, reasonable benchmark tests of those items.

5. **Selecting the environment.** Based on all the information acquired about the candidate hardware and software systems, the systems can then be evaluated. This evaluation can be detailed and extensive if project resources for such an effort are available, or it might be accomplished in a short amount of time and based on limited data. By comparing the results of the evaluation, the project team can select the software and hardware for the project. As with domain selection, the relative weights of the criteria are determined by the particular circumstances of the project and cannot be determined on an absolute basis. For example, a tight budget may force cost considerations to be paramount.

6. **Subsequent steps.** The next steps are to acquire and install the software and hardware that were selected if they are not already in-house. If there will be a long time before the systems are available, project staff should consider whether it is possible to start learning about a system before delivery. For example, vendor courses on the use of a hardware or software system could be taken before system delivery. Also it may be possible to borrow hardware until the ordered system arrives or to visit a site where the hardware or software is available.

After a hardware-software environment has been selected and installed, if there remains any doubt that the environment can support the project, the match between the system and the problem domain should be tested as soon as possible. It might be useful early in the system development process to try to develop a small prototype of the problem using the environment. This prototype should include, to the extent possible, examples of all the types of reasoning, knowledge representations, input and output types, and so on that will be present in the final system. If a clear mismatch is found, consider modifying or extending the environment (for example, developing specialized system software that the project needs; adding memory to the hardware), selecting a different environment that better fits the problem, or redefining the specific problem (if that is possible) so that the environment and the problem are a better match.

When we started the domain search that led to *COMPASS*, we also started a separate and parallel project task to select the development environment.

Prior to the beginning of the *COMPASS* project, the Knowledge Based Systems Department had gone through an extensive effort to choose development hardware to purchase. A group selected to look into the options and evaluate alternatives contacted vendors and collected vendor information. Many of the considerations described later in this chapter were discussed and quantified when possible, and the decision turned out to be very close. We decided to purchase several Xerox Lisp machines based on the general agreement that they had provided an excellent development environment at a relatively reasonable cost.

When we started selecting the development environment for *COMPASS*, we did not give a great deal of thought to any possible hardware other than the department's computers. After the department's recent and extensive hardware selection process and the expenditure of considerable amounts of money on the Lisp machines, we were not at all sure that we had an option to choose different machines. Even if we could, there did not seem to be any major reason to do so, and there were several reasons to stay with the department machines:

■   Project personnel had already become familiar with these computers through their work on other projects.

■   The use of the department's machines would keep the project in uniformity with the other department projects, thus allowing the sharing of expertise and software.

■   The selection of the computers had been recently made, and we knew of no major hardware changes that had occurred in the intervening time to affect the decision.

■   There was nothing about the potential expert system domains we were looking at (which, of course, included the *COMPASS* domain) to indicate that a different hardware choice would be better.

■   Since the department machines were recently purchased, it would have been difficult to convince management to buy even more new computers.

The situation with regard to software tools was completely different. No one in the department or elsewhere at GTE Laboratories had yet used a knowledge engineering software package since this project was the first at the laboratories, and in the entire GTE Corporation, to build a major expert system. We gave strong consideration to using a knowledge engineering software tool in order to concentrate as much as possible on acquiring and implementing the knowledge. On the other hand, if no tools available could provide capabilities we required, the excellent programmers on the project team could provide any system facilities we might need—although this would be at the cost of diluting our efforts on the rest of the project, especially the knowledge implementation.

The decision of whether to use a knowledge engineering tool, and, if so, which tool to use, would strongly influence the project. It would affect the knowledge representations used, the speed and effort needed in implementing the expert system, and the performance of the system and its portability. It would determine how much effort we would have to put into system programming. Furthermore because we were the first in the corporation to develop a major expert system, we felt (and it proved to be true) that any decisions made on tool selection might have a major influence on similar selections to be made later by other parts of the corporation.

Because of the importance we attached to the selection of the project's knowledge engineering tool, we made it a major phase of the project. Another project member and I surveyed the available knowledge engineering tools and found seventeen to consider, from university tools to large, commercial packages. For each tool, we collected information from product literature, technical papers and reports, discussions with developers and salespeople, and, when possible, discussions with users. We were able to see demonstrations of several of the tools and to get copies of some of the tools to try out at GTE Laboratories.

I developed a set of points to consider about each tool (they are the basis of the set of selection criteria that form the latter part of this chapter) and used them as a guide to compare the tools against each other and against the possibility of doing the entire implementation directly in a programming language. We narrowed the selection to four major candidates and looked further into these. We finally selected KEE (Knowledge Engineering Environment) from IntelliCorp. The other candidate knowledge engineering tools did not provide all the paradigms of KEE, did not have as good a user interface and editing facilities, were not as well supported, were not as portable, and/or were not available on our machines. The option of development without use of a software tool, although allowing the most customization, was rejected because it would require us to develop and later maintain many of the features already in KEE.

7.2   CRITERIA AND PARAMETERS FOR COMPARING SOFTWARE TOOLS OR HARDWARE

The remainder of this chapter contains an extensive list of criteria and points to consider when selecting the software tool or the hardware for an expert system development. Not all of the issues discussed apply in every case, and many situations are special, but these criteria and points should provide a good basis for the selection process.

Many of the points pertain to both hardware and software, and the term *system* shall be used to refer to either. Where a point does not apply to both, this will be specified clearly. For ease of reference the option of directly using a programming language (an AI language such as Lisp or Prolog or a conventional language) to develop the expert system will be included as another possible software tool. The related option of developing a shell and then using it for the expert system will be treated similarly.

Most of the criteria in the remainder of this chapter were used by the group that selected the department's computers (which we used for *COMPASS*) or by the *COMPASS* project's software selection team, who chose the project's knowledge engineering tool.

7.3   OBTAINING THE SYSTEM

The first issues to consider are related to obtaining the system, including the important topic of cost.

7.3.1 AVAILABILITY

The system (either hardware or software) should be available when the project needs it. Selecting a system that is already in-house is the best situation. Almost as good is a system that is off-the-shelf and available as soon as purchased. But in many cases, a system may not be immediately available. It may be a new product soon to be put on the market, a new release, or a new version of an existing product. A hardware system may be on the market but not readily available due to a backlog in orders. When the system cannot be obtained right away, the vendor will usually promise that the system will be available by a certain date. Here the environment selectors on the expert system project should consider four important points:

1. Does the date promised for system availability fit in with the project schedule?

2. From what can be found out about the reputation and track record of the vendor, how likely is it that the date promised will be met?

3. What is the likely slippage?

4. If the date promised does slip, how disastrous would that be to the project?

Project leaders should estimate when the project will need the system to be available. The date should be no later than the estimated date by which the domain would have been selected, domain experts would have been chosen, and some early knowledge acquisition would have gone on. Move that date forward to allow time for installation of the system, integration of the system, and training. Obviously if the date promised (including the likely slippage) is far beyond this date, the system should not be selected. The greater the likelihood that the system will not be available when needed, the more the system should be downgraded as a possible candidate for the project.

> The computers used for *COMPASS* were already in-house when we started the project. The KEE system we selected for *COMPASS* was available after a delay while the contractual agreement was negotiated and signed.
>
> When we started working on *COMPASS-II*, the expanded version of *COMPASS*, and were planning to reimplement the *COMPASS-I* program, we had the option of changing the project's software tool. We decided to reimplement *COMPASS* using a new upgraded version of KEE announced by Intelli-Corp. This choice seemed to be the best alternative for the project since we

were generally satisfied with KEE (having found ways to work around any deficiencies we had found) and had gained a great deal of experience using it.

IntelliCorp promised that the new version would be available before we thought we would need it. My general conservatism in project leadership has always made me cautious about basing my project's success on the promises of others, but the time cushion seemed adequate, and so we decided to use the new KEE for *COMPASS-II*. The new version of KEE was delivered to us somewhat late but in time for us to use it.

7.3.2 COST

The cost of obtaining the system is usually a paramount issue. When calculating the comparative costs of two systems, remember to include all related costs, such as the costs of maintenance, expected future upgrades, system installation, training, needed consulting, and project personnel time for performing system-level work. Take into account any warranties included and any bundled features. If there will be several developers, include the costs of multiple copies of the development system, and if there are expected to be several copies of the final expert system program, include the costs of that many system copies (using the cost of a delivery version of the system if such is available). If many copies of the system are needed, ascertain if there is a quantity discount.

For estimating future costs, it is important to remember that both the areas of expert system hardware and knowledge engineering software tools are dynamic. It is hard to be sure what system will be used for deployment in a year or two. Also prices are continually going down and the capabilities of both hardware and software products are continually rising.

A major factor related to cost is whether any hardware or software systems already purchased by the company are in-house and available to the project. If so, these systems should be given strong consideration, especially if major expenditures have been made. But the project should be able to choose a new system if there are compelling reasons to do so.

We knew we needed three or four copies of the knowledge engineering tool for the developers and eventually several more for testing and deployment. KEE was one of the most expensive systems considered. Its large cost was probably its major negative point. Although it did not help us initially, a quantity discount plan from IntelliCorp significantly decreased the cost of later copies.

7.3.3 LEGAL ARRANGEMENTS

The project team should try to ascertain the legal arrangements that must be agreed to in order to obtain the system. For example, must a long-term maintenance contract be agreed to? Is there any proprietary information of the vendor delivered with the system that must be protected by the buyers? Are there any hidden costs or obligations?

> GTE lawyers were concerned about several points in the KEE contract. They negotiated these with IntelliCorp's lawyers and settled on a mutually accepta- ble contract. This negotiation process, however, added an unanticipated delay to the initial delivery of KEE.

7.3.4 INTEGRATION INTO ENVIRONMENT

The system must be able to be integrated into the total computing envi- ronment of the developers. Clearly, at a minimum, if a software tool and a hardware platform are being selected, the software must be able to be run on the hardware, and both should be able to be integrated into the overall environment. If either the software or hardware has already been selected or purchased, the complementary system must be able to run it or run on it.

If some effort must be put into integrating a candidate system into the existing environment, the project should consider the cost and ease of this work and the operational smoothness of the resulting integrated system. If the expert system will be embedded into a larger system, the integration issue is critical.

> At the time we looked for a software tool, we had essentially already selected our department's Xerox computers for the project. This prior choice provided a typical nontechnical real-world constraint on the software tool selection process.

> In addition to KEE, another tool we investigated was Inference Corporation's ART. There were some important differences between the two; however, the overriding practical difference was for us that KEE could run on the depart- ment computers and ART could not. Thus the only way we could select ART was if it seemed so overwhelmingly superior to KEE that its use alone could justify purchase of new hardware. We could not justify choosing ART over KEE on this basis and so eliminated ART from consideration.

7.3.5 UNIFORMITY WITH OTHERS

It is beneficial to choose a system that is already in use in the corporation. If other corporate groups physically or organizationally close to the expert system development project already are using the system, they provide a ready pool of experienced personnel to help project staff learn about it and also might combine forces with the project for system operation and main- tenance. If the potential maintainers or operators of the expert system are already using the hardware or software, they would find it easier to main- tain or operate the expert system eventually produced. Finally, if any groups in the corporation are using a potential system, the expert system project might benefit because vendors often give a quantity discount based on purchases by the entire corporation.

> Since our department was the first in GTE to purchase an AI workstation and our project was the first in GTE to purchase a knowledge engineering tool, considerations of uniformity did not apply to our decisions. But later, when other GTE groups made similar decisions, they did take this into account and in many cases followed our lead.

7.4   BACKGROUND AND PROSPECTS

The background and history of the vendor and the system should be considered.

7.4.1 VENDOR TRACK RECORD AND PROSPECTS

The prestige, reputation, track record, and future prospects of the system vendor should be scrutinized. The system may be the company's first AI product or its one hundredth. The company may be a small start-up company or in the Fortune 500. The company may have made or be making a major commitment to AI, or it may be dabbling in it. The developers of the system may be major names in AI or unknowns (but watch out for companies that get top AI people to put their names but not much else into a product). All of these factors should go into judging the vendor.

An important consideration is the likelihood that the vendor will still be in business maintaining and upgrading the hardware or software for the life of the expert system. Small start-up companies have a way of disappearing. Big companies with small commitments can easily change their minds about continued effort or can starve an unimportant small part of the company by giving it minimum funding. However, systems with a large installed base are likely to be maintained by or taken over by someone, even if the original company no longer supports the system.

> When our department selected the Xerox computers, we knew that Xerox was an early leader in Lisp machine development and that there was a relatively large installed base of Xerox Lisp machines. This consideration did not, however, stop Xerox from spinning off their Lisp machine business eventually. Support has continued to be available, and therefore the *COMPASS* deployment on these computers has not been hindered as yet. However, this situation might cause problems for *COMPASS* in the future and might eventually require the porting of *COMPASS* to other computers.

> When we looked into software tool companies, we found that IntelliCorp, the developer of KEE, was relatively small, although it seemed to be a strong

company. We did count as a disadvantage the fact that it might not survive through the full life of our expert system.

7.4.2 SYSTEM HISTORY

Any major successes by prior users of a candidate system in developing deployed and working expert systems should be counted as a positive attribute for the system. It is even better if some of these successful expert systems are similar to the present project's expert system in size, scope, application area, and so on. Although prior success is not a guarantee that the system is the best one for the project, it can certainly add to one's confidence in selecting the system.

On the other hand, if the system has been used successfully only for demonstration expert systems, that should be considered as a negative point. The same is true if the system has been used successfully for only a narrow class of applications that significantly differ from the application the project will tackle.

> We felt that both our hardware and software choices were among the most powerful systems that we could have selected. They were being used to develop real expert systems, although we did not base our selection of them on the success of any particular expert system project. We did feel that they were general purpose and would not be restricted to a narrow class of problems.

7.4.3 STAGE OF DEVELOPMENT

Consider the stage of the development of the system. If it was recently released, it may not be stable, it may be missing some important facilities that the vendor plans to add later, and it may not have complete or correct documentation. There may be system bugs that have not yet been found and corrected. These same problems may also be found for a newly released version of an established system.

The expert system project does not want to be the one that finds the bugs in a system or the inaccuracies in its documentation. Instead it needs a system with minimal bugs and with accurate documentation. Therefore hardware and software selectors should be wary of being among the first to use a completely new system or a new system version and should lean toward selecting a mature system.

> Neither the Xerox computers nor KEE were new when we purchased them. Their previous commercial use did not completely eliminate bugs and inaccurate documentation (we found some of both for each product), but prior usage by other customers had lessened some of these problems by allowing errors to be found and fixed. Some of the other systems we looked into were newly available commercially, and we downgraded these somewhat in our evaluation.

7.4.4 SYSTEM UPGRADING

It is a positive attribute of a hardware or software system if an improved version of the system is under development. It means that a better system with additional features will be available in the future. But some issues in this regard should be investigated. If the upgraded system will be available soon, consideration should be given to waiting for the new system, possibly using the old one for some small initial programming. (But before deciding to wait for the upgrade, remember to consider the reliability of the promised delivery date of the new system version.) Another issue is whether a considerable effort will be required to take a program developed using the present version of the development system and use it on future system upgrades. If new versions of the system will not accept previously developed programs without major modifications, that might be an important negative attribute of the system.

> Both Xerox and KEE introduced system upgrades during the development of *COMPASS*—evidence of continuing effort by the vendors to improve their products. We handled the Xerox upgrades as they came. It took some effort on the part of system programmers to get the new releases installed and working, but we did not have to modify more than a very small fraction of our software. We developed *COMPASS-I* and *COMPASS-II* with different major releases of KEE. Small upgrades within the release were handled with no problem. Because we completely rewrote *COMPASS* for *COMPASS-II*, we did not have to worry about moving *COMPASS-I*'s implemented knowledge to the new KEE release. We did have a potential problem in the slipping of the scheduled release for the new KEE version but had allowed enough time so that it had little impact.

7.4.5 SYSTEM MAINTENANCE BY THE VENDOR

The expected level of future maintenance of the software tool or hardware by the vendor should be considered. Try to determine how extensive is the hardware vendor's field support group and if it will respond quickly and with skilled people to problems. For both the system programs of a computer and software tools, get an idea of how soon software bugs will be fixed and whether there is a mechanism for collecting bug reports and rapidly responding to them. Information on the responsiveness of maintenance personnel might be obtained by talking to present users of the system.

> In the *COMPASS* hardware and software evaluation, we had difficulty estimating the level of system maintenance that each vendor would provide. We questioned the vendors about this area and, where possible, asked present system users. In many cases, however, our judgment on this issue was derived from our overall assessment of the quality of the vendor company.

7.5   LEARNING TO USE THE SYSTEM

The more complex the system and the less experienced the users, the greater the importance of the attributes related to learning to use the system.

7.5.1 TRAINING MATERIALS

A system should come with written materials to aid the project's implementers in learning to use it. Easy-to-use, well-written training manuals and other training materials (such as on-line tutorials) are important, especially for novice users. Superior training materials allow the training of users of different levels of sophistication by providing tutorial information at different levels.

The standard system documentation also plays an important role in aiding new users to learn to use the system. The documentation should be written and organized to be easily accessible and usable by the inexperienced.

> KEE came with a training manual that led a naive user through some of the basics of the system. Although this did not include a lot that more advanced users require, it was useful.

7.5.2 TRAINING COURSES

Vendor-provided training courses in system use are valuable, especially for hardware and for more complex knowledge engineering tools. If there are such courses, project personnel should consider their cost, whether the courses are optional or bundled into the system price, and whether the courses are given frequently and at convenient locations and convenient times. Ascertain if such training courses can be given at the project team's site, which might be less expensive (due to saving of travel expenses and travel time) and allow more people to participate.

> The hardware and software vendors each provided a training course. Xerox personnel led a training course at our site that almost every member of the department attended. Because it was attended only by our people, the course was somewhat informal and customized to our desires.
>
> IntelliCorp's formal KEE training course at their location turned out to be at a low level relative to the expertise of our two participants (myself and another project member). Since we were the only two participants at that time, we were able to take the course at our own pace, finishing in 6 hours rather than 3 days. IntelliCorp allowed us to use the remaining time for planning and implementing an initial version of our knowledge representation, with IntelliCorp personnel acting as valuable consultants. Later during *COMPASS* development, when a major new release of KEE became available, an IntelliCorp programmer spent a few days at our laboratories to provide training for all *COMPASS* personnel.

7.6   SYSTEM USABILITY AND GENERAL FEATURES

The ease of using the system and the features it provides are important issues to consider.

7.6.1 SYSTEM INTERFACE

The system should have a well-designed and friendly user interface. For example, hardware should have a clear display, a good graphics and windowing system, a well-laid-out keyboard, and so on. Software should have a convenient and unconfusing syntax, easy-to-use and powerful input mechanisms, and flexible output mechanisms. Both should have system-level functions that are simple to use and understand, helpful error messages, and easy recovery from disasters.

> The Xerox computers and KEE scored well in this attribute. The Xerox Lisp machines had the best interface available at the time. Together with its programming support features, its overall user environment was excellent.

> One of KEE's best points was its user interface, which we rated as very user friendly. It allowed relatively easy creation and movement around knowledge bases, object hierarchies, and rule groups.

> When considering the option of developing our program without using a software shell, we felt that our experienced programmers could probably develop and customize a version of any selected set of features from any of the tools we investigated. Furthermore we thought that some of the best features of certain software shells might be wasted on us if we did not require them, and thus we would be paying for unneeded features. But the one feature that we were sure to need was a good interface for the expert system developers. Although we thought we could develop such an interface, it was beneficial not to have to devote our resources to this task.

7.6.2 SUPPORTIVE PROGRAMMING ENVIRONMENT

The development system should provide a supportive environment for developing programs or other knowledge structures. This may be provided by the computer, the software shell, or both. A basic need is a good editor for programs and for rules and other knowledge representational structures. A good "Help" system is useful. A good developer's interface facilitates rapid development. Facilities for debugging are very important. Added features, such as a rule cross-indexer, can be useful. In general, the more features available, the more powerful they are, and the easier they are to use, the better. Sometimes, however, there is a trade-off. For example, the most powerful editor may be the hardest to use. System selectors should remember not just to count system features but to compare them and to evaluate them relative to the skills of project personnel.

The Xerox computers and KEE excelled in this area. Both had excellent programming environments—better than their competition. The editing and debugging facilities were excellent and did not require a great amount of training or study to master.

7.6.3 EFFICIENCY OF THE PROGRAMMING ENVIRONMENT

System selectors should not only focus on the features provided by the programming environment but should also consider the efficiency of the programming environment. For example, a system with a long response time is difficult to use. Language compilers make code run faster, and rule compilers make rules run faster. Both can make development and deployment versions of the expert system more efficient. If such compilers are present, also consider their speed of compilation.

The Xerox computers and KEE had reasonably efficient programming environments.

7.6.4 SOFTWARE ENGINEERING-RELATED FACILITIES

Developing an expert system is developing software, albeit a special kind of software requiring some special approaches. Many of the same software engineering goals that one would have in developing a conventional computer program must be fulfilled. For example, the expert system program should be developed with long-term maintainability in mind. Facilities should be in place to allow the expert system to be developed by multiple developers if that is required.

Thus system selectors should examine any software engineering-related features provided by the system being evaluated. In general, many of the features desired to aid software development and to promote maintainability are not provided by software tools or hardware and must be built by the expert system developers. (In Chapter 11 we discuss ways to build such features.) Any software engineering features provided by the software tool or the hardware will probably prove to be very useful and should count as a positive attribute.

Neither the Xerox computers nor KEE provided a full package of software engineering features, so we developed our own (as described in Chapter 11). A few useful features were provided. For example, KEE makes it easy to break up an implementation into many knowledge bases. We utilized this facility to modularize the expert system program.

7.6.5 DOCUMENTATION

Documentation is a significant feature of any system, hardware or software. In order to use a system well, developers require good system documentation. The documentation should be complete and detailed—covering all aspects of the system, describing common situations with many examples, and including a tutorial section for beginners and a reference manual. It should be up to date, with new system features and recent changes fully documented.

The documentation should be well written, nicely packaged, and easy to access through good organization and good indexing. Online documentation is a useful feature, but it must be easy to use to be effective.

The documentation should be accurate. Inaccurate documentation can cause system users to waste considerable amounts of time, since it often causes errors difficult to debug. Therefore it is desirable that the vendor have a mechanism to correct quickly any documentation errors found, such as by frequent updates of individual documentation pages during the time between the release of major documentation versions, or by some kind of "bulletin" system.

> The Xerox and KEE documentation were both moderately good. They were uneven and had some errors, which usually were not corrected until the next major release of the system.

> When selecting a software tool, we found several that had poor documentation and downgraded those accordingly.

7.6.6 PERFORMANCE

The expected performance provided by the development environment is important. The environment may be inherently slow due to its design, which might be seen from demonstrations of the system. However, often the slowdown in performance occurs when the expert system program starts to get big. This potential problem is hard to determine from demonstrations and small trials of the system, where limits are not being tested. It might be possible to learn about system performance for a larger program by speaking to users of the hardware or software who have developed or are developing large expert systems.

If an environment has poor performance, development may be difficult or, at least, very inconvenient. It may make it difficult to run the developing expert system for the many test cases that are usually necessary during development.

Performance is often most important in deployment. If the development environment will be the deployment environment, run–time performance may be a critical concern during development. For a real–time expert system, poor performance may make it impossible for the expert system to meet its objectives.

> Our environment seemed to have reasonable performance during most of *COMPASS*'s development; however, as *COMPASS* developed into a very

large system, test cases took a long time to run—inhibiting development at times.

COMPASS in deployment is run offline, not in real time, and thus the speed of a run is not critical to its use. But clearly better performance would allow more *COMPASS* runs per day on one computer, cutting the overall operating costs.

7.6.7 SIZE

The difference between the amount of memory provided by the hardware and the memory requirements of the software tool with associated software gives an indication of the amount of memory available to the expert system itself; however, the amount of knowledge that can be stored is also related to the efficiency of the software tool's representation (and, of course, the skill of the programmers). For a small expert system, memory limitations may cause no problems; however, as the expert system program gets larger, its performance may worsen since its size may be approaching the available memory. Thus it is advisable to consider the expected size of the expert system and then to choose a hardware and software tool combination that allows adequate room for the expert system.

Our performance problems stemmed primarily from the large size of *COM-PASS* added to the size of KEE and Lisp. The total almost filled the Xerox computer, causing a great deal of swapping at times.

7.6.8 SYSTEM INTERFACES

The system selected should be able to interface to whatever inputs and outputs are required by the expert system. If the interfacing is an important aspect of the expert system, the ease of developing the interface and the speed of using it may be significant features to consider. For example, an expert system may require extensive interaction with a large database or access to existing conventional programs. In either case, a software tool that includes special features to implement such interfaces should get added consideration, and a tool that does not allow or strongly restricts such interfaces should be rejected. Also, to take a hardware example, if an expert system requires constant monitoring of multiple processes, a computer that facilitates that kind of monitoring—provides the necessary number of ports, provides the interrupt capabilities needed, and so on—would be greatly preferred.

The *COMPASS* task required data from a single source—the RMCS system that collected the output data from a No. 2 EAX. Collecting these data and extracting the information needed by *COMPASS* from the raw data was a formidable task. However, the method of expert analysis performed by *COM-*

PASS required that all the data be collected before any of the expert system processing started. Thus there was no need for an active data interface during the main knowledge processing of *COMPASS*. The primary data transfer was done before the expert system part of *COMPASS* started running. This data transfer from an RMCS could be (and later in *COMPASS*'s development and deployment was) performed outside the main *COMPASS* environment, on an auxiliary computer.

7.6.9 SECURITY

Security of the program and of the knowledge in the program may be important to the project. The program being developed may turn out to be a valuable product. More important during development is that the knowledge being acquired may need to be protected. It may be critical knowledge of corporate expertise or corporate strategies, which if disclosed might hurt the company's competitive advantage, or it may be knowledge that would be politically embarrassing or legally threatening if disclosed. The expert system may use data that require secure treatment, such as company-private data or information classified as secret by the government. There may be other reasons to avoid unauthorized access to the expert system program. If security is an issue, any mechanisms that the software tool or hardware being evaluated provide for protection should be considered in rating the system.

Security was not an important concern for the *COMPASS* project; however, possible sales of *COMPASS*, especially to international locations with weak copyright laws, may require better security.

7.6.10 USER SUPPORT AND CONSULTANTS

There should be some provision to aid system users when a question is raised or when trouble occurs, such as a user assistance telephone service. For inexperienced system users, it is useful if the vendor has a consulting service available. If the project might want this service and it does exist, project personnel should check on the availability of the service and the cost.

We considered the expected availability of user assistance from the vendor when rating potential hardware and potential software tools. We found that both Xerox and IntelliCorp provided designated people for users to call when there were problems.

During the period of *COMPASS* development, we received varying levels of service from both companies. Xerox usually worked with us over the telephone to find and correct problems. They provided service calls when needed. IntelliCorp also provided telephone contacts to resolve problems. Because our programmers were high level and very experienced, we sometimes found it easier to work around a problem rather than to make the calls to track down the answer to a question.

When *COMPASS* was being run by GTE Data Services, at times they found it easier and quicker to ask questions of and get support from GTE Laboratories than to deal with the vendors' support personnel.

7.7 SPECIAL FEATURES RELATED TO SOFTWARE

Some features relate primarily to the evaluation of software, such as the paradigms a tool provides and the amount of access a tool allows to a general-purpose computer language.

7.7.1 BUILDING OR BUYING A SOFTWARE TOOL

An expert system group may consider developing its own knowledge engineering tool and then using that tool to develop the expert system. A software tool built in-house has certain advantages over one offered commercially. There are no purchase, maintenance, or other costs that would be associated with a commercial tool. When the expert system is deployed, there would also be no license fees or purchase costs for each of the deployed expert systems, especially important if the final system is expected to be put in widespread distributed use. A tool developed in-house could be customized specifically for the expert system project, with the goal of giving the expert system developers a tool that has every feature they desire and where each feature is at exactly the level (of sophistication, user friendliness, and so forth) that matches the expert system group's needs. An in-house tool can be modified as necessary to meet any new or unexpected requirements, whereas once a project is wedded to a commercial tool, any unexpected requirements must be met within the constraints of the tool.

Nevertheless, there are several negative aspects to having a custom knowledge engineering tool developed in-house. The cost savings may be more than eliminated by the costs of the personnel and equipment needed to develop it. The tool development might divert attention from the development of the expert system. Unless personnel, money, and talent are readily available, the large amount of resources and talent needed might leave less of each available for the expert system project. Also rather than having the maintenance of the tool (and associated documentation) taken care of by a vendor, this continuing commitment—for the life of any expert system utilizing the tool—must be made in-house. Moreover, to equal a commercial vendor, the in-house maintenance group might have to keep up continually with the state of the art, such as by making the tool more efficient, adding new features, and making it available on additional hardware platforms.

Thus unless there are special circumstances, buying a commercial tool is often better in the long run. There are some special circumstances where in-house development may be warranted: when there are several expert system projects to split the internal cost of tool development; when the expert system will be sold or is being developed under contract, and the long-term costs of in-house tool development and maintenance could be included in the price (without affecting sales); when a large number of copies of the expert system will be made, making the licensing or purchase costs of large numbers of commercial systems prohibitive; when the expert system requires certain capabilities not available in any commercial system; and when the development of the in-house tool has its own justification, such as the possibility of the tool's becoming a product. Except for situations such as these, it is usually best to let the commercial tool developers develop the tools and for the expert system project to put its efforts into the expert system.

> The *COMPASS* development team had some excellent programmers who probably could have developed an excellent knowledge engineering tool with just the capabilities needed by *COMPASS*. But after considering seriously the possibility of developing our own tool, we decided that the effort would divert us from our main task, expert system development, and that the continuing requirement for tool maintenance would become a long-term burden.

7.7.2 KNOWLEDGE REPRESENTATION PARADIGMS

Some knowledge engineering tools support a single knowledge representation paradigm, such as backward-chained production rules. (When no tool is used and the expert system is programmed directly in a computer language, this situation may also be considered to be employing a single paradigm.) Several tools make multiple paradigms available. A hybrid or multiple-paradigm tool allows the user the capabilities of two or more interacting knowledge engineering paradigms—say, rules and frames, or rules, frames, object-oriented programming, and direct access to a programming language. Also a tool may furnish mechanisms to facilitate certain knowledge structures, such as a blackboard system or particular techniques to represent uncertainty. In addition, a tool may provide special features, such as a truth-maintenance system to help deal with hypothetical and nonmonotonic reasoning (where a proposition can be thought true at one time and false later on).

Hybrid tools are more general than those with a single paradigm. Having two or more paradigms in which to represent expert knowledge allows the user more power. Multiple-paradigm tools also provide greater flexibility than a single-paradigm system. They can deal with a larger range of problem types and thus provide more confidence about being able to cope with unforeseen issues. Therefore they are a good choice if the project's tool must be selected before the domain is chosen.

A multiple-paradigm tool is usually based primarily on one main paradigm. A tool based primarily on production rules has a slightly different character to it than a tool based primarily on frames. Which is better depends on the domain and the types of reasoning to be utilized but may in the end be a matter of personal choice. In any case, a good hybrid system should have a smooth integration of the paradigms.

Specialized single-paradigm tools do offer some advantages. They often are easier to use and easier to learn than multiple-paradigm tools and may save work for the user (such as by predefining much that must be specified in a more general system). Frequently they are more efficient than more general tools since they can be optimized for the single paradigm. Because they are usually less complex, they might make it easier to develop and maintain the knowledge. (However, a single-paradigm tool might make it more difficult to develop and maintain the knowledge if the use of its single paradigm forces an awkward knowledge representation while the use of multiple paradigms would allow a simpler, clearer, more elegant representation.)

Not only should the particular paradigms offered by a tool be considered but also the power of each offered paradigm. For example, several tools may offer a production rule package or a frame system, but each package is different. These packages should be investigated to see which offers the greatest power, convenience, and flexibility. For example, production rule packages may offer the user full, limited, or no control over conflict resolution (that is, rule-firing priority). Their rule languages may differ in their ability to express complex concepts. They may offer forward chaining only, backward chaining only, both types of chaining separately, or both types integrated. Frame systems may offer one fixed inheritance mechanism or many types of inheritance. They may or may not allow dynamic inheritance or multiple parents. Tool selectors should examine and evaluate these and any other differences between the paradigms offered by each tool.

One of the main reasons we rated KEE over most other software tools was its furnishing of multiple knowledge representational paradigms. KEE provided a frame structure, production rules, object-oriented programming mechanisms, and easy incorporation of Lisp code. We expected to be developing a large, complex expert system but were choosing the tool before we knew a great deal about the domain and the scope of the domain expert's knowledge. Therefore it was important to have as many different capabilities and as much power available as possible. When *COMPASS* was implemented, we used all the paradigms and almost every feature of KEE. For example, most of *COMPASS*'s data storage was accomplished using frame structures, and most passing of programmatic control was accomplished via object-oriented programming messages.

7.7.3 INCORPORATION OF A COMPUTER LANGUAGE

One important issue related to the knowledge representation paradigms is whether the software tool allows the use of a computer language in situations where the other paradigms furnished by the tool cannot be used or cannot be used well. If so, then there need be less concern about whether the tool might not be able to provide some capability found to be necessary later on. The ability to use general-purpose computer code gives the developers great flexibility. If the tool's paradigms can do what is needed, they can be used. If there is something that the provided facilities cannot do, that capability can be implemented using the programming language.

> The ability to utilize a programming language when needed was one great advantage that KEE had over many of the other software systems we examined. KEE allowed us to drop to Lisp at any point in the program where we felt it was necessary. This meant that we could cover up any weaknesses (from our standpoint) of KEE. For example, if KEE's rule system did not provide a certain needed mechanism, we could write a function (callable from a rule) to perform the required task. Since the implementation of *COMPASS* turned out to include several hundred Lisp functions, we certainly took advantage of this feature.

7.7.4 MATCH TO PROBLEM

All expert system building tools are not equally applicable to every potential use. The best tool for one problem may be poorly suited to another. Some tools may be applicable primarily to a certain problem type (such as diagnostic problems), while others, especially those providing many knowledge representation paradigms, are much more general. Although most tools can be used for a wide variety of domains, some tools are designed for particular domain types and provide special features likely to be needed by developers of expert systems in those areas.

If the domain (or a small list of possible domains) is known before the software tool is selected, the requirements of the problem(s) should be analyzed to see how well a particular tool matches them. The types of general reasoning tasks (e.g., backward chaining from hypotheses) and the kinds of knowledge that need to be represented for the expert system's domain should match the facilities made available by the software tool.

In addition, special capabilities offered by particular tools may be very important in certain applications and not in others. For example, some software tools offer facilities to aid in accessing external data or external databases; some provide a good subsystem to generate explanations of the expert system's reasoning. If such capabilities are important requirements of the problem, the tools offering them should be strongly considered.

> We selected KEE as a powerful general-purpose system before we knew a great deal about *COMPASS*'s No. 2 EAX maintenance domain. In retrospect we felt that we had made a proper choice since we did use almost all of KEE's facilities for the *COMPASS* implementation.

7.7.5 ACCESS TO SOURCE CODE

A tool is usually provided as a black box. The tool's source code is generally proprietary and kept from the user. But some vendors may provide the user access to some or all of the tool's implementation. This may be a valuable feature for advanced programmers. They may be able to modify the tool for their own purposes, overriding aspects they do not like and adding facilities they desire.

Performing such modifications does present a problem: the project (and eventually the ultimate system maintainers) from then on will have to maintain the modified part of the tool's code themselves. They must make the modifications again each time a new tool release is installed. Also a less-than-expert programmer may, while modifying the tool's code, inadvertently make a change to another part of the tool—possibly a subtle change that may be hard to diagnose. Thus it may not be wise, even if the facility is available, to open up a tool's source code to modification by project programmers.

Nevertheless access to the code may provide project programmers with insight into how the tool works. Furthermore if a portion of the tool's implementation uses the tool itself, project programmers can use access to that part of the implementation to see paradigmatic examples of how to best use the tool.

> A good deal of KEE was implemented using KEE itself and was partially accessible by the user. This occasionally helped the *COMPASS* programmers by allowing us to see how certain parts of KEE worked. Although we considered altering the core KEE implementation, we decided against it because we did not want to have to maintain the modifications when new KEE versions were released or risk the possibility of introducing subtle errors in the KEE system, and we felt there might be some problems if a major revision was made of KEE's internal structure.

7.8 SPECIAL FEATURES RELATED TO HARDWARE

Some features apply to the evaluation of hardware for the expert system, including the type of computer, the system software and file system provided, and the number of different software tools available for the computer.

7.8.1 COMPUTER TYPE

As software tools for developing expert systems become available on greater numbers of platforms, the choice of hardware for developing an expert system is expanding. Hardware selectors for the expert system project can consider a wide variety of possibilities, including special-purpose AI symbolic processors (e.g., Lisp machines), workstations, PCs, minicomputers, mainframes, and some combinations of these. Each has benefits and disadvantages that will depend on the particular situation of the project and on what options are available from the dynamic hardware market. Clearly one minimum criterion is that the hardware should be capable of running the desired software tool. Other factors may include the need, or lack of need, for such capabilities as large memory capacity, integration with other systems, shared access, security, and ability to be moved from location to location (physical size, weight).

> Our department chose an AI symbolic processor, a Lisp machine, not specifically for the *COMPASS* project but for all our AI work at the time. Such a specialized workstation seemed to be the best platform for direct (without a tool) development of AI programs. It also proved, in the *COMPASS* project, to be a good environment to use with a tool such as KEE.

7.8.2 SYSTEM SOFTWARE AND FILE SYSTEM

A computer's system software should be efficient and mature. Bugs should be found only infrequently. Although the technology behind the hardware is constantly changing, it is obviously preferable to choose a computer that uses up-to-date base technology and one whose vendor can be expected to keep up with the latest technology.

A computer that loads and unloads files slowly can be inconvenient for development and, later, for operation. The speed of the file system becomes even more important as the expert system gets larger. A large expert system can take many minutes and sometimes hours to load. If it takes a long time to load an expert system then it takes away a lot of flexibility in development.

If the expert system project has or can get access to candidate hardware systems, benchmark tests of loading and saving might be performed with small and large amounts of data. The computer should be tested on loading and saving to local storage and on loading and saving to a networked file server if that will be utilized.

> These issues were not major concerns in the *COMPASS* hardware selection process. The Xerox system software was relatively mature, and file system performance was not an issue we examined carefully when evaluating computers. However, as *COMPASS* got progressively larger, we took increasing notice of this feature because it took longer and longer to load and save *COMPASS*, a major inconvenience.

7.8.3 SUPPORT FOR MULTIPLE TOOLS

It is beneficial if the hardware supports many AI software tools, even if one particular tool has already been selected for the project. When an expert system development is completed or when project plans are changed, the project's computers are usually made available to the successor project or to other projects. An expert system project should not necessarily utilize a computer just because it is available, yet the availability of a computer is usually an issue in the selection and often the paramount issue. Thus although it may not be important for the present project, a computer that can run many software tools is valuable for its future flexibility.

> The Xerox computers were originally selected to be used by all department projects. Since the other department projects at the time did not utilize knowledge engineering tools, the subject of support for multiple tools was not an important issue at the time.

7.9   ISSUES RELATED TO DEPLOYMENT

When selecting an expert system development environment, it is important to consider the eventual deployment of the system. Clear savings of time and effort can be gained by deploying the expert system using the same software tool and hardware used for development. If this approach is followed, deployment concerns should be taken into account when the development environment is selected.

On the other hand, often it is advantageous to use the best available development environment for developing the expert system and then to choose a deployment environment that is best suited to deployment needs. Also in the dynamic expert system world, there are often benefits to deferring the choice of the system. But if no consideration is given to deployment until the prototype is completed, it may turn out that the deployment choices have been confined to ones that are not optimal for the expert system. Thus even when the development and the deployment environments will differ, it is beneficial to give consideration to the ultimate deployment of the expert system when choosing the development environment. Some issues related to deployment, such as performance and vendor maintenance of the hardware or software, have been mentioned. Here some additional issues are discussed.

7.9.1 USE AS DEPLOYMENT VEHICLE

A significant issue is whether the hardware or software system being evaluated can be used as the deployment vehicle for the final expert system implementation. Some of the factors used in selecting hardware and software for development have a different relative importance when a deployment environment is being chosen. For example, system speed that is acceptable in a development system may be completely unacceptable performance for deployment. The cost of a deployment system may be of much greater concern to potential users or buyers than the cost of a development system is to the expert system project (or vice-versa). Additional issues that pertain primarily to deployment systems include reliability, availability, maintainability, serviceability, and the ability to integrate into the existing operational situation.

It may be difficult at the beginning of the project to determine what the deployment environment might be. On the other hand, in many situations, the deployment environment is determined or mandated at the project's inception or is limited to being the same environment as the development environment. (We discuss the selection of a deployment environment further in Chapter 13.) If the hardware system or software tool under consideration could be (or will be) used for system deployment, there is no chance of problems—possibly major problems—in transferring the expert system to another environment for deployment. This should be considered a major plus for a potential system.

> We did not know how *COMPASS* would be deployed as we looked into hardware and software tool choices. When we chose to use KEE on the Xerox computers, it seemed at least possible that the final system might be deployed on that combination (as it was). However, had we been able to envision the changes in hardware and software possibilities that would become available after we made our selections, we might have given more consideration to other options.

7.9.2 EASY TRANSFER TO DEPLOYMENT VEHICLE

If the final expert system will not (or probably will not) be deployed using the development environment, the system selectors should investigate to see if there is a possible or obvious deployment system to which the final program can be transferred.

Some hardware companies produce specially designed deployment computers—stripped-down, less expensive versions of their development computers. If such a deployment computer is a good vehicle for deploying the expert system, that would be a positive point toward selecting a corresponding development computer.

Most software tools can be utilized on more than one (often many) platforms. This portability allows the expert system to be developed using the tool on a good development computer and then transferred to a computer better for deployment. For example, it may be advantageous to develop an expert system on a Lisp machine and then deploy it on a PC. If the deployment computer is not known at the project's inception, it is usually safer to select a tool that can be used on many computers. The more computers on which a tool can be used, the more choices will be available later. Also the more aggressive a tool company seems to be today in putting its tool on new hardware options, the more likely that they will have it available on the hardware desired at the time the deployment environment is selected (though that hardware may not even be in production at the project's inception).

Another possibility to consider is that some software tool companies offer a delivery version of the tool, usually a stripped-down version of the tool without some or all of the development aids. An expert system developed using the full version tool should be easily transferable to the delivery version. Assuming this is true, the delivery version might offer several benefits over the full system. It might have better performance, it might allow deployment on computers where the full tool cannot be used, and it might be less expensive than the full system. If the development tool has such a delivery version available, that might be important benefit to consider.

It may be possible, especially for less complex software tools, to consider developing the expert system using the tool and then rewriting it for deployment without the tool—thus saving the cost of multiple tool copies. If this scenario is reasonable for the project, then any support the tool gives for it is clearly a positive feature.

> When we chose our software tool and hardware, we did not know how *COMPASS* would be deployed. However, KEE was (or was expected to be at the time we considered it) available on several platforms and available in a relatively small delivery version—positive factors in our consideration. Later KEE's portability allowed several deployment options for *COMPASS* to be considered.

7.9.3 OPERATION AND MAINTENANCE OF THE DEPLOYED EXPERT SYSTEM

In addition to the maintenance of the software tool and the hardware related to the deployed expert system, the deployed expert system itself must be operated and maintained. It is a valuable attribute of the deployment software tool and hardware if they make that operation and maintenance easier. This is especially important if the deployed expert system will be operated and/or maintained by groups other than the expert system developers.

For example, the final expert system should be easy to access and run. It should be easy to navigate around the expert system to locate problems. Good debugging and editing features should be available to maintainers. The knowledge base should be easy to read, modify, and update by non-developers. It may be beneficial if simple changes could be made by one class of people, such as users or low-level maintainers, and only complex modifications need be made by the high-level maintenance group. The hardware and the software tool should facilitate all of these features.

We did not know how complex a system *COMPASS* might turn out to be when we were selecting the environment. We did think that some of KEE's major strengths were in its graphics and its interface and that its editing facilities were very good. These capabilities we felt should aid (and did) in development, as well as in later maintenance.

Checklist for Selecting the Hardware and the Software Development Tool

☐ Recognize that all computers and knowledge engineering software tools are not equally applicable to a particular expert system development project.

☐ If possible, select the hardware and software for an expert system development as part of the project rather than having the decision made before the project begins.

☐ Start evaluating software tools and hardware early enough in the project to allow the development environment to be available by the time needed— certainly by the time enough knowledge has been acquired to make implementing of the knowledge desirable. Allow time for selecting, acquiring, and installing the development environment and for training project staff.

☐ Make a survey of computers and software tools that might be usable by the project, collecting information and opinions about the potential systems.

☐ Arrange to see a demonstration of all systems that are good possibilities.

☐ Arrange to use a potential system in-house, if possible, to allow for an in-depth analysis.

☐ Evaluate the available hardware and knowledge engineering tools utilizing the points described in this chapter and making use of the information collected about each system and the opinions formed from demonstrations and in-house use. Based on this evaluation, select the best available hardware and knowledge engineering tool for the project.

☐ Make sure that the system will be available when the project needs it; be conservative in believing vendor-promised dates.

☐ Consider all aspects of cost, including costs of purchase, maintenance, upgrades, installation, training, consulting, and additional copies.

☐ Ascertain what kind of legal arrangement must be agreed to with the vendor. There may be hidden costs or obligations that may cause problems.

☐ Select a system that can be integrated into the overall environment. The software tool must be able to run on the hardware selected.

☐ Consider the benefits of selecting a system already in use within the corporation.

☐ Consider the prestige, reputation, track record, and future prospects of the system vendor.

☐ Give some weight to a system with a history of major successes, especially if the successful expert systems are similar to the present project's expert systems.

☐ Consider the development stage of the system, and lean toward selecting a mature system.

☐ If an improved system version is under development, count that as a positive attribute, but investigate its time of availability and the ease of upgrading to it.

☐ Select a vendor expected to provide a high level of future maintenance.

☐ Vendor-provided training courses can be very useful. Investigate their availability and cost.

☐ Investigate whether a candidate development system has a friendly, well-designed user interface.

☐ Ascertain whether the development system has a supportive environment for developing the expert system software, including such features as a good editor, a "Help" system, and good debugging facilities.

☐ Since developing an expert system, whatever else it may be, is still developing software, count positively any software engineering-related features that the system may provide, particularly features that assist in making the final expert system more maintainable and, if needed, features that aid development by multiple developers.

☐ Examine the documentation that comes with the hardware or software. Good documentation is an important feature of any system.

☐ Evaluate whether the system's training manuals and related written materials are easy to use and well written.

☐ Evaluate the performance of the system, especially for a large expert system. Good performance is valuable during development. It is often more important—possibly critical—for deployment.

☐ Choose a software and hardware combination that provides adequate memory for the expected size of the expert system.

☐ If security of the program being developed or of the knowledge contained in it is an important concern, evaluate the security capabilities of the system.

☐ Ascertain if the system vendor provides a user assistance service, such as a telephone contact for questions.

☐ Determine if the system vendor provides a consulting service, either bundled with the system or for a reasonable additional cost. This type of service may be useful to a project, especially to inexperienced developers.

☐ Make certain that the development system is able to interface to the necessary input sources and output destinations of the expert system. The system should facilitate the development of needed interfaces. The speed of the interfaces should match the requirements.

☐ Investigate whether to build or buy a knowledge engineering tool. A tool built in-house will probably cost less than a commercial tool, and it can be customized as desired. But in-house tool development may divert resources from the expert system and may entail a long-term tool-maintenance burden. Therefore give strong consideration to buying the tool.

☐ Consider the set of knowledge representation paradigms a knowledge engineering software tool makes available. This is probably the most important feature of a tool. Multiple-paradigm tools are more powerful and more flexible than single-paradigm tools, though they may be more difficult to learn and to use.

☐ Have concern not only about which particular knowledge representation paradigms are offered by a software tool but also the power of each paradigm offered. One production rule system may be much more powerful than another.

☐ Ascertain whether a software tool allows the use of a general-purpose computer language in situations where the paradigms provided by the tool cannot be used or cannot be used well. This is a valuable feature.

☐ Explore the match between the problem being solved and a potential software tool. Some tools are primarily applicable for certain types of problems (e.g., diagnostic problems).

☐ Limit consideration to the types of computers—PC, mainframe, AI workstation, etc.—that will meet the needs and situation of the project. The computer must be able to run the chosen software tool.

☐ Determine if the computer has good file system performance and efficient and mature system software.

☐ Give weight to a hardware platform that supports many software tools. Even if the project's software tool has been chosen before the computer is selected, this capability gives added flexibility.

☐ Consider that the use of the development environment as the expert system deployment vehicle eliminates the possibility of major problems that could occur while porting the expert system to another environment for deployment.

☐ If a development system will probably not be used for deployment, then it is a very positive situation if there is an obvious deployment path, such as a delivery version of the development system.

☐ If the development system (or a delivery version of it) may be the final deployment system, ascertain whether it will allow the final expert system to be easy to operate and maintain.

Prerau, Developing and Managing Expert Systems (Addison-Wesley)

CHAPTER 8

Selecting the Domain Experts

- Why is it important for the expert system development team to be able to choose the domain experts for an expert system project?

- What are the technical and nontechnical criteria for selecting a project expert?

- What is an effective process for selecting a project expert?

- Is it better to use a single domain expert?

- How can multiple experts be used effectively?

- How can consulting domain experts be utilized to assist and guide the project?

Once the domain of the expert system has been selected, the next important task is to select the domain expert or experts who will work with the project.

The purpose of an expert system undertaking is to produce a system with a high degree of domain expertise. The most important (and often the only) source of domain expertise for the project is the domain expert or experts. The selection of experts, therefore, is an important step in the development process.

8.1 RESPONSIBILITY FOR SELECTING THE EXPERTS

Sometimes expert system project personnel have no choice as to who will provide the project's domain expertise, because only one expert in the domain is available to the project. The company may have only one expert in the domain. The company may not employ any experts in the domain but may have access to certain particular experts. There may be situations where there are several available experts but only a few can participate in the project. In other cases, there may be several experts in or available to the company, but someone in management has selected a particular one or small group of them to work with the project. This selection may be for good reasons (as far as the project is concerned), such as that management feels that the selected people are the best of the available experts. Or it may be for bad reasons (as far as the project is concerned), such as that management does not want to spare any of its most valuable experts.

Because of the central role that domain experts play in an expert system project and because there are several criteria to consider in selecting experts, it is important that the project team be able to select the experts, if at all possible. Even if management assigns a top expert to the project, those who made the selection probably had little knowledge of many of the aspects to be considered.

Often if in-house domain experts are to be used, they may come from parts of the company far removed organizationally from that of the expert system team. Thus there may need to be continuing political negotiations between the project (or the project's upper management) and the managers of the potential project experts.

When and if the project does choose its own experts, the team should take the time and effort necessary to select the best people available. They should identify the potential experts, ensure that they have at least the minimal qualifications to be able to work with the project, and evaluate them to select the best. Even if there is only one potential expert, the project team should ensure that that expert meets the minimal project qualifications.

It has proved valuable in evaluating potential experts to utilize a set of the attributes desired in a good project expert. The next section provides such a set of attributes.

The *COMPASS* project team selected the project's No. 2 EAX expert. We knew that there were expert analysts of No. 2 EAX maintenance problems and that we could find a few good candidates at GTE telephone companies. We had full backing of our local management to contact potential experts, interview them, and attempt to arrange the participation of the selected expert.

8.2   ATTRIBUTES OF GOOD DOMAIN EXPERTS

The desired attributes for domain experts relate to both technical skills and the nontechnical parts of the expert's role. Probably no project experts will fully meet all of the desired attributes discussed in this section. Furthermore when there are not many available experts, project personnel may have to focus on only a few of the most important attributes. Nevertheless it is important to know what makes a good domain expert in order to maximize the possibility of selecting good experts from the available alternatives.

8.2.1 EXISTENCE OF DOMAIN EXPERTISE AND EXPERIENCE

The domain should be established to the extent that there is expertise and experience. There should be recognized experts who are demonstrably better than amateurs in performing the task. Primary sources of these experts' abilities should be their special knowledge, judgment, and experience.

If an area is too new or too quickly changing, there may be no experts. Such a domain should have been eliminated in the domain selection process. Here, during the expert selection process, is another opportunity to find another domain or at least to shift the domain slightly to a related area where there may be experts. However, if the project is saddled with the task of trying to produce an expert system for a domain with no experts, the best that can be done is to find a person with a great deal of expertise and experience related as closely as possible to the task domain.

The analysis of maintenance messages of the No. 2 EAX is a task where a considerable amount of domain expertise and experience exists.

8.2.2 LEVEL OF EXPERTISE

Potential project experts should, if at all possible, be leading domain experts. The expert system that will be built can be expected to have only a fraction (hopefully a large fraction) of the experts' task knowledge. If the project's domain experts are not much above mediocre practitioners, the expert system will likely function at a mediocre level at best. This may result in the expert system's never being used in the field or being used to a lesser extent than it might have been. It would certainly be unfortunate if all of the effort and resources that went into the creation of an expert system were to be of no avail because of the use of too low a level of expert.

Because top-level experts perform valuable (often vital) services in their usual jobs, it is frequently difficult to have such top-level experts made available to the project. There may be a high cost to the project. There may need to be difficult political negotiations, possibly at a high management level. The experts' immediate management (and possibly higher-level management) might fight the assignment. Thus there is often a temptation to save the effort, the political capital, or the money by accepting lower-level domain experts for the project. It is advisable to resist this temptation.

In some situations, an expert system based on the knowledge of average domain practitioners might be used, such as when many of the people who perform the task are much below the average level or when there is a great advantage to uniform decision making (even at an average level). But even in such cases, the use of the system would be wider and the payoff from applying it greater if the system is based on the knowledge of high-level experts.

> From the beginning of the *COMPASS* domain selection process, we set our sights on getting one of the best No. 2 EAX experts to work with us. Our choice was the leading No. 2 EAX expert at GTE-Southwest (GTESW)—and one of the best in the country.

8.2.3 EXTENSIVENESS OF EXPERIENCE

A project expert should have had lengthy experience working on the task that the expert system will be addressing. During this long period of task performance, the expert should have had the experience necessary to be able to formulate the insights into the area that result in heuristics, which will be the core of (and the major feature of) the expert system.

> The *COMPASS* expert was a switching services supervisor at GTESW. Prior to his involvement with the *COMPASS* project, he had worked in telephone switching for 15 years, including about 5 years specifically on the No. 2 EAX.

8.2.4 REPUTATION

The knowledge, experience, credentials, and reputation of the project's experts should be such that if the final system is able to capture a portion of the experts' expertise and experience, the system's output will have credibility and authority.

The reputations of the experts upon whose knowledge the system was based are sometimes the major determinant of the credibility of the deployed expert system. In domains where an accepted test for goodness of result exists, high marks for the system in such tests may be important credibility factors, and the reputations of the experts may not be of great concern. In other domains, the most credible tests may be those that confirm that the system agrees with the experts on the same problem. These results may lack weight in the user community unless the experts have notable reputations or substantial credentials.

> The *COMPASS* domain expert has an excellent reputation for his knowledge of the No. 2 EAX.

8.2.5 FINDING EXPERTS WITH THE RIGHT EXPERIENCE

The experts chosen should have expertise and experience in the specific aspect of the domain that is the basis of the expert system. Thus for a diagnostic expert system, expertise should come from an expert diagnostician, not an expert designer or manufacturer. Although the designer of an automobile engine may know more about the intricacies of the engine than anyone else, the designer usually cannot diagnose problems in the engine as well as a top-level experienced mechanic can. The top mechanic knows from long experience the symptoms of various problems. For example, a certain noise, a certain vibration, a certain odor, or some combination of all of these may indicate the likelihood of a particular problem. Or the mechanic might know that one type of problem almost never occurs unless another type of problem occurs concurrently. These heuristics, generalized from encountering many real problems, are not usually known by the designer. Thus for an expert system for repairing automobiles, it is the expertise and experience of expert mechanics, not expert designers or expert manufacturers, that is required.

> The *COMPASS* expert obtained his experience analyzing and repairing switch problems. An attempt to do the same kind of expert system with a top No. 2 EAX designer (assuming one were available) would probably not have been as successful as *COMPASS*. For example, a large number of expert rules in *COMPASS* concern the following situation:
>
>> The data have been analyzed to the extent possible. Due to ambiguity in the data, we have been unable to narrow the cause of the problem to a single switch fault. The best we (or anyone) can conclude from the data is that the fault is one of three possible faults. Now what?
>
> Our *COMPASS* expert was able to supply a set of rules from his long experience, which said, in effect,
>
>> *If* the data indicate that the fault in the switch can be Fault A, Fault B, or Fault C,

> *Then,* in my experience with this type of situation, the actual fault is
> usually Fault B, less likely Fault C, and least likely Fault A.

A switch designer would not have the experience to formulate such a rule
accurately.

There was a case where an expert system was built by a leading AI university
under contract to a large corporation. The endeavor utilized a leading designer as the expert. A significant effort was put into the task, and it can be
assumed that the development was done at a high level. When the time ar-
rived to put the system into use in the field, field personnel would not accept
the system because it had the experience of the designer but not the field
expertise that they needed.

8.2.6 COMMUNICATION SKILLS

It is clear that domain experts for an expert system project should have
skill in the domain. Almost as important (and more easily overlooked in
the expert selection project), they should have skill in communicating their
knowledge, judgment, and experience and the methods they use to apply
these to the particular task.

Good project experts not only should have the expertise and experience
but also the ability to impart these to the project team, whose members
usually know little or nothing about the subject area. Project experts should
be articulate. They should be comfortable dealing with people who are
unfamiliar with domain jargon and who may not quickly grasp domain
concepts that seem very obvious. They should be good teachers since they
will probably spend a good deal of time explaining domain concepts and
procedures to neophyte project members. Any actual experience teaching
domain concepts is clearly beneficial.

In addition good project experts should be introspective, able to examine and analyze their task procedures and reasoning processes. They
should be organized thinkers, able to describe these processes in a structured way. (If an expert has written anything describing domain concepts,
this is a good indication of the ability to organize the concepts of the
domain well.) Finally project domain experts should be able to describe
those reasoning processes clearly to the project team.

The *COMPASS* expert was an excellent communicator, first in teaching the
COMPASS knowledge engineering team the basics of the No. 2 EAX and then
in relating and explaining to them the methods he used to analyze No. 2 EAX
maintenance messages.

In interviewing experts, we met a potential expert who was articulate and
knowledgeable, with excellent communication and teaching skills and was excited about our project. Unfortunately his primary expertise was the No. 1 EAX
(another common switch in GTE telephone companies), and he could not be

considered a top expert on the No. 2 EAX. We had already decided that it was better for the project to implement an expert system for the No. 2 EAX rather than the No. 1 EAX since the No. 2 EAX was newer and in more widespread use. However, this expert seemed so ideal that we were strongly tempted to change the domain of the system to the No. 1 EAX. We were considering this possibility when we met with our eventual *COMPASS* expert. He seemed to be about as good a potential expert as the No. 1 EAX expert, and he was a true No. 2 EAX expert; therefore we chose him. The interest in a No. 1 EAX *COMPASS* would have been less than for the No. 2 EAX *COMPASS,* and *COMPASS* may therefore not have made as much of an impact as it did. The important point here was that we so strongly felt that the communicative skills of an expert were vital to the success of the project that we did consider using a related but different domain in order to get an excellent expert.

8.2.7 TEMPERAMENT

Project experts should have the correct temperament to fill the role of a project expert. One part of this is the temperament needed for the teaching that is required. However, a large part is a combination of self-assuredness and openness that can let people allow their thinking processes be dissected and challenged.

The role of domain expert for an expert system project is difficult. They have to examine in detail the way they make decisions. Techniques that they have used for years are thoroughly scrutinized by people who, though probably inexperienced in the field, are usually very bright and sometimes have much higher levels of educational background. Domain experts are asked to put into words abstract feelings on why they pursue one alternative rather than another. They are pressured to quantify judgments they think they make qualitatively. They are asked to describe in great detail every heuristic used in every decision and then to let other experts in the field (e.g., the consulting experts) examine and criticize these details. If a domain expert does not have the right temperament to accept this kind of scrutiny, there may be problems.

The *COMPASS* expert had the temperament to work well as a project expert. He was patient enough to endure grueling knowledge acquisition sessions and self-assured enough to stick to his decisions even in the face of arguments from the knowledge acquisition team. But even he occasionally felt pressured by the constant probing. He was often hard put to define exact breakpoints between two situations but handled the situation well. He was able to open up to the consulting experts his No. 2 EAX knowledge (which we had captured during knowledge acquisition) and had no problem making the changes they suggested without feeling possessive toward his own rules and procedures.

He was able to work well during the knowledge acquisition sessions for some parts of *COMPASS* that were not based on his direct experience but on his general expertise. He was able to accept strong questioning about his suggested rules and procedures from the knowledge acquirers (with their newly found knowledge of No. 2 EAX switching combined with their more extensive background in probability and combinatorics). This kind of questioning did not occur to the same degree when the rules and procedures were based directly on his experience.

8.2.8 COOPERATIVENESS

Project experts should be cooperative and eager to work on the project. At worst they should be nonantagonistic.

Sometimes experts consider participation in the project to be a minor inconvenience or an unimportant break from their usual important work. Sometimes they are assigned by management to the project against their will and may prefer to work on their usual domain tasks. Sometimes they feel that the expert system may eventually be a job threat and are antagonistic.

Domain experts who are not interested in or are resentful about being on the project may not put in the full effort required or, worse, may withhold portions of their knowledge. To guard against this, expert system developers should try to find eager experts or convince not-so-enthusiastic experts to be excited about the project. There are several reasons why experts might become more interested and excited about working with the expert system project:

■   Experts who are interested in computers and in learning something about expert systems may feel (or be convinced by the project team to feel) that AI is an exciting field and that they can only be helped in their careers by being involved. It should be made clear that by the end of the project they could possibly become, at their usual jobs, the local authorities on expert systems and AI.

■   Experts who see a big potential payoff in the expert system may want to be involved with it. It cannot hurt a person's career to be a major contributor to a big winner. The experts' names will be mentioned (sometimes prominently) in publicity about the completed expert system directed to the company organizations directly involved and in general domain literature both within and without the company. The experts may attend meetings and system demonstrations with top management and possibly win incentive awards and other honors.

■   It can reasonably be said that it is an honor to be selected as a domain expert for an expert system. The selection says that yours is the expertise and experience that we want to capture and distribute and that others will now start doing their job your way.

■   Some experts consider the construction of an expert system based on their experience to be a way (albeit a small way) to be immortalized. Long after the experts are finished with the project, and possibly long after they have left the company, retired, or even died, their expertise and experience will be there, in the expert system, solving problems.

Project personnel should attempt to foster these feelings in potential project experts.

> The *COMPASS* expert was interested in and enthusiastic about the project. He put in more effort than was expected. He became an advocate for *COMPASS* within the telephone companies. He learned a good deal about AI and expert systems and became familiar with the Lisp machines being used.
>
> His involvement with the *COMPASS* project allowed him to receive a good deal of visibility with his management. His participation was featured in several articles in his company newspaper. He made presentations before top management of his company and of the entire GTE Corporation. And he eventually shared with us in a major award for *COMPASS*, the highest technical award in the GTE Corporation.

8.2.9 WORKING RELATIONS

It is helpful if the project experts are easy to work with. Domain experts spend a lot of time with the project team, especially the knowledge acquirers, since knowledge acquisition sessions may go on for days at a time. Concentrated meetings can be difficult for any group and may be more difficult when the kind of scrutiny that is the basis of knowledge acquisition is involved. If an expert's manner and personality blend well with the rest of the team, the work is easier.

> We had an excellent working and personal relationship with our *COMPASS* expert. Since meetings usually lasted a week, it was important that the group was able to work well together.

8.2.10 AVAILABILITY

The domain experts for an expert system project should be willing to commit a substantial amount of time to the development of the system. Depending on the scope of the project, knowledge acquisition may require many hours, days, or weeks of meetings with the knowledge acquisition team. The experts' commitment thus may involve spending a good deal of time away from their primary jobs, over an extended period, and possibly may require extensive travel and long intervals away from home.

> The project expert made a commitment to work on *COMPASS* one week each month for a lengthy period (eventually two years). Also he was willing to travel from his home city of San Angelo, Texas, to our site outside Boston each month. His commitment was one important factor in the success of *COMPASS*.

8.2.11 MANAGEMENT SUPPORT FOR EXPERT INVOLVEMENT

There should be strong managerial support, as high up in management as possible, for the project experts' commitment of a substantial amount of time over an extended period to the development of the expert system. Each expert's management should be able to agree to set aside ample time in the expert's schedule for the knowledge acquisition meetings to occur and should agree that interruptions during the time allotted to the expert system project will be kept to a minimum. To have the time commitment needed for a successful project, experts cannot squeeze in their work with the system developers. The knowledge acquisition should be an official task of theirs—part of their work load—and the rest of their responsibilities should be diminished accordingly.

Getting the experts' management to commit their time to an expert system project is often a problem. The best experts, in the most important corporate areas, are usually the ones who can be least spared from their usual position. Remember that some of the important reasons for selecting an application area for the project involve selecting one where expertise is scarce or expensive or where the experts are overworked. In any of these cases, the direct management of top-level experts would clearly, and understandably, not want to lose their services, even part time. However, it is the top-level experts who should be the ones whose knowledge is used as the basis of an expert system. Higher-level management is often less concerned about the effect of the loss of one person part time and so should be courted if possible.

Even if the domain experts' management has agreed to their involvement in the project, the stronger the commitment (and usually the higher management level it comes from), the better. The stronger the managerial commitment is, the less likely it will be that any of the experts will have continual interruptions while working on the project, will be pulled off the expert system project temporarily as crises occur, or, worst, in the middle of the system development will be reassigned permanently to a new project or new position that management feels is more important. Furthermore, in addition to losing the services of the experts while they are working on the project, their management will be concerned over the cost of their salaries for the period of the project and the cost of travel expenses, if required. A strong commitment by the experts' management will make an agreement easier to come by as to who will support the experts during their time on the project.

Changing domain experts for an expert system (or for a specific subdomain of an expert system) in midstream is technically difficult, and, especially when unplanned, could be disastrous. There are major difficulties in adding the partial heuristics of one expert to those of another. Moreover a replacement expert would have to learn almost everything the original expert had already learned about the project, about AI and expert systems, and so on. Even more important, a new expert would have to learn and understand the concepts defined in the knowledge acquisition up to that point. If the new expert used a somewhat different approach to the same analysis and therefore did not agree with some of the definitions, concepts, rules, and procedures already found, the knowledge acquisition might have to be completely reviewed and some or all parts redone. Even if the already acquired knowledge was accepted, the replacement expert would not have been there at its creation and might lack insights as to why certain choices were made or miss some subtle points.

If there is a possibility that experts might be changed in mid-project, project leadership should employ all available political and other influence to prevent this from happening. The project team should ascertain the degree of enthusiasm and commitment to the project of the management of a potential project expert. It is clearly advantageous for the team to do all it can to convince the expert's management that they should strongly back the project. If possible, a formal commitment of the expert's time for the duration of the project should be obtained, such as a contract or an internal written agreement. It might be a major blow to the project if the amount of time an expert was available to the project or the funding for the expert's time and travel were cut in the middle of the project.

> We were able to obtain from the management of GTE-Southwest, our expert's company, a commitment of one week per month of our expert's valuable time for the duration of the *COMPASS* project—over two years. Any smaller commitment of time would have significantly affected the speed of the project, and a major cutback would have made it almost impossible to achieve the excellent technical results that we did.

> During the two years, the strong commitment of GTESW was kept although during that period our expert received a promotion and moved to a new and more important position at GTESW. A small number of times we mutually agreed with the expert to shift the week of our meeting with him to the following week, but never did he miss any time from *COMPASS* knowledge acquisition due to his management's holding him back. GTESW management paid for the expert's time while on the project and his travel and lodging expenses.

8.2.12 COMPUTER AND AI BACKGROUND

It is helpful (although not vital) to select experts with some interest in and knowledge about computers. Any background an expert has related to AI is valuable.

Many aspects of standard computer technology may be involved in an expert system program, such as data communications, database access, and graphics. The programming may or may not be in a conventional language, but it is still programming. The more knowledge the domain experts have of the basics of computer technology, the more they can understand and participate in project discussions related to computers, and the more they can aid the project in this area. They might be able to learn to operate the expert system program or to make editing changes to the program's knowledge, thus allowing them to participate more fully in the project. Also if the expert system is eventually tested or put into production use at the experts' job sites, they might be able to function as system operators or administrators.

Experts with some knowledge of AI can more easily understand the project team's desired structures for knowledge representation, allowing them to tailor the delineation of their domain knowledge. It also may be possible for knowledge acquirers to use less obvious AI knowledge representation paradigms (such as frames instead of rules) directly as knowledge documentation if the experts understand them. In addition, knowledge of AI and expert systems will enable the experts more easily and accurately to describe the project to their management and other domain personnel and to understand both the potential and the limitations of the project. The knowledge engineers often have computer backgrounds and a strong understanding of mathematics. If the experts have some background in these areas, they can understand more easily any mathematical or computer-related terms or abstractions that the knowledge engineers may discuss or propose as knowledge representational devices.

> Prior to his involvement with the project, the *COMPASS* expert had had a good deal of exposure to and had shown some personal interest in computers. In his jobs in telephone company central offices, he had constant contact with computers. For example, the common control part of a No. 2 EAX— the part of the switch that controls the switching—is a computer system, as is the RMCS. Moreover he had built a home computer for personal use and had had some programming experience. This computer background made it easier for him to understand our computer-related problems and sometimes to participate in their solution. Also he could easily understand the use of tables, functions, binary numbers, and so forth. He had no background in AI or expert systems but was able to pick up fairly quickly from the project team a basic introduction to these areas.

8.2.13 EXPERTS AS DOMAIN REPRESENTATIVES

The selection of project domain experts who have a good understanding of the wants and needs of the user community is advantageous. In most cases, the project experts are the only people on the project who have dealt with the potential users of the system. They may hold now or have held the same job as the potential users or may have worked with people holding that job.

Potential users should help shape the expert system—its capabilities, the forms of its inputs and outputs, the ways it could be introduced to minimize negative impact to the working environment, and other areas directly related to users. There is a great benefit if a project's domain experts can act as user spokesmen as well. (Although project consulting experts can act as user spokesmen to some degree, they are involved with the project on a low-level, intermittent basis, while the primary domain experts are involved on a deep and continuing basis.) From the beginning of the domain experts' involvement with the project, they can help focus the project tasks on the areas most desired by the user community and with the most payoff and can help obtain agreement by domain area personnel on the specific tasks selected. Their knowledge of user desires can be used to guide the emerging system design on a day-to-day basis in the direction that will maximize the utility of the system and the degree to which the system will actually be used.

The domain experts might be able to identify or foresee potential political problems and suggest ways to ameliorate them. Their knowledge of the domain might allow them to predict forthcoming changes in procedures, organizational structures, or some other area that may occur between the time the expert system venture is initiated and the time it is to be put into the field. Then they may be able to guide the evolution of the expert system to take into account these changes.

Knowledge of potential users might enable the experts to suggest the best method to phase the expert system into use in the field, thus determining the relative importance of possible system features and the order in which they will be addressed by the project. They might be able to assist in efforts to quantify the potential benefits of the system—to help justify funding and support of the project or to help later in getting support for deployment or sales of the finished system.

The project experts' familiarity with the user community might help the project when demonstrations of the system are given. For example, they might have good ideas about what features would be the most impressive to domain personnel and therefore should be emphasized in a demonstration. At a system demonstration or other meeting, they might be able to explain the system to domain personnel better than the AI people.

No. 2 EAX maintenance technicians are the primary users of the output of *COMPASS*. Based on his over 15 years' experience in telephone switching, the *COMPASS* expert understood the maintenance technician position, the kinds of people who fill these positions, the principal problems they have, the information they usually know and do not know, the ways they like to work, the working environment, and so on.

Using his familiarity with user problems, the expert provided guidance on what subdomain should be the initial focus of the project. Based on his opinion we selected NR20 maintenance messages as first area to examine. This selection proved to be the correct choice. The consensus of domain area personnel to whom we later spoke was that NR20 messages was the area they were most concerned about and the area that should be the priority of a maintenance system.

The expert's familiarity with the user community helped throughout the project. For example, one of the tasks we gave him was to specify the phrasing of the sentence or paragraph that *COMPASS* would output for each type of suggested maintenance action. His experience with field personnel allowed him to use the correct level of jargon. Moreover he was able to give the output an appropriate length—succinct for common maintenance situations where lengthy information would be unnecessary and more detailed for maintenance situations that rarely occur and for which the switchperson needs additional support.

8.2.14 EXPECTATIONS

It is helpful to select as project domain experts people who have realistic expectations about the project. As AI outsiders, domain experts may have heard something about expert systems and may have formed erroneous opinions. They may have too high or too low expectations for the system that will be developed. If so, it is desirable that they be able to accept the opinions of the project's AI experts on the realistic expectations for the project. They should understand clearly, for example, that the system will likely be limited in scope and may not always produce optimal or correct results.

The *COMPASS* expert had not heard much about AI or expert systems before we started and did not come into the project with any preconceived expectations.

8.3   THE PROCESS OF SELECTING DOMAIN EXPERTS

As soon as the domain has been identified, it is time to start the process of selecting domain experts for the project (assuming the project is able to keep that responsibility). An effective selection process is to compile a list of possible domain experts, utilize meetings with the leading candidates to evaluate them, and select the best to be the project expert(s). To begin this process, the project staff member or members who will make the selection might speak to contacts in the domain area (those made during the domain selection process and any others), stating the need for project experts and briefly describing the domain expert's role. Some of the more important points to stress are that:

- The project needs the best available experts.

- An expert should be someone who will give credibility to the ultimate system.

- The present goal is just to find people with whom to explore the possibility of working with the project—there is no commitment involved at this point.

These initial contacts may provide other contacts, and eventually the selection team will get a few names of potential project experts.

At this point, the selectors might try to narrow the list to a few leading candidates. After that, much depends on how easy it is to arrange meetings with the candidates and how much effort and expense can be devoted to this process. There may be brief informal interactions or lengthy meetings. The meetings might be held at the candidates' places of business, or the candidates might be invited to visit the project site (which might allow them to see demonstrations of other expert systems or of expert system-related hardware and software). If it is expected that the project's knowledge acquisition meetings will be held at a site remote from the experts' job locations, then a meeting at that site can give potential experts more of an understanding of the eventual project and can give the project staff an idea as to whether there will be any problems with the experts' travel.

At a meeting with a potential project expert, project staff should introduce AI and expert systems, explain the purpose of the project, and detail the kind of involvement needed from the project expert. The project staff clearly should be trying to sell the project to the expert. The publicity about AI and expert systems may have done the job already. If not, mention might be made of some of the following:

- The possibility of being involved with "the exciting new 'high-tech' field of artificial intelligence and expert systems."

- The possibility of participating in a project that might result in a big payoff—with the corresponding potential rewards.

- The honor of being an expert for an expert system project. ("Your expertise and experience are what we want to capture and distribute.")

- The importance that a project expert will have in determining to a large extent the way the task will be performed by practitioners in the future.

- The immortality aspect of having one's knowledge used for many years.

- The likelihood of high visibility.

- The possibility of learning about the latest in expert system and computer technology.

At the same time that the project staff is selling the project, they should be scrutinizing the expert, considering each of the attributes of a good project expert. It is difficult for project members to judge the level of expertise of an expert in a field new to them. They will probably have to rely on reference checks with the project's domain contacts or other domain personnel and on any other information they can find about the expert's reputation. Thus they should use the meeting to look for other desirable features: communication skills, personality, interest in the project, cooperativeness, temperament, and computer and AI background. Also, they should try to ascertain the expert's availability and the likelihood of management support for the commitment required.

Probably the most important trait to look for is the ability to communicate well. One possible way to use the meeting to get some information on an expert's communication skills—and to start the project's task of learning about the domain as well—is to ask the expert to deliver a tutorial talk covering some aspect of the domain or possibly an introduction to the whole domain. It can be a prepared presentation or spontaneous. In either case, it should be informal, with the project people asking a lot of questions (somewhat simulating a knowledge acquisition session). The way the talk is presented and questions are answered should give some idea of the expert's capability to communicate and teach.

Based on findings from the meetings with the potential experts and the other information available and giving consideration to the desired attributes for project experts (which have been discussed in this chapter), project personnel then select the best of the potential experts.

Once one or more domain experts are selected, the next step is to secure their participation. If an expert does not work for the company, a contractual arrangement probably is needed. For experts from within the company, approval of appropriate management usually must be secured. Sometimes this approval is easy to get; sometimes it is not. If obtaining consent for a domain expert's participation is difficult, project leadership should negotiate with the expert's management. This negotiation is another sales job, similar to selling the expert on the project, and some of the items to mention are the same. Here are some useful points to make:

■   The possibility of their organization's being involved with "the exciting new 'high-tech' field of artificial intelligence and expert systems."

■   The possibility of their organization's participating in a project that might result in a big payoff for the corporation, with the corresponding potential rewards for all.

■   The potential of a big payoff to the organization itself from using the developed system, especially if they have previously identified the problem to be handled by the system as a major problem in their operation.

- The likelihood of high visibility, which will include the experts' management.

- The way that their organization will determine the way that the task will be done in the future. Every other group using the expert system will have to follow their techniques.

- The possibility that some of their staff will learn about the latest in expert system and computer technology.

In addition and if necessary, project management might consider some possible incentives to the expert's management that might seal the agreement:

- Their organization will be the site of the first demonstration or field test of the system.

- Their organization will be the first recipient of the expert system, and therefore they will get the first benefits from it.

- Their organization will be able to influence the direction that the project takes and help select exactly which tasks within the domain are handled by the expert system.

- The expert system project will pay travel expenses and/or part of each expert's salary.

With these arguments and incentives, there may be no problem getting approval for an expert's participation. But if even these incentives do not convince an expert's management to make the full commitment needed, the expert system project's leaders can try to go over the head of direct management and convince the expert's upper management of the benefits of the project. If even this step does not succeed, project personnel may decide to pursue the next best potential experts.

It is only reasonable that the project leaders not offer more than is required to gain agreement. It is dangerous to oversell the project, promising capabilities the system cannot possibly have by a deadline the developers cannot possibly meet. If domain experts or their management are expecting more than the system can reasonably deliver, there may be major problems down the road. In fact, once there is a firm commitment from the experts and their management, it is probably best for project personnel to downplay somewhat the potential of the system.

Early in the *COMPASS* project, we developed many of the criteria for selecting a project expert, and we used them throughout the selection process.

We thought as we started the selection process that we would be able to find at least a few people in GTE with enough expertise on the No. 2 EAX to act as the domain expert. Each of GTE's telephone companies has No. 2 EAXs, and each has three or four levels of maintenance experts for them. The leading No. 2 EAX expert or experts in each telephone company seemed to have the potential to be a project expert.

We then spoke with several people in the domain area, making the contacts primarily through our project's corporate interface person. We explained our need for a project expert and some of our criteria. These interactions yielded a small list of potential No. 2 EAX experts for our project.

The more promising of these experts we asked to come separately to our laboratories for one or two days. At these meetings, we outlined the project and its goals, gave the potential expert a little background on AI and expert systems in general, talked about the potential participation of the expert in our project, and asked the potential expert to talk about No. 2 EAX maintenance. Throughout the meetings, we tried to see how well the potential expert met our selection criteria. Based on these evaluations, we selected the *COMPASS* expert.

Although not a factor in our selection, it turned out that the selected expert was from GTE-Southwest, the telephone company of the vice-president who had first suggested the *COMPASS* domain. With this high official's approval behind us, we had fewer problems than might otherwise have occurred in getting the expert's management to approve his participation. Still there was some reluctance from the expert's direct management—and understandably so—in losing the services of an excellent employee for the one-quarter time we were asking. We explained the potential benefits of the project to them and offered to try to install the first test system at GTESW. They soon agreed to the expert's participation. Throughout the remainder of the project, they supported our efforts.

8.4   WHEN NO EXPERTS ARE AVAILABLE

The fundamental goal of an expert system endeavor is to create a computer program that embodies the heuristics that leading experts have formulated over lengthy experience performing a task. However, often managerial or political pressure is put behind an application area for which there are no experts or no available experts. When there is no expert, there is no direct source of the heuristics for the expert system. In some domains it might be possible to use only printed sources, such as manuals and textbooks, to develop an expert system, but in most cases there are no sources other than an expert for the kinds of heuristic knowledge that an expert knows and could provide. To attempt to develop an expert system without an expert takes the project beyond the basic expert system development process (which is very difficult in itself) and thus is not technologically conservative.

One approach might be to change the domain. Project developers might try to convince management that attempting this particular application is not worth the risk that the final system may never work well enough to be used at all. But there may be no way to change the selected domain. In that situation, the project leadership might attempt to redefine the task slightly to some related area where some experience exists or start the project with a subtask for which there is an available expert so at least an important part of the system is based on direct experience.

On the other hand, it might be a good decision to pursue the selected domain if the task is so important and the payoff so large that it is worth the risk of failure to make the attempt. One can attempt to use related expertise in lieu of direct experience. If this is to be done, it is important for the project leadership to make it clear to its own top management, to the expert and his management, to potential users, and to anyone else interested in the system that the project is going beyond a standard expert system approach and the probability of a successful system may be less than it otherwise would be.

An important part of COMPASS—the analysis of SMA110, SMA111, and SMA112 messages—was not based on our expert's direct experience but used his general expertise at analyzing No. 2 EAX maintenance messages. This task was not assigned to the project. We, the system developers, chose to attempt it after a substantial part of COMPASS was working and we had gained confidence in the basic methodology.

Due to the large amount of data that had to be analyzed for the three SMA message types and the ambiguity in the messages, even the best No. 2 EAX experts could not analyze these messages as well as they could other message types. But COMPASS could preprocess the data for the three SMA messages in ways hitherto unavailable to an expert. Therefore rather than just trying to duplicate our expert's direct experience in analyzing these messages, we felt that COMPASS could do better by making its analysis after a better preprocessing and basing that analysis on our expert's general expertise. Had COMPASS's superior preprocessing been available to the expert before he performed his usual manual analyses, he would have done a better job. Over time he would have formulated heuristics based on his experience doing this new analysis. But since he did not have the preprocessing available, he had not formulated any pertinent heuristics. Therefore we attempted to develop these heuristics for COMPASS based on our expert's general expertise in the domain and based on parallels he and we could make with the proven COMPASS methodologies for analyzing other message types.

We felt that this approach was riskier than our standard development techniques, and related this belief to people interested in the project. But we felt fairly confident of success because we were basing the new techniques on proven COMPASS methodologies for situations that were somewhat similar. We felt that we were not taking much of a political risk. If we succeeded (as we did), COMPASS would be able to perform analyses in this particular subdomain that would be significantly better than those performed by even the best experts. If we failed, we could always go back to standard COMPASS development, and we were confident that we had a good chance to put into COMPASS a version of the limited manual techniques that the expert used.

8.5   THE NUMBER OF DOMAIN EXPERTS

As the primary source of domain expertise, the expert system development project may utilize one domain expert or a number of them. The use of a single expert is usually preferred, but there are many cases in which it is useful or necessary to utilize multiple domain experts. For example, no one available person may be an expert in all the areas of the domain covered by the system.

8.5.1 USING A SINGLE EXPERT

If possible, the expertise for the system—or at least that pertaining to each distinct subdomain—should be obtained principally from a single expert. This approach avoids several problems.

Even if two or more experts generally agree on conclusions, they may often disagree on problem-solving techniques. It is difficult for an expert system project to develop a consistent body of knowledge on a specific area of expertise by acquiring the knowledge partially from each of two experts and then combining portions of each expert's reasoning processes. Even if two experts agree on the end results of an analysis and on their macrolevel steps and techniques, there will usually be differences (sometimes very subtle and sometimes very great) in the way they go about their microreasoning.

To illustrate, if the system's knowledge about a particular expert analysis step is made up of the heuristics of Expert Able for the initial part of the analysis and the heuristics of Expert Baker for the remainder of the analysis, the total body of knowledge may be inconsistent. Baker's heuristics for the later stages of the analysis were developed to be applicable to the situation that exists after the initial Baker heuristics have been applied. These later heuristics are probably not fully applicable to the situation existing after Able's initial heuristics have been applied. The two experts may make different assumptions, weigh factors differently, or proceed in a different sequence. Expert Able might weigh a particular factor strongly in the early reasoning and not so strongly later in the analysis. Expert Baker might weigh the same factor less at the beginning of the analysis and more toward the end. These two approaches might yield the same results in most cases. But if Able's early reasoning is combined with Baker's later reasoning, the factor might get too much weight, possibly yielding incorrect results. Some of the problems generated by the combining of two or more experts' reasoning processes may not be noticed for a long time, producing latent bugs in the reasoning process.

Clearly there is even a greater problem in attempting to combine the knowledge and reasoning of two or more experts who often disagree on conclusions. In some fields it is not uncommon for leading experts to disagree on major points, a situation that can lead to many problems. If one leading expert says "Yes" and another says "No," what should the expert system say? For example, two world-famous economists may, for the same situation, have very different economic predictions and very different policy recommendations. Can these two experts be combined in a single expert system? No. However, it would still be a great benefit to be able to have the expertise and experience of either one of these experts available in an expert system. Getting some of the knowledge of a top expert into an expert system is very useful, and we must, at least for the near term, be satisfied with that.

A related problem often occurs when a panel of peer domain experts is used to provide knowledge for the system on a particular domain area. The use of a panel brings some advantages, which we will discuss in the next section, but problems may occur when the panel is not unanimous. If four members of the panel say "Yes" and two say "No," does that mean that the four are right? And what should be done if they split three to three? Often this means that a knowledge engineer—not an expert in the domain at all—might have to determine which group of three to follow.

In addition to avoiding the problems just mentioned, the use of a single domain expert has other advantages. A single expert used for the development of the whole system—or even for the development of the parts of the system related to more than one subdomain—might identify more parallels between the subdomains than otherwise would have been seen. Appreciation of these parallels might allow one subdomain's structure or even its reasoning techniques to be used, or modified for use, in other subdomains. Also during the expert system development sessions, a domain expert gains experience in how to be a good project expert and forms a working relationship with the group. The expert learns about AI and expert systems and about the kinds of knowledge the knowledge acquisition team is looking for and the best ways to present that knowledge. All of this must be duplicated if additional experts are to be used.

> We thought that we would be able to utilize a single domain expert to get knowledge on No. 2 EAX maintenance. Our one expert was able to supply all of the knowledge *COMPASS* needed, and we were able to maintain his commitment to the project for the entire length of *COMPASS* development.

> We probably could have used a different expert for some of the different No. 2 EAX message types; however, many of the parallelisms we used in the *COMPASS* structure for the different maintenance messages would have been unclear to a new expert, and he would have had to spend a good deal of time trying to understand the existing parts of *COMPASS*. Also he would have had to pick up the knowledge of expert systems and the goals of our project that our expert already had learned. It would have been much more difficult to have had a new expert take over in the middle of the work on the analysis for a message type. Another expert might have had to revise much of what had been done, or we may have even had to start over.

8.5.2 USING MULTIPLE EXPERTS

No single expert may be available for the total amount of time required by the project, and thus the use of multiple experts may be unavoidable. Project management should strive to get a desired expert with the complete commitment required, but this situation may prove impossible to attain.

Multiple experts may also be required if no single expert (or at least no single available expert) has the breadth of expertise in subdomains to be able to act as a project expert for the entire system. Even if an expert knows something about all subdomains, he may not be the top expert we would want in every one of these areas. The project may have to consider a trade-off between using the same expert for all subdomains versus using one or more additional experts. The additional experts would bring more knowledge than the original expert in particular subdomains, but using them might entail some of the problems discussed.

If multiple experts are utilized, it is wise to try to divide the domain into distinct subdomains and use a single expert for each one. Then each subdomain can be treated as a mini-expert system. If this is done, it is desirable to have one expert act as the overall system expert, responsible for integrating all the subdomain knowledge into a single system.

The use of multiple experts, even within a subdomain, brings certain advantages that may be very valuable. It can strengthen the technical authority of the resulting expert system. This factor may be important to the project, especially in a domain where there is no test of the correctness of the expert system or where the results of the system will be strongly challenged. The use of multiple experts representing different organizational entities might allow the project to avoid political problems that might have occurred had only one of these entities supplied an expert to the project. For example, it might avoid a "Not Invented Here" attitude, which otherwise might affect the possibilities for the success of the expert system. The project might attempt to get the same authority and political benefits of multiple domain experts by having a single primary domain expert and several consulting experts, but that may not be enough.

If multiple experts are to work together in a particular subdomain, one of them should be designated the lead subdomain expert with final authority to allow all the expertise to be filtered through a single person's reasoning process. It should be noted, however, that some techniques have been found—in disciplines outside of AI such as economic modeling and technological forecasting—to allow the combining of inputs from many different experts. For example, the Delphi method has been used to allow the opinions of a panel of experts to be combined into a consensus viewpoint.

> We were able to use a single No. 2 EAX maintenance expert for *COMPASS*. He had the breadth of expertise needed to cover all the areas we considered. We used consulting experts but not multiple primary experts.

8.6   CONSULTING DOMAIN EXPERTS

As an alternative to using multiple domain experts for the expert system, it may be possible to use a single primary expert and a group of consulting domain experts, peers of the primary expert. Even if multiple primary experts are used, a panel of consulting experts may still prove valuable.

The consulting experts act as senior advisers to the project and do not need the deep involvement (and corresponding time commitment) of a primary expert. They are available for discussions with the primary domain expert or experts. They participate in major reviews of the expert system. They sometimes act as representatives for the potential users of the system or for their own organizations and might help evaluate the correctness or effectiveness of the final expert system program.

When there is a single primary domain expert and that expert has a question about a domain-related matter, members of the development team usually cannot help because they typically have little or no knowledge of the domain and rarely have top-level domain expertise. When such a question surfaces, it is beneficial that the project have consulting domain experts who can discuss the matter with the primary expert. Occasionally the primary expert needs a sounding board for crystallizing thoughts on a detail of the expert process, and the consulting experts can be available for that purpose. They can help ensure that the primary expert has not, through oversight, omitted any important pieces of domain knowledge. A group of consulting experts can, in addition, provide broader background and experience than the primary expert. They can aid the primary expert in subdomains where he is not as expert as one of them.

The consulting experts might act as representatives for the eventual users of the system. They may be able to look at the system in a more detached way than a primary expert. If they are from or are familiar with parts of the user community remote from that of any primary expert, they may be useful in answering such important questions as: "Will the expert system be applicable, without modification, to all potential users?" "If the system must be modified, what modifications will be needed?" "Does every potential user group have the same data sources available?" "Could every potential user utilize the same output format and level of detail?" "Are there special circumstances that pertain to certain users but are not covered by the expert system?" "How can the system be designed to minimize the need for customization?"

Consulting experts can provide strengthened technical authority to the expert system, as well as the benefits from the participation of several political or organizational groups. These advantages accrue in a manner as discussed for multiple primary experts in the previous section but in a somewhat diminished way because of the consulting experts' lower level of project participation.

A panel of consulting experts—either the same group used during the development or a new group—might be used in testing and evaluating the project. They can check the output of the expert system and analyze the internal reasoning of the system to confirm its validity. They might be asked to read through the knowledge document (which should contain the output of the knowledge acquisition in readable form) to find any mistakes or omissions.

It is highly desirable that consulting experts think of themselves as members of the project team, not as outside critics. This feeling should be reinforced throughout their participation in the project. Therefore project personnel should give strong weight to any recommendations that the consulting experts might have and take any criticism from the consulting experts as constructive. If the consulting experts consider themselves project members, often they will become advocates of the expert system when the development is complete.

> Four consulting experts participated in various parts of the *COMPASS* project. They represented three of GTE's telephone companies, one of which was GTESW, the domain expert's company. Thus in addition to the individual participation of these experts, the project received the views of and some backing from two GTE companies in addition to the company of our expert.

> Three of the consulting experts participated in a three-day meeting held to examine *COMPASS-I* just after it was completed. The results of this review meeting gave us confidence that *COMPASS-I* was working well and, additionally, furnished a consensus about where the project should head. The consulting experts provided the important information that, in their opinions, *COMPASS* would be applicable without modification in all GTE telephone companies. Their positive reviews were very useful in getting backing for *COMPASS* from management.

> Three of the consulting experts also attended a similar meeting to examine *COMPASS-II*. This meeting had similar results and benefits for the project.

> Throughout the development of *COMPASS*, our primary expert occasionally called the consulting experts to review domain questions. The consulting experts also helped set up and run the initial *COMPASS* field trials at switch sites in the three companies. Later three of the consulting experts served as *COMPASS* field trial coordinators for their respective companies, and one participated in the *COMPASS* deployment.

Checklist for Selecting the Experts

☐ The expert system project should have the responsibility for selecting the project experts.

☐ There should be real expertise and experience in the domain.

☐ Project experts should be top-level domain experts (mediocre practitioners usually will not do).

☐ Project experts should have had lengthy experience on the task of the expert system.

☐ Project experts should have experience and expertise in just the aspect of the domain that is related to the expert system. Thus, base a diagnostic expert system on the expertise of diagnosticians, not designers.

☐ Project experts should have good communications skills (this is important but sometimes overlooked until too late).

☐ Project experts should be introspective, able to examine and analyze their task procedures and reasoning processes.

☐ Project experts should be good teachers (they will probably have to teach the project staff a good deal about the domain, including basic concepts and jargon).

☐ Project experts should have the required temperament: the self-assuredness and openness to allow their thinking processes to be dissected and challenged.

☐ Project experts should be cooperative and eager to work in the expert system project. If they are not, project personnel should try to convince them to be enthusiastic about the project.

☐ Project experts should be easy to work with. They and the project staff will be spending a lot of time together.

☐ Project experts should be willing to commit the substantial amount of time and effort needed for their roles in the system development.

☐ There should be strong support by the experts' management, as high up as possible, for the experts' participation in the project. The best experts, in the most important areas, are usually the ones who can be least spared from their usual positions—but these are the experts needed.

☐ Compile a list of potential experts through the recommendations of domain contacts. Tell them that the project requires the very best experts.

☐ Meet with the top candidate experts. Sell them on the project while analyzing how effective they would be as project experts.

☐ Select the experts that best meet these criteria.

▭ Secure the approval of the management of the selected experts by convincing them of the value of the project and possibly promising some direct benefits to their organization.

▭ Try to utilize a single project expert, at least for each subdomain. There are some advantages to using multiple experts, but these are outweighed in many cases by the disadvantages.

▭ Utilize peers of the primary expert(s) as consulting domain experts. They can act as senior advisers and consultants to the project, participate in major system reviews, act as user spokespeople, assist in evaluating the correctness of the final expert system program, and provide additional credibility to the system.

Prerau, Developing and Managing Expert Systems (Addison-Wesley)

CHAPTER 9

Acquiring the Knowledge

■ Why is knowledge acquisition the most important task of an expert system system development, once the domain has been selected?

■ What considerations of knowledge acquisition should be taken into account from the beginning of the project?

■ What are some practical factors to keep in mind when setting up the knowledge acquisition sessions?

■ How can the knowledge acquisition get started?

■ What are some practical techniques for knowledge acquisition that have proved successful?

■ How might the knowledge be recorded at the knowledge acquisition sessions?

■ What are some good practices for documenting the knowledge?

Knowledge acquisition is the process by which expert system developers find the knowledge that domain experts use to perform the task of interest. This knowledge is then implemented to form the expert system program. The essential part of an expert system is its knowledge; it is what distinguishes an expert system from a conventional program and gives the system its power. Therefore, once the domain has been selected, knowledge acquisition is very likely the most important task in an expert system development.

Knowledge acquisition for expert system development is a relatively new field, and there is a need for (and interest in) research into better methods of knowledge acquisition, including techniques to automate the process. But for the foreseeable future, most of the knowledge for any practical expert system in a complex domain will be obtained through the interaction of knowledge engineers and domain experts.

Acquiring knowledge from an expert can be very difficult. Most of the time, experts do not realize all that goes into the decisions they make. An expert's briefly considered decision often actually encompasses a very large amount of information and judgments. Remember the simple example in Box 2.1: when the traffic light turns green and the experienced driver makes the seemingly simple decision to start the car going forward, this decision is actually based on many pieces of information that have been collected and on several judgments that are made almost instantaneously. Experts often do not realize the large extent of the knowledge they use to make what they consider simple or obvious judgments. Furthermore, sometimes an expert's actions are performed almost unconsciously, based on years of successful performance. For example, I have asked experienced drivers (including myself) the following question: "Approximately how often do you look into the rearview mirror when driving on a highway in normal conditions: every 10 seconds? every 30 seconds? every minute? every 5 minutes?" They almost always have absolutely no idea how often they do this task, but they know they do it, and their years of good performance indicate that they do it at a reasonably expert level. This illustrates another problem for knowledge acquisition: getting expertise from experts who do not have a firm notion of exactly how they do their tasks.

This chapter describes techniques related to practical knowledge acquisition, starting at the beginning of an expert system project and proceeding more or less in the order that knowledge acquisition-related concerns might occur during the project. Initial sections of the chapter cover the knowledge acquisition considerations in selecting an appropriate domain for the expert system and in choosing an expert. The next sections consider some points related to getting started: how to set up the knowledge acquisition meetings, what the first meetings should cover, and what knowledge acquisition techniques can be used at these initial meetings. The remaining sections cover the core issues of knowledge acquisition: the techniques for acquiring, recording, and documenting the knowledge. Some of the key points on which we will focus concern the importance of:

- taking knowledge acquisition concerns into account when selecting the domain
- taking knowledge acquisition concerns into account when selecting an expert
- using test cases to elicit knowledge
- using generated test cases to multiply the effectiveness of test case analysis
- using good knowledge recording and documentation practices.

9.1 CONSIDERING KNOWLEDGE ACQUISITION AT THE PROJECT'S BEGINNING

Even before knowledge acquisition begins, two decisions crucial to its success are made: the choice of the project's domain and the choice of the project's expert(s). If considerations of the subsequent knowledge acquisition process enter into these decisions, the knowledge acquisition will have a much better chance to succeed.

9.1.1 SELECTING THE DOMAIN WITH A VIEW TOWARD KNOWLEDGE ACQUISITION

Knowledge acquisition can be substantially facilitated if the domain selected has certain characteristics. Since knowledge acquisition is of critical importance to the ultimate success of the expert system development, it is wise to keep it in mind even in the initial stages of the project when the domain is being selected. Thus it is not surprising that some of the criteria listed in Chapter 6 for selecting a good expert system domain are related to the likelihood of successful knowledge acquisition.

It is beneficial to knowledge acquisition if the expert system domain selected is such that an initial expert system covering just part of the domain can be developed first and then expanded to cover other subareas. Also it is helpful if the task can be decomposed into subtasks. If both of these goals obtain, then discussion at each knowledge acquisition session can be focused on one subtask for one subarea of the domain. Such focusing greatly facilitates the knowledge acquisition. It is much easier to examine an expert's techniques in a narrowly defined situation than to try to discuss a broad domain all at once.

Furthermore it is valuable to the knowledge acquisition effort that the domain selected is fairly stable. If during the system development the domain situation changes in a way that invalidates a significant portion of the knowledge already acquired, a substantial part of the knowledge acquisition process might have to be redone. Changes in data can often be easily handled, but if there are many domain changes that affect an expert's procedures and heuristics, a large part of the knowledge found early in the knowledge acquisition may no longer be valid, and it may not be possible to continue the knowledge acquisition without redoing most of the early work.

> For *COMPASS* knowledge acquisition, we were able to concentrate on one class of No. 2 EAX maintenance messages at a time. The analysis of each class of messages could be considered a separate area of interest. (In one case, two maintenance message types indicated the same kind of switch problem; we treated these two message types as if they were a single message type.)

Occasionally when we found a needed modification to a rule for one maintenance message type, there would be a corresponding rule for another message type, which we would then consider modifying. But for the most part
each maintenance message had a large number of new rules and procedures
specific to itself. Thus the expertise for each message type was treated as separate from that for the other message types, and knowledge acquisition concentrated on one type at a time.

We selected the *COMPASS* domain not knowing whether it was decomposable; it turned out to be very useful to the knowledge acquisition that the
COMPASS procedure for each message type could be divided into five phases
and that these could be further divided into nine steps (see Figure 10.1). Thus
during knowledge acquisition for a particular maintenance message type, we
could further focus on a particular stage of the *COMPASS* process for that
message type. This focusing made the knowledge acquisition process, difficult
as it was, much better and faster. It was as part of our initial knowledge acquisition that we discovered that there were several phases and stages to the
COMPASS task. Our expert did not realize this decomposition when we
began.

9.1.2 SELECTING EXPERTS WITH A VIEW TOWARD KNOWLEDGE ACQUISITION

Domain experts are the primary source of the knowledge for an expert
system. Because of this, among the important attributes of a domain expert
discussed in Chapter 8 are several related to knowledge acquisition. These
attributes primarily relate to the degree that an expert will function well in
the role of knowledge source.

An expert should have developed domain expertise by task performance over a long period of time. The primary objective of the knowledge
acquisition is to find the expert heuristics related to the task. It is these
heuristics that most distinguish the knowledge in an expert system from
that in a conventional program. Project experts should have had enough
experience to have been able to develop the domain insights that result in
these heuristics.

An expert's communication skills are important to knowledge acquisition. Experts should be capable of communicating their knowledge, judgment, and experience and the methods they use to apply these to the
particular task. Each expert's temperament, cooperativeness, and working
relations with the project team can have a major impact on the success and
the speed of the knowledge acquisition.

A factor of great consequence pertaining to the role of experts in
knowledge acquisition is their availability. If they cannot devote the necessary time to the project, it is unlikely to succeed. The knowledge acquisition process can often be slow and laborious, especially for a complex

task. If the availability of an expert limits the effort, there may not be enough time to specify completely the important domain heuristics. Weak, approximate versions of these heuristics may wind up in the final expert system, or worse, they could be missing completely. Without key heuristics, the system performance will be significantly diminished, possibly to the point of uselessness.

Significant time and effort should be given to the selection of the expert or experts who will work with the expert system project. A key part of this task should be evaluating the capability of potential experts for their role in knowledge acquisition and their availability, as well as considering their domain expertise.

> We spent a good deal of time and effort in the process of expert selection for *COMPASS*. We used an interviewing process to determine whether the potential experts had, in addition to their domain expertise, the attributes to be good knowledge sources during the knowledge acquisition process: communication skills, cooperativeness, correct temperament, and so on.

> The expert selected proved to be excellent for the knowledge acquisition. He had lengthy experience related to *COMPASS*'s task of analysis of the No. 2 EAX maintenance messages and had developed numerous heuristics for each of the major phases of the analysis. Furthermore he was an excellent communicator and had most of the other related attributes for being an excellent knowledge source. These characteristics greatly facilitated our knowledge acquisition throughout the project. Finally, he made a major commitment of time and effort to the project and was fully backed by his management.

9.2   KNOWLEDGE ACQUISITION MEETINGS

The setting up and scheduling of knowledge acquisition meetings are important practical concerns.

9.2.1 MAXIMIZING ACCESS TO THE EXPERTS

The knowledge acquisition meetings should be organized so as to maximize access to the domain experts. How to accomplish maximum access depends on the situation. Since the rest of the expert system team is probably working full time on the system, their schedule is usually more flexible than that of the domain experts, who have other commitments. That fact should be taken into account when scheduling the meetings. On the other hand, we have discussed the desirability of having the experts and their management make strong commitments to the project. If this commitment has been made, certain scheduled blocks of each expert's time should be set aside to work on the expert system, and the experts and their management should not expect them to work on their primary jobs during those times. This arrangement is obviously superior to having the experts squeeze the knowledge acquisition into their schedules at random times, and project leaders should strive to obtain such an arrangement.

If part of the knowledge acquisition is to be done by observing experts performing their expert functions in their usual environment, it is best to have scheduled blocks of time with the experts before and after these observations to discuss the task further in a more controlled atmosphere.

> We were able to obtain a firm commitment from the *COMPASS* expert's management, with our expert's concurrence, for one-quarter of his time— one week each month—for knowledge acquisition. *COMPASS* knowledge acquisition meetings were held at our laboratories in Waltham, Massachusetts, and the expert flew up from San Angelo, Texas, to attend them. Since the trip the expert had to make was long (about eight hours of traveling each way, including waiting for connections), it seemed reasonable to schedule the meetings one solid week each month. We scheduled each meeting week one to three months in advance and tried to select a time in which neither the expert nor the knowledge engineers had other commitments. If the situation on or off the project changed, we mutually agreed on alternative dates, and occasionally the expert came for a shorter or longer period than a week. This schedule proved to be generally effective for us, but there were times when we might have preferred some additional flexibility, such as having the expert available two days every other week.

9.2.2 ALLOWING THE EXPERTS TO DEMONSTRATE THEIR EXPERTISE

The knowledge acquisition meetings should be organized so as to maximize the capability of the domain experts to demonstrate their expertise. Sometimes the best way to do this is to have the knowledge engineers observe or follow the experts while they are performing their primary jobs in their usual environments, but often providing a good atmosphere for knowledge acquisition is all that is needed.

The experts may not be able to function at their usual level of expertise in environments different from those to which they are accustomed. At unfamiliar sites they might be unable to recreate mentally their usual environments, and thus the analyses they do there. If the job sometimes is performed under pressure (e.g., piloting an airplane), it may be that the procedures an expert describes while sitting calmly in an office differ from those actually used. If the expert works as part of a team and has considerable interaction with others doing related jobs (e.g., an air traffic controller), it may be difficult or impossible to reproduce the environment. Moreover, at an expert's job location, there may be certain unique equipment, data sources, and so forth crucial to decision procedures that are not available elsewhere. Experts may even utilize some components of their usual environments without realizing it. If any of these factors pertains, it is imperative to attempt to hold at least some of the knowledge acquisition meetings at the experts' job sites.

> The *COMPASS* analysis is done by analyzing computer RMCS printouts of No. 2 EAX maintenance messages. Our belief that there was no need to have the expert perform the analysis at a switch site or an RMCS site proved correct. There was some switch-specific data he occasionally needed that was available in hard-copy binders at switch and RMCS sites, but it was relatively easy for us to get copies of the pertinent data.

9.2.3 MINIMIZING INTERRUPTIONS

The best experts—the ones desirable for an expert system project—are usually the ones who can least be spared from their usual positions. Often such experts have jobs where they are consulted frequently for major and minor crises or because they know the most about certain areas. Thus knowledge acquisition meetings held at or near an expert's work site are likely to have many interruptions. Some of these could stretch into hours or days because high priority emergencies related to the expert's primary job almost always take precedence over work on an expert system development process, which is often viewed as a sidelight to the primary job.

It is obviously desirable for the knowledge acquisition meetings to proceed with the minimum number of interruptions. Therefore if the knowledge acquisition does not require being at an expert's site, the knowledge acquisition meetings should be held at a site remote from the expert's place of business. Even a meeting room in another section of the building is better than meeting across the hall from the expert's office.

> In the *COMPASS* expert's regular job in Texas as switching services supervisor, randomly occurring problems frequently required his immediate attention, and he usually worked on them until they were solved. Some of these were very high impact problems; sometimes they involved large sums of money for the GTESW telephone company or restoring telephone service to large geographic areas with many telephone subscribers. By having our scheduled knowledge acquisition meetings in Massachusetts, we minimized, but did not completely eliminate, the times when he was called upon to help in such crises. Once or twice during major problems when he could not be spared from his primary job, we had to reschedule his trip to Waltham (and thus our knowledge acquisition meetings). However, once the expert was in Massachusetts, we could count on his uninterrupted availability except for occasional telephone calls. No problem ever occurred that necessitated his flying back to Texas in the middle of one of our week-long meetings.

9.2.4 ACCESSING THE IMPLEMENTATION

Knowledge acquisition meetings should be set up so as to allow access to the partially implemented expert system program (based on the incomplete knowledge that has thus far been acquired), for several reasons:

■   Many times during knowledge acquisition sessions, program runs of a certain type or with certain input data are desired that were not anticipated before the session began.

■   Implementation of major chunks of acquired knowledge usually must await the period after the knowledge acquisition sessions, but often it is beneficial during a knowledge acquisition session to make some modifications and additions to the existing implementation of the thus-far-acquired knowledge in order to add new knowledge that was acquired during the session. Then new runs of the program can be made and the results compared with those of a domain expert, allowing an immediate evaluation of the newly acquired rules and procedures.

■   Knowledge acquisition is frequently aided by using the output of one part of the developing program as test input for knowledge acquisition of a succeeding part of the program. Program runs to obtain this test input should be performed before the knowledge acquisition session when possible; however, often a run is desired that was not anticipated in advance or that is based on changes just made.

■   Effective knowledge acquisition for certain domains requires the knowledge acquisition team to utilize the results of running the developing expert system program on the very latest data. For example, an expert's decisions may be based in part on knowledge of recent events (for example, the weather, the status of a process, or recent local actions).

■   Processes in certain domains have a significant time dependence, and in such domains it may be important for the knowledge acquisition team to make a series of runs of the developing expert system program during the knowledge acquisition period or to run the system continuously. For example, the knowledge acquisition team may want to compare one run against a later run to track a changing situation.

To run the program during knowledge acquisition, it is therefore important to plan for the knowledge acquisition team to have access to the developing expert system implementation during the sessions.

One advantage of having the *COMPASS* knowledge acquisition meetings at our Waltham site was that it provided immediate access to the developing *COMPASS* program on our computers.

We frequently ran *COMPASS* during the knowledge acquisition. Sometimes we ran the current implementation of *COMPASS* on new or archived data on which that particular version had not been run before—for example, to test if the current version of *COMPASS* had some possible problem that had just occurred to us. Many times we used the output of an implemented step as the input to our discussions of the next step. For this purpose, we often required *COMPASS* runs that we had not thought in advance that we would need.

Also during the knowledge acquisition sessions, we frequently found small problems in the knowledge. Then we found changes in the knowledge that we thought would solve the problems, implemented the changes, and reran the system to see if the fixes did indeed solve the problems.

Finally for a selected No. 2 EAX we sometimes ran the *COMPASS* implementation over a series of days during a week-long knowledge acquisition session to allow us to compare *COMPASS* analyses over the period and to follow specific switch problems over time.

9.2.5 LOCATING MEETINGS AT THE PROJECT TEAM'S SITE

If the project domain experts and the project knowledge engineers are not colocated, there are some advantages to having the knowledge acquisition sessions at the project team's site. For example, it takes the experts away from the demands at their own locations and allows access to the partially implemented expert system program. Also it might yield decreased travel expenses if there are fewer experts than knowledge engineers attending the meetings. Moreover if knowledge engineering programs, equipment, or other aids are available at the knowledge engineers' site, holding the meetings there provides access to these specialized facilities.

There may be some negative aspects to holding knowledge acquisition meetings at the project team's place of business. It will likely increase the possibility of interruptions due to the knowledge engineers' other commitments and could lead to problems if needed domain data or tools are not available.

By having the *COMPASS* knowledge acquisition meetings at our Waltham site, we minimized travel expenses, because one expert rather than two or more knowledge engineers had to travel. It allowed attendance at the knowledge acquisition session as needed by all expert system development personnel and facilitated use of our techniques for recording the knowledge and for updating documentation. A negative aspect was that the knowledge engineers sometimes were called away singly or in a group to attend meetings. Such incidents did delay the knowledge acquisition at times. However, we tried, whenever possible, to reschedule our other meetings so that they would not conflict with the knowledge acquisition. Furthermore, since *our* primary job was developing *COMPASS* (as opposed to the expert's primary job: his work at GTESW), we were able to schedule these other meetings so that we were rarely called away for more than an hour or two at a time.

9.3   BEGINNING THE KNOWLEDGE ACQUISITION

Beginning at the first knowledge acquisition meeting, certain steps can be taken to help the knowledge acquisition process get off to a good start.

9.3.1 MEETING ATMOSPHERE

The leader of the knowledge acquisition effort should try to control the atmosphere at the knowledge acquisition meetings so as to maximize the likelihood of long-term success. For a major expert system development, the knowledge acquisition group will be together for many long intervals, over a long period of time. An informal atmosphere will probably lead to the most productive results. A spirit of mutual respect should be fostered. The domain experts are expert in their fields, but the knowledge engineers are (at least relative to the domain experts) experts in the fields of AI and expert systems.

The domain experts should be made to feel part of a team, not occasionally visiting outsiders, necessary evils, or conversely, exalted visiting gurus. As team members, their desires should be taken into account when project decisions that involve them are made, but theirs should not be the only votes.

As *COMPASS* project leader and leader of the knowledge acquisition, I tried to maintain a friendly, informal atmosphere at the knowledge acquisition sessions. The meetings usually went on for one week without interruption, and often with intense discussions, so I felt it was important to promote a casual and congenial tone. Whenever possible we used a conference room seating about fourteen, although we almost never had more than four or five people at the meeting. The conference room allowed us some space to spread out and be comfortable. We had coffee and soft drinks available in the room at all times. Although we could have had lunch served in the conference room, I felt we needed the break of walking to the company cafeteria. As part of our friendly environment, we eventually established a tradition of going out to a restaurant for lunch on the last day of each session, to reward ourselves for our hard work.

Since the knowledge engineers knew very little, if anything, about telephone switching and certainly nothing about the details of the No. 2 EAX while the *COMPASS* expert knew very little about AI and expert systems, an atmosphere of mutual respect developed. We probably impressed each other with unfamiliar jargon and concepts from our respective fields.

We stressed from the beginning that the expert was part of our team and tried to take his wishes into account whenever possible. Although he spent most of his time in the conference room used for knowledge acquisition sessions, we assigned him a permanent desk, an office with a nameplate on the door, and a mailbox, and placed his name on most of our mailing lists. We invited him to any GTE Laboratories or department meetings or gatherings that occurred while he was at our site and that he could properly attend. In short, we tried to make him feel like a permanent member of our department rather than a visitor.

9.3.2 FOCUSING THE KNOWLEDGE ACQUISITION

The leader of the knowledge acquisition should try to keep the focus of the meeting on the work at hand, usually by concentrating on the test case under consideration. As experts discuss the domain and the task of interest, they may want to get into detailed anecdotes. Some of this is good, giving the knowledge engineers the flavor of the domain, but the amount should be controlled. Also, some experts may want to spend a lot of time discussing obscure, complex cases and how they handle them, since the simpler cases may interest them less. But it is usually more important for the knowledge acquisition to focus on the simple, everyday test cases, at least at first.

This issue was not a large problem in the *COMPASS* knowledge acquisition. Short anecdotes by the expert often provided a brief break from the knowledge acquisition while giving the knowledge engineers a broader general background about the way telephone companies operate.

9.3.3 GETTING BACKGROUND DOMAIN KNOWLEDGE

Knowledge engineers are often completely unfamiliar with the domain of the system. Thus part of the knowledge acquisition process should be devoted to providing them with some background in the domain. Some of this background may be obtained from good written materials, but in many cases these do not exist for the expert task being considered. Another way is for the project to jump right into the knowledge acquisition at the start of the first session with an expert, and let the knowledge engineers try to pick up the domain information bit by bit. This approach will work eventually but may be inefficient. A more effective strategy might be to devote a large portion of the initial period of knowledge acquisition directly to the task of giving domain background to the knowledge engineers. Thus at the first meeting or meetings, an expert can give the knowledge engineers an informal tutorial on the domain and the domain terminology.

Although there is a natural impatience to get right into the actual knowledge acquisition, references to domain concepts and terms occur over and over in the knowledge acquisition meetings, so it is usually useful to invest some time initially discussing the domain in general without focusing on the specific task. The amount of time spent on these discussions depends on the familiarity of the knowledge acquirers with the domain, the availability of other sources of information such as texts, the complexity of the domain, the amount of nonstandard vocabulary (jargon) used by domain practitioners, and the scope of the project. If the project is a major expert system development whose knowledge acquisition sessions might go on for several months or more, spending a significant amount of early time on domain background is a good investment.

One negative aspect is that after some meetings with an expert, there may not be a single piece of acquired knowledge to show anyone—most important, the project's upper management or the expert's management. If this situation might be a problem, one approach is to interleave the tutorial with some straight knowledge acquisition so that the sessions can display some early results. Another possible negative aspect is that none of the experts may have ever prepared anything like a tutorial. However, we discussed in Chapter 8 the worth of selecting project experts who communicate well, so this may not pose a large problem. In fact, it might be a good way to verify the judgment made on the communication skills of the experts involved. Nevertheless if the experts do have a problem with preparing or presenting a informal tutorial and if the project cannot or does not want to change experts, perhaps an informal question-and-answer session about the domain in general might accomplish the same purpose.

> The entire first week of knowledge acquisition meetings with our expert was devoted to a tutorial on telephone switching in general and on the No. 2 EAX structure. We asked the expert in advance to prepare the tutorial, and he was able to organize the material for us and provide a good overview of the domain—at least the parts of the domain that might be related to the *COMPASS* task.
>
> During this week, there was no mention of the specific task of *COMPASS*: the analysis of maintenance messages. Instead the knowledge engineers learned a lot of basic telephone switching ideas and No. 2 EAX jargon—information that would prove useful during the remainder of the knowledge acquisition. Furthermore when the actual discussions of the expert's task began, we did not have to interrupt to ask for definitions of terms or explanations of concepts nearly as much as we might have otherwise. Therefore the knowledge acquisition flowed more smoothly.

9.3.4 PREPARING A TUTORIAL DOCUMENT

It is useful to ask project domain experts to prepare a tutorial document on the domain. Depending on the skill of the experts in writing and preparing such a document and the availability of literature on the field, it could be nothing more than a compendium of pertinent pages photocopied from notes, reports, manuals, and data sheets, or it could be a full synopsis of the domain written especially for the knowledge acquisition team by the project experts. The document can be used initially as the basis of the tutorial and later as a reference. It can be made be available to knowledge engineers who join the project at later stages as well to aid them in learning about the domain.

> The *COMPASS* expert prepared a tutorial document by making a package of pertinent excerpts of several existing No. 2 EAX reports and publications. It gave the knowledge engineers a useful reference during and after the tutorial week. A copy of the document was given to each of the three new project members who eventually joined the project. The expert gave them private minitutorials as needed based on the document.

9.3.5 GIVING THE DOMAIN EXPERTS SOME AI BACKGROUND

Providing the experts a little background in AI, expert systems, computers, and related topics early in knowledge acquisition will allow them to understand better what the project is to accomplish, give them a start toward learning some AI jargon they might hear, and allow them to understand the purposes for the questions they will be asked. If it will not overwhelm the experts, project personnel may give them a brief tutorial and possibly prepare a tutorial document or recommend an introductory book or article.

> We gave a short overview on AI and expert systems to the *COMPASS* expert at our first meeting. We provided a few introductory articles but made sure that he did not feel pressured to read them. We felt that his time spent with us was making enough of an initial impact on his regular job and did not want him to feel that we were giving him homework.

9.3.6 USING WRITTEN MATERIALS FOR INITIAL KNOWLEDGE

Once the knowledge engineers have some basic background in the domain, it is time to start the actual knowledge acquisition. Books, manuals, or other written materials discussing the domain can form the basis of an initial knowledge base. In such written material, an expert has already extracted and organized some of the domain expertise. This organized knowledge might prove useful in building the system.

If detailed written material exists that is pertinent to the task, the analysis of this material may form a major part of the work on the expert system. For less complex domains this analysis might make unnecessary some (or even all) of the knowledge acquisition meetings with domain experts.

> We used the existing No. 2 EAX reports and publications to gain knowledge about the No. 2 EAX in general. Not surprisingly, however, there were not any written materials explaining the kind of analysis process our expert went through to find and repair problems in the switch or any written documentation of expert heuristics. Therefore we were unable to get any initial knowledge acquisition rules directly from books or reports.

9.3.7 INITIAL STEPS

An effective way to begin the knowledge acquisition is to have a domain expert methodically describe the task or, if the task is large, the first subtask that the knowledge acquisition will focus on. The expert should slowly step through the task for some test cases—at a speed far below normal—explaining in detail every step.

This process is often very difficult for an expert. One alternative is for the knowledge engineers to observe the expert performing the task in a real situation. Another alternative is to have the expert perform the task on a test case at close to normal speed, verbalizing whenever possible. In either case, the knowledge engineers can take notes or, better, audiotape or videotape the task performance. Videotaping has the advantage over audiotaping of capturing more of what is happening: the expert's movements, expressions, and surroundings, any diagrams or visual inputs utilized, and what the expert is looking at when each judgment is made. Audiotaping is cheaper, easier and faster to set up, and less obtrusive. Another possibility is to make a transcript of an expert's task performance for some real or test cases by having someone directly take down what happens, by transcribing from an audiotape or videotape of the expert performance, or, if the task involves interface with a computer, by keeping a record of the expert's interactions with the computer.

Whatever recording method is used, the expert should be asked to follow along with the task record, discussing in detail each step performed and each decision made. An audiotape or videotape of task performance can be played back one short segment at a time, and similarly a written transcription can be analyzed one line at a time. At each point, the knowledge engineers attempt to find out from the expert exactly what is being considered, what decisions are made, and why they are made.

> We initially used audiotapes in *COMPASS*, with the expert going through the task at close to normal speed and attempting to verbalize his decision processes. We obtained some initial idea of his domain techniques by this approach. However, after using this method for a brief time, it became clear that the expert was able to step slowly through his analysis while we interrupted him at each step to probe for his methodology. This approach seemed easier to use, and we adopted it.

9.4   DOCUMENTING THE KNOWLEDGE

In order to discuss more fully the techniques that can be used to elicit the knowledge, it is useful to describe first what that knowledge will look like and what techniques can be used to document it.

9.4.1 USING QUASI-ENGLISH KNOWLEDGE ACQUISITION RULES

An effective technique for documenting the expert domain knowledge is to use quasi-English *if-then* rules whenever possible. When rules cannot be utilized reasonably, quasi-English procedures can be used.

When an expert describes a heuristic for a particular circumstance, it can be formulated by a knowledge engineer into an *if-then* rule. The formulation is examined by the expert to see if it is acceptable. If not, the knowledge acquisition team and the expert discuss how to modify the formulation so that the expert can accept it.

Utilizing *if-then* rules for documenting the knowledge acquisition allows the knowledge to be acquired in independent chunks in a way that might become a basis for a rule-based implementation. This technique, however, in no way forces the implementation to utilize the rule paradigm, and thus a knowledge acquisition rule might be implemented, for example, as part of a frame structure or as a piece of programming language code.

The project's domain experts should be able to understand the *if-then* rule method of knowledge representation more easily than other AI paradigms. After some exposure, they might be able to relate some of the domain knowledge to the knowledge engineers utilizing this paradigm directly by stating their heuristics in the form of *if-then* rules. Moreover other experts in the domain who are involved in program evaluation or technology transfer should be able to read and understand the documentation in the form of quasi-English rules.

> In the *COMPASS* knowledge acquisition, we almost always used quasi-English *if-then* rules for knowledge documentation. They proved to be an easy-to-use and easily understandable way to formulate most of the expert's knowledge. A rule from the *COMPASS* system documentation is shown in Figure 9.1. The full English equivalent of this rule is shown in Figure 9.2. Occasionally we used other forms of knowledge documentation. For example, a complicated looping procedure was documented as a quasi-English procedure (Figure 9.3). Additionally when a large amount of data was found related to some items, it was documented in tabular form.

> The *COMPASS* domain expert could easily read and refer to the documented rules. Other No. 2 EAX experts asked to evaluate *COMPASS* could read the rules and procedures directly as written. They therefore were able to under-

NR 20 XY ANALYSIS RULES

. . . . .
. . . . .
. . . . .

BC DUAL EXPANSION ONE PGA DOMINANT LARGE NUMBER MESSAGES
ANALYSIS RULE

If   There exists a BC Dual Expansion One PGA Dominant Problem
and
      The number of messages is five or more
Then
      The fault is in the PGA of the indicated expansion (.5)
and
      The fault is in the PGA of the silent expansion (.3)
and
      The fault is in the IGA (.1)
and
      The fault is in the Backplane (.1)
Because
      Most messages are in one expansion, so the problem is
      probably in that PGA.

. . . . .
. . . . .
. . . . .

FIGURE 9.1 A rule from the *COMPASS* documentation

stand the knowledge inside the system with little prior briefing on *COMPASS*
and expert systems in general and with no knowledge of expert system
knowledge representation paradigms.

We were often able to implement a knowledge acquisition rule by one or
more implementation rules in KEE (usually with associated Lisp functions).
When this could be done, it allowed a nice isomorphism between the knowledge and the implementation, which would not have been possible if the
documented knowledge were not in rule form.

9.4.2 THE KNOWLEDGE DOCUMENT

The expert rules and procedures should be documented as they are found.
It is valuable to keep them in a formal knowledge document, which is
generated incrementally and maintained continually during the entire course
of the knowledge acquisition.

The knowledge document should be a primary tool of the project's
knowledge engineers and domain experts, frequently referenced during the
knowledge acquisition process. Other domain experts can examine it to
help them understand and evaluate the system. In addition, since the

BC DUAL EXPANSION ONE PGA DOMINANT LARGE NUMBER MESSAGES
ANALYSIS RULE

If   The analysis process, thus far, has identified a group of
      Network Recovery 20 maintenance messages as corresponding
      to a "BC Dual Expansion One PGA Dominant Problem" (that
      is, the problem has been identified as pertaining to the part of
      the network related to the B-switch and the C-switch, there
      are two expansions, and the maintenance messages for paths
      related to the Preliminary Grid Assembly card in one of the
      expansions clearly dominate in number over the maintenance
      messages related to the Preliminary Grid Assembly card in the
      other expansion)
  and
      The number of messages in the group of Network Recovery
      maintenance messages is five or more
Then
      A possible site of the fault causing the group of maintenance
      messages is the Preliminary Grid Assembly card in the
      expansion with the dominating number of maintenance
      messages, with an estimated likelihood of 0.5
  and
      A possible site of the fault causing the group of maintenance
      messages is the Preliminary Grid Assembly card in the
      expansion with the smaller number of maintenance messages,
      with an estimated likelihood of 0.3
  and
      A possible site of the fault causing the group of maintenance
      messages is the Intermediate Grid Assembly card in the
      network unit, with an estimated likelihood of 0.1
  and
      A possible site of the fault causing the group of maintenance
      messages is the back of the network units (the backplane),
      with an estimated likelihood of 0.1
Because
      Most of the maintenance messages are in one of the two
      expansions, so the cause of the problem is probably the
      Preliminary Grid Assembly card in that expansion.

FIGURE 9.2 Full English equivalent of the rule in Figure 9.1

knowledge document describes all the domain knowledge that must be
implemented in the expert system program, it can be considered a specification for the knowledge implementation.

The knowledge document should become part of the final documentation of the project. When the rule paradigm is used for implementation
and the rule language allows the implementation rules to be readable and
to correspond closely to the knowledge acquisition rules, it may be possible

SMA 63 POSTCLUSTERING

SUB-STEP 3 PROCEDURE

1. Find the largest remaining Possible Sender Cluster, "X".

2. Apply the SENDER PROBLEM RULE and the BORDERLINE SENDER RULE to X.

3. If X is a Sender Problem or a Borderline Sender Cluster, remove X from the remaining Possible Sender Cluster list and go to Line 1, above. Otherwise, compute the average size of all the Possible Sender Clusters remaining (including X) and round up. This is the "Average Unbroken Sender Cluster Size". Then delete all remaining Possible Sender Clusters including X.

4. Apply the BORDERLINE/DEFINITE TRUNK RULE.

FIGURE 9.3 Documentation of a *COMPASS* procedure

for the knowledge document, or at least parts of it, to be generated from the corresponding implementation.

The *COMPASS* knowledge document was used extensively throughout the project, and it was an important part of the final documentation. We referred to it continually in every knowledge acquisition session. When we wanted the consulting experts to validate the knowledge in *COMPASS*, we sent them copies of the knowledge document.

9.4.3 READABILITY OF THE KNOWLEDGE DOCUMENTATION

The knowledge acquisition team should devise conventions for documenting the knowledge to improve readability and clarity. Since the documentation of the knowledge will be used for several purposes by people of varying backgrounds, it must not be ambiguous or confusing.

The rule from the *COMPASS* knowledge document in Figure 9.1 shows the manner in which we documented *COMPASS* rules. Note the use of capitalization and indentation to make the rule more readable.

All the conventions we used were clearly defined and used consistently. For example, the *COMPASS* knowledge document makes clear (though not shown in the figure) that a number in parentheses in the rule is the likelihood that the fault is in the cited location.

9.4.4 TERMINOLOGY USED IN THE KNOWLEDGE DOCUMENTATION

The rules and procedures in the knowledge documentation should use standard domain terminology, categories, and jargon that practitioners of the domain will understand. Any special conventions used should be clearly specified.

Since knowledge engineers often begin an expert system project unfamiliar with domain terminology, it should not be too difficult for them to accept the standard usage within the domain. The terms may seem awkward or, worse, counterintuitive, but they are grounded in usage. The knowledge engineers should acquire proficiency in the use of these terms through repeated use during knowledge acquisition sessions. Moreover knowledge acquirers, by their very nature, should be people who find it relatively easy to talk with people from completely different fields from their own, using the terminology of that field.

It is more difficult for domain experts to adopt terminology differing from that which they usually use and may make their roles in knowledge acquisition much more difficult for them. Furthermore consulting domain experts and other domain personnel who spend only a small amount of time working with the expert system project will likely have difficulty reading knowledge documented with nonstandard terms.

> The *COMPASS* knowledge document employs standard No. 2 EAX terminology and jargon throughout. In the rule shown in Figure 9.1, domain terms such as *expansion* and *backplane* are used. Domain acronyms such as *PGA* (Preliminary Grid Assembly) are used without expanding them, as is standard practice among domain personnel.

> We used the standard domain terms from the beginning of the knowledge acquisition. The knowledge engineers were able to learn fairly rapidly to use the correct terminology. A few domain terms caused some problems. For example, NOT, meaning "Network Outlet Terminal" is a common No. 2 EAX term, but it caused us confusion. Did a rule called "NOT ADJACENT RULE" apply to the situation when a NOT was adjacent to something or to the situation when there was not any adjacency? We finally had to establish our own convention: we would never use *not* for negation—instead we used *no, isn't, doesn't,* and so on. Following this convention was not (that is, *wasn't*) very easy.

9.4.5 DEVISING TERMINOLOGY FOR DOCUMENTATION AND DISCUSSION

During the knowledge acquisition it is likely that terms will be needed to denote some concepts for which there are no existing domain terms. An expert's inner reasoning usually includes many intermediate concepts that neither the expert nor anyone else in the field ever had to name. The knowledge acquirers and the expert have to agree on terms for these concepts. When coining new terms, they should make sure that the devised terms do not conflict with or have the possibility of being confused with any existing domain terminology or jargon, and they should define the new terms as clearly and completely as possible.

The definitions of these terms should be part of the documented knowledge. If any definition changes as the project evolves, the new definition should be agreed on explicitly and revised in the knowledge documentation.

It may seem convenient to use simple but slightly inaccurate terms for these concepts rather than more accurate but unwieldy terms. This approach can lead to trouble. It is easy for someone to misuse a newly defined term when its meaning in the context of the project differs from the common meaning of the term. Thus the knowledge acquisition team should reject the use of a term whose coined meaning disagrees with its inherent meaning.

In the *COMPASS* knowledge acquisition sessions, we coined terms for concepts for which no domain terms existed. For example, although the *COMPASS* expert and all maintenance personnel who perform No. 2 EAX analyses group together sets of maintenance messages that have certain commonalities, there was no term to denote one of these groups of messages—probably because these groups are an intermediate result in the analysis process. In the *COMPASS* knowledge acquisition, however, these message groups were major subjects of discussion, referenced in many knowledge acquisition rules. Therefore we needed a term to refer to them and decided to call them *Clusters.*

The word *Cluster* itself was a good selection and caused us no trouble, but there was some difficulty in terminology related to its use. After some Clusters are eliminated for various reasons, each Cluster that remains corresponds to a problem that *COMPASS* has found in the No. 2 EAX. Therefore we started calling the same group of messages a *Problem* (as used in Figure 9.1). The use of two terms, *Cluster* and *Problem,* to mean more or less the same thing led to difficulties for us. When was a set of messages a Cluster, and when did it become a Problem? This simple situation often led to confusion. We could have avoided this situation had we made rigorous definitions of terms.

On the other hand, from the outset we always made a clear distinction between what we meant by a Problem and what we meant by a Fault (that particular part of the No. 2 EAX that must be repaired). Thus we had no troubles caused by the use of both of these concepts together, as in Figure 9.1.

Even in well-defined fields with long histories it still may be necessary to coin terms. For example, in an earlier work of mine studying automated recognition of printed music notation, I was surprised to find that there is no term in music literature for the class of symbols made up of the sharp, the flat, and the natural. These symbols are called *accidentals* when they precede a note and modify its pitch but are also used in key signatures to denote the key of the music. From a literature search and discussions with musicologists, I was unable to find a term in music to denote this class of symbols independent of syntactic use. Undoubtedly the reason for this is that a general term for the set of symbols has never been needed. In automated recognition, however, there are many instances when the same procedures can be used for symbol recognition without regard to the syntactic use of a symbol. My program, *DO-RE-MI*, often was able to determine that an unknown symbol was a "sharp or flat or natural" and would then invoke procedures to determine which of the three symbols it was. Consequently the class consisting of symbols that are a "sharp or flat or natural" was a concept *DO-RE-MI* frequently employed. Therefore I found it very convenient to have a name to refer to this symbol class and coined the term *sofon*, an acronym for "sharp or flat or natural." I thought it very interesting that a concept so seemingly basic had never been named in hundreds of years of widespread use of music notation.

9.4.6 IDENTIFYING THE KNOWLEDGE ACQUISITION RULES AND PROCEDURES

It is usually good practice to give the knowledge acquisition rules unique descriptive names—lengthy if necessary—rather than identifying them by short phrases or numbers. The rule name should be descriptive enough to ensure that it will be unique.

The set of rules will be changing continually during knowledge acquisition, sometimes rapidly. These changes continue throughout the life of the program, including later in program maintenance. Rules are regrouped, new rules are added, and old rules are deleted, combined, or split. If rules are numbered, they must be renumbered continually. Use of short names often requires a name to be changed to distinguish it from a newly found rule in a closely related area. Lengthy names are cumbersome, but they clearly define the rule and usually remain constant while the ruleset is changing. Also the use of descriptive names helps the knowledge acquisition team remember the function of a rule when it is tracing through the rules or when it considers a rule it has not examined for a while.

In Figure 9.1, the *COMPASS* rule name "BC DUAL EXPANSION ONE PGA DOMINANT LARGE NUMBER MESSAGES ANALYSIS RULE" indicates, however awkwardly, that this is the expert rule to be applied in the Analysis stage of the task under the following specific situation: the system has narrowed the problem to the BC portion of the switch, there are two expansions, the number of messages for one of the two PGAs is significantly more than (dominates) the number of messages for the second PGA, and the total number of messages is large (as defined in this rule as "five or more"). The very long rule name stayed with the rule throughout the development, while other rules changed. In the *COMPASS* implementation, the KEE rule that implements this knowledge rule is given the same name (within allowable rule name syntax).

9.4.7 ORGANIZING THE KNOWLEDGE ACQUISITION RULES AND PROCEDURES

The knowledge acquisition rules and procedures should be organized to make the knowledge documentation easy to use. For example, the documented rules should be grouped into divisions that are meaningful to the domain. This organization aids in locating particular rules in the documentation and puts related rules together, which facilitates document editing. If possible, the implementation should follow this grouping, but organizing the documented rules is useful even if the implementation cannot correspond.

> In the *COMPASS* knowledge document, we organized the rules by the maintenance message type being analyzed. Within that, we grouped the rules by the stages of *COMPASS* processing, and within that by common characteristics that are meaningful in the domain. For example, in Figure 9.1, **NR 20 XY ANALYSIS RULES** refers to a group of rules that all relate to a particular class of switch problems and that all apply during a particular stage of processing. Specifically they are the set of rules that apply in the Analysis stage of *COMPASS* for NR 20 messages and that deal with switch problems that an expert would consider to be of the "XY" type.

9.4.8 UTILIZING AN EXPLANATORY CLAUSE

Including an explanatory part of each knowledge acquisition *if-then* rule is very helpful. An explanatory clause (such as a BECAUSE clause) appended to an *if-then* rule provides additional information on a domain expert's justification of a rule.

Although by design the explanatory clause should have no effect on the operation of the expert system, it helps experts and knowledge engineers remember why they defined certain rules as they did. It is not an infrequent occurrence for the knowledge acquisition team to look at a knowledge acquisition rule they defined a month or more ago and have no idea why it had certain provisions and lacked other ones, why certain bounds to its use were set, or why certain parameter values were used. The explanatory clause can document why these decisions were made.

The explanatory clause also can document these decisions to aid consulting domain experts and, later, the maintainers of the system. The explanatory clause also might be used in an explanation or justification component of the system. It could, for example, be produced when the system is queried as to why a certain rule holds.

> The *COMPASS* rules originally did not have an explanatory clause. Occasionally we found that when we examined a knowledge rule that we had not looked at in a while, we could not remember exactly why something was done a certain way. We had to utilize valuable knowledge acquisition time

reconstructing our previous reasoning. Furthermore we found related problems occurred when the *COMPASS* rules were read by persons outside the *COMPASS* development team (such as outside domain experts examining the knowledge base or personnel involved with program maintenance). Sometimes they found it difficult to understand the reasoning behind certain parts of *COMPASS*. The addition of BECAUSE clauses to *COMPASS* knowledge rules that were not self-explanatory has minimized these problems.

9.4.9 DOMAIN DESCRIPTION AND GLOSSARY

Users of the documented knowledge who may be unfamiliar with the domain, such as the expert system developers, system operators, and system maintainers, will find helpful a description of the aspects of the domain that most relate to the expert system. This description might be put in an introductory part of the knowledge documentation, in an appendix, or at selected points throughout the documentation.

Such users will also benefit from the inclusion of a glossary of pertinent domain terms. Even more important, a glossary can provide definitions of all the terms coined by the knowledge acquisition team to denote concepts for which there were no domain terms or to denote parts of the expert system and its structure. It can include any computer- and AI-related terms that may be needed by domain experts or other non–AI people referencing the documentation.

The introductory part of the *COMPASS* knowledge document included a brief discussion of the No. 2 EAX domain. Some domain-clarifying discussions were included as needed at various points of the documentation.

The knowledge document contained an extensive glossary of close to 150 terms. A majority of these were specific No. 2 EAX terms (such as *Intermediate Grid Assembly, NUC,* and *Junctor Grouping Frame*), while several others were telephone switching or general telephony terms *(Tip, Trunk,* and *Service Circuit)*. The preponderance of these terms in the glossary reflected our goal of documenting the knowledge using domain terms whenever possible. Other important entries in the glossary were terms denoting intermediate or previously undefined concepts in the analysis such as *Cluster,* and *Unidentifiable Linked*.

9.5   ACQUIRING THE KNOWLEDGE

The major portion of the knowledge acquisition process is the lengthy time spent with domain experts eliciting and modifying the domain knowledge.

9.5.1 BASIC KNOWLEDGE ACQUISITION CYCLE BEFORE IMPLEMENTATION

Early in the project and other times when there has not been a significant amount of implementation of a particular area of knowledge, an effective technique for knowledge acquisition is to follow a basic cycle of (1) elicit, (2) document, and (3) test, as shown in Figure 9.4. A simple example of this approach was shown in Box 2.1. This technique is useful when not enough knowledge has been found about the subtask of interest to warrant meaningful implementation. In addition it is useful when the knowledge found is likely to have continuing and major changes. In this case, it may be easier to use a paper version of the knowledge than to implement the knowledge and constantly have to change the implementation. A third situation where this technique is useful occurs when the implementation of the knowledge is being developed but the implementers have not caught up to the knowledge acquirers. In all of these cases no computer implementation of the knowledge is available to aid the knowledge acquisition, and the following knowledge acquisition technique, in which the knowledge already documented is hand simulated, can be used (Figure 9.4):

1. Elicit knowledge from a domain expert. During early knowledge acquisition, obtain this knowledge from written materials (if available) or the expert's initial descriptions of the task methodology. Later obtain it from the results of the testing (Step 3).

2. Document the elicited knowledge.

3. Test this new knowledge (in conjunction with all of the previously acquired knowledge) by the following technique:

■   Have the expert analyze a new situation (a new set of data) in the normal task manner, or utilize the results of a prior analysis by the expert.

FIGURE 9.4 Knowledge acquisition cycle with hand simulation

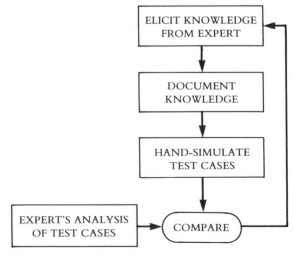

■   Analyze the same situation (the same data) using hand simulations of the documented knowledge. For example, if all the knowledge is in rule form, decide which rule would fire first, which rule next, and so on until the analysis is completed.

■   Compare the results of the expert's analysis against those of the hand simulation.

■   If the results differ, find the rules or procedures that produced the discrepancy: have the expert and the knowledge acquisition team follow the reasoning of the hand simulation step by step until a difference from the expert's reasoning is found.

■   Go back to Step 1 and elicit new knowledge from the expert on how to modify the rules and procedures that caused the discrepancy to make them come into agreement with the expert analysis.

The knowledge acquisition process continues to cycle through these three steps, revising and expanding the documented knowledge, until a body of knowledge has been found and implemented.

> We followed the elicit-document-test cycle when we began the *COMPASS* knowledge acquisition. Afterward we used this knowledge acquisition process each time we initially examined a new area of reasoning. We continued using it until we had built up enough fairly stable knowledge about the area that it seemed reasonable to begin implementation.

9.5.2 BASIC KNOWLEDGE ACQUISITION CYCLE AFTER IMPLEMENTATION HAS BEGUN

An effective technique for knowledge acquisition when an implemention of the already-acquired knowledge is available is to follow a basic cycle of (1) elicit, (2) document, (3) implement, and (4) test, as shown in Figure 9.5.

As the knowledge acquisition proceeds and a small body of somewhat stable knowledge has been found, the knowledge should be implemented. Note that a major distinction between expert system development and conventional software development is that in developing an expert system, implementation of the system starts very early—well before anything close to the total specification of what is to be implemented is known.

When a computer implemention of the knowledge is available, the following knowledge acquisition technique (Figure 9.5) can be used:

1. Elicit new knowledge from a domain expert using the hand-simulation technique or the results of the testing (Step 4).

2. Document the elicited knowledge.

3. Implement the elicited knowledge by adding to or modifying the existing expert system program.

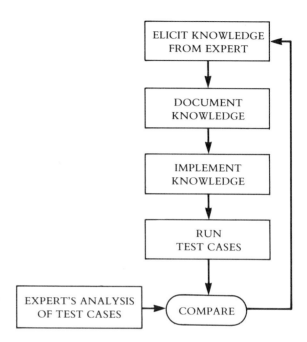

FIGURE 9.5 Knowledge acquisition cycle with program runs

4. Test this new knowledge (in conjunction with all of the previously acquired knowledge) by the following technique:

■ Have the expert analyze a new situation (a new set of data) in the normal task manner or utilize the results of a prior analysis by the expert.

■ Run the newly modified expert system program for the same situation, using the same data.

■ Compare the results of the expert's analysis against those of the implemented program. (Sometimes a comparison is not necessary. The program may produce obviously wrong results or may not run through to the end. Either of these cases indicates incomplete or incorrect heuristics or mistakes in the implementation. Often the causes of such problems are not hard to find, and the problems can be corrected immediately.)

■ Where the results differ, find the rules or procedures that produced the discrepancy: the expert and the knowledge acquisition team can examine in the documented knowledge the set of rules and procedures related to the discrepancy and hand simulate small parts of the analysis to see if these rules and procedures agree with the expert's analysis. To aid this process, the computer implementation might be used to produce a trace of the system's reasoning or to provide intermediate results.

■ If the hand simulation of the documented knowledge agrees with the expert, look for an implementation error in the program. If they do not agree, go back to Step 1 and elicit new knowledge from the expert on how to modify the rules and procedures that caused the discrepancy to make them come into agreement with the expert analysis.

This process continues, cycling through the four steps, for the remainder of the knowledge acquisition in the area of knowledge. In this way the expert system program as well as the documented knowledge are continually revised and expanded.

This cycle was the methodology that we used repeatedly throughout the *COMPASS* knowledge acquisition. It was most useful when a large section of knowledge had been completed, and we wanted to refine it.

9.5.3 USING TEST CASES TO ELICIT EXPERT KNOWLEDGE

When considering a new area of the domain, the knowledge acquisition team can go through several test cases with a domain expert, formulating and documenting for each test case the rules and procedures that the expert used to perform the task. Then a large number of additional test cases can be used to expand and modify the initial knowledge.

For each test case, the existing rules and procedures are used to attempt to perform the task. This process can be done by hand simulation or, if the pertinent domain knowledge has already been implemented, by machine. For each case, the expert examines the reasoning of the system, step by step, and finds all points of disagreement. The expert and the knowledge acquisition team then try to modify and expand the existing rules and procedures so that they work correctly—that is, their reasoning agrees with that of the expert. As the system gets bigger and the implementation grows, the expert's final results can be compared with those of the system, and only those cases where there is disagreement would be examined in detail.

We went through each test case with the *COMPASS* expert. He tried to explain each substep in as much detail as he could, and we formulated knowledge acquisition *if-then* rules or procedures to document each substep. We discussed each rule with the expert and modified it until he was satisfied. Since he knew that each rule was to be considered just as an initial version and would be subject to much change, he did not feel that accepting a rule was a major decision requiring long and deep thought.

We continued going through numerous test cases with the *COMPASS* expert. Rules and procedures were continually changed. At some points fairly early in the process, we (including the expert) thought that we were almost finished.

Subsequently we would find test cases that opened up completely new areas to consider and other test cases that pointed to major required changes and expansions to the existing rules and procedures. There were many subtle decisions and checks that the expert made in his analysis that he did not realize he was making until a test case pointed them out.

9.5.4 USING ACQUIRED KNOWLEDGE TO GUIDE RELATED KNOWLEDGE ACQUISITION

When the knowledge acquisition session begins to consider a domain area similar to another area for which knowledge has already been acquired, knowledge acquisition can be substantially facilitated by utilizing the acquired knowledge as a guide. Also when a mistake or needed modification is found for one rule, it is useful to consider corresponding rules in parallel areas to see if they need the same changes. These techniques are similar to the way humans modify their knowledge of a situation for use in comparable but unfamiliar circumstances.

In many cases, parallel situations require at least somewhat parallel rules and procedures. The number, organization, and structure of the rules and procedures for parallel or related situations may be similar. Therefore one way to aid the eliciting of knowledge from an expert is to use previously acquired knowledge for a parallel or related area as a template for the new knowledge. Sometimes this technique is of no use at all, but frequently it is helpful as a way to bring up issues of likely concern. Furthermore if subsequently the expert finds that changes need to be made to one of the rules or procedures, later effort can be saved by considering whether the same change is needed in analogous structures.

Often we were able to modify rules and procedures for one *COMPASS* maintenance message type for use with another message type. The organization of the rules and procedures was often quite similar.

Within a message type, we sometimes were able to modify a group of rules for one situation and use it for a corresponding situation. For example, rules for analyzing a No. 2 EAX A-Switch Problem were similar to rules for B-Switch Problems, C-Switch Problems, and so on. When we began looking into B-Switch rules, we copied the A-Switch rules, changed the As to Bs, and asked the expert to examine this new set of rules for applicability. In some cases the proposed new rules did not require much modification.

This technique is a way to speed knowledge acquisition, not a way to reuse knowledge. Each new message type or new area still had to be examined by the expert. We discussed with him whether simple modifications of the parallel rules and procedures might apply to the new situation and, if so, how the modification should be made.

9.5.5 USING KNOWLEDGE ACQUISITION FORMALISMS DIRECTLY

Having experts define their reasoning directly in terms of the types of knowledge acquisition *if-then* rules and procedures that will appear in the knowledge documentation is convenient. Early in the knowledge acquisition, it is beneficial to explain to the experts the ways the knowledge will be documented. As the knowledge acquisition process continues, interested experts begin to understand the use of *if-then* rules and other AI concepts (just as the knowledge engineers begin to understand some of the deeper concepts of the domain). This understanding may enable the experts to describe their domain knowledge by using the knowledge acquisition formalisms directly, thus speeding the knowledge acquisition process. In addition, it will help the experts interpret the knowledge base being built and will provide them a foundation to participate eventually in the maintenance of the expert system implementation.

> As the knowledge acquisition process continued, the *COMPASS* expert became increasingly familiar with the rule formalism used and was often able to formulate his domain expertise in that form. (At the same time, the knowledge engineers slowly became No. 2 EAX miniexperts.)

9.5.6 UPDATING THE KNOWLEDGE DOCUMENTATION

As the expert knowledge is acquired and revised, the knowledge documentation should be continually updated. During the the knowledge acquisition sessions, each knowledge engineer and expert should have an up-to-date copy of the knowledge documentation. When knowledge is being acquired and modified rapidly, new versions of the documentation should be made available as soon as possible.

> The *COMPASS* knowledge document was in our word processor and was updated and reprinted after every one-week knowledge acquisition session at least. When knowledge acquisition was rapid, we updated and reprinted it daily or even more frequently.

9.5.7 DEFERRING SPECIFICATION OF CERTAIN DETAILS

It is sometimes effective to use general phrases initially to define and document some knowledge acquisition rules and procedures instead of attempting to determine precise definitions immediately. For example, a general phrase might be used temporarily if an expert has trouble detailing or quantifying a specific knowledge item. This technique obviates the knowledge acquisition sessions' having to consider minor details before more important problems have been solved. It also takes some pressure off an expert at the beginning of the knowledge acquisition for a new area because some possibly difficult decisions, such as on precise breakpoints between two types of situations, can be deferred. Moreover it allows the expert to think more of the big picture at first. Later in the knowledge acquisition, the general phrase can be replaced by a specific quantity where possible, or techniques for dealing with uncertainty can be used.

> During *COMPASS* development, when the expert could not easily specify in detail some part of a knowledge rule, we tentatively used a phrase denoting the general concept. For example, when formulating some rules, the expert said that certain decisions could be made for a particular cluster of maintenance messages only if there were a sufficient number of messages in the cluster. He could not immediately define how many messages constituted a sufficient number but thought it was somewhere around five. Rather than spend valuable knowledge acquisition time to determine the definition of "sufficient number" at a time when we were just formulating basic rules, we decided to use the phrase "a sufficient number of messages" tentatively as part of several rules. A rule might state:

> *If* X is true,
>   *and* Y is true,
>   *and* there are a sufficient number of messages,
> *Then* conclude Z."

> The phrase was given a working definition of "five or more messages" to allow initial rule implementation. Only after several months was the phrase replaced in the rules by a specific number. The number turned out to be different for different rules in which the phrase was used.

> By being willing to use a general phrase when formulating the rule, we did not at that time have to delve into the question of how many messages were sufficient. It allowed us to concentrate on the higher-level issues, deferring the detail until later. Also it resulted in saving knowledge acquisition time since some rules using this phrase were eventually discarded completely and so any time spent defining those rules in detail would have been wasted.

9.5.8 GENERATING TEST CASES FROM TEST CASES

In many domains, each test case can be used to generate many additional test cases. Consider a particular test case in which some parameter X has the value 5. After a knowledge acquisition rule has been formulated based on this test case, the knowledge acquirers might ask the expert whether the rule would be the same if X were 1, or if X were 10, and so on (as long as these values of X were valid.) If the rule still holds, the applicability of the rule can be expanded. If not, the knowledge acquisition team can give consideration to the new situation, with the altered value of X. However, by considering this situation in the middle of the discussion of the original test case, the entire context of the new test case does not have to be discussed again in order to come to the point at issue. This technique often quickly generates several new knowledge rules.

> This technique worked very well in *COMPASS*. It frequently allowed us to examine several different situations based on a single test case.

9.5.9 ESTABLISHING A DEFAULT FOR CLOSE DECISIONS

Establishing one or more default meta-rules—basic assumptions to use for close decisions—is a valuable practice. When there are choices of which way a rule might be formulated (for example, more inclusive or more exclusive, more rigid or more flexible, more conservative or more liberal), a default meta-rule can provide guidance. The meta-rules should be part of the knowledge acquired from the experts and should come directly from domain concerns—is there generally more of a risk, more of a payoff, and so forth in slanting one way rather than another way? The meta-rules should be documented in the knowledge document and maintained, just as every other piece of acquired knowledge.

> After discussions with the *COMPASS* expert, we formulated a major Assumption about the No. 2 EAX maintenance domain. We documented it in the knowledge document as follows:
>
> > ASSUMPTION: In this domain, it is better to not find a problem that exists than to find a problem that does not exist (that is, false positives are worse than false negatives). A problem not found will probably be found on a subsequent *COMPASS* run. A false problem found entails unneeded work by switch personnel and may entail repair work on good components.
>
> Based on this assumption, we were able to decide many close calls. Should a rule identifying possible switch problems be more inclusive or more exclusive? Under the Assumption, the rule should be more exclusive, identifying only those potential problems that the knowledge acquisition team is fairly sure actually correspond to real problems.

9.5.10 FINDING THE EXTENT OF RULES

Generated test cases can often be used to find the edges of applicability of acquired rules and procedures. If Rule A (or Procedure A) applies in a certain situation and Rule B (or Procedure B) applies in a different but somewhat similar situation, a generated test case in between the two situations might help clarify the boundaries of A and B. For example, if a domain expert has defined one rule that applies for $X = 10$ and another rule that applies for $X = 20$, it is valuable to ask the expert to specify which rule applies if X were 15, 17, and so on. This type of question may make the expert uncomfortable because rules of thumb often do not have sharp boundaries. After some thought, however, the expert may be able to pick a reasonable cutoff point or might conclude that more information is needed, leading to an additional direction for the knowledge acquisition.

If an expert is unsure as to which of two rules applies for a certain situation, the expert system may not be too far wrong if it used either one. Hence the expert's selection of which rule applies for marginal cases may not be critical. Also here is where a default meta-rule can be very useful. If the expert is unsure as to whether $X = 17$ comes under Rule A or Rule B, a meta-rule can provide guidance, if one applies to the situation.

> We frequently used generated test cases to determine the extent of *COMPASS* rules, a technique that worked well. Often the *COMPASS* expert felt pressured as we tried to pin him down to specifying the exact cutoff point between two rules. He usually could make a reasonable decision, however, on rule extent, especially when we reminded him of the assumption that false positives were worse than false negatives and that if either of two rules seems to apply to a boundary case, then it may not matter which is used.
> The decisions he made on close cases were sometimes among the work he discussed with the consulting experts.

9.6   RECORDING THE KNOWLEDGE

Good techniques for initially recording the knowledge as it is acquired should support and speed the knowledge acquisition sessions while ensuring the accuracy of the final knowledge documentation.

9.6.1 FLEXIBILITY

When a new piece of domain knowledge is found at a knowledge acquisition session (for example, a rule for a particular situation is agreed upon), a record should be made of the new piece of knowledge. A member of the knowledge acquisition team can act as recording secretary and write down each new rule. Other possibilities might be considered; for example, each new rule might be entered directly into a word processor, or the whole session might be tape recorded, with agreed-upon rules transcribed later.

The method in which the knowledge is initially recorded at the knowledge acquisition sessions should allow for frequent changes in rules while they are being discussed and, if needed, should facilitate transfer of the knowledge to the knowledge documentation when the discussion is completed. It is wise to use the recording technique best suited to the knowledge acquisition—entering the recorded knowledge into the knowledge documentation at a later time if necessary—rather than to delay the knowledge acquisition sessions while the knowledge documentation is being produced. To speed the recording of the knowledge, it is worthwhile to define some reasonable conventions.

During *COMPASS* knowledge acquisition sessions, we wrote the knowledge acquisition rules and procedures on a whiteboard and, when a rule or procedure was agreed upon, took an instant photograph of the board. The knowledge document was updated as soon as possible after a day's knowledge acquisition session using the photographs (which were kept on file for reference). This technique proved useful in *COMPASS*, but did require that a project member spend a significant amount of time transcribing the information from the photographs.

A color code for different categories of information was helpful initially: black for new rules, blue for revisions of old rules, green for comments, and so on. After several sessions, as we became familiar with our knowledge recording and transcribing process, we abandoned the color coding.

9.6.2 RECORDING REMINDERS

During a knowledge acquisition session, the team sometimes comes upon topics to discuss or actions to take that are beyond the scope of the current discussion—for example, an obscure case that is complicated enough to require a significant amount of knowledge acquisition on its own. It may seem that the choice is to divert the knowledge acquisition session into a very detailed area and away from the main train of thought or, alternatively, to neglect considering the obscure case. Here it is useful to have a formal mechanism to record reminders. These reminders can be used to trigger a knowledge acquisition session at a later date. They should be made part of the knowledge document and treated as other acquired knowledge.

Reminders were treated as an outcome of knowledge acquisition, similar to the rules and procedures. They were updated, deleted, or expanded, just like the other knowledge, and were documented in a separate section of the knowledge document. Occasionally the knowledge acquisition team reviewed the reminders to determine if any item should be immediately treated or if any were no longer needed and could be deleted. If we decided to treat a reminder right away, it became the basis of the next knowledge acquisition discussions.

9.6.3 RECORDING BENEFITS OF THE EXPERT SYSTEM

Recording potential payoffs, benefits, and advantages of the expert system as the knowledge acquisition proceeds can be advantageous. During the knowledge acquisition sessions, sometimes a potential advantage or payoff that the expert system will offer is discussed. Although the major potential payoffs of the system should be clear, compiling a list of other advantages of the system is useful. Some of these may relate only to very specific situations and thus may be forgotten if not recorded.

During the course of the development of the expert system, the subject of potential system benefits may come up many times, such as when management requires cost justification of the system or when project personnel make presentations about the system or attend meetings where the system is discussed. For such purposes, having a long list of benefits is frequently important and is, at least, impressive.

> A separate section of the *COMPASS* knowledge document listed advantages of the expected final system. These advantages were treated as an outcome of knowledge acquisition; they were updated, deleted, or expanded just like the reminders, and were documented similarly.

CHECKLIST FOR ACQUIRING THE KNOWLEDGE

- ☐ Consider knowledge acquisition when selecting the domain.

- ☐ Choose a domain such that an expert system partially covering the domain is useful, at least initially; this selection allows knowledge acquisition to concentrate on one subdomain at a time.

- ☐ Choose a domain task that is decomposable, allowing knowledge acquisition to concentrate on one subtask at a time.

- ☐ Choose a domain that is fairly stable, thus minimizing the need to redo parts of the knowledge acquisition.

- ☐ Consider knowledge acquisition when selecting domain experts. As a major part of the process of selecting an expert, evaluate each expert's potential as a knowledge source.

- ☐ Select domain experts who have had enough domain experience to have been able to develop the domain insights that result in heuristics.

- ☐ Select experts who communicate well.

- ☐ Select experts who can commit the substantial time required for knowledge acquisition.

- ☐ Organize knowledge acquisition meetings so as to maximize access to the project's domain experts.

- ☐ Set up knowledge acquisition meetings so as to maximize the capability of the experts to demonstrate their expertise to the knowledge engineers—in the experts' usual environments if necessary.

- ☐ Organize knowledge acquisition meetings so as to minimize interruptions, possibly at a site remote from the experts' places of business.

- ☐ Consider the benefits of having the knowledge acquisition meetings at a site where the knowledge acquisition team can have access to the implementation.

- ☐ Weigh the advantages and disadvantages of having the knowledge acquisition meetings at the project team's business location. An advantage is to allow access to knowledge acquisition aids that may be available there; a disadvantage is the possibility of interruptions.

- ☐ Devote an initial period of the knowledge acquisition to an expert's giving the knowledge engineers a tutorial on the domain and the domain terminology, without any actual knowledge acquisition going on.

- ☐ Have the domain experts prepare a tutorial document on the domain for the knowledge engineers.

▭ Use books or other written materials discussing the domain to form the basis of an initial knowledge base.

▭ Begin the knowledge acquisition by having an expert go over a typical problem, explaining each step in detail.

▭ Use some form of quasi-English *if-then* rules to document expert knowledge whenever possible; use quasi-English procedures when rules cannot be reasonably utilized.

▭ Keep acquired rules and procedures in a knowledge document.

▭ Develop conventions for documenting the knowledge acquisition rules to add clarity.

▭ Use jargon standard to practitioners of the domain for the rules and procedures in the documented knowledge.

▭ Devise accurate terms for concepts for which no domain terms exist. Define the terms clearly, and document the definitions.

▭ Give the knowledge acquisition rules unique descriptive names (lengthy if necessary).

▭ Organize the documented rules and procedures to facilitate access and editing.

▭ Include an explanatory clause as part of each rule.

▭ Include a full glossary with the documented knowledge.

▭ When little or no knowledge has been implemented, follow a basic knowledge acquisition cycle of: (1) elicit, (2) document, and (3) test.

▭ When a significant amount of knowledge has been implemented, follow a basic knowledge acquisition cycle of: (1) elicit, (2) document, (3) implement, and (4) test.

▭ Initially elicit expert techniques by using a few test cases.

▭ Use a large number of additional test cases, when available, to expand and upgrade the initial knowledge.

▭ Get domain experts to define their reasoning in terms of knowledge acquisition rules and procedures, if possible.

▭ As the knowledge is acquired and revised, generate and continually update the knowledge documentation.

▭ Use general phrases to define knowledge acquisition rules and procedures initially, thus deferring concern about detail until higher-level items are decided.

▭ Use each test case to generate many additional test cases where possible.

▭ Establish default assumptions to guide close decisions in formulating rules.

☐ Use the generated test cases to find the extent of applicability of each rule.

☐ At the knowledge acquisition sessions, record acquired knowledge in a flexible manner.

☐ Use suitable conventions for knowledge recording.

☐ Record reminders to defer overly detailed or secondary items.

☐ Record potential payoffs of the expert system as they are discussed.

Prerau, Developing and Managing Expert Systems (Addison-Wesley)

CHAPTER 10

Representing the System Knowledge

- What techniques can be used successfully for representing expert knowledge for implementation?

- How can problem decomposition aid in knowledge representation?

- What are the strengths of each major knowledge representation paradigm?

- How can multiple knowledge representation paradigms be used together to best advantage?

- What are the benefits of reconsidering the representation later in the project?

As the expert system project acquires domain knowledge, the project's knowledge representers decide on the best ways to represent that knowledge in a computer program. They must find a means to represent every pertinent item, concept, relationship, and structure in the domain and in the expert reasoning about it. They can employ any or all of the AI paradigms made available by the project's selected knowledge engineering tool. The chosen representation scheme will be the basis of the knowledge implementation.

Knowledge representation is an important and difficult step in the development of an expert system. A well-chosen representation should enable the domain knowledge to be described clearly and concisely. It should be at an appropriate level of detail—emphasizing the more important domain concepts, including everything that is significant, but excluding all irrelevant detail. It should allow for the efficient implementation of the knowledge.

In this chapter, we discuss techniques that have proved useful for representing expert knowledge. We examine the major expert system knowledge representational paradigms, the advantages and disadvantages of each, and how groups of paradigms might be used together in a multiparadigm system.

10.1 DECOMPOSING THE PROBLEM

It is beneficial to the knowledge representation effort if the expert system task is decomposable into a set of steps. A domain task may have an obvious decomposition, at least to an expert, or a decomposition may be found during knowledge acquisition. Some problems, however, do not partition cleanly.

If a task decomposition can be found, it allows the expert system program to be modularized in a meaningful, convenient way. The knowledge representers can organize the representation around the task steps. Each step might be the basis of a separate representational structure. All the knowledge, data, and other items associated with the task step can be represented as parts of the corresponding structure or as other closely related structures. Each of these task step structures might eventually correspond to a separate program module, such as a knowledge base or a ruleset.

> The *COMPASS* developers, including the expert, did not know at first that the task of analyzing No. 2 EAX maintenance messages was decomposable. Therefore our initial knowledge representation for the *COMPASS-I* analysis of NR20 maintenance messages did not make use of any segmentation of the knowledge. After some time, we saw that the task could be decomposed into five major stages: Input, Identify, Analyze, Suggest, and Output. As we acquired more knowledge from the expert, we found that the expert analysis, and thus the knowledge representation, could be broken down further into nine steps within the five stages (Figure 10.1). Not only were these steps separable, but they were performed sequentially, with little or no backtracking.

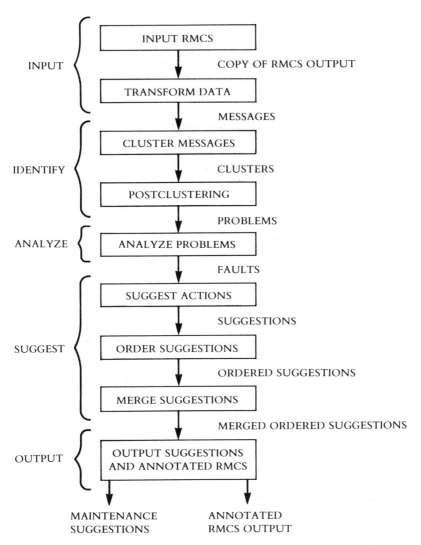

FIGURE 10.1 Nine steps of *COMPASS*

When *COMPASS* was expanded to cover other maintenance messages, we discovered that the five stage–nine step structure found for analyzing NR20 maintenance messages fit the added maintenance message types well enough to keep the same stage and step representation for all *COMPASS* maintenance message types. (To achieve this nice uniformity, we did, in a few instances, have to squeeze a knowledge item into a not exactly perfect representation. The gain of using a uniform mechanism throughout *COMPASS*—a mechanism already proved, represented, implemented, and debugged in *COMPASS*-1—outweighed the problems caused by occasionally having to use a nonideal representation.)

The *COMPASS* knowledge representation parallels the expert's nine-step procedure in analyzing the No. 2 EAX maintenance messages. To illustrate, Box 10.1 describes the nine steps for the analysis of NR20 maintenance messages.

BOX 10.1
THE NINE STEPS OF *COMPASS*'s NR20 ANALYSIS

COMPASS employs a nine-step process (Figure 10.1) to analyze each of the No. 2 EAX maintenance messages it covers. This process follows the steps of the *COMPASS* expert. The *COMPASS* analysis of NR20 maintenance messages illustrates this process.

1. **Input RMCS Step.** The maintenance message data—in this case, NR20 messages—from the No. 2 EAX being analysed are obtained from the RMCS connected to the switch (which has collected the switch's output). When performing the analysis manually, a No. 2 EAX maintenance person (such as the *COMPASS* expert) gets these data by typing a series of commands at the RMCS terminal to request that the desired data be collected from the RMCS and printed by the RMCS printer. *COMPASS* parallels this operation by connecting to the specified RMCS, requesting the maintenance message data, and accepting the data.

2. **Transform Data Step.** Once the No. 2 EAX maintenance messages are received, *COMPASS* transforms them into an internal form that it can handle—KEE frame structures. This step, necessary for *COMPASS*, does not correspond obviously to a step in the expert's analysis but might be considered as paralleling his reading the printed text of the RMCS output.

3. **Cluster Messages Step.** From this point on, *COMPASS* and the expert perform the same steps (except for any subtle points of the expert's analysis that might have been missed in the *COMPASS* knowledge acquisition). In this step, switch problems are identified by grouping messages into clusters, where a *cluster* is defined as a set of messages that are (expert analysis indicates) probably all caused by the same physical problem in the switch.

What is the idea behind the clustering? Each NR20 maintenance message indicates an electrical path across the switch through which the No. 2 EAX could not complete a telephone call. Therefore somewhere on the path there is a faulty component. Moreover the expert assumption is that there is only one faulty component. The maintenance message, however, does not indicate where on the path the fault occurred. (The No. 2 EAX does not have the time available or the capability to isolate a fault within a path; when it finds that a path is faulty, it aborts the call and prints a maintenance message, indicating the full path in which the fault occurred.) Thus there is no way to find the location of a fault from a single message. However, if several faulty paths all contain the same element or group of elements (e.g., a particular relay or wire), it is possible that the shared element is the cause of all the maintenance messages indicating those paths. Therefore, *COMPASS* groups together all maintenance messages that have certain commonalities that experts would consider physically meaningful. These clusters will be analyzed later to determine if the switch fault indicated by commonality does indeed seem to correspond to an actual physical fault in the switch.

As an example of clustering, consider the messages in Figure 10.2. (The figure presents only pertinent excerpts of the messages to simplify the explanation.) Message 18 and Message 24 do not seem very similar. They differ almost everywhere except in the first three digits of the last grouping of digits. However, experts would recognize the commonality shared by the two messages as meaningful. It indicates a specific No. 2 EAX problem, which is called an FGA problem. They would group these two messages in the same cluster (along with any other messages that are identified as having the same commonality) and would refer to the cluster as "FGA 8.2.0.3.x.x.x.x". Messages 24 and 37 are much more similar than Messages 18 and 24, differing in only a few digits. However, experts would recognize that the particular correspondence of Messages 24 and 37 is not meaningful; it does not indicate that the two messages may have been caused by the same switch problem. Therefore these two messages would not be grouped together in a cluster.

The Cluster Messages Step yields a large set of message clusters. Each cluster contains all the messages that have some particular physically meaningful commonality. For example, an output of this step might be as shown in Figure 10.3.

4. **Postclustering Step.** *COMPASS* employs expert techniques to clear up the many ambiguities that remain after clustering. These ambiguities often are very complex.

A large set of clusters is found in the Cluster Messages Step. After clustering, there almost always are some—and commonly a very large number of—ambiguities left concerning the cluster with which each message should be associated. These ambiguities occur because frequently many of the maintenance messages fall into two or more clusters; that is, maintenance messages often have physically meaningful commonalities with two or more other messages or groups of messages. For example, in Figure 10.4, Messages 39 and 47 have a "DE-TV 15.0.3.2.x.x.0.1" commonality, while Messages 47 and 52 have a "PGA 15.3.0.1.0.x.x.x.x" commonality. Thus the Cluster Messages Step will determine that Message 47 is in (at least) two clusters, the "DE-TV 15.0.3.2.x.x.0.1" cluster (Cluster 2 of Figure 10.3) and the "PGA 15.0.1.0.x.x.x.x" cluster (Cluster 8 of Figure 10.3). In *COMPASS*, clusters that contain one or more common messages are called *overlapping clusters*.

Some overlapping clusters are caused by random matches. The number of these random matches is increased significantly by the fact that a large part of the archi-

FIGURE 10.2 Excerpts of three No. 2 EAX maintenance messages (RMCS-formatted version). Only the first two messages have a meaningful commonality.

```
MESSAGE 18:   8   0.3.2.1.1.1.0.2   3.0.2.2.1.0.3   2.0.3.0.3.2.2
MESSAGE 24:   8   2.1.1.2.3.0.1.2   1.1.2.1.2.0.3   2.0.3.1.1.0.1
MESSAGE 37:   8   2.1.1.3.3.0.1.3   1.1.3.1.3.0.3   3.0.3.1.1.0.1
```

CLUSTERS
CLUSTER 1: BC 7.x.3.2.0.x.x.0.2
Composed of: MESSAGES 5, 6, 12, 13, 14, 15, 17, 21
CLUSTER 2: DE-TV 15.0.3.2.x.x.0.1
Composed of: MESSAGES 39, 42, 47, 58
CLUSTER 3: FGA 8.2.0.3.x.x.x.x
Composed of: MESSAGES 24, 29, 37, 53
CLUSTER 4: C-TO-D 7.3.3.3.2.x.2.x
Composed of: MESSAGES 8, 9, 10, 11, 30
CLUSTER 5: A-SWITCH 8.0.2.2.0.3.x.x.x
Composed of: MESSAGES 44, 45, 48, 49
CLUSTER 6: FGA 7.2.2.3.x.x.x.x
Composed of: MESSAGES 3, 12, 13, 17, 21
CLUSTER 7: PGA 8.0.2.2.0.x.x.x.x
Composed of: MESSAGES 44, 45, 48, 49
CLUSTER 8: PGA 15.3.0.1.0.x.x.x.x
Composed of: MESSAGES 47, 52, 61
CLUSTER 9: E-SWITCH 15.2.0.1.3.x.x.x
Composed of: MESSAGES 39, 42, 47, 58
CLUSTER 10: BC 7.x.3.2.0.x.x.0.3
Composed of: MESSAGES 62, 64, 65

. . . . .

FIGURE 10.3 Typical information found by the Cluster Messages Step

tecture of a No. 2 EAX is based on each path at each point having four options, and therefore most of the "digits" in the No. 2 EAX maintenance messages are really quaternary numbers, 0 to 3. Because there are just four choices for each number rather than ten, a random agreement of small sets of digits for two messages is more likely.

There are many meaningful combinations of corresponding numbers that will form a cluster. The expert assumption is that each message is caused by a single fault, and, based on this assumption, a set of heuristics is used to eliminate random clustering. For example, in Figure 10.3 Message 47 is in both Clusters 2 and 8. In the Postclustering Step *COMPASS* analyzes all the maintenance messages in each cluster and concludes that Message 47 belongs in Cluster 2 and that its commonalities with the messages in Cluster 8 are random. Thus *COMPASS* determines that messages 39 and 47 of Figure 10.4 have a commonality because they were both caused by the same switch fault, while the commonality of Messages 47 and 52 is random.

Another common source of overlapping clusters is the situation where an identical set of messages is identified as several different problem clusters. In Figure 10.4, Messages 39 and 47 would be found by an expert to have several other commonalities besides the DE-TV commonality mentioned. Thus they would be together in several

```
MESSAGE  39:    15    1.0.2.1.0.2.3.2    0.3.2.2.1.0.1    2.0.1.3.0.0.3  ⎤─ DE-TV 15.0.3.2.x.x.0.1
MESSAGE  47:    15    3.0.1.0.2.0.3.2    0.3.2.1.0.0.1    2.0.1.3.0.2.1  ⎦
MESSAGE  52:    15    3.0.1.0.3.1.1.3    0.1.3.1.0.1.3    3.1.3.1.0.1.0  ⎤─ PGA 15.3.0.1.0.x.x.x.x
```

FIGURE 10.4 Excerpts of three No. 2 EAX Messages (RMCS-formatted version). The second message clusters with both the first and the third.

clusters. For example, in addition to the DE-TV cluster, the two messages would be found in the "E-Switch 15.2.0.1.3.x.x.x" cluster (Cluster 9 of Figure 10.3), which is made up of exactly the same messages as Cluster 2. Postclustering uses expert precedence relationships to disambiguate this type of situation. In our example, Cluster 2 would be selected as the real cluster and Cluster 9 would be eliminated.

The Postclustering Step contains expert heuristics to disambiguate several other complex cluster relations, such as clusters that are *associated* (related to switch parts tied together by circuit elements called junctors) and clusters that are *adjacent* (related to paths physically adjacent on connectors). Where possible, *COMPASS* determines with which cluster a message should be associated and thus disambiguates overlapping clusters.

This overlapping of clusters can get extremely complex, especially for No. 2 EAX message types SMA111 and SMA112. Although a particular SMA111 or SMA112 problem is caused by a single switch fault, the corre- sponding No. 2 EAX messages identify two different paths through the switch, only one of which contains the actual fault. There is no indication as to which of the two messages contains the switch fault. Therefore half of the paths identified by these messages have no faults and can be considered spurious data. The spurious messages greatly increase the complexity of the overlapping and the difficulty of the analysis. In some cases, there is not enough information to allow the disambiguation of the overlap between two clusters. Postclustering contains expert techniques to handle this situation.

The output of the Postclustering Step is a set of clusters of messages, each corresponding to one problem in the switch. We call these remaining clusters "problems." For example, an output of this step corresponding the data shown in Figure 10.3 might include the data shown in Figure 10.5.

5. **Analyze Problems Step.** *COMPASS* uses expert heuristics to analyze each problem cluster identified by the prior analysis and determine the single fault in the No. 2 EAX causing all the maintenance messages in the problem. The analysis is frequently complex. Although the expert assumption is that a single fault is causing all the maintenance messages, of almost all cases the No. 2 EAX maintenance message data are such that the best expert analysis will not be able to narrow the cause of the group of maintenance messages to a single switch fault. Instead the best result achievable is the production of a set of possible specific switch faults, any of which might have caused all the messages in the cluster. For example, the best expert analysis may determine that a certain cluster of messages was caused by either a malfunction in a particular circuit card, a malfunction in a second circuit card, or a defect in the wiring between them. However even the best expert would not be able to determine from the data which of the three faults actually caused the messages.

PROBLEMS

PROBLEM A: BC 7.x.3.2.0.x.x.0.2 + ADJACENT BC
Composed of: MESSAGES 5, 6, 12, 13, 14, 15, 17, 21, 62, 64, 65
PROBLEM B: DE–TV 15.0.3.2.x.x.0.1
Composed of: MESSAGES 39, 42, 47, 58
PROBLEM C: C–TO–D 7.3.3.3.2.x.2.x
Composed of: MESSAGES 8, 9, 10, 11, 30
PROBLEM D: FGA 8.2.0.3.x.x.x.x
Composed of: MESSAGES 24, 29, 37, 53
PROBLEM E: A–SWITCH 8.0.2.2.0.3.x.x.x
Composed of: MESSAGES 44, 45, 48, 49
PROBLEM F: PGA 15.3.0.1.0.x.x.x.x
Composed of: MESSAGES 52, 61
. . . . .

FIGURE 10.5 Typical information produced by the Postclustering Step.
Six problems were found from the ten clusters of Figure 10.3.

COMPASS typically finds one to five possible switch faults corresponding to each switch problem it has identified.

Each possible fault found for an identified No. 2 EAX problem is given an associated likelihood. This likelihood is the domain expert's estimate, based upon his years of experience, of the relative probability that the fault was the actual cause of the messages. Therefore for every No. 2 EAX problem, the output of the Analyze Problems Step is a list of the possible specific No. 2 EAX faults causing the problem, each with an associated likelihood. An example is shown in Figure 10.6.

6. **Suggest Actions Step.** For each possible fault identified for a particular switch problem, *COMPASS* determines one or more possible maintenance actions that could be suggested to the switchperson. This determination is based on expert knowledge of maintenance procedures. For example, for a possible bad circuit card, one maintenance suggestion would be to run a switch diagnostic test on the card while it remains in its slot in the switch. A second possible suggestion would be to replace the card with a spare card.

Each fault has one to four corresponding possible suggestions. The total list of suggested actions for a problem cluster usually has between three and twelve items. For every No. 2 EAX problem, the output of the Suggest Actions Step is a list of the possible suggested actions for each of the No. 2 EAX faults that may be causing the problem (Figure 10.7).

7. **Order Suggestions Step.** For each switch problem, *COMPASS* collects all the suggested actions for all the problem's faults and puts them in priority order. The prioritization utilizes expert heuristics and is based on these primary factors:

■ The likelihood that the corresponding fault is the actual cause of the switch problem.

PROBLEM FAULTS

PROBLEM A: BC 7.x.3.2.0.x.x.0.2 + ADJACENT BC
POSSIBLE FAULTS:
- Backplane/Piggyback Connector Fault
  Likelihood: 0.9
- PGA 7.0.3.2.0.x.x.x.x Fault
  Likelihood: 0.08
- IGA 7.3.0.2 Fault
  Likelihood: 0.01
- IGA 7.3.0.3 Fault
  Likelihood: 0.01

PROBLEM B: DE-TV 15.0.3.2.x.x.0.1
POSSIBLE FAULTS:
- IGA 15.0.3.2 Fault
  Likelihood: 0.35
- FGA 15.3.0.1 Fault
  Likelihood: 0.35
- TVCA Fault
  Likelihood: 0.2
- Backplane Fault
  Likelihood: 0.1

. . . . .

FIGURE 10.6 Typical information produced by the Analyze Problems Step

- The likelihood that the maintenance action will be effective, that is, will find or remedy the fault (assuming the fault is real).
- The ease of performing the maintenance action.
- The potential disruption that could result from performing the maintenance action (for example, the act of performing certain maintenance actions can disrupt service for a number of customers, and so experts try to perform such actions only when they are clearly required.)

The expert heuristics take all of these factors into consideration and put all the suggested maintenance actions into an ordered list. Thus for every No. 2 EAX problem, the result of the Order Suggestions Step is an ordered list of suggestions (Figure 10.8).

8. **Merge Suggestions Step.** Sometimes two or more maintenance actions can be performed simultaneously. For example, instead of a No. 2 EAX diagnostic test being run on a path through a particular circuit card and a second diagnostic being

SUGGESTIONS FOR PROBLEM FAULTS

PROBLEM A: BC 7.x.3.2.0.x.x.0.2 + ADJACENT BC

POSSIBLE FAULTS:

- Backplane/Piggyback Connector Fault
  SUGGESTIONS:
    -Perform Physical Test of Backplane/Piggyback
    Connector
- PGA 7.0.3.2.0.x.x.x.x Fault
  SUGGESTIONS:
    -Replace Circuit Card PGA 7.0.3.2.0
    -Perform Diagnostic on Path through PGA 7.0.3.2.0
- IGA 7.3.0.2 Fault
  SUGGESTIONS:
    -Replace Circuit Card IGA 7.3.0.2
    -Perform Diagnostic on Path through IGA 7.3.0.2
- IGA 7.3.0.3 Fault
  SUGGESTIONS:
    -Replace Circuit Card IGA 7.3.0.3
    -Perform Diagnostic on Path through IGA 7.3.0.3

. . . . .

FIGURE 10.7 Typical information produced by the Suggest Actions Step

ORDERED SUGGESTIONS FOR PROBLEMS

PROBLEM A: BC 7.x.3.2.0.x.x.0.2 + ADJACENT BC

ORDERED SUGGESTIONS:

1. Perform Physical Test of Backplane/Piggyback Connector
2. Perform Diagnostic on Path through PGA 7.0.3.2.0
3. Replace Circuit Card PGA 7.0.3.2.0
4. Perform Diagnostic on Path through IGA 7.3.0.2
5. Perform Diagnostic on Path through IGA 7.3.0.3
6. Replace Circuit Card IGA 7.3.0.2
7. Replace Circuit Card IGA 7.3.0.3

. . . . .

FIGURE 10.8 Typical results of the Order Suggestions Step

run on a path through a second card, often a single diagnostic can be run on a path through both cards. *COMPASS* uses expert knowledge of No. 2 EAX maintenance procedures to analyze the suggested maintenance actions for a problem. If two or more maintenance actions are found that may be performed simultaneously, they are merged into a single suggestion. For every No. 2 EAX problem where this merging occurs, the result of the Merge Suggestions Step is a revised ordered list of suggestions with all mergeable suggestions merged. For an example, compare Figures 10.8 and 10.9. Experts know that a single diagnostic test performed on Path 7.0.3.2.0.x.x.0.2.x.x.x.x will test a path through IGA 7.3.0.2, as well as a path through PGA 7.0.3.2.0. Thus, the second and fourth suggestions in Figure 10.8 can be merged into the single suggestion shown in Figure 10.9.

9. **Output Suggestions and Annotated RMCS Printout Step.** In the manual task, experts annotate the RMCS printout as they find problems. Depending on the circumstances, they may perform the recommended maintenance actions themselves (following the priority order) or ask other (usually lower-level) switch personnel to perform the tasks. When dealing with these other switchpeople, they use the accepted domain terminology and jargon, and they provide more detailed instructions for maintenance actions that are less frequently performed.

Correspondingly *COMPASS* prints two outputs. Its primary output is a prioritized list of suggested maintenance actions, using switch terminology and jargon. It gives greater detail about maintenance actions that are less familiar to the switchperson, while producing terse indications for common types of actions. The secondary output is a reproduction of the RMCS printout with a reasonable duplication of the annotating that an expert would do on it by hand. Samples of the two *COMPASS* outputs are shown in Figures 5.8 and 5.9.

MERGED ORDERED SUGGESTIONS FOR PROBLEMS

PROBLEM A: BC 7.x.3.2.0.x.x.0.2 + ADJACENT BC
MERGED ORDERED SUGGESTIONS:
1. Perform Physical Test of Backplane/Piggyback Connector
2. Perform Diagnostic on Path 7.0.3.2.0.x.x.0.2.x.x.x.x
3. Replace Circuit Card PGA 7.0.3.2.0
4. Perform Diagnostic on Path through IGA 7.3.0.3
5. Replace Circuit Card IGA 7.3.0.2
6. Replace Circuit Card IGA 7.3.0.3

. . . . .

FIGURE 10.9 Typical results of the Merge Suggestions Step. Compare with Figure 10.8.

10.2 PARADIGM(S) FOR REPRESENTATION

Presumably when the project is starting work on the knowledge representation, the software tool already has been selected, and thus the knowledge engineering paradigms available for knowledge representation are known. Based on what is known at the time about the domain and the expert analysis, the knowledge representers should consider the kinds of knowledge that need to be represented and try to select for each the best representation possible from among the available paradigms.

If only a single paradigm is available, such as in the use of a tool based solely on production rules or the development of an expert system directly in a programming language, that paradigm will have to be used to represent all the knowledge of the expert system—active knowledge and static knowledge, declarative knowledge and procedural knowledge, domain knowledge and program control. However, if multiple knowledge engineering paradigms are available, they should be used where they are most effective. In Section 7.7.2 we discussed the relative merits of using a software tool with multiple paradigms versus a tool that supports a single paradigm or the direct use of a computer language. Although hybrid tools have some negatives, from the standpoint of knowledge representation it is advantageous to have multiple paradigms in which to represent expert knowledge. They allow more power and greater flexibility in the representation, so that the knowledge representers should be able to produce a better, clearer, more elegant, more effective knowledge representation. In the following sections we consider for what purposes the different AI paradigms are well suited, assuming that the software tool gives some choice of representations.

To analyze switch maintenance messages and suggest maintenance actions, *COMPASS* utilizes a large amount of diverse knowledge, all of which must be represented. In the *COMPASS* program, knowledge in the following areas (among other things) must be represented:

- Generic structure of No. 2 EAX switches
- Structure of each individual No. 2 EAX switch being analyzed
- Makeup of switch maintenance messages
- Message commonalities that allow clustering
- Techniques for disambiguating message clusters
- Switch faults
- No. 2 EAX maintenance actions
- Techniques for prioritizing maintenance actions
- Techniques for merging maintenance actions
- Possible *COMPASS* outputs in No. 2 EAX terminology

- Expert techniques for relating all of the above
- Flow of *COMPASS* control

COMPASS represents this knowledge efficiently and effectively by utilizing KEE's multiple AI paradigms: object-oriented programming, frames with demons, inheritance, production rules, and Lisp programming.

In implementing *COMPASS,* we utilized all of these paradigms (and almost all other features provided by KEE). We tried to use each KEE paradigm to represent and implement those aspects of *COMPASS* for which it was best suited.

10.3 FRAMES, INHERITANCE, AND DEMONS

The important concepts and objects in the application area can be represented by frames, where each frame contains all the information related to its corresponding domain item. In a multiple-paradigm expert system, frames can form the basis of the implementation.

The use of interframe relations, such as subclass and instance, allows a frame structure to be built. Generic objects can be represented by class frames. A complex hierarchy of frame classes can be built corresponding to the way a part of the domain is organized (physically or conceptually). For example, a frame structure could represent the organization of a corporation, the taxonomy of a plant species, an expert's unique way of categorizing certain domain items into 12 categories with 26 subcategories and 47 subsubcategories, or the steps and substeps of the expert system program itself. Specific individual items would be represented by instance frames, inheriting information from the generic class frames. Information on relationships between classes and between objects, such as PART-OF, can be represented using interframe relations.

Frame structures can provide an easy-to-use mechanism for storing and retrieving data. Static data related to domain items can be stored in frames and referenced during a program run. Dynamically created data can be stored in precreated frame slots or in dynamically created slots. If the amount of data to be stored or retrieved gets very large, consideration might be given to using a standard database management system and having the expert system access the database. (Some software tools offer special mechanisms by which the tool allows easy access to large databases.)

In addition, a frame structure can be used to pass information to new objects created during a program run, without explicit action of the expert system program. A great deal of general information related to the members of a class can be stored in a generic class frame. Then when a new class member is found during a program run, a frame corresponding to the new member can be created dynamically as a child of the generic class frame, causing the frame inheritance mechanism to associate the generic information with the new frame automatically. For example, the knowledge acquisition rule,

> *If* a problem is identified to be "no fuel,"
> *Then* the remedy for the problem is to fill the gas tank

can be implemented implicitly using a frame structure rather than explicitly with a rule or with some programming language code. The REMEDY slot in the generic frame for the Class NO–FUEL–PROBLEM can be set to *Fill-the-gas-tank*. When a new object of Class NO–FUEL–PROBLEM is identified, say NO–FUEL–PROBLEM#18, a NO–FUEL–PROBLEM#18 frame is created as a child of the generic NO–FUEL–PROBLEM class frame. When this new frame is created, it automatically (that is, without specific action of the expert system program) inherits from the generic NO–FUEL–PROBLEM frame a REMEDY slot with value *Fill-the-gas-tank*. When this type of property passing is very common, frame inheritance proves convenient and useful.

Frame structure can be used to organize the program and make the locating of specific parts of the program easier and more natural (assuming that the software tool provides a good interface for viewing and manipulating frames). Other program paradigms can be associated with parts of the frame hierarchy. For example, methods associated with class NO–FUEL–PROBLEM can be stored in slots in the generic NO–FUEL–PROBLEM frame. Each child of NO–FUEL–PROBLEM inherits these methods. Rules related to objects of class NO–FUEL–PROBLEM might be placed in the generic NO–FUEL–PROBLEM frame or in an associated NO–FUEL–PROBLEM-RULES frame.

Demon mechanisms can be used in frame slots to delay computation until necessary and to initiate computation only when certain conditions occur. For example, rather than computing all values that might be required, a demon can be structured to activate computation only when the corresponding value is needed. The demon mechanism can cache computed values in slots to avoid unnecessary recomputation of values. An example of the use of the demon mechanism is discussed in Section 2.5.2.

> Most of the important concepts and objects in *COMPASS* are represented by KEE frames (called "units" in KEE). At the beginning of a run, *COMPASS* contains over 1,000 frames, with a total of over 15,000 slots. These numbers grow significantly as new frames are created during a run.
>
> Frame structures are used throughout *COMPASS* to organize and store knowledge. For example, Figure 10.10 shows a portion of the *COMPASS* frame hierarchy representing maintenance actions that *COMPASS* might suggest. This SUGGESTIONS hierarchy shows that there are several major classes

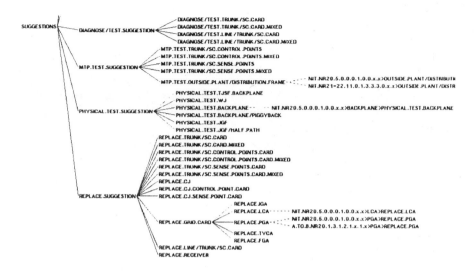

FIGURE 10.10 Portion of the tree of frames representing the SUGGESTIONS hierarchy

of maintenance suggestions, each with subclasses and some with subsub-classes (the subclass relation is represented in the figure by a solid line). The subclass frames that are the leaves of the SUGGESTIONS subclass tree (that is, the ends of the solid-line tree in Figure 10.10) represent the generic maintenance actions that a No. 2 EAX maintainer might take. Each frame contains generic information about the correspondence maintenance action.

For each of the many specific maintenance suggestions determined by *COMPASS* during a run, a corresponding frame is created as an instance of the pertinent generic frame. These generated frames thus inherit all of the information from their generic frame parent. Figure 10.10 shows some instance frames created during part of a *COMPASS* run (the instance relation being represented by broken lines). For example, for the possible Backplane Fault of the NIT.NR20.5.0.0.0.1.0.0.x.x Problem, *COMPASS* determined that a Physical Test Backplane action should be suggested. It then created a corresponding frame instance, which it named

"NIT.NR20.5.0.0.0.1.0.0.x.x>BACKPLANE>PHYSICAL.TEST.BACKPLANE",

as a child of the generic PHYSICAL.TEST.BACKPLANE frame (as shown in the figure). This new frame inherits from the generic frame all the properties that apply to every Physical Test Backplane maintenance action, such as the information that all Physical Test Backplane maintenance actions should be performed only during the low telephone traffic part of the day (since testing the switch backplane entails some risk of putting subscribers out of service).

A portion of the details of the generic SUGGESTIONS frame is shown in Figure 10.11. Each subclass frame of SUGGESTIONS (that is, each generic suggestion type) inherits each slot shown. Note, for example, the ATTACKABILITY slot (which indicates whether the particular suggestion type can be performed anytime or whether it is risky and should be performed only during low traffic) is inherited to each subclass. In each subclass frame, an ATTACKABILITY value is stored, based on knowledge about the corresponding suggestion type.

In addition to its value, each slot may have any of several facets, such as an inheritance mode, a value class for type checking or for designating a method, cardinality information (number of values allowed), and a comment. These facets are inherited. The ATTACKABILITY slot in SUGGESTIONS uses the ValueClass facet to restrict the set of acceptable values for the inherited ATTACKABILITY slot in each of its subclass suggestion-type frames to either "ANYTIME" or "LOW.TRAFFIC". The ATTACKABILITY slot for the subclass frame is thus restricted to one of these two values, and that value inherited to all the instance frames of the suggestion type created during a run. For example, all Physical Test Backplane maintenance actions should be performed only during low telephone traffic periods, and therefore the value of the ATTACKABILITY slot for the PHYSICAL.TEST.BACKPLANE subclass is set to "LOW.TRAFFIC." This value is inherited by the

NIT.NR20.5.0.0.0.1.0.0.x.x>BACKPLANE>PHYSICAL.TEST.BACKPLANE

frame and all other instances of PHYSICAL.TEST.BACKPLANE that might be created.

Lisp functions that relate to all suggestion frames are stored as methods in SUGGESTIONS and then inherited to all generic and instance suggestions. In Figure 10.11, the slot CRLF! contains a method used when data about each found suggestion are output.

COMPASS frames are also used to store data, such as the information related to the configuration of specific No. 2 EAXs in telephone companies. This information is static, changing about once a year. COMPASS uses this type of frame information as it would use a small database.

The COMPASS frame hierarchy is used to give structure to the data and rules. All rules reside in frames, which are grouped as children of ruleset frames. The Lisp code in COMPASS is accessed by calls to method slots in the related frames. By using the frame hierarchy effectively, we were able to structure the data and significantly reduce the number of rules required. A pure rule-based system probably would have required several hundreds or thousands of additional rules.

Demon mechanisms are used to increase the power of KEE rules by allowing a rule's slot access to invoke a complex function. For example, a rule might access the number of messages related to Network Unit Controller Copy 0 (NUC.0) by retrieving the value of the NUMBER.MESSAGES.NUC.0 slot, a simple slot value retrieval that the rule system allows. By use of a demon in the

```
The SUGGESTIONS unit
Unit: SUGGESTIONS in knowledge base SUGGEST
Created by ASG on  9-Oct    14:23:58
Modified by RER on 21-Feb    15:21:48
 Superclasses: (ENTITIES in KB GENERICUNITS)
 Subclasses: REPLACE.SUGGESTION, PHYSICAL.TEST.SUGGESTION,
MTP.TEST.SUGGESTION, DIAGNOSE/TEST.SUGGESTION, DIAGNOSE.SUGGESTION,
CALL, AWAIT.SUGGESTION, ANALYZE.SUGGESTION,
ADJACENT.MTP.TEST.SUGGESTION, UPDATE.SUGGESTION,
UNPLUG/REPLUG.SUGGESTION
 Member of: (CLASSES in KB GENERICUNITS)
─────────────────────────────────────────────────────────
MemberSlot: *ACTION from SUGGESTIONS
   Inheritance: OVERRIDE
   ValueClass: WORD
   Cardinality.Max: 1
   Values: Unknown

MemberSlot: *ATTACKABILITY from SUGGESTIONS
   Inheritance: SAME
   ValueClass: WORD (ONE.OF ANYTIME LOW.TRAFFIC)
   Cardinality.Max: 1
   Values: Unknown

MemberSlot: *CRLF! from SUGGESTIONS
   Inheritance: (METHOD in KB KEEROLES)
   ValueClass: (METHOD in KB KEEDATATYPES)
   Cardinality.Min: 1
   Cardinality.Max: 1
   Comment: "Return the character for carriage return/line feed"
   Values: CRLF

MemberSlot: *FAULT.TYPE from SUGGESTIONS
   Inheritance: SAME
   ValueClass: (SUBCLASS.OF FAULTS)
   Cardinality.Max: 1
   Values: Unknown

MemberSlot: *GENERIC.LOCATION from SUGGESTIONS
   Inheritance: OVERRIDE
   ValueClass: WORD
   Cardinality.Max: 1
   Values: Unknown

MemberSlot: *LIKELIHOOD from SUGGESTIONS
   Inheritance: SAME
   ValueClass: NUMBER |[0 1]
   Cardinality.Max: 1
   Values: Unknown

MemberSlot: *OUTPUT.TEXT from SUGGESTIONS
   Inheritance: OVERRIDE
   ValueClass: LIST
   AVUNITS: CREATE.OUTPUT.TEXT
   Cardinality.Min: 1
   Cardinality.Max: 1
   Comment: "The output form for this suggestion"
   Values: Unknown

MemberSlot: *OUTPUT.TEXT.FORMAT from SUGGESTIONS
   Inheritance: OVERRIDE
   ValueClass: LIST
   Cardinality.Min: 1
   Cardinality.Max: 1
   Comment: "The form to be filled in to create the OUTPUT.TEXT"
   Values: Unknown
```

FIGURE 10.11 Portion of the SUGGESTIONS frame

slot, however, this access calls a function that will go to the MESSAGES knowledge base, examine the pertinent maintenance message data, and compute the number of messages related to NUC Copy 0. The demon mechanism is also used to delay computation until necessary and to cache computed values in slots to avoid recomputation. Thus, if the number of NUC.0 messages is never needed, it will never be computed, and if it has already been computed and is needed again, it will reside in the slot and can be accessed without the demon function's being called. Demons also provided a means for transferring data between knowledge bases.

10.4 PRODUCTION RULES

The use of production rules is probably the most common technique for representing knowledge in expert systems. Furthermore, production rules are frequently the best way in a multiple-paradigm program to represent the active knowledge—the basic knowledge acquisition rules found from an expert. If the rule language is well constructed and flexible, the implemented rules can correspond to the knowledge acquisition rules and sometimes might look very much like them. Production rules are declarative and to some degree are independent of each other. Thus in many cases they can be treated modularly and added, deleted, and modified independently. This independence is convenient for development, but care is necessary: rules are not always as independent of each other as they might seem. Frequently they are quite interdependent, and sometimes the dependency relationship between two or more rules might be very subtle.

We discussed some of the basic ideas pertaining to production rules in Section 2.5.1. Rules can be used to represent several types of knowledge, such as situation/action, premise/conclusion, sufficiency, and definitions. They can represent uncertain situations by having some measure of uncertainty attached to a rule or a clause of a rule. Forward-chaining rules can be used to represent reasoning that is data driven, following a set of data to its conclusions. Backward-chaining rules are more appropriate when the reasoning is hypothesis driven, determining which of several hypotheses should be selected. If the task calls for it and the development system allows it, both chaining mechanisms can be combined.

Knowledge represented and implemented in rules is often easier to maintain than if another paradigm (such as programming language code) had been used. The ease of maintenance is due to the following factors:

1. Correspondence of knowledge acquisition rules and implementation rules. During program maintenance, when a needed change to the expert system knowledge has been determined and must be implemented, the correspondence of knowledge acquisition rules to implementation rules usually makes it easy to find where in the program a change should be made to implement the knowledge change. Also when it has been determined that a knowledge acquisition rule is correct but has been implemented incorrectly, the rule correspondence facilitates locating the implementation of that knowledge acquisition rule.

2. Readability. Because of the regular and often simple structure of rules, they are usually easier for maintainers to read and understand than other paradigms, such as program language code. Even if the rule language is such that the implemented rules appear obscure, the rule language is generally very restricted—certainly more so than a general purpose programming language. Therefore once maintainers learn the rule language, they usually find the rules much simpler to understand than a complex subroutine written in a general-purpose programming language.

3. Modularity. Rule modularity usually allows a rule to be modified for maintenance without necessitating changes in any other part of the implementation. It is generally much more difficult when making a change in program code to be sure that no other part of the program will be affected.

Sometimes a rule language is close to English. This closeness may be useful because it makes the rules easy to read. It may, however, cause more problems than it prevents since it is very easy for English-like implementation rules to be misinterpreted. Frequently such constructs are read erroneously due to the multiple meanings, shades of meanings, and ambiguities of English. Also large numbers of English-like rules may seem repetitious and verbose.

Production rules are good for hiding details. A knowledge acquisition rule beginning:

If the average height of a basketball team is greater than 7 feet,
Then . . .

can be represented by an implementation rule such as:

(RULE:
    (IF (GET-AVERAGE-HEIGHT *team*) GREATER-THAN 7)
    (THEN . . .))

where *team* is a variable. This rule representation corresponds closely to the knowledge acquisition rule, which makes the implementation rule relatively easy to be read and maintained. It hides the details related to finding the average height by using a call to the function "GET-AVERAGE-HEIGHT". The function is called when the rule's antecedent is tested for a particular team. It does all the work of actually getting the heights of each player on the team (probably by accessing the team frame, getting the set of players, and accessing the HEIGHT slot in each player's frame), averaging the heights, and returning the result. A similar result might be obtained if the average height was found from a slot value, access to which would in turn activate a demon.

COMPASS uses KEE production rules to represent many of the knowledge acquisition rules acquired from the expert. It contains over 400 KEE rules.

Since the expert's COMPASS analysis was data driven, we used KEE forward-chaining rules. For example, the knowledge acquisition rule shown in Figure

9.1 is implemented in the *COMPASS* program using the KEE rule shown in Figure 10.12. Each rule resides in a KEE frame, and the rules are grouped into rulesets. The rules in each stage of *COMPASS* are organized in a hierarchy, first broken down by maintenance message type and then by rulesets for each maintenance message type for each stage. Figure 10.13 shows a portion of the Analysis Stage rule hierarchy for analyzing SMA110-112 messages. The SMA110-112.XY.ANALYSIS.RULES ruleset shown in the figure groups all Analysis Stage rules for SMA110-112 messages that pertain to problem types an expert would call Type XY. When, for example, SMA111 problems of type XY are identified, only these Analysis rules apply.

Note that we used likelihoods in rules to represent uncertainty. The primary area where uncertainty entered the analysis was in the determination of the fault in the No. 2 EAX that caused a certain cluster of maintenance messages. In the Analysis Stage, an expert (and thus *COMPASS*) can narrow the possibilities for the fault causing the maintenance messages to a few. But in most cases even the best expert with unlimited time and all the available data cannot narrow the possibilities to a single one. The best that an expert can do in these cases is to provide an estimate of the likelihood that each of the possibilities is indeed the actual physical fault in the switch. In *COMPASS*, these likelihoods were made part of the Analysis rules, as shown in the *COMPASS* rule of Figures 9.1 and 10.12. Since KEE did not provide a good mechanism for combining these uncertainties, we had to implement the likelihood mechanisms ourselves.

10.5   OBJECT-ORIENTED PROGRAMMING

In addition to the use of objects and relations between objects to represent and store knowledge, an object–oriented programming system can furnish a good mechanism for representing the passing of control around an expert system program. A method in an object can send message to another

FIGURE 10.12 Implementing the *COMPASS* rule of Figure 9.1

```
[IF (AND (?X IS IN CLASS NR.PROBLEMS)
         (THE PROBLEM.TYPE OF ?X IS BC.DUAL.EXPANSION.ONE PGA.DOMINANT)
         (GEQ (THE NUMBER.OF.MESSAGES OF ?X)
              5))
   THEN
   [AND (THE FAULTS OF ?X IS (QUOTE ((PGA INDICATED.PGA)
                                      .5)))
        (THE FAULTS OF ?X IS (QUOTE ((PGA SILENT.PGA)
                                      .3)))
        (THE FAULTS OF ?X IS (QUOTE (IGA .1)))
        (THE FAULTS OF ?X IS (QUOTE (BACKPLANE .1]
   DO
   (FAULT.IDENTIFIED.SIGNAL (QUOTE
              NR20.BC.DUAL.EXPANSION.ONE.PGA.DOMINANT.LARGE.NUMBER.MESSAGES.ANALYSIS.RULE)
              ?X
              (QUOTE BC.DUAL.EXPANSION.ONE.PGA.DOMINANT)
              (LIST (QUOTE ((PGA INDICATED.PGA)
                             .5))
                    (QUOTE ((PGA SILENT.PGA)
                             .3))
                    (QUOTE (IGA .1))
                    (QUOTE (BACKPLANE .1]
```

object. The message activates a method in the recipient object and thus effectively passes control to the second object. For example, a piece of code in a method might contain:

(IF (GRADE-OF-ROAD GREATER-THAN .10)
(SEND-MESSAGE "STEEP-HILL" CONTROLLER))

The CONTROLLER object would receive the message "STEEP-HILL" and would continue the processing based upon that information, effectively taking control of the program. In many systems, STEEP-HILL would be the name of the method invoked in the CONTROLLER object.

This technique for passing control provides a great deal of power to the programmer because it enables program control to be sent to almost any part of the program at any time. (This power can entail some problems, which we consider in Section 11.3.6.)

COMPASS made great use of object-oriented message passing for both data manipulation and control passing. The *COMPASS* program contains over 400 different object-oriented messages that can be sent, many invoked several

FIGURE 10.13 Portion of the rule hierarchy for SMA110–112 Analysis Stage Rules

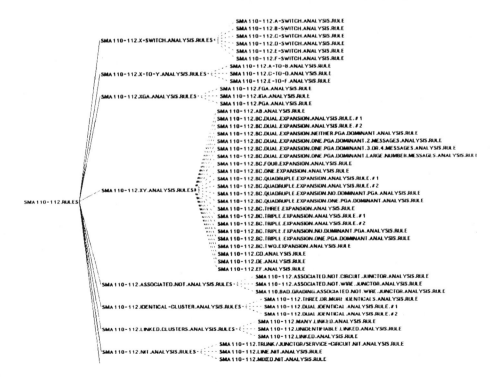

times in a run for different frames or with different arguments. Much of the flow of procedural control is accomplished through message passing. Each KEE frame is an object in KEE's object-oriented programming environment, and methods in a frame can be invoked by sending that frame a message indicating the method (along with its arguments, if any). In some cases, the invoked method is meant to run a short time, determining a piece of information and then returning a value to the calling method. But when *COMPASS* is using object-oriented messages to pass program control, the invoked method assumes control of the program for the time being. This technique was used to pass control within a knowledge base and also from one knowledge base to another. It proved to be a powerful technique but had to be limited to promote maintainability (see Section 11.3.6).

10.6 PROGRAMMING LANGUAGE CODE

The code of a general-purpose programming language can, in principle, do everything that any of the other knowledge representation paradigms can do and can provide a power and flexibility that the others cannot. Thus in a multiparadigm system good programmers frequently want to implement everything in code and minimize the use of other paradigms. This policy is often a mistake; as discussed in Section 11.3.3, in many cases it is beneficial to minimize the amount of programming language code used. However, access to a general programming language is extremely valuable when implementing a multiparadigm program in that the language furnishes a means by which the programmers can provide themselves with any facility found to be missing or weak in any paradigm of the development tool. It is for this purpose that programming language code is most useful. For example, referring to the basketball team example in Section 10.4, the rule language may not provide a convenient way to represent the process of finding the average height. It may be difficult to express with rules the simple procedure whereby the frame structure is examined, the frames in a certain class are identified, data from slots in those frames are accessed, and calculations are made using those data values. But a small function written in a program language can easily implement this capability.

> In *COMPASS* we tried to use Lisp code only where KEE provided no other convenient paradigm. We found many pieces of domain knowledge that could not be represented in KEE in any way other than by Lisp code. In other cases, we used Lisp code when there was a way to use other KEE paradigms but the resulting representation would be obscure, highly complex, or extremely impractical. The final *COMPASS* program contains over 500 Lisp functions.
>
> Frame methods embodied in Lisp code initiate the object-oriented messages that governed the flow of program control. The methods are also used as

part of the rules to facilitate predicate testing on the different types of *COMPASS* objects. In addition, certain pieces of domain knowledge are procedural by nature. For example, Figure 9.3 shows Substep 3 of the Postclustering Step for SMA63 maintenance messages. Although this substep utilizes rules within the procedure, the overall procedure would most naturally be represented in a programming language. Therefore it was programmed in Lisp.

10.7 REPRESENTING AND REREPRESENTING

An effective method for producing an expert system is to develop successively more complete instances of the system. For example, first an initial feasibility prototype system can be developed, then a full prototype system, and then a production system. While the knowledge acquisition is essentially cumulative through this process, the knowledge representation can (and possibly should) change from one project phase to the next, especially between the initial and the full prototype. The change may be radical. The major decisions that influence the design of the knowledge representation for a project phase are made primarily in the earlier parts of the work. Between those decisions and the beginning of the next project phase, the knowledge representers' understanding of the domain and of the structure and elements that need to be represented probably has improved significantly. Therefore when the next phase begins, the knowledge representers may be able to design a dramatically improved knowledge representation.

In an ideal situation, the reconsideration of the representation is a planned part of the project. In this case the prototype phases of the expert system are developed with the understanding that the knowledge representation will be reviewed fully when the project team begins working on the subsequent phase. At that point the knowledge representation is examined, and it is modified or completely revised based on the project team's latest understanding of what needs to be represented. Any representation structures that were found powerful and useful in the previous representation can be incorporated into the new representation, but only after a complete reconsideration of the design.

Using this approach, knowledge representers in at least the initial prototype project phase do not have to be overly concerned with the effectiveness or the completeness of the representation. They can allow the representation to evolve as the acquired knowledge evolves. They do not have to wait until a large body of knowledge is acquired before they design an initial representation, and once this initial representation is designed, the knowledge implementation can begin. If later in the project phase the knowledge representers are required to represent unexpected new items or structures that do not fit neatly into the expert system architecture, they can squeeze them into or paste them onto their existing structure. If the overall design gets complex or messy, that situation does not have to cause alarm because the representers know that the representation will be completely reexamined in the next project phase.

One additional benefit might come from a full reconsideration of the knowledge representation at the start of a new phase of the project. Between the beginning of the previous phase and the beginning of the present phase, a new release of the knowledge engineering tool or a totally new tool may have become available. If the project team decides to use a new release or tool for the next phase of development, a new represention effort would be able to make good use of the additional structures and facilities that the new release or new tool might provide. These added capabilities might allow the revised representation to be significantly better than the old representation.

> We began our initial knowledge representation and program design for *COMPASS-I* after we had learned something about the No. 2 EAX domain and the expert's analysis process and had acquired a small number of knowledge acquisition rules. Based on that limited knowledge, we developed a representation that seemed to cover all the concepts, objects, and structures that we thought would be needed. As additional knowledge was acquired, however, the knowledge representation proved deficient and had to be expanded and modified. New knowledge constructs that needed to be included were identified. In addition, many of the existing items in the representation had to be expanded, split into several parts, reorganized, or eliminated. The knowledge representation paradigms we used, especially the use of object-oriented programming constructs and rulesets, enabled us to make these additions, deletions, and modifications reasonably quickly and aided us in developing the *COMPASS* feasibility prototype rapidly. But use of these paradigms did not ensure that the final knowledge representation structure would be well designed—and in certain aspects it was not. However, since our plan was to reconsider the *COMPASS-I* representation and revise it completely if needed when we began the next phase, we were not greatly concerned by the non-optimal overall design.

> Moreover although *COMPASS-I* analyzed one maintenance message type (the NR20), the future expansion of *COMPASS* would probably cover several types of maintenance messages. If we had expected to employ the *COMPASS-I* representation for the entire development, we would have had to take great care in developing the *COMPASS-I* representation to leave structural space for other maintenance messages types. However, since we expected to rework completely the knowledge representation after finishing *COMPASS-I*, we did not have to be concerned about future possibilities and could concentrate solely on representing the NR20 analysis. Thus we saved a good deal of un-

necessary complication in the initial *COMPASS* representational structures, which simplified and speeded the work. Furthermore a sizable part of the additional design and implementation work that would have been done to allow for other maintenance message types would have been wasted because many of *COMPASS-I*'s representational structures were modified several times (and some were eliminated) before the final *COMPASS-I* representation was complete.

When we began work on *COMPASS-II*, as planned we completely reconsidered the knowledge representation. We decided that the basic *COMPASS-I* knowledge representation could form the basis of the *COMPASS-II* representation and also that many decisions made for the *COMPASS-I* knowledge representation worked well and should be retained. However, we rerepresented several parts of the *COMPASS-I* knowledge representation that had proved to be poorly structured or awkward or had caused us difficulties. For example, in *COMPASS-I*, the use of a single PROBLEM object to represent all aspects of a No. 2 EAX maintenance problem caused complications when multiple implementers were involved. Therefore we changed the representation for *COMPASS-II* to allow different aspects of a No. 2 EAX problem to be represented by different, related objects.

As work on *COMPASS-II* was beginning, a new release of the KEE software became available, and we installed it. This release had many added features and capabilities that increased the power of the KEE knowledge representation. Therefore these additional constructs were primary factors considered in the rerepresentation of *COMPASS* for *COMPASS-II*. Had we not planned to rework the *COMPASS* representation, either we would have reworked the representation anyway, though unplanned, to take advantage of the new capabilities of KEE or would have not taken advantage of the additional power made available by the new version of KEE. In the former case we would have wasted effort in perfecting the *COMPASS-I* knowledge representation; in the latter we would have wound up with a *COMPASS-II* knowledge representation that was not as powerful as it could have been.

A principal matter of interest during the rerepresentation of *COMPASS* was the expansion from one maintenance message type in *COMPASS-I* to several (eventually ten) maintenance message types in *COMPASS-II*. In many instances we reused parts of or concepts from the *COMPASS-I* knowledge representation but modified them to allow the inclusion of multiple maintenance messages. The modularization of the *COMPASS-I* representation to correspond to the subtasks of NR20 analysis seemed to apply to the other maintenance message types in most cases. Therefore this overall structure was modified and used in *COMPASS-II*. Many of the *COMPASS-I* frame structures could be modified to handle multiple maintenance messages and then used for *COMPASS-II*. A level in their frame hierarchies had to be added to allow for the different maintenance message types, and one or more slots had to be added to the frames of the structure (for example, a slot to identify the maintenance message type). More complex naming conventions were needed to distinguish by maintenance message type the messages input to *COMPASS*, the No. 2 EAX problems found by *COMPASS*, and many of the frames created by *COMPASS*. Of course, all of the information and structure related to the nine additional maintenance messages was new.

Finally, in the *COMPASS-II* knowledge representation, we gave a good deal of emphasis to representational features that would foster the long-term maintainability of *COMPASS*. This issue strongly affected our thinking in developing the representation for *COMPASS-II* but did not concern us much in *COMPASS-I*.

For the final *COMPASS* production system, the core of *COMPASS-II* was unchanged, and the main work was on input and output. Thus the *COMPASS-II* knowledge representation was not revised. Certainly some improvements could have been made to the *COMPASS* knowledge representation had it been completely revised again at this point in the development, but the possible gains did not seem to warrant the cost in effort and the possible introduction of errors.

CHECKLIST FOR REPRESENTING THE KNOWLEDGE

☐ Choose the representation so as to be able to describe the domain knowledge clearly, concisely, and in a manner allowing efficient implementation.

☐ Represent the domain knowledge at the appropriate level of detail, including all important concepts and excluding all irrelevant detail.

☐ If the expert system task can be decomposed into a set of steps, consider making each task step the basis of a separate representational structure.

☐ When a multiple-paradigm expert system tool is used, make full use of the available paradigms, using each paradigm where it is most effective.

☐ Utilize frames to represent the important concepts and objects of the domain.

☐ Make use of frame hierarchies with interframe relationships to represent complex taxonomies, structures, and organizations.

☐ Consider frame structures as an easy-to-use mechanism for storing and retrieving data, including dynamically created data.

☐ Take advantage of frame structures to pass generic information to newly created objects during a program run without explicit action by the expert system program.

☐ Use demons in frame slots to delay computation until necessary or to trigger functions on slot access or change in value.

☐ Consider using production rules to represent the active expert knowledge. Production rules are usually more readable and modular than other representational paradigms.

☐ Explore the use of object-oriented messages for passing control around the expert system program.

☐ Use a programming language for knowledge representation when other available paradigms prove ineffective or when efficiency is an important concern.

☐ Reconsider the knowledge representation at the beginning of major project phases, especially when going from the initial feasibility prototype phase to the full prototype phase. Reuse any powerful and useful structures, and revise or redesign the rest of the knowledge representation.

☐ Use the expectation of the planned reexamination and revision of the knowledge representation to speed the early knowledge representation.

Prerau, Developing and Managing Expert Systems (Addison-Wesley)

CHAPTER 11

Implementing the System

■■■■ What makes the specification of an expert system program different from that of a conventional program?

■■■■ What makes the implementation of an expert system program different from conventional software implementation?

■■■■ What techniques can be used successfully for implementing an expert system?

■■■■ What techniques can be used to accommodate multiple developers?

■■■■ What implementation approaches can aid in making the ultimate expert system more maintainable?

When some expert knowledge has been acquired and a knowledge representation has been determined, the project's implementers develop the expert system program to implement the acquired knowledge. We discuss in this chapter techniques for implementing the expert knowledge. There are some significant differences between the implementation techniques used for developing conventional computer programs and those used for developing expert system programs, and we consider these differences. We also examine two areas critical to expert system development that are often not handled satisfactorily by knowledge engineering tools. One relates to methods for managing an expert system implementation where there are multiple developers and the other to techniques that can be used during implementation to promote the maintainability of the expert system program.

11.1 EXPERT SYSTEM IMPLEMENTATION COMPARED WITH THE IMPLEMENTATION OF CONVENTIONAL PROGRAMS

The implementation of an expert system program has many aspects that are similar or identical to the implementation of a conventional program; however, there are some important differences.

11.1.1 IMPLEMENTATION WITHOUT A FULL SPECIFICATION

The cyclic process (Figure 9.5) used for all but the earliest part of knowledge acquisition includes a critical implementation step. Knowledge is acquired from experts and documented, and then this knowledge is implemented. The newly expanded and upgraded program is run with test cases, and the results of the runs are compared against the experts' analyses of the cases. The cycle repeats as new expert knowledge is acquired based on the comparison and then is implemented.

The acquired expert knowledge specifies the functionality of the expert system program. Accordingly the documentation of the knowledge can be thought of as the formal specification of the program. But the knowledge in the documentation is not complete—or considered fully correct—until close to the end of the expert system development. Some partial specification of the program may be determined at the outset of the implementation and remain unchanged, but the major part of the specification—the acquired expert knowledge as documented—continually changes and expands throughout the expert system development, as the knowledge acquisition process goes through its Elicit-Document-Implement-Test cycles.

Therefore in expert system development, the full program specification cannot be determined completely before the implementation begins. To the contrary, the specification and the implementation slowly evolve concurrently. Furthermore they cannot be strictly separated; their mutual development is intertwined, each dependent on the other.

Because there is never a complete program specification available to guide programming efforts, expert system implementation is significantly different from the implementation process used for more conventional software. A full top-down process cannot be used. In most cases, neither the complete set of concepts to be represented in the program, the overall organization and flow of the program, nor a good modularization of the program is known until the project is well into the implementation. Thus a complete design of the program architecture cannot be developed before programming begins. In addition, it is never clear when the specification—and thus the corresponding implementation—is complete. A new test case can open up a whole new area of knowledge that might have been overlooked. Thus the implementation task ends not when the specification is fully and correctly programmed, as is the case for conventional development, but when the implemented knowledge meets some criteria of goodness—for example, agrees with a domain expert to a sufficient degree.

Instead of the conventional approach, a process of incremental development and refinement generally is used for expert systems. A small program is written implementing the first few chunks of expert knowledge found. The small program is refined and enlarged incrementally as the comparisons between the experts' analyses and those of the existing program yield new incremental chunks of knowledge to be implemented. This method of expert system program design and development is supported and promoted by the use, where possible, of modular implementation techniques. Modular implementation systems, such as production rules or an object-oriented programming system, minimize the interactions of the implementations of different knowledge chunks, even if those knowledge chunks will ultimately be used simultaneously. If the implementations of two pieces of knowledge do not interact, each can be implemented independently, without the implementer of one having to know anything about the other. Thus the first-found piece of knowledge can be implemented even before the knowledge acquisition process has found the second.

Figure 11.1 expands the knowledge acquisition cycle outlined in Chapter 9 with a more complete description of the implementation process. In addition to the major Elicit-Document-Implement-Test loop, there are inner loops. One inner loop represents software testing and evaluation: the acquired knowledge is represented and implemented, and then the program is tested by the programmer to ensure that the knowledge has been represented and implemented correctly. The other inner loops show that the

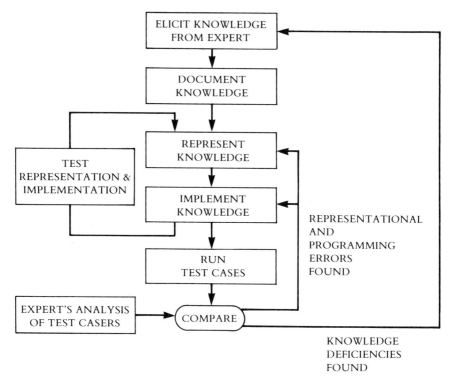

FIGURE 11.1 Knowledge acquisition and implementation cycle

comparison of the program's results against those of an expert can, in addition to indicating knowledge deficiencies in the developing expert system, also identify the presence of errors in representation or in implementation.

The *COMPASS* knowledge representation and implementation process began after three week-long meetings with the expert. By that time, we had learned something about the No. 2 EAX domain and the expert's analysis process and had acquired a small number of knowledge acquisition rules. Because we were starting the implementation from scratch, we had to devote a major portion of our first efforts to designing an initial overall architecture and to implementing some base structures (as well as to our learning to use KEE, which we just had obtained). Interspersed with the times when we were trying to implement the acquired knowledge were additional knowledge acquisition sessions. Frequently as a result of these sessions, the documented knowledge was changed to a great extent. Established (and possibly implemented) rules were often severely altered or discarded completely. New classes of objects and classes of rules appeared, and older ones (possibly already implemented) often changed, disappeared, or were reorganized. Thus while trying to catch up to the knowledge acquisition, the *COMPASS* implementers not only did not have a complete specification for the software, but they had a moving target—at both the higher, architectural, level and at the lower, individual rule, level.

Eventually the implementation caught up to the knowledge acquisition. From then on, we went through a series of Elicit-Document-Implement-Test cycles, trying (though not always succeeding) to implement all that was found at one knowledge acquisition session before the beginning of the next session. Thus we interspersed specification and implementation. Our knowledge document and our program's design and implementation grew concurrently and incrementally.

11.1.2 REIMPLEMENTING THE IMPLEMENTATION

Work on implementing the expert system program is performed in each of the development phases of an expert system project—for example, in developing an initial feasibility prototype, developing a full prototype, and developing a production system. Section 10.7 described some of the benefits of reconsidering some or all of the existing knowledge representation at the beginning of a new development phase. Similarly when starting a new development phase, there may be many advantages to reimplementing some or all of the program code of the previous phase.

When a new expert system development phase begins, the programmers have a much better concept of what needs to be implemented than they did when they generated the code for the previous phase. They very likely can devise a much better, cleaner, and more efficient program organization than was used in the previous phase.

Depending on the ultimate use of the code developed, the goals of implementation differ from one phase to the next. For example, although maintainability and efficiency of code are important goals of later phases of expert system program development, they frequently are not crucial objectives in the implementation of an initial prototype. Instead the primary implementation goal of this phase usually is to implement the desired functionality as rapidly as possible. (However, if large parts or all of the code developed in a project phase are expected to be used as part of the final production system, then the maintainability and efficiency of that code are of high importance.)

There is another benefit to rewriting the program in large measure when a new phase begins. If such rewriting is planned, it makes it much more reasonable to reconsider at the beginning of the phase the hardware and software choices made earlier in the project. Based on an updating of the project's survey of available hardware and software and the additional understanding of project needs garnered during the previous project phase, project personnel can consider whether a change of hardware or software might be warranted. Strong consideration should also be given to changing to a new release of the software or a new upgrade or system software release of the hardware if such have become available.

Finally when the approach of rewriting early software is decided upon in advance, less—possibly a great deal less—effort (and therefore time and expense) is required in the earlier phase to produce its code. Knowledge implementers can concentrate on making sure the program displays the desired functionality and can minimize their other concerns. If knowledge implementers know that they are developing throwaway code, they do not have to try to optimize the code for efficiency (although some minimal effort toward efficiency may be needed to make the program fast enough to be convenient for knowledge acquisition, for field tests, and for demonstrations). They do not have to worry about following any practices for promoting the maintainability of the program, such as enforcing uniformity of style, and they can use makeshift input and output communications. Thus this approach speeds the development while reducing its costs—two considerations that may be of paramount importance.

If rewriting the entire implementation seems too great a step, a possibility is to develop some portions of an implementation with the objective of long-term use and other portions with the expectation that they will be recoded in a future phase. Often some portions of the implementation seem clearly to be permanent parts of the system, reusable in all subsequent phases, while other parts may seem subject to change or growth. Obviously it is wise to invest more time and effort in initially coding the likely-to-be-permanent program parts. Consider salvaging from the old program only those parts developed with final implementation in mind (and therefore in "final" form already) and those parts that will not form part of the final production system anyway (such as some utilities or communications programs that will be rewritten based on deployment decisions not yet made). Even if the full reimplementation concept is accepted, there will probably be small pieces of the program that can be and will be reused in the next phase.

> From the beginning of project planning, we intended to rewrite completely the *COMPASS* feasibility prototype implementation. Thus we could implement *COMPASS-I* without great concern for program efficiency, uniformity of style, maintainability, readability, efficiency, comments, documentation, and so on. The approach did cause some problems; for example, some of the code turned out to be very obscure and understandable only by its developer. This approach, however, allowed for rapid development of the large and complex *COMPASS-I* program.
>
> Just as we began work on *COMPASS-II* implementation, a new and more powerful release of KEE became available. We used this new release to reim-

plement the NR20 program of *COMPASS-I* completely. This time, we consciously, and for the most part conscientiously, based the implementation on our understanding that much of the program we were writing, if not almost all, would be part of the final, fielded system. We instituted and utilized practices, including some based on principles of software engineering, to make the system more maintainable. We used a much more uniform style and more comments than in *COMPASS-I*, and tried to eliminate all obscure code.

The final *COMPASS* implementation is described in Box 11.1.

BOX 11.1
THE IMPLEMENTION OF *COMPASS*

COMPASS is implemented in 18 KEE knowledge bases, as shown in Figure 11.2. Seven of these are active knowledge bases—PREPROCESS, PATTERNS, CLUSTERS, POSTCLUSTERS, ANALYZE, SUGGEST, and OUTPUT—which correspond to steps in the expert's analysis procedures. The CONTROL, ACCESS, EVENTS, and UTILITIES knowledge bases provide support functions. The remaining knowledge bases gather and provide data.

Many features of the *COMPASS* implementation are discussed in Chapter 10 and in this chapter. Most of the important concepts and objects in the No. 2 EAX application area are represented by KEE frames (called "units" in KEE). Each frame is an object in KEE's object-oriented programming environment. As *COMPASS* operates, it constructs new frames in some of the knowledge bases. These frames represent the specific items in the situation under investigation. Frame inheritance is used to pass generic information to these created frames. Active knowledge is generally implemented by KEE rules and Lisp code. Demons are used to expand the functionality of KEE rules. Much of the procedural control in the system is accomplished through object-oriented message passing.

KNOWLEDGE BASES PROVIDING DATA

■ **COMMUNICATIONS.** The COMMUNICATIONS knowledge base interacts with *COMPASS*'s external communications computer, an Apple Macintosh, to provide the input data needed by *COMPASS*—the maintenance messages for a No. 2 EAX. The input data are put on an input queue, which is managed by this knowledge base. *COMPASS* automatically looks for arrivals on the input queue and processes an input file when available. This capability allows *COMPASS* to be run for several No. 2 EAXs (with selected syndromes for each) without *COMPASS* operator intervention beyond initiating the communications process. When *COMPASS* finishes a run, the output report is placed on an output queue, which is also managed by the COMMUNICATIONS knowledge base. The external communications computer picks up files from this queue for distribution to the users.

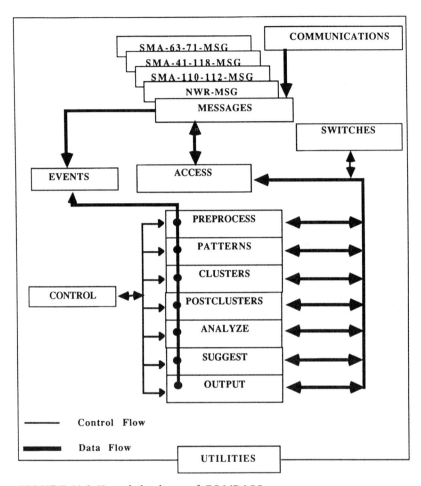

FIGURE 11.2 Knowledge bases of *COMPASS*

■   **MESSAGES.** The MESSAGES knowledge base provides the means and the location to store *COMPASS*'s input data. It contains frames representing the content of the RMCS messages. A regular expression grammar is used to parse each message. The data may contain garbled sections due to problems in communications. Generic frames are used to represent different message types. During *COMPASS*'s Transform Data Step, a frame instance is set up for each maintenance message received from an RMCS. Frame inheritance is used to pass properties from the generic frames to the frames representing individual messages. The MESSAGES knowledge base also contains an optimized quicksort, specifically tailored to the various types of sorting of No. 2 EAX messages that must be done by *COMPASS*.

■ **NWR-MSG, SMA-63-71-MSG, SMA-41-118-MSG, and SMA-110-112-MSG.** Four auxiliary knowledge bases—NWR-MSG, SMA-63-71-MSG, SMA-41-118-MSG, and SMA-110-112-MSG—are utilized by MESSAGES to provide a pool of precreated KEE frames. Using these knowledge bases saves the significant amount of time that would otherwise be required to create these frames during a *COMPASS* run.

■ **SWITCHES.** The SWITCHES knowledge base contains site-specific information about No. 2 EAX switches. Each switch that *COMPASS* analyzes is represented by a hierarchy of frames in this knowledge base. The site-specific data specify information on the structure of the switch, the switch's trunks (lines going out to other central offices), the equipment related to the switch, and the exact wiring—called the "grading"—of each switch. (Although the vast majority of wiring in each No. 2 EAX is standard, each switch has some switch-specific wiring.) The grading data is used by *COMPASS* analyses to find interconnections within the switch. In addition, *COMPASS* has a separate utility that allows instant access to these data (see Section 13.6.2).

The SWITCHES knowledge base also contains information on which of *COMPASS*'s outputs should be generated for each switch—whether the ordered suggestion list should be output alone or together with the annotated version of the RMCS data.

KNOWLEDGE BASES PROVIDING SUPPORT FUNCTIONS

■ **UTILITIES.** The UTILITIES knowledge base contains software tools developed to aid in the implementation and running of *COMPASS*. It provides a set of methods for loading and saving knowledge bases and the support files associated with a knowledge base. Data-driven methods are used to accommodate a knowledge base in development mode, intermediate mode, or production mode (where everything is compiled). An additional frame of UTILITIES contains methods for setting system-wide parameters.

■ **CONTROL.** The active knowledge bases are invoked through the CONTROL knowledge base. As shown in Figure 11.2, all high-level control flow in *COMPASS* passes through the CONTROL knowledge base. CONTROL determines when a particular stage of *COMPASS* will be executed. Each active knowledge base has a special CONTROL frame that receives messages from the CONTROL knowledge base. The CONTROL frame in turn sends messages to frames within the knowledge base to cause the appropriate stage of *COMPASS* to be performed.

■ **ACCESS.** The ACCESS knowledge base provides the mechanism for interknowledge base data access in *COMPASS*. It provides two techniques that can be used to allow one knowledge base to access data in another knowledge base: an access gateway and an import-export mechanism.

■ **EVENTS.** The EVENTS knowledge base centralizes control of *COMPASS* output. All output data in *COMPASS* are channeled through EVENTS. When, in an active knowledge base, an event occurs that requires a *COMPASS* output, that knowledge base sends the output data to EVENTS.

ACTIVE KNOWLEDGE BASES

■   **PREPROCESS.** The PREPROCESS knowledge base contains methods that perform preprocessing of the No. 2 EAX maintenance messages. For example, sometimes the No. 2 EAX retries a failed call on exactly the same path that the call failed on, yielding two identical maintenance messages produced within seconds of each other. PRE-PROCESS identifies such situations and, as an expert would do, eliminates from consideration one of the messages. It also eliminates certain erroneous messages caused by a known bug in the No. 2 EAX software.

■   **PATTERNS and CLUSTERS.** In *COMPASS*'s Cluster Messages Step (see Box 10.1 for a discussion of this and the other steps of *COMPASS*), No. 2 EAX maintenance messages are grouped into clusters, where a cluster is a set of messages that expert analysis indicates were all caused by the same switch problem. For each maintenance message type, the PATTERNS and CLUSTERS knowledge bases contain knowledge about all the particular sets of commonalities that a group of messages of that type may share to form a cluster. The PATTERN frame hierarchy has leaf nodes that represent different fields in a No. 2 EAX message that can indicate a pattern for clustering. The CLUSTERS knowledge base includes a CLUSTER frame hierarchy in which all subclass frames represent specific cluster types made up of these fields. The structure of the CLUSTER hierarchy is based on a set of expert-derived cluster properties. A complex hashing technique is used to provide an efficient way to determine the clusters for a large set (up to several hundred) of maintenance messages. Each message can be—and often is—a member of several clusters.

The KEE rule language proved inadequate for representing knowledge about clustering. Thus although the expert knowledge for the Cluster Messages Step is in rule form, the active parts of the step are implemented primarily as Lisp functions attached to slots.

The output of the Cluster Messages Step is a set of cluster instance frames in CLUSTERS, each representing a cluster that *COMPASS* has identified. Each identified cluster is an instance of a particular generic cluster type, and each contains pointers to the frames in the MESSAGES knowledge base that represent the messages making up the cluster.

■   **POSTCLUSTERS.** The POSTCLUSTERS knowledge base implements *COMPASS*'s Postclustering Step, which uses expert techniques to determine which of the large number of clusters produced by the Cluster Messages Step are "real," that is, which represent actual problems in the switch.

Because each maintenance message can be in more than one cluster, the message sets of the different clusters can intersect—partially or completely. For each message in more than one cluster, the POSTCLUSTERS knowledge base determines the single cluster to which the message actually belongs. Clusters with no (or very few) messages remaining are determined to be spurious; the rest of the clusters are determined to be real.

POSTCLUSTERS imports from the CLUSTERS knowledge base the information it needs on each cluster and puts that information in its own CLUSTERS hierarchy. Each cluster instance points to an instance of a SWITCH.PART hierarchy that represents the location of the specific switch problem that caused the maintenance messages making up the cluster. POSTCLUSTERS utilizes a set of rules in a POSTCLUSTER-

ING.RULES hierarchy to determine the real clusters. Because of the complexity of POSTCLUSTERING, the processing is broken into up to ten substeps (depending on the maintenance message type).

■ **ANALYZE.** The Analyze Problems Step of *COMPASS* determines, for each real switch problem cluster, a set of possible specific faults in the switch, any of which might have caused all the messages in the cluster. This process is implemented in the ANALYZE knowledge base.

The ANALYZE knowledge base imports from POSTCLUSTERING the information it needs on the set of real clusters that have been found. These have now been identified as relating to actual switch problems. For each identified problem, an instance is created of the corresponding generic problem type in a PROBLEMS hierarchy.

The ANALYZE knowledge base contains a hierarchy of ANALYZE.RULES (a portion of which is shown in Figure 10.13). These rules analyze the data in the maintenance messages related to a specific problem and determine a list of possible specific switch faults that might have caused the problem. ANALYZE.RULES, just like all other complex groups of rules in *COMPASS,* is split into several rulesets for efficiency and ease of understanding. When specific switch faults that correspond to a particular problem have been identified, a frame corresponding to each fault is created as an instance of its generic fault type, in a FAULT frame hierarchy. There are generally several possible faults for a given set of messages. Each problem frame has pointers to all of its corresponding FAULT frames.

The ANALYZE rules associate with each fault a likelihood, which is the expert estimate of the relative frequency of the fault for the specific type of problem. This is stored in a LIKELIHOOD slot in each FAULT instance frame.

■ **SUGGEST.** The SUGGEST knowledge base is used to implement the three steps of *COMPASS*'s Suggest Stage: Suggest Actions, Order Suggestions, and Merge Suggestions. It imports from the ANALYZE knowledge base the information it needs on the faults found for each problem. It puts this information into created frame instances in its local versions of the PROBLEM and FAULT hierarchies, with pointers between each problem and its corresponding faults.

Each created fault instance frame inherits information from its generic-fault-type parent frame on the possible maintenance actions an expert switchperson might take to repair the fault. *COMPASS* builds a suggestion list for each problem frame by combining the suggestions for each of the problem's possible faults. In addition, for each specific maintenance suggestion, a new frame instance is created as a child of its generic-suggestion-type in a SUGGESTION frame hierarchy (as shown in Figure 10.10). These suggestion instance frames inherit information on the characteristics of the suggestion type, such as whether a suggested maintenance action may be performed anytime or only during low telephone traffic periods.

Next expert rules from a SUGGESTION.RULES hierarchy are utilized to prioritize suggestions. An ordered list of suggestions is produced in a slot in each problem frame.

Finally the SUGGESTIONS knowledge base contains expert rules in a MERGING.RULES hierarchy that search through the suggestion list to see if there are two or more maintenance actions that can be performed simultaneously. If so, the rules cause these suggestions to be merged into a single suggestion.

■   **OUTPUT.** The OUTPUT knowledge base contains information needed for the Output Suggestions and Annotated RMCS Printout Step of *COMPASS*. The primary function of the knowledge base is to format the results of *COMPASS* and produce the *COMPASS* output listings. It makes extensive use of the facilities of the EVENTS knowledge base to produce the desired outputs.

The OUTPUT knowledge base uses the *COMPASS* import mechanism to get from the SUGGEST knowledge base all the data it needs on the suggested maintenance actions. It produces (through the EVENTS knowledge base) both the primary output of *COMPASS*, an ordered list of suggested maintenance actions, and its secondary output, an annotated version of the RMCS output (which is *COMPASS*'s input). Data in the SWITCHES knowledge base tell *COMPASS* whether to produce just the primary output or both outputs.

11.2 SOME TECHNIQUES FOR KNOWLEDGE IMPLEMENTATION

Implementing an expert system is similar to conventional programming in that many of the most effective techniques are learned by experience. Reading about programming does not alone make an excellent programmer. Therefore it is advisable for implementers to experiment with the software and hardware environment as soon as it is available. In addition, it is useful to look at examples of successful code. Talking with programmers experienced with the software tool, paradigms, or language being used can be helpful.

Each tool, paradigm, and language is different, and there are valuable implementation techniques specifically associated with each one. In addition some general techniques for knowledge implementation have proved useful, as we shall now discuss.

11.2.1 CORRESPONDENCE OF KNOWLEDGE ACQUISITION RULES AND IMPLEMENTATION RULES

Where possible, it is beneficial to implement a knowledge acquisition rule by a corresponding implementation rule (or, if necessary, by a set of corresponding implementation rules). The implementation rule(s) should have close to or exactly the same name as the knowledge acquisition rule and should, to the extent possible, read like the knowledge acquisition rule.

By following this procedure, the knowledge implementers create a clear correspondence (one-to-one where possible) between the acquired and the implemented rules. This produces a strong correspondence between the knowledge documentation and the implementation—that is, between the program specifications and the program code. This clear specifications-to-code relationship benefits the development effort and later the program maintenance, and it greatly aids technology transfer. It identifies the correspondence between a piece of rule knowledge and the section of code that implements it whenever either must be changed during development and maintenance, and it allows the knowledge documentation to act as a pointer into the knowledge implementation.

In implementing *COMPASS,* we tried where possible to have a one-to-one correspondence between the knowledge acquisition rules and the KEE rules. Each KEE rule was given the same name as the corresponding knowledge acquisition rule (within the limits of the rule-naming facility of KEE). Thus for SMA110-112 maintenance messages, the knowledge acquisition rule for prioritizing suggestions that is called the "Replace CJ Card Before CJ Control Points Suggestion Rule" is implemented by a KEE rule called:

"SMA110-112.REPLACE.CJ.CARD.BEFORE.CJ.CONTROL.POINTS. SUGGESTION.RULE".

Beyond the names of the rules, we tried to make each rule implementation agree as well as possible with its corresponding knowledge acquisition rule. Compare the knowledge acquisition rule of Figure 9.1 with its implementation shown in Figure 10.12. Note that the IF and THEN clauses of the implementation conform somewhat closely to the corresponding clauses of the knowledge acquisition rule. The BECAUSE clause of the knowledge acquisition rule is, by design, not implemented, and the DO part of the implemented rule is used solely to generate a signal for the EVENTS output mechanism (Section 11.3.7).

Sometimes a knowledge acquisition rule is implemented by multiple KEE rules, either because of weaknesses in the rule language or because we wanted to make the implementation cleaner. When this one-to-many implementation is done, the implementation rules are given the same name as the knowledge rule, with an identifier number added. Thus the *COMPASS* NR20-22 knowledge rule "F-Switch Analysis Rule" is implemented by two KEE implementation rules:

"NR20-22.F-SWITCH.ANALYSIS.RULE.#1" and
"NR20-22.F-SWITCH.ANALYSIS.RULE.#2".

11.2.2 GROUPING RULES IN RULESETS

When implementing a large set of rules, it is usually wise to group the rules into rulesets where possible (provided the software tool supports rulesets). We discussed in Section 9.4.7 the virtue of grouping the documented rules into reasonable divisions rather than leaving them unstructured. The same is true for the implemented rules. Such a grouping gives a logical structure to the rule implementation and helps developers and, later, maintainers locate the rules in the expert system program. It is even better if the grouping of the implementation rules can be made to match the grouping of the knowledge acquisition rules because this makes the knowledge document closely correspond to the implementation.

Depending on the rule system being used, it may be possible to invoke rulesets independently. If all parts of the expert system's knowledge might apply during any part of the analysis, then all of the program's rules might fire at any time and all rulesets must be considered simultaneously. However, sometimes the rules can be divided into situational rulesets, where each rule in a ruleset requires the same prerequisite situation before it has a chance to fire. Then when one or more of the particular situations occurs, the rule processor need consider only the rules in the corresponding rulesets—not the entire body of rules. This approach allows the overall rule implementation to be more efficient. Furthermore each rule in a situational ruleset no longer has to contain in its antecedent the items that define the situation in which the ruleset applies since the rule will be considered only when that ruleset applies. For example, consider an implementation rule that begins:

```
(IF (AND (SPEED-LIMIT IS UNLIMITED)
     (ROAD-CONDITION IS EXCELLENT)
     (CAR-SPEED IS MAXIMUM-CAR-SPEED)
 THEN . . . .
```

If that rule is made part of a ruleset called

SPEED-UNLIMITED-ROAD-CONDITION-EXCELLENT-RULESET,

which is invoked only when the program finds that SPEED-LIMIT is UNLIMITED and ROAD-CONDITION is EXCELLENT, then the rule can be simplified to begin:

```
(IF (CAR-SPEED IS MAXIMUM-CAR-SPEED)
 THEN . . . .
```

This kind of simplification makes each rule easier to read and implement and makes the program's set of rules more efficient to run.

The *COMPASS* knowledge was such that the rules could be divided into several situational rulesets that generally followed the organization of the knowledge document. The structure of a typical ruleset structure is shown in Figure 10.13. Although *COMPASS* had over 400 KEE rules, no ruleset contained more than 20 rules. Thus at any one time, the rule processor had to consider no more than 20 rules.

11.2.3 IMPLEMENTING AND DEBUGGING

Debugging an expert system program is different in several notable ways from the debugging of conventional programs. In the development of a large conventional program, each module is well defined and has a complete specification. Therefore the modules usually can be developed independently. Frequently in the development of large conventional programs, all the program modules are not integrated together as one large program until late in the development process. A good deal of effort must go into module debugging, to ensure that most programming bugs in the modules have been eliminated before program integration.

In contrast, expert system programs are developed and debugged incrementally rather than by module and are integrated and tested as a whole early in development. Figure 11.1 shows that the implementation of each new or updated piece of acquired knowledge is tested and debugged when implemented. A newly added part of the expert system program may be a whole new module but is most often a more incremental change to the program, such as a few new rules or frames or some modifications to existing rules and frames.

Even more in contrast to conventional development is the use of the comparisons of the knowledge acquisition cycle to test the developing program. A major step in each knowledge acquisition cycle is to run the entire developing program—as much as has been implemented—and compare its results against those of an expert (Figure 11.1). This process finds weaknesses and gaps in the knowledge, which lead to the acquisition of new knowledge. But at the same time, as shown in the figure, this knowledge acquisition process continually tests the partially developed program code and identifies the presence of programming errors.

Discrepancies between the expert and the program may be due to incorrect or missing knowledge in the program, but they may also be caused by incorrect implementation. The primary task of knowledge acquisition is to find inaccuracies in the expert system knowledge that cause these discrepancies and thus upgrade the program knowledge. While this task is being performed, errors in the program code are frequently found to be the cause of discrepancies. These bugs must be immediately corrected, for they may be masking real knowledge errors in the program. Therefore the main process of expert system knowledge acquisition includes "automatically" a constant program-debugging component.

We used the Figure 11.1 development cycle throughout all but the early *COMPASS* knowledge acquisition. As part of this process, we frequently found discrepancies between the expert and the program that were due to program coding errors. In fact, when we found that a discrepancy was due to such an implementation error, we were usually relieved. It was easy (at least for us, as experienced programmers) to fix program bugs once they were found, but it was sometimes very difficult to determine the appropriate knowledge changes and additions that would repair weaknesses in the program caused by its incomplete knowledge.

Using our expert system development process, we were almost always able to have the latest version (or, if some programming changes were in the process of being made, a very recent version) of the complete partially developed program available in a state where it could be run and where it had relatively few programming bugs. This allowed us, among other things, to be able to demonstrate *COMPASS* at almost any time, even on short notice. Since there was a lot of interest in AI, expert systems, and *COMPASS* itself, we were often asked to do just that.

11.2.4 DOCUMENTATION

Documentation is not often the favorite word of computer programmers. Expert system implementers are no exception. Although everyone agrees that documentation is necessary, not many programmers relish the task. There is a tendency to skimp on documentation during system development and then to complete it quickly and sometimes haphazardly at the end of a project. Clearly expert system project leaders should try to avoid this situation.

Standard techniques of documentation can be used where applicable for documenting expert system programs. For example, reports can be written describing for each program module its purpose, inputs, outputs, and so on. But beyond such standard techniques, there are some aspects of expert system implementations that may allow additional types of documentation.

If a knowledge documentation is compiled and kept updated as part of knowledge acquisition, it becomes a significant piece of program documentation. It is a program specification that is constantly up to date and relevant. If the documented knowledge has clear parallels to the implementation (by rule correspondences, naming conventions, specific references, and other means), it can act as a pointer to the program code.

Associating each item (function, frame, slot, message, rule, and so on) in a large program with a comment or other documented description that explains its particular role and its implementation is a useful form of documentation. It is advisable to make full use of whatever comment and description facilities are available. For programming language functions, the standard comment capabilities of the language can be used. Rule systems often provide for a comment to be associated with each rule or each ruleset. Frame systems may provide for a comment to be associated with each frame and for a comment facet to be associated with each slot in a frame. If such facilities are not provided, frame creators might create their own COMMENT slot in each frame they create and their own COMMENT facet in each slot.

> To document the *COMPASS* implementation, we included full and extensive comments in the *COMPASS-II* software. We utilized the facilities of KEE to associate comments with most frames and with many slots within frames, except where we felt that the function of the frame or slot was exceedingly obvious. We commented rulesets in some cases but felt the clear correspondence between the implementation rules and the knowledge acquisition rules in the knowledge document lessened the need for additional rule documentation in the program.

> We prepared a full set of *COMPASS* documentation for operators and maintainers. This set includes several reports, some published papers, and a listing, as follows:

> - "The *COMPASS* Knowledge Document" (4 volumes)
> - "*COMPASS* Knowledge Bases" (3 volumes)
> - "*COMPASS* Knowledge Engineering Tools"
> - "Field Test Techniques and *COMPASS* Field Results"
> - Three published papers on *COMPASS*
> - Complete *COMPASS* source code listing

> Excluding the papers and source code listing, the documentation contains 1.1 million bytes.

11.3 MANAGING THE IMPLEMENTATION AND PROMOTING MAINTAINABILITY

Current expert system development tools generally do not provide good support for two aspects of expert system implementation important to practical expert system development: managing the implementation and promoting program maintainability.

First, expert system developers need facilities that will help them perform implementation management tasks, such as configuration management, but in expert system development tools, such facilities—common in conventional programming—are often lacking or weak. For example, for the development of larger expert systems implemented by several programmers, tools generally do not provide good mechanisms for the coordination of the programmers, which is necessary to speed development and prevent errors.

Second, expert system programmers need tools and techniques that will help them develop easy-to-maintain programs. Expert systems for business and industry in many instances are maintained by some group other than the developers. The maintaining organization may not have great experience with expert systems tools and techniques, and even if they are experienced, they still must be able to read and understand implementations that are often very complex. Thus developing the expert system program to maximize maintainability becomes an important issue. Ideally this goal should be achieved without sacrificing the power needed to produce working systems rapidly.

> On beginning the implementation of *COMPASS-II*, we reexamined the implementation techniques used in the development of *COMPASS-I* and decided that there should be more formal coordination of the programmers. Clearly the relative independence programmers in *COMPASS-I* development had led to the rapid implementation of a complex program. However, it also led to some problems of coordination, which we expected would get worse as *COMPASS* staff changed and expanded. In addition, we tried to anticipate problems that might occur when *COMPASS* was transferred. We had seen that several nondevelopers had had difficulty following and understanding the *COMPASS-I* implementation and felt that a potential problem might be that the *COMPASS* program—large, complex, and implemented using multiple paradigms—would prove to be difficult for maintainers to understand and maintain.

> Thus we concentrated on trying to formulate techniques that would improve our development approach in two main areas: coordinating the development activities of the implementation team and producing a system that could be understood and maintained by personnel other than the developers. These standard problems were often cast in a nonstandard way because of the nature of expert systems and the development environment. We developed several useful techniques related to the two areas—some new techniques and others derived from traditional software engineering but modified to fit expert system development. The *COMPASS* project was possibly the first application of some of these software engineering concepts to the development of a large expert system.

11.3.1 SOFTWARE MODULARITY AND TASK ASSIGNMENT

Modularity is an issue in any software development project. It makes a program easier to develop, read, understand, and maintain and is a primary mechanism for allowing multiple programmers to implement a large system. In expert system development, modularization is complicated by the desire to make the structure of the system reflect the structure of expert knowledge. Any modularity of the implementation probably will make the expert system program easier to read and understand. But much of the development and the maintenance processes for an expert system involve upgrading the knowledge of the system and then changing the implementation to reflect the changed knowledge. Thus it is wise to make the mapping between the knowledge and the implementation as transparent as possible.

Knowledge engineers, therefore, cannot define the modularity of an expert system solely in a way that is convenient for software development; it must roughly follow the modularity of the expert knowledge. The separate parts of the system may thus be more interdependent than is desirable for software engineering purposes.

Expert systems should be modularized in such a way that a developer can work on a system module without too much dependence on other developers, and yet the modularity of a system should roughly follow the modularity of the expert knowledge. Since the complete program specification is not known as implementation begins, the structure of the knowledge, and therefore the final decomposition of a program into modules, is not known as well. The modularization may not solidify until many Elicit-Document-Implement-Test cycles have been completed. However, if the analysis of the domain task has been able to decompose the task into several distinct steps or into several distinct areas of knowledge, these steps or areas (or possibly both) can form the basis of a modularization of the program. For example, each step or distinct knowledge area might be implemented as a separate module, such as a ruleset or a knowledge base (provided the software development tool supports it). Although the use of multiple modules brings several benefits, it also can bring added complexity and some potential difficulties related to configuration control, intermodule data flow, and intermodule control flow. (Sections 11.3.4–11.3.6 discuss techniques to minimize these problems.)

The mechanism we utilized for modularizing the COMPASS program was the use of multiple knowledge bases. We divided the program into 18 separate KEE knowledge bases as shown in Figure 11.2 and discussed in Box 11.1. Of these, seven correspond to recognizable subtasks of the expert task and actually perform the expert analysis. The remaining eleven provide necessary abstractions or facilities; they are knowledge bases in structure only and do not contain actual expert knowledge.

The expert task performed by COMPASS is noninteractive; the system (just as a human expert) gets a group of messages, processes them, and produces a list of suggested actions. At first it was not obvious to the knowledge acquirers or the expert that the problem could be neatly decomposed. But after many sessions of knowledge acquisition, it became clear that the expert's No. 2 EAX maintenance message analysis, and therefore the *COMPASS* implementation, could be broken into a series of nine steps (as shown in Figure 10.1 and discussed in Box 10.1).

I assigned the entire implementation of each step of *COMPASS* to a single programmer. Thus each of the four programmers (including myself) had complete responsibility for the implementation of one or more steps. In most cases, each step was implemented by a separate knowledge base. Where there was not a one-to-one mapping between steps and knowledge bases, the correspondence between the expert's analysis steps and the *COMPASS* implementation was still made very clear.

Parts of the implementation that did not perform active analysis (such as support systems or static data about individual switches) were separated into modules by the use of more traditional modularity criteria. Where possible, modules that provided clean, useful abstractions were specified. I assigned the implementation of each of these modules as well to a single programmer. Each module became a separate knowledge base in most cases.

The knowledge bases were implemented using the KEE system's facility for creating and utilizing multiple knowledge bases. Each KEE knowledge base has its own name space. Each knowledge base can be, independently and as a single entity, loaded into the computer, displayed, modified, and saved.

The partitioning of the program into multiple knowledge bases was on the whole very successful, allowing the simultaneous development of the *COMPASS* program by four programmers with a minimum of complications. The use of multiple knowledge bases did cause some difficulties in configuration control, data flow, and control flow, which we attempted to minimize.

11.3.2 UNIFORMITY OF STYLE

If the expert system program is being implemented by more than one programmer, it is advisable to try to ensure that the system has a uniform "look" to aid program maintainability. Even though each programmer may use the same language or paradigm set, each has an individual, sometimes highly personalized, programming style. Thus parts of a large program implemented by multiple programmers may be written in very different styles. This nonuniformity of style makes the program look fragmented and makes it more difficult to maintain. The problem is identical to that encountered in developing traditional software, with two exceptions. First, expert system developers, especially in a multiple-paradigm environment, often have a wider variety of options than programmers of conventional systems. Second, it may be more difficult to get some expert system programmers who are used to "freestyle" AI programming methods to adapt their programming to a common style.

One way to approach the problem of nonuniformity of style is to adopt a set of programming-style conventions. These conventions can be discussed, at length if necessary, among the project programming staff but should be enforced when agreed upon. Conventions might prescribe, for example, a uniform way to name system elements. Rule names might always be by convention nouns (Problem-Identification-Rule) or always verbs (Identify-Problem-Rule). Frame names might be all capitals and rule names upper and lower case. Method names might be distinguished from slot names. Conventions might prescribe which of alternative techniques should be used to program a common construct. Conventions at a higher level might establish that a certain type of knowledge should always be implemented in rules, whereas another type of knowledge should always be implemented in programming language code. Depending on the available paradigms, the flexibility of the software system, and the creativity and number of programmers, the list of conventions can be long and detailed or can consist of a few guidelines.

For the development of the initial prototype system, some decisions about naming conventions and other programming style issues can be decided, but enforcement may not have to be strict. However, when development of the final system begins, all conventions should be agreed upon and strictly enforced.

> No stylistic constraints were put on the system developers for the development of *COMPASS-I*. As a result we found that different parts of *COMPASS-I* were sometimes written in very different styles. This made it difficult for a nondeveloper to understand the implementation. However, this situation was tolerable for a feasibility prototype, and the freedom given the programmers helped speed the implementation. But this same situation was unacceptable for *COMPASS-II*, since we expected most of this implementation to form the basis of the fielded version of *COMPASS*. One problem I found as the project leader was that it was sometimes difficult to get the best, most experienced AI programmers to abandon their personal AI programming methods and to follow rigid conventions.
>
> After some discussions, we established a set of programming guidelines. I tried, fairly successfully, to attain compliance by keeping the number of guidelines to a reasonable size and by enforcing compliance by mutual agreement rather than a strict enforcement structure. I could consider this somewhat informal approach because there were never more than three other programmers besides myself, but it would be difficult to utilize in a project with a larger staff.
>
> Some guidelines referred to program structure. For example, we agreed to put all rules in rulesets (see, for example, Figure 10.13). Some guidelines referred to documentation. Thus to ensure adequate in-code documentation, we agreed that each method would contain header comments describing its functionality. One large part of the guidelines included agreements on naming

conventions. Some naming conventions were that only capital letters were to be used, that each blank in a slot name was to be filled by a period, and that the names of all method slots were to end with an exclamation point. These conventions yield a method slot name such as "GET.ASSOCIATED.NOT!". We also agreed to give names to implementation rules that were as close as possible to the name of the corresponding knowledge acquisition rule. We further agreed to construct fault names based on the name of the associated problem and to construct suggestion names based upon the associated fault names, according to a standard process. This convention led to suggestion names such as

"NIT.NR20.5.0.0.0.1.0.0.X.X>BACKPLANE>PHYSICAL.TEST.BACKPLANE".

11.3.3 USE OF PARADIGMS THAT PROMOTE MAINTAINABILITY

When there is a choice of paradigms, it is beneficial to favor a more-maintainable paradigm over a less-maintainable one. Furthermore when programming using any AI paradigm, it is usually worthwhile to sacrifice some efficiency for readability and maintainability.

Production rules and frame structures are easier to maintain than programming language code in most situations. They are simpler and more fixed in their structure than programming code, and that generally makes them easier to read and understand, and thus more maintainable. They usually offer the programmer fewer possibilities for using sophisticated but obscure programming devices, which a reader of the program might misunderstand or miss completely. Finally, the use of production rules rather than program code to implement knowledge acquisition rules makes the knowledge as implemented in the system more isomorphic to the acquired knowledge.

The use of rules or frames rather than programming code also yields an important benefit if the expert system is ever ported to different hardware while using the same software tool—a reasonably possible occurrence sometime in the life of the program. The software tool vendor will probably ensure that the AI paradigms the tool provides (rules, frame system, and so on) work on the new machine without the necessity of major rewriting or, at worst, will provide conversion software or instructions. However, the programming language parts of the system may need some changes (possibly many) to make them work on the new hardware, and these modifications will probably have to be done by the expert system group, not the software tool supplier.

In most cases programming language code is more efficient than rules or frames. But efficiency of implementation is usually not the most important goal of programming an expert system. The long-term maintainability of the program is, in most cases, of greater concern. It is now generally accepted that in most instances the largest costs in the life cycle of a computer program are for program maintenance. This may be true to an even greater degree for an expert system program, where the knowledge as well as the code must be maintained. Therefore even when programming within any one paradigm, maintainability should take priority over efficiency. This means, for example, programming in clear code and forgoing, if at all possible, the use of complex or nonobvious coding techniques whose only purpose is to increase efficiency.

Efficiency may be critical in situations where speed is paramount (such as for a real-time system), and this consideration may override any concerns about maintainability. (Surely if a program cannot meet its minimum requirements as to speed, there is no need to worry about its long-term maintenance.) But in most other cases, beware of false economy. A more efficient program that is harder to maintain will usually cost more in maintenance over the long term than whatever is gained by the greater program speed. On the other hand, efficiency should not be forgotten. A faster-running program is easier to develop (since it is easier to do test runs), easier to use, and clearly costs less to run. A reasonable compromise might be to implement the program with maintenance as the prime concern and then to consider making more efficient those parts of the program that most affect the overall run time.

Hard as it is to get experienced AI programmers to modify their programming style, it is usually even more difficult to get experienced programmers to program inefficient code intentionally. Often the fun, the challenge, and the skill of programming is in minimizing the size or the run time of a program. It goes against the nature of many programmers to, say, use a set of slow-running, verbose rules to do what a faster, shorter piece of programming language code can do, even though the use of rules may make the program much more readable and maintainable. Therefore project leaders may have to push hard for clear and maintainable but plain and somewhat inefficient code.

Maintainability can be downplayed during the development of an initial prototype; however, when work on the final system begins, some goals should be agreed upon, such as: "Use production rules instead of programming language code if at all possible." The paradigm(s) of choice will depend on many factors—type of problem, projected environment for the final product, efficiency considerations, skill level of users, and so on.

We were not concerned about maintainability when implementing *COM-PASS-I*, although we did not give much stress to efficiency either. Thus implementers used their programming skills in their accustomed way, which resulted in code that was relatively efficient but sometimes obscure. This made it difficult for nondevelopers to understand the *COMPASS-I* implementation;

moreover there were parts of the *COMPASS-I* code that could not be understood by any of the *COMPASS* programmers other than the programmer who wrote it. We accepted this situation for *COMPASS-I*, knowing that by making no restraints on the programmers, we speeded the implementation while producing a program that would perform somewhat better.

For *COMPASS-II*, we put an emphasis on maintainability, especially since *COMPASS* was designed to run offline, and therefore efficiency, though important, was not a critical concern. We felt that KEE frames and production rules generally would be easier to maintain than Lisp code, and therefore we tried to use frames and rules whenever possible. For example, the NR20 knowledge acquisition rules for prioritizing suggested maintenance actions were implemented in Lisp code in *COMPASS-I* but were reimplemented in KEE rules for *COMPASS-II*. In many cases, we felt that Lisp code would have provided a more efficient implementation than did frames or rules but that this efficiency would have been at the expense of maintainability.

I found as project leader that there were some experienced programmers whose techniques were so ingrained that they found it very difficult to program somewhat inefficiently in order to increase maintainability, even when urged to do so. The only approach that worked (to a degree) was to monitor the code of such people.

11.3.4 CONFIGURATION MANAGEMENT AND CONTROL

Configuration management and control is an area where many existing expert system development tools are weak. Tool developers generally concentrate on facilities related to the AI paradigm or paradigms that form the basis of their tool (such as tool speed, flexibility, ease of use) but often provide few system management capabilities, although such capabilities can be very useful. For example, it is often beneficial to have a mechanism facilitate the maintenence of all the files associated with a program or with a module of a program such as a knowledge base. Also it is useful to have an easy way to ensure that developers have consistent, complete copies of software.

If such capabilities are not provided by the development environment being used, it is often worth the effort for the expert system implementers to develop their own set of utilities for these purposes. The project should more than regain the effort extended in developing the configuration facility through improved knowledge engineering and savings in development time. The uniform configuration control characteristics of a central utility can prevent many software engineering mishaps and lead to a better control of development. Also depending on how the expert system is productized, the configuration utility might be usable by the expert system maintainers. Although a configuration facility may be developed for one particular project, it is not domain dependent, and if it is developed with sufficient generality, it could be used for other expert system projects.

As we worked on the implementation of *COMPASS,* we found that our environment did not supply the necessary configuration management and control capabilities. Therefore we put in place some mechanisms of our own for configuration control. For example, we needed a way to avoid multiple concurrent updates. If two programmers concurrently made modifications to a knowledge base, then the second to store the knowledge base would overwrite the knowledge base stored by the first, erasing the modifications made by the first programmer. We solved this problem by agreeing that no more than one person at a time would update a knowledge base. We set up a central location where we recorded which programmer (if any) was currently working on each knowledge base. This approach was somewhat cumbersome and failed occasionally when programmers forgot to record their status. Failure could mean that some programming effort had to be redone. Later in *COMPASS* development, we handled this problem by lessening considerably the need for two programmers to work on the same knowledge base. We did this by the use of the ACCESS mechanism (discussed in the following section).

To provide the additional configuration management and control features that we needed, we developed a UTILITIES knowledge base. UTILITIES contains information on the knowledge bases under development and can save and load the knowledge bases and their associated files.

Most of *COMPASS*'s knowledge bases are large—some having more than 250 frames and 50 or more methods in the frames. Each knowledge base was to be saved to and loaded from the shared file server many times during development by any or all of the (usually) four developers who worked on *COMPASS.* UTILITIES supervises this saving and loading. Each knowledge base has associated with it one or more files. These associated files contain method definitions, data structure declarations, and other items related to the methods. File names were keyed to their associated knowledge base; for example, the ANALYZE knowledge base had associated files ANALYZEFNS1, ANALYZEFNS2, ANALYZEFNS3, and so on. Facilities built into UTILITIES support configuration version control of a knowledge base and the set of files associated with it. For example, when a save to a new destination directory is requested, special handling in UTILITIES ensures that all files in the set are correctly saved.

Although UTILITIES was developed specifically for the *COMPASS* project, the ideas behind it proved of sufficient generality to be used on other projects to supplement the capabilities of commercial tools.

11.3.5 DATA FLOW AND ACCESS

In a large expert system program with multiple modules (e.g., rulesets, knowledge bases), data requirements and data access paths are usually unrestricted and are often unclear. It is desirable to utilize data abstraction and data flow restrictions to clarify and standardize the flow and to protect the data. Well-defined, standardized data-flow paths aid in development because they make it easier for developers to follow the movement of data in a complex system. Similarly they increase the maintainability of the expert system by making the data flow more intelligible to maintainers.

For an expert system program with multiple implementers, restricting the data flow can provide a way to coordinate the use of data among the implementers, as well as provide some protection for the data. One problem that occurs with multiple implementers is that one implementer may make knowledge representation changes that affect data structures referenced by other implementers. For example, when an implementer, possibly as part of a major change in the representation of a knowledge structure, changes the name of a data item in a module from SPEED to VELOCITY, other implementers' program modules that use the value of SPEED will no longer find it and will suddenly (and seemingly inexplicably) not work correctly. A more complex case of the problem would occur when an implementer changes the paradigm of representation for a set of data that other programmers utilize, such as rerepresenting a matrix, which was originally represented in program language code, as a group of frames in a frame structure. In both cases, a standard for data flow could require the implementer of a module containing externally referenced data to provide those data in a standard form, no matter in what way the module is later altered. It is also useful to have a mechanism to prevent an implementer from making changes to the data or data structures in other implementers' program modules. This type of facility may not be provided in the software tool. A standard for data flow could provide some protection for the data in a module to prevent such tampering.

A complex, multiple module program might achieve clarification, standardization, and protection of data flow if the implementation team restricts data flow by adopting a set of data access conventions and abstractions and by employing a formal mechanism for intermodule data access. A module would then be required to use certain standard structures to request data from another module. Each module that might be a source of data would be required to have mechanisms to respond to standard requests for data. These mechanisms would have to supply the data according to the agreed-upon convention. Thus in the above example, the intermodule data access mechanism should provide a way for the module to supply the data value now known as VELOCITY in response to the same standardized request to which it previously returned the value of SPEED.

> In the implementation of the *COMPASS-I* feasibility prototype, no restrictions were made on how one knowledge base could access data in another knowledge base. As a result a programmer occasionally found that his code did not

work because someone had changed a data structure that he accessed in another knowledge base. This happened, for example, when a slot named FAULT was renamed FAULTS. These problems were sometimes hard to track down. When the feasibility system was completed, it was difficult for someone outside the project team to understand exactly what the data access paths were and how a change would affect the system.

These kinds of problems are commonplace in software development. In the case of *COMPASS,* the situation was aggravated by the fact that some of the system decomposition into knowledge bases was based on a functional partitioning of the expert task and thus was not partitioned based on software concerns.

In *COMPASS-II,* we wished to ensure clean data interfaces but did not want to make strong restrictions on how the various knowledge representations available in KEE could be used. To do so would reduce the usefulness of the available paradigms. Therefore we placed restrictions on data access but only on the data access between knowledge bases. This approach gave each developer independence in designing his knowledge base's internal knowledge representation while requiring specification of the nature of the inputs he would get and the outputs he would have to produce.

The ACCESS knowledge base provides the framework of the data access scheme for transferring knowledge among the *COMPASS* knowledge bases. There are two different mechanisms for retrieving data in another knowledge base: an access gateway and an import/export mechanism. The access gateway consists of a single frame (always called ACCESS) in each active knowledge base. The ACCESS frame is a subclass of a generic ACCESS frame that resides in the ACCESS knowledge base. This arrangement allows the access gateway mechanism to be propagated easily throughout *COMPASS.* When a function or method needs data, it always assumes that the needed information is in a slot in its own knowledge base. If the data must be obtained from another knowledge base, a method in the original knowledge base's ACCESS frame is invoked by means of demons. The invoked method fetches and returns the desired value. The access gateway mechanism thus ensures that interknowledge base data requests are done in a uniform way.

For large amounts of shared data, the access gateway may not be an efficient approach. For example, *COMPASS* constructs a frame in the MESSAGES knowledge base for each of possibly hundreds of maintenance messages. It would be not be very efficient for the CLUSTERS knowledge base, which requires access to the same data, to create another frame for each maintenance message. To avoid this possibility, we created in the ACCESS knowledge base a framework for data abstraction, again based on demons, that allows data structures to be imported and exported. In essence, the exporter of knowledge structures provides an abstraction of whatever structure is used so that it looks like a record to the importer. The importer is freed from worries about the data structures someone else is using. Furthermore the transfer of data across knowledge bases is done in a standard way, which increases system maintainability.

The ACCESS knowledge base provides generic import and export structures. The developer of a knowledge base that must export structures builds a demon that will collect pointers to the structures to be exported and also creates an access function, which provides the importing knowledge base access to the various fields in the data structure.

This approach does not completely eliminate the need for communication among developers because when an importer requires data that are not already set up to be exported, he and the exporter must agree on what must be exported and how the export should be structured and invoked. But using the import/export mechanism does make it much easier for the user of an exported structure to find out what can be accessed. It allows the developer of each knowledge base the flexibility of changing the data representation many times during the development of the system without disrupting the development of other knowledge bases.

Note that the import/export mechanism does not allow the importer to change the exporter's data structures or values. Thus the mechanism provides data protection when it is used (although it does not, by itself, prevent anyone from not using it and instead directly accessing and modifying someone else's knowledge base).

11.3.6 CONTROL FLOW

Control flow can be obscure in a complex expert system. This lack of clarity may impede implementation to some degree, especially if there are multiple implementers, and it will certainly make program maintenance more difficult. It is therefore beneficial for the implementation team to develop a means by which the flow of control can be clarified and made more orderly.

For example, a large object-oriented expert system may have complex control flow paths—not just within objects but also between objects and between knowledge bases. Unconstrained coding in an object-oriented programming environment may result in control passing continually and rapidly between objects in different knowledge bases. Such complex control flow is difficult to document and is difficult for nondevelopers to follow and maintain. Too much restriction on control flow, however, may take away much of the power of the object-oriented paradigm. Thus some approach is needed whereby there is some constraint on control flow but the constraint is not strong enough to be overly restrictive.

The approach to defining and limiting control flow depends on the structure and modularity of the implementation. In an expert system implementation consisting of several independent modules, a useful technique is to develop a top-level module that defines the control flow and to adopt a set of conventions for initiating action within a module. Such a structure can be refined for a system with a more complex control flow.

> When programmers who were not developers of COMPASS looked at the COMPASS-I implementation, they found the flow of control in the program difficult to follow. Program control leaped from an object in the middle of one knowledge base to a seemingly unrelated object in the middle of another knowledge base, and from there to a third object somewhere else, and so on. Object-oriented messages seemed to be moving in all directions, and the outside programmers had trouble tracing the path of control flow.

> We decided that for COMPASS-II we needed to put some restrictions and standardization on control flow. As with data flow, we did not wish to restrict what an individual developer could do about control flow within a knowledge base because this restriction would significantly diminish the power of the object-oriented programming paradigm. Therefore we decided to place constraints only on interknowledge base control flow.

> We accomplished these constraints by creating the CONTROL knowledge base. This knowledge base provides a centralized branching point for control flow in the system. It also serves as a storehouse for systemwide variables and provides a standardized framework for initiating actions in the active knowledge bases.

> The CONTROL knowledge base is the clearinghouse for knowledge base invocation. All knowledge bases that perform some part of the COMPASS analysis receive control from the CONTROL knowledge base. After one of these knowledge bases has completed a task, it returns program control back to the CONTROL knowledge base. Thus control is never passed from one active knowledge base directly to another.

> A generic frame, GENERIC.CONTROL, has instances (always called CONTROL) in each active knowledge base. The instances inherit method slots that contain templates for functions to initialize a knowledge base and to initiate actions in a knowledge base. These templates are filled in by the individual knowledge base implementers. When COMPASS executes, the CONTROL knowledge base passes program control to a particular knowledge base by sending a message to that knowledge base's CONTROL frame.

> The top-level control format produced by the use of the CONTROL knowledge base assists both implementer and maintainer. It provides a standard mechanism to run any knowledge base and a good starting point for someone trying to track down a bug in a knowledge base.

11.3.7 INPUT/OUTPUT

In a complex expert system program, there may be a scattering of input and output statements throughout the program, each written for a specific input or output device. If this circumstance pertains, there may be little flexibility to accept a change in the appearance of the input, to make a change in the appearance of the output (even a simple change such as the use of a different font), or to accept input from or redirect output to different peripheral devices. Furthermore problems in maintenance may occur if it is hard to locate the source of specific input/output commands within a large program. Knowledge engineering tools and environments are strong in providing input/output options but often are weak in providing an organized, simple-to-understand way of accessing those options.

The maintainability and flexibility of an expert system program's input and output may be improved by a mechanism that channels all of the input and output through one identified part of the program. One way to do this is to create a program module that will serve as a central clearinghouse for input and output.

> We found two major problems related to the output of *COMPASS*. One was the difficulty in dealing with different classes of peripheral devices. *COMPASS* was developed in an environment based on the Xerox Lisp machine and its associated equipment, with bitmapped output devices. Without any special centralized input and output facilities, this situation could result in difficulties if *COMPASS* is moved to an environment where the available input and output devices are different. For example, when *COMPASS-I* was installed at GTE Data Services, GTEDS had no bitmapped hard-copy devices connected to their machines. Revising the *COMPASS* output statements throughout the code for use on a different output device was time-consuming. Also this revision had to eliminate all font changes and other graphical information.

> The second problem was the difficulty involved in changing the appearance of the output—such as changing fonts, reformatting the layout of reports, or redirecting output to different files or windows. For example, for a *COMPASS* demonstration, we might want to increase the font size of all the output for readability. Accomplishing this task for *COMPASS-I* was cumbersome because the output statements were dispersed throughout the code and because it was not easy to determine which of the many functions and rules in the system was producing the output.

> Our solution to these kinds of output-related problems was to create the EVENTS knowledge base. It provides facilities for device independence of output, easy redirection of output streams, and centralized control of all output parameters. When an event occurs that requires information to be output, the knowledge base in which the event happened, rather than producing the output, calls a standard function that channels the output data to the EVENTS knowledge base for output. An "Event" can be an occurrence such as the finding of an intermediate result (a possible fault for a No. 2 EAX problem was identified), the finding of an error (two suggestion-ordering rules produce opposite ordering for two suggestions), or the production of part of the final output. For example, in Figure 10.12, the DO clause is a call to a function, FAULT.IDENTIFIED.SIGNAL, that signals to EVENTS that a set of possible switch

faults has been identified and sends information to EVENTS on the rule fired and the faults found.

The EVENTS knowledge base allows an implementer to set up frames for a variety of output streams, each representing a type of logical output and a physical device to which that output will be sent. Each stream frame is set up to inherit slots from the appropriate class frames in a hierarchy of both logical and physical device frames. The logical device frames partition the output into different types, such as Report, Trace, Break, and Error. Physical device frames describe the specific output devices that are available, such as bitmapped windows, laser printers, and line printers.

Value slots and method slots in the stream frames contain the information needed to format and direct the output of text and graphical information. For each logical type of output, a default physical device can be set. Inappropriate commands, such as font changes on devices that do not support fonts, are automatically suppressed. Page size information is included in the knowledge base to allow line wrapping and automatic form feeds. By simply changing a few slot values in the EVENTS hierarchy, the same output could be directed to a different window, to a file, or to another type of display device.

Because *COMPASS* had no input problems similar to the problems on output, the *COMPASS* version of EVENTS was limited to use on output. EVENTS will be extended to use for program inputs when this proves to be needed on other projects.

CHECKLIST FOR IMPLEMENTING THE SYSTEM

☐ Develop an expert system program by a process of incremental development, starting with a small program and refining and enlarging it incrementally. Because the specification of an expert system (that is, its knowledge) cannot be completely specified before implementation, do not attempt a full top-down approach.

☐ Investigate the possibility of rewriting some or all of the expert system program code when entering a new development phase.

☐ When using a production rule system, implement a knowledge acquisition rule by a corresponding implementation rule (or, if necessary, by a corresponding set of rules) if possible.

☐ Group rules into rulesets.

☐ Utilize the knowledge acquisition cycle as a major means of "automatically" debugging the expert system program.

☐ Plan to use the documented knowledge as a significant piece of program documentation. Write the knowledge documentation with that purpose in mind.

☐ Put comments in the program liberally—not just in the programming language code but also in all program elements, such as rules, frames, and frame slots.

☐ Modularize the overall program architecture in such a way that developers can work relatively independently but also in such a way as roughly to follow the modularity of the expert knowledge.

☐ Where possible utilize modular implementation techniques, such as production rules and object-oriented techniques, to minimize the interaction of the implementation of different knowledge chunks.

☐ Adopt a set of programming-style conventions to give the program a uniform look.

☐ Favor a more maintainable paradigm (such as production rules) over a less maintainable paradigm (such as programming language code).

☐ Sacrifice some program efficiency to attain better readability and maintainability, unless speed of program execution is a paramount concern.

☐ Utilize configuration management and control facilities; develop them if the software system being used does not provide them.

☐ Enforce well-defined, standardized data-flow paths to make the system's data flow clearer to developers and maintainers.

☐ Limit control-flow paths to clarify the flow of program control for developers and maintainers.

☐ Channel input and output through one identified program part to allow simplicity and flexibility in controlling input/output.

Prerau, Developing and Managing Expert Systems (Addison-Wesley)

CHAPTER 12

Testing and Evaluating the System

- How does the expert system knowledge acquisition cycle inherently provide repeated validation and verification testing of the expert system program?

- How can meetings with the project's consulting experts provide testing of the expert system during development?

- Under what circumstances can the correctness of an expert system be confirmed absolutely?

- How can an expert system be validated by comparison with human experts, and when should an outside expert or group of experts be used?

- How should field trials be arranged?

- What techniques can be used for expert system verification?

- What amount of effort should be put into expert system evaluation, and what standards should be used?

This chapter discusses techniques for testing and evaluating the quality of an expert system to determine the level of expertise and accuracy that can be expected from it. Other aspects of the expert system—its reliability, maintainability, integratability, ease of use, and so forth—should be appraised as well, and these issues are discussed in Chapter 13.

Any software system that is to be deployed should undergo evaluation to determine if it performs acceptably. For conventional programs, there are several established techniques for this purpose. In this chapter, we look into aspects of program evaluation that are unique to or most applicable to expert system programs.

Program evaluation generally can be separated into two components: validation and verification. **Validation** refers to determining whether the *right system* was built, that is, whether the system does what it was meant to do and at an acceptable level of accuracy. Validating an expert system involves confirming that the expert system performs the desired task with a sufficient level of expertise. **Verification** refers to determining whether the system was *built right,* that is, whether the system implementation correctly corresponds to its specifications. Therefore verifying an expert system means confirming that the program accurately implements the acquired expert knowledge as documented.

12.1 VALIDATION AND VERIFICATION DURING EXPERT SYSTEM DEVELOPMENT

The development of expert systems, as opposed to that of most conventional programs, inherently includes repeated validation and verification testing as part of the development process.

12.1.1 VALIDATION AND VERIFICATION AS INHERENT PARTS OF KNOWLEDGE ACQUISITION

The knowledge acquisition cycles of Elicit-Document-Test and Elicit-Document-Implement-Test are based on a repeated validation testing of the evolving expert system. The primary purpose of the Test Step in each cycle is to find deficiencies in the expert system's knowledge by comparing the present version of the documented knowledge or its implementation against a human expert's reasoning. In addition to this validation testing, it is important to note that the knowledge acquisition process automatically performs verification tests, checking the evolving software for implementation bugs. Each time the partially completed expert system program is run to test the knowledge in the program, all aspects of the operation of the program are tested as well. Thus as shown in Figure 12.1, the process of developing the expert system inherently includes a large amount of program testing—both validation and verification.

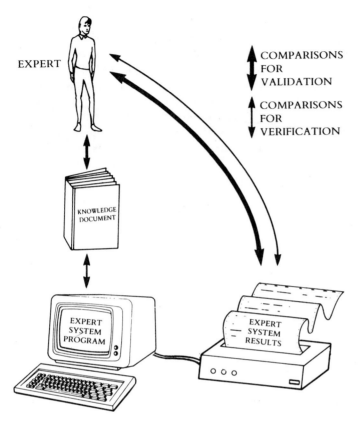

FIGURE 12.1 Validation and verification testing during expert system development

Frequently as part of knowledge acquisition, runs of the evolving program are made to test the knowledge. But if the program aborts its execution, clearly there is a programming error that must be corrected before knowledge acquisition (or at least that aspect of knowledge acquisition) can continue. Moreoever if the program runs to completion and its results disagree with those of an expert, frequently the cause of the discrepancy is not an error in the acquired knowledge but rather a programming mistake. Thus in addition to finding weaknesses in the knowledge, the knowledge acquisition cycle finds and corrects programming errors. Often the locations of errors in the program are found by the same process that knowledge acquirers use to find errors in the expert system knowledge—by comparing an expert's step-by-step reasoning against that of the program and finding the points where they diverge. At first only small parts of the ultimate program are tested by the knowledge acquisition process, but as the program grows toward its final size and structure, increasing portions of the system are evaluated.

In most instances, the knowledge acquisition cycle is used to develop the expert system program cumulatively, and the entire program is run and evaluated many times as it grows. Thus most parts of the growing program are evaluated and reevaluated repeatedly—possibly a great many more times than would be part of any reasonable postdevelopment testing. In some expert system developments, different modules of the program are developed separately. In these cases, the program as a whole may never be evaluated during development, although each module is tested many times. But even then, for domains with clearly defined intermediate results, testing each module may be tantamount to testing the entire program.

> The *COMPASS* knowledge acquisition made repeated use of the Elicit-Document-Implement-Test knowledge acquisition cycle, through which we found and corrected errors in the knowledge. This process also identified many programming errors. Sometimes we found that when using the cycle to test one part of the program, a poor result would lead us to find an implementation error in a completely different part of the program. As we reached the end of the knowledge acquisition of *COMPASS* for each maintenance message type, we tested full runs of *COMPASS* many times against the expert's analyses. *COMPASS* generally performed very well in these tests, and the discrepancies found were usually the result of easy-to-repair errors.

12.1.2 VALIDATION TESTING BY CONSULTING EXPERTS

One way to perform validation testing during expert system development is to have a group of consulting experts evaluate the expert system at points throughout the project. They should examine many expert system runs and identify any results with which they disagree. Sometimes the discrepancies found will be due to differences in technique or knowledge between the consulting experts and the project's primary experts, but often they will lead the system developers to find and correct errors in the expert system's knowledge or implementation.

If the domain permits, each expert individually can analyze a series of test cases before being told the expert system's results for the cases. Then their independent results can be compared against those of the program. In addition to examining system inputs and outputs, consulting experts can analyze in detail the internal reasoning of the system and confirm that it is valid. This analysis might be facilitated by having a system developer or primary expert walk them through several test cases, closely detailing the reasoning of the system. The experts also might be asked to read through the knowledge documentation, examining every rule (or other knowledge unit) to determine whether there are any mistakes and omissions in the acquired knowledge.

When the expert system is completed, project consulting experts or other domain experts might be asked to participate in the validation of the completed system.

During *COMPASS* development, we had a number of meetings with a group of consulting domain experts and used several approaches to aid them in evaluating the program. We gave the consulting experts a set of test cases and asked them to perform their usual analyses. Then their results were compared with those of *COMPASS*. Their results generally agreed, although in some cases errors in the *COMPASS* knowledge or implementation were found (and corrected). Sometimes when the experts disagreed with a *COMPASS* result, later and more detailed analysis showed that *COMPASS* was right and that all of the experts were wrong. This situation usually occurred in cases where *COMPASS* performed certain subanalyses that the experts skipped. The experts knew about these lines of reasoning but bypassed them in practice because they were time-consuming and were, by the experts' meta-heuristics, unlikely to produce useful information. *COMPASS* could perform these subanalyses very quickly and therefore did so in all runs. In the infrequent cases where the subanalyses proved fruitful, *COMPASS* outperformed all the top experts.

We also walked the consulting experts through many *COMPASS* analyses in full detail. They almost always agreed that the methodology was correct. On occasion they would state that although *COMPASS*'s approach was correct, their methodology would have been somewhat different. These sessions sometimes allowed experts to find subtle points where the knowledge needed to be changed.

In addition to detailing *COMPASS*'s methodology to the consulting experts at meetings, we sent all of them complete copies of the *COMPASS* knowledge document periodically and before each meeting. They thus were able to examine all of *COMPASS*'s knowledge and reasoning in great detail at their own pace. They discussed with the primary expert any errors they found, and corrections were made to the knowledge document and the corresponding implementation.

12.2 VALIDATION OF THE DEVELOPED EXPERT SYSTEM

When the expert system has been developed, it should be validated as shown in Figure 12.2. Several techniques can be used; the choice depends on the nature of the application.

12.2.1 VALIDATING ABSOLUTELY

Several aspects of an expert system's domain affect the techniques required for validation. In some domains, the correctness of an expert system's results can be confirmed absolutely, as in the following examples:

■ *An expert system that attempts to find the answer to a complicated mathematical or puzzle-like problem.* Although it may be very difficult to find the correct answer, once it is found, it may be relatively simple to determine that the answer is correct.

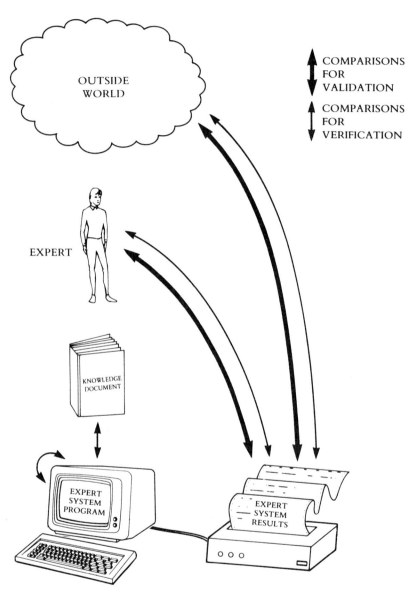

FIGURE 12.2 Validation and verification of the developed expert system

- *An expert system that attempts to find malfunctions in a device.* The system can be run for real devices to see the degree to which it actually can pinpoint the malfunction. These runs can be done as special tests or may be part of a field trial.

■ *A predictive system for which old data are available.* Based on the old data, the system can predict an outcome, and this result can be compared against what actually occurred.

In domains such as these, the degree of competence of an expert system may be determined absolutely against the outside world, without need for comparison against human experts' results. It should be remembered, however, that the actual utility of the expert system usually depends on how its competence compares with that of typical domain practitioners. The expert system should not be considered a failure because it makes some mistakes unless the same degree of error could not be tolerated in a human performing the task.

COMPASS produces a list of recommended actions for each switch problem. Therefore there are (at least) two criteria by which to judge COMPASS's performance:

1. Will COMPASS correct the problem—that is, will one of its recommended actions repair the problem?

2. How quickly will COMPASS correct the problem—that is, how high on COMPASS's list of recommendations is the successful recommendation?

The first criterion is the more important. If a problem is not corrected by any of COMPASS's recommendations, then all the recommended actions were performed with no useful result, and the analysis of the problem must be re-done manually—probably by a higher-level switchperson (such as a local expert or a regional expert). If COMPASS does not do well on the second criterion, the cost is not as great—the switchperson might have performed some maintenance actions that were not the most likely to find the problem, but the problem would eventually be found.

Ideally COMPASS should always select for first repair the most likely cause of the problem found. But the most likely cause many times is not the actual one. We found numerous cases where COMPASS made the best recommendation—the one top domain experts would make—but the actual problem turned out to be due to some other less likely cause. There is therefore no way that COMPASS could be perfect by the second criterion—that is, could always choose the correct repair action to make first.

The actual results of COMPASS field trials have shown that in over 98 percent of the cases, COMPASS determined the correct maintenance recommendation. In over 60 percent of these cases, COMPASS was successful in its first recommendation other than a recommendation to run a switch diagnostic test. (Although expert experience has shown that switch diagnostics usually do not find the cause of a problem, running a switch diagnostic is usually the first recommendation of both COMPASS and top experts because running a diagnostic test is an easy and quick action.)

12.2.2 VALIDATING AGAINST EXPERT PERFORMANCE

Some domains that do not have an absolute test of correctness have the property that experts will generally agree on the correctness or optimality of a result. If there is no clear notion of result correctness, an equivalent property is that experts will generally agree on whether a decision is good, reasonable, or at least acceptable. Expert systems for such domains can be validated by comparison against expert performance.

To compare an expert system against a human expert, one technique is to compare the expert system's results against actual operational expert judgments. This comparison can be done only if all the pertinent data available to the expert in the operational situation can be made available to the expert system. Another technique is to get the expert system's results on a set of test cases and compare these against the results obtained by human experts. The technique preferred depends on the application area and the kinds of data available. In many situations, the comparisons can be made using the expert or experts who participated in the expert system development. It is often enough to show that the system's results are close to those of a project expert.

Furthermore for domains where experts often strongly and irreconcilably disagree, such as economic forecasting, developers and users have to be satisfied with a system that implements, to the degree possible, the expertise of a single expert or a small group of experts. In such cases, the expert system's results clearly should be measured against the results of the particular expert or experts involved.

Validating the expert system with an expert or a group of experts other than those involved in the expert system development provides the important advantage of removing possible biases, although it is often more difficult (and sometimes more costly) to arrange. This approach might also provide a better technical result since it could reveal subtle problems in the reasoning of project experts that would not be identified by the project experts themselves. It also provides the nontechnical benefit of giving the validation more—sometimes a great deal more—credibility.

As with the utilization of multiple experts to develop an expert system, there are both advantages to and problems inherent in utilizing multiple experts for system validation. A major advantage of the use of several experts is that it gives added credibility to the validation. However, a process must be set up to deal with those cases where the evaluating experts disagree, and such a process might not be effective or easy to use. One simple approach is to consider as correct the majority decision of the experts. More accurate but more difficult to employ are techniques such as the Delphi technique that try to obtain expert consensus. Another approach is to measure the expert system's degree of agreement with the expert majority and to compare that against the degree to which each individual expert agrees with the majority.

In addition to appraising *COMPASS*'s success in recommending actions to repair actual switch problems, we also compared *COMPASS*'s recommendations
in field situations against those of the primary expert. There was complete
agreement in over 93 percent of the cases. (Note that for problems where
they do not agree completely, *COMPASS*'s list of recommendations usually
contains many of the same recommendations that the expert would make.
Thus even when *COMPASS* does not completely agree with the expert, it still
often recommends a maintenance action that corrects the switch problem.)

12.2.3 VALIDATION BY FIELD TESTING

When the domain and organizational conditions permit, it is valuable to
evaluate the expert system's performance by running the program in the
field under actual operational conditions. This evaluation could be done as
part of a field trial of the expert system or by testing the expert system in
its initial routine production use. Such field tests can be an important part
of a total evaluation of the expert system. In addition, successful results
from the field often do more to convince potential users of the merits of a
system than the success of much more extensive and accurate laboratory
tests.

If the domain is such that individual errors by the expert system have
small cost and there are no problems getting the cooperation of a field
organization, it is certainly advisable to set up field tests—formal field trials
or tests of the system in initial production use. But if poor decisions made
by the expert system can have major negative effects, conducting actual
field trials may not be possible. Certainly in such cases the field trials should
not be done until other available techniques of evaluation have been employed and have shown that the system performs well.

When field testing cannot be performed, one possible approach is to
run a parallel field trial, where the expert system is run in a nonoperational
setting paralleling the actual operation. In such a situation the expert system
is run on real data and makes decisions under circumstances similar to the
actual operation (for example, the same time constraints), but its decisions
are not acted upon. Instead they can be compared to the actual operational
decisions made, and they can be analyzed in detail by experts.

Field tests should be carefully controlled to ensure that no factors unrelated to the expert system's competence can be the cause of poor results.
Field personnel should understand the function of the expert system, operate it correctly, and utilize its results correctly. After an expert system
has been in production use for an extended period, operational people get
accustomed to it. They understand how to operate it and how to make use
of its results, and they adjust their operating procedures to incorporate it.
But in a field trial or in initial production use, none of these circumstances
can be assumed. Furthermore some field personnel—possibly seeing a threat
to their jobs—might be actively opposed to the expert system and

might attempt to influence the test results. Also for a field trial some field personnel might not want to be bothered participating in a test of a system that is not a final product. All of these possibilities should be considered when setting up the field testing.

Moreover since in most cases the primary objective of field testing is to determine the level of expertise and accuracy of the expert system, careful consideration should be given to the types of data collected for this purpose. The data gathered should be such that they accurately reflect the task performance of the system and will be convincing to others. Field tests can also provide valuable data on important operational factors related to the expert system such as run speed, ease of use, installation costs, training needs, and many others. Mechanisms should be set up to gather accurately the data related to all important factors, while imposing as little burden as possible on users.

> We ran carefully controlled field trials on the *COMPASS* system, using several sites at three different GTE telephone companies. We set up procedures with supervisors to ensure that the No. 2 EAX switch personnel would utilize *COMPASS*—and only *COMPASS*—to determine problems with their switch. The field personnel agreed to follow *COMPASS*'s recommendations—whether or not they believed them to be correct. This agreement occasionally proved important. In its very first field trial, *COMPASS* recommended some maintenance actions with which the switchpeople disagreed. It identified a set of problem symptoms that were already known to switch personnel. They and their local No. 2 EAX experts had been trying unsuccessfully for several weeks to pinpoint the switch fault causing the problem. *COMPASS* suggested that the cause of the problem was located in an area of the switch far from where the local people thought the fault would be found. Although the switch personnel were sure that *COMPASS* was wrong, they followed *COMPASS*'s advice because they had agreed to do so and were very impressed when *COMPASS*'s recommendation did indeed solve the problem.

> We collected data on how well *COMPASS*'s recommendations succeeded in correcting the switch problems. The results, as mentioned in Section 12.2.1, were excellent. *COMPASS* also did very well in later field trials performed when it was transferred to GTE Data Services.

12.3   VERIFICATION OF AN EXPERT SYSTEM PROGRAM

Verification of an expert system program confirms that the expert system program has been built correctly. The program should accurately implement the acquired expert knowledge. The knowledge acquisition process by its nature includes repeated runs of parts of the developing program, which uncover errors not only in the knowledge but in the knowledge implementation. It is likely that this process will result in a final expert system program that not only agrees very well with the knowledge documentation but also contains fewer program bugs than a typical conventional program. In addition, by the same mechanism, the implementation of the knowledge in the final expert system program will be tested as part of any validation process. Errors in the knowledge implementation often are caught during validation when errors or weaknesses in the program's results are investigated.

The implemented expert knowledge should have no internal errors (independent of whether the acquired knowledge is correct and complete). For example, in a production rule system there should not be any redundant rules, unreachable rules, subsumed rules or clauses, rules with the same name, rules with incorrect syntax, sets of circular rules, and so forth. In a frame system, there should not be any slot values (preset or created) that are illegal, frames with the same name, slot multiple-inheritance conflicts that are unresolved, circular inheritance paths, and so on. These situations can be checked without knowing if the knowledge itself is correct. Most rule systems check for syntax errors, and some rule systems provide automated rule checkers, which can check a knowledge base for many of the other potential problems listed. Frame systems often provide automatic checks, such as type checking of slot values, and these are provided for both the original entry of the stored expert system program and frames created dynamically during processing. If the absence of important potential problems is not confirmed automatically, the expert system testing team should examine these areas.

As part of the verification process, the base program that implements the knowledge engineering paradigms should be verified as operating correctly—production rules properly processed by the inference engine, slot value inheritance in a frame system properly performed, and so on. This aspect of verification should be pursued to the extent that the expert system verifiers suspect errors in the knowledge engineering software tool. It may be minimized if the project is using a standard, commercial software tool that is in wide use.

> During the *COMPASS* knowledge acquisition process, the program was run numerous times. In addition to finding weaknesses in the knowledge, many programming errors were found and corrected. During field trials and field use, any errors found in *COMPASS*'s results were investigated and corrected, including those caused by programming mistakes. In deployment few programming errors were discovered, which we felt indicated the benefits of the expert system knowledge acquisition process as a verification technique.
>
> In addition, the KEE system provided several verification checks on the *COMPASS* program, both static and dynamic. It performed checks on rule syntax, slot value type, proper inheritance, and so on. Moreover the *COMPASS* devel-

opers felt that KEE, being a widely used commercial tool, would itself produce few errors that were not known or not found during program implementation.

When *COMPASS* was transferred to GTE Data Services, the *COMPASS* group there performed several verification tests on the program. For example, they traced through the rules to determine if there were any nonreachable rules, redundant rules, and so on. Rather than use actual switch data, they put together a set of data that included many possible types of problems on which to test *COMPASS*.

12.4 EVALUATION EFFORT AND STANDARDS

The amount of effort put into evaluating the performance of an expert system program should be strongly related to the task performed by the system. If the domain is such that a large evaluation process is necessary, the resources and time needed for that task should be included in the plan for system development.

Expert systems in some domains require a sizable evaluation effort. For example, if a major error by the expert system would have disastrous effects, a great deal of resources should go into evaluating the program. Such systems should not be put into operational use until the deployers and users are convinced that it performs at the level required. Another circumstance where a large evaluation effort may be required is in a domain where experts perform only slightly better than average practitioners. Here the expert system may have no payoff in quality of performance (though there may be an automation payoff) unless it can be shown to be very close to the level of an expert. Also in a domain where the primary payoff is in automating work done by large numbers of people who perform at approximately the same level, the system probably would not be accepted unless it can be shown to have at least that level of performance.

On the other hand, there are many applications for which a small effort at evaluating the expert system may be all that is required. In a domain where experts have vastly superior performance to that of the average practitioner, the system may need to show only some small degree of expert performance to be acceptable. A precise measurement of its level of skill might not be necessary. In domains where mistakes are not crucial, it may be possible to prove the system in operational use. If so, it would make it unnecessary to devote a great deal of developmental resources to system evaluation.

As with level of effort, standards of evaluation for an expert system program should reflect the task. In critical applications, standards clearly should be very high. Where errors are not costly, lower standards might be employed. As with conventional software, there is no way to prove that a system is perfect. If the standards of evaluation are too high, there is a risk of not approving a system that would be useful. This possibility must be weighed against the alternative, usually worse, possibility that if the standards are too low, a nonacceptable system might be approved.

When setting standards for evaluating the expert system, it is important to bear in mind that different types of errors of the system may have different degrees of significance. The knowledge acquired from an expert may include information on which ways the system might shade its reasoning so that it minimizes the impact of errors. This type of knowledge, obtained from the experts or potential users, should also be used to weigh the results of expert system validation tests.

> Incorrect No. 2 EAX maintenance diagnoses are common, even by experts, since the No. 2 EAX data are ambiguous. A mistaken maintenance action does not have a disastrous result, although it does have a cost (in wasted switchperson time). Furthermore the skill of a top No. 2 EAX maintenance expert is far greater than that of the average journeyman No. 2 EAX switchperson, the primary user of *COMPASS*. For these reasons, we felt (and it proved true) that if *COMPASS* could be shown to perform at close to the level of the *COMPASS* primary expert (and therefore could be shown to have significantly greater expertise than the average No. 2 EAX switchperson), then it would not be necessary to measure its skill level with great accuracy or expend great resources on an evaluation process prior to field use. In the *COMPASS* domain false positives (finding a problem that is not really there) are worse than false negatives (not identifying a problem that actually exists). We took this important difference into account when evaluating performance.

CHECKLIST FOR TESTING AND EVALUATING THE SYSTEM

☐ Use the cycle of Elicit-Document-Implement-Test not only for knowledge acquisition but also as a way to test the evolving expert system program continually.

☐ In a domain where the correctness of an expert system's results can be determined absolutely, measure the competence of the system by the degree of its agreement with the known correct results. To determine the overall worth of the system, this measured competence should be compared, in most cases, not against a standard of perfection but against the proficiency of typical domain practitioners.

☐ In a domain where experts usually agree, evaluate the system by comparison against human experts.

☐ In a domain where experts often disagree strongly and irreconcilably, compare the expert system's results against the results of the project's expert(s) and be happy with a system that has expertise close to that of the project expert(s).

☐ When the domain allows, utilize for system evaluation an expert or experts not associated with the project, as long as the gains in impartiality of evaluation and credibility of result outweigh any difficulties and costs.

☐ If the domain allows, use multiple experts for system evaluation when the gains in credibility of result outweigh the problems that occur when the evaluating experts disagree.

☐ Use meetings with consulting experts to evaluate system results and also to evaluate the detailed reasoning and internal processes of the system.

☐ When domain and organizational conditions permit, test the expert system in the field. Set up a field trial to evaluate the expert system's performance under actual operational conditions, or test the system during its initial routine production use.

☐ If live field testing cannot be performed, consider running a parallel field trial, where the system is run on real data but in a nonoperational setting that parallels actual operation.

☐ Control field testing carefully to ensure that procedures are followed correctly and that field personnel understand the expert system and know how to use it. Try to ensure that no factors unrelated to the expert system's competence can be the cause of poor results.

☐ Give careful consideration to the types of data that will be collected during a field test. They should accurately reflect the performance and other important factors related to the expert system and should be convincing to others.

☐ Set up mechanisms that allow the gathering of the accurate field test data while imposing as little burden as possible on users.

☐ Verify that the program accurately implements the acquired expert knowledge. The knowledge acquisition process by its nature will likely result in a final expert system program that agrees very well with the knowledge documentation.

☐ Verify that the implemented expert knowledge contains no internal errors (independent of the completeness or correctness of the knowledge itself), such as redundant rules, sets of circular rules, and illegal slot values. Utilize automated checking systems if available.

☐ Verify that the base program that implements the knowledge engineering paradigms operates correctly. This aspect of verification may be minimized if the project is utilizing a standard, commercial software tool in wide use.

☐ Put the amount of effort into system evaluation that the particular system warrants. Invest substantial effort in a large-scale evaluation if errors by the expert system would be disastrous or if knowledge of the exact competence level of the system is critical. Invest less evaluation effort if system errors are not crucial and any performance close to an expert's is valuable.

☐ Set standards of evaluation for the expert system based on domain requirements. In critical applications, standards should be very high. When errors are not costly, consider using lower standards to gauge success.

Prerau, Developing and Managing Expert Systems (Addison-Wesley)

CHAPTER 13

Transferring and Deploying the System

■■■■■ What techniques can be used successfully for transferring an expert system, such as from a development group to a deployment or operating group?

■■■■■ What technical and nontechnical factors should be considered during deployment?

■■■■■ What type of training do the recipients of an expert system transfer need?

■■■■■ What techniques can be used successfully for transferring general expert system technology skills from a technically advanced part of a corporation to other parts of the corporation where the skills are needed?

■■■■■ How can an expert system be developed with technology transfer and deployment in mind?

In this chapter, we consider issues of technology transfer and deployment related to an expert system. Chapter 3 discussed technology transfer and deployment as they affect the planning and managing of the expert system project. Here we examine several other important factors pertaining to these issues, emphasizing areas where the technology transfer and deployment processes for expert systems are significantly different from the corresponding processes for conventional programs.

There are two aspects of expert system technology transfer: (1) the transfer of an expert system *program* from one group to another, such as from a development group to a deployment or operating group, and (2) the transfer of general expert system *technology skills,* such as from a corporate laboratory to an operating unit of the corporation. The techniques and requisites for both types of transfers will be examined. We also discuss ways to take technology transfer and deployment into account throughout the expert system development process, factors to consider when deploying an expert system, and techniques to aid in gaining user acceptance of the system.

13.1 DEVELOPING AN EXPERT SYSTEM WITH TECHNOLOGY TRANSFER AND DEPLOYMENT IN MIND

If the developers of an expert system know from outset of the project that the expert system program will be transferred to some other group for deployment or for operation and maintenance, they can try to take this forthcoming transfer into account in their work. In addition, whether or not the program developers will deploy the expert system themselves, they should consider issues related to the eventual deployment of the system starting from the early phases of the project and continuing throughout development.

13.1.1 ISSUES RELATED TO DOMAIN SELECTION

Several attributes of an expert system domain might affect the success of the technology transfer and deployment of an expert system. For example, the problems of transferring an expert system from the unit of a corporation that developed it to an operating unit of the corporation can be lessened significantly if the domain was selected such that the project is strongly supported by a senior manager of the operating unit and there are no political problems related to the control of the system. Furthermore domain managers and system users will be more likely to accept the deployed expert system if the domain was selected such that:

■ Domain personnel have previously identified the need to solve the problem that the system attacks.

■   Domain personnel have helped define the specific tasks of the expert system.

■   The expert system can be introduced into the working environment with minimal disturbance of current practices.

■   Users have no fears that the automation provided by the system would negatively affect their job security.

■   There are no users who will resist the system because they think that they might be adversely affected by the decisions made by the system (e.g., on allocation of funds).

■   Domain experts can agree on whether the system's results are correct (allowing users to be able to ascertain unambiguously the level of correctness of the expert system).

■   The task's payoff is simple to measure (allowing users to determine if the system merits the costs).

■   The task's payoff is significantly large.

Operation and use of the deployed system are made somewhat easier if the domain selected is fairly stable, so there is less need to retrain operators or users frequently. A domain that is fairly stable or at most slowly changing also facilitates maintenance of the deployed system; the maintenance effort can focus on correcting errors in the knowledge and in the program rather than on keeping up with a shifting situation. Maintenance is also simplified if the domain is such that knowledge changes do not require major alterations in reasoning processes but instead require only modifications that can be made relatively easily in expert systems, such as the revising of specific rules or frame attributes or the adding or deleting of entire knowledge structures.

Technology transfer might be facilitated if the expert system does not have to perform the entire task in order for the system to be useful. This attribute makes it possible for the system to be phased into use gracefully. For example, a limited but useful version of the expert system program might be transferred initially to a deployment group. Later one or more expanded versions of the expert system might be transferred. The early transfer of a relatively small system should smooth the transfer process. It allows the receiving group to start its work earlier and thus possibly spread it out over a longer period of time. It also allows the group to avoid having to learn about and deal with an entire large system all at once.

> The *COMPASS* domain satisfied many of these attributes. For example, domain experts agreed on the correctness of *COMPASS*'s results. Also, its decisions did not adversely impact anyone, and so no one had motivation to disagree with its results and fight its deployment for that reason. On the other hand, the deployment of *COMPASS* might have been facilitated if a senior manager in the operating units had acted as its champion.

The No. 2 EAX domain was very stable. The hardware design of the switch was well established and unlikely to change. Thus we expected (and it turned out to be true) that program maintenance personnel would not need to be concerned about having to update the deployed program's knowledge due to domain changes.

13.1.2 ISSUES RELATED TO KNOWLEDGE REPRESENTATION AND IMPLEMENTATION

Technology transfer of an expert system program is facilitated when the system knowledge representation is clear and easy to understand, when the program is easy to read and understand, and when the program is well documented. If so, the transferring group may be able to reduce its efforts in training, in providing consultation to the receiving group, and since a clearer program might require less detailed documentation, in preparing the documentation. In addition, the receiving group may be able to devote less time to formal training and to other efforts toward learning about the system.

A clear, easy-to-understand knowledge representation and a clearly written, well-documented expert system program aids deployment. System operators are able more quickly to track down problems that occur during program execution. Maintenance of the deployed expert system is facilitated because program errors are more easily found and repaired. Deployment is facilitated if the implementation is easy to modify and update.

Some of the principal attributes that make an expert system program more understandable and maintainable are the following:

- The expert system program utilizes a hardware platform and a software tool that are well documented and relatively easy to learn and whose vendors supply good training and support.
- The program is divided into several well-defined modules.
- The program is written using a uniform programming style.
- A uniform naming convention is used throughout the program.
- The bulk of the knowledge is implemented utilizing paradigms that are relatively easy to maintain.
- Program data flow is clear.
- Intermodule data access is standardized.
- Program control flow is clear.
- The knowledge documentation is well written and clearly specifies the domain knowledge.
- The program documentation is well written and complete.

The more of these attributes an expert system program has, the easier it will be to deploy, operate, and maintain.

> While we were working on the representation and implementation of *COMPASS,* we understood that it would be transferred out of GTE Laboratories and would be deployed and maintained by others less experienced than ourselves. Therefore we provided the *COMPASS* program, as best we could, with all of the attributes listed above.

13.2 TECHNOLOGY TRANSFER

There are two aspects of expert system technology transfer: the transfer of an expert system program and the transfer of general expert system technology skills. First consider the transfer of an expert system program between two different groups. This transfer may be performed because the two groups have differing capabilities or because they have differing roles. For example, the skills to develop a prototype expert system differ from those needed for productization of an expert system, which in turn differ from those needed to operate or maintain the system. Developers need great experience and knowledge of expert system development techniques, deployers have more need for experience and knowledge in such areas as producing efficient software products, integrating a system into an operating environment, and selling a system (literally or figuratively), and operators and maintainers must be able to keep the system running and updated while dealing with users and meeting their needs.

In many circumstances there may be more than one transfer in the life of an expert system—for example, from a group that develops it to a group that productizes and deploys it and then to a third group that operates and maintains it. On the other hand, for many expert systems the life cycle does not include any transfer at all because the group that develops the system becomes the deployment and maintenance group.

The transfer of the expert system program might be accomplished in various ways, including the following:

■ **Formal transfer.** The expert system program could be transferred formally on a specified day. The program would be handed over to the receiving group, along with full documentation. The transferring group might provide some initial training or consulting services.

■ **Gradual transfer.** The transfer could be a gradual process of transition. This option is available when the two groups in the transfer can work together over an extended period of time. Personnel of the receiving group might work for some time with the transferring group, learning about the program in detail. Over time, responsibility could gradually be shifted to the receiving group, until it took full responsibility for the system.

- **Transfer with associated transfer of personnel.** The transfer of the system could be accomplished concurrently with the organizational transfer of personnel from the transferring to the receiving group. This approach obviously accomplishes the transfer of expertise about the expert system program. It should aid as well in the transfer of expert system technology skills.

The second aspect of technology transfer to explore is the transfer of expert system technology skills from a part of a corporation more skilled in expert system technology to a part of the corporation that is new to or less skilled in it. Since skill and experience in developing, operating, and maintaining expert systems are often not available in the parts of a corporation where they might be required, there is frequently a need for such a transfer. This kind of technology transfer consists of a transfer of knowledge and possibly also a transfer of actual systems that support expert system activity:

- **Knowledge transfer** is the sharing of training, methodologies, techniques, information, experiences, and requirements. The transfer also includes the providing of technical support and consultation services.

- **Systems transfer** is the transfer of operational development tools, inference engines, software utilities, machines, and any other software or hardware that might aid in the development or maintenance of an expert system, especially those developed by the group making the transfer.

Even when the goal is to transfer general expert system technology, the transfer of a real expert system program can provide a focus for the transfer process, which might not be obtained by general training or by a review of examples of AI technology.

All transfers require time. Even the formal transfer requires time for training and consulting. Furthermore it is evident that the transfer of expert system technological skills cannot be accomplished instantaneously (other than by direct transfer of experienced personnel) and must be done over a possibly long period of time. Therefore the two groups participating in the transfer should be prepared for extended work with each other. Beyond being prepared for the transfer process, it is certainly beneficial if they are enthusiastic about their involvement. Positive attitudes go a long way toward smoothing any difficulties.

> The *COMPASS* project was involved in both aspects of technology transfer. One project technology transfer goal was to transfer the *COMPASS* expert system program to an operation and maintenance group. Another important project goal was to encourage the spread of AI and expert system technology in the corporation by transferring some of our expert system development expertise to other GTE groups.

Our goal of transferring the *COMPASS* program followed from GTE Laboratories' charter as the corporate research center, which did not include operation or long-term maintenance of a system such as *COMPASS*. We successfully transferred the *COMPASS* program to two different groups: initially to GTE Data Services for testing and limited deployment and later to the GTE telephone companies for full deployment. Both transfers were successful, and both recipient groups proved able to deploy and run *COMPASS* for extensive production use in telephone company switch maintenance operations.

The transfer of AI expertise took place in several ways. In the transfer of *COMPASS* to GTEDS, we also transferred general skills related to expert system technology. At the time we were developing *COMPASS*, GTEDS had no personnel trained or experienced in expert system technology, and we felt a valuable function of our project would be to help GTEDS in establishing a technology base in expert systems. GTEDS management regarded expert systems as an important area and welcomed our assistance. Their objective was to obtain the skills required not only to be able to deploy and operate *COMPASS* but also to be able to develop other expert systems. The transfer of a real application such as *COMPASS* provided a tangible focus for the process of transferring expertise.

When *COMPASS* was transferred to the GTE telephone companies, the goal of the receiving groups was more limited than that of GTEDS—they wanted to be able to operate and maintain *COMPASS* for use by their switch maintenance personnel. As telephone company people grew familiar with *COMPASS*, however, they became interested enough to want to learn more about general expert system technology. We provided guidance and informal support for this effort.

In addition, we were able to utilize the *COMPASS* project to assist another GTE group in getting started in expert systems. We helped a major corporate business unit start an expert system group and helped them select their application domain—an expert system to aid in the maintenance of the GTD-5 switch. We participated in the training of some of their personnel and gave them a copy of the *COMPASS* program, which they were able to use as a basis for their own program.

The *COMPASS* project was instrumental in encouraging the formation of other AI groups in GTE. *COMPASS* became a major item of discussion among GTE personnel interested in AI, such as at internal GTE corporate AI workshops. Information about the expert system development techniques of *COMPASS* was presented to several of these other groups, and *COMPASS* personnel were often consulted as these groups were forming.

13.3 ORGANIZATIONAL ROLES AND ACTIVITIES IN TECHNOLOGY TRANSFER

For technology transfer from a corporate expert systems group (such as at a corporate laboratory) to an operating unit of the corporation, let us consider possible organizational roles of the two groups involved in the transfer process, as well as the role of the ultimate users of the system:

1. The role of the expert systems organization transferring the technology. The role of the expert systems group may include developing expert system prototypes for well-selected applications, discovering and demonstrating techniques for expert system development, providing guidelines and standards for using and deploying expert system technology, and providing training, support, and consultation services. In addition, the group should have personnel designated to participate in technology transfer. These people need adequate time and technology resources to work with and later consult with the recipients of a transferred expert system and to synthesize general knowledge of expert system development into deliverables.

The outputs of the activities of the expert systems group that can be transferred to the operating unit may include:

- Expert system programs, either as prototype systems or operational systems.

- Specification of the environment needed to support the deployment, operation, and maintenance of the systems.

- Technical papers and internal reports related to the technology and techniques of expert system development.

- The development of general expert system methodologies and guidelines for developing and engineering expert systems.

- Consulting services for the recipient groups.

- Training services for the recipient groups.

2. Role of the operating unit receiving the technology. The role of the group in the corporate operating unit that accepts the outputs from an expert system group includes operating and/or maintaining the transferred systems. These systems may be product or service offerings for corporate users or external customers. The group should establish a base of skilled AI technical people through training or hiring, establish an active AI environment, install appropriate computing equipment and tools, and be able to accept, operate, and maintain expert systems. Acquiring these capabilities may require formal and on-the-job training for the personnel in the receiving organization. If the organization desires the capability to develop expert systems on its own, its personnel require additional training, and resources are needed for a full development environment. In this case, the receiving organization's management must be prepared to invest added resources and possibly accept short-term losses to be able to enter this field and eventually deliver valuable expert system products.

The receiving group may produce some or all of the following:

■ Testing and evaluation of the expert systems.

■ Selection of the expert systems' deployment hardware and software.

■ Specification and implementation of the expert systems' integration into their deployment environments.

■ Operation of expert systems.

■ Long-term maintenance of expert systems.

■ User training.

■ User consultation.

■ Technical support for user-operators.

■ Technical support for user-maintainers.

■ Demonstrations of the technology for user groups and corporate management.

In addition to accepting expert system programs from more advanced expert system groups, an operating unit group might desire to acquire expert system development skills and produce their own expert systems. If so, a key objective would be the building of a base of expertise in the development, engineering, and operation of expert systems. A reasonable charter for such a group would be:

■ To accept large expert systems developed by the corporation's advanced expert systems groups or elsewhere.

■ To develop smaller expert systems.

■ To deploy and maintain expert systems from both sources.

Groups with this charter could be started in many or all parts of a large corporation.

3. The role of the user groups. The user groups utilize the products and services provided by the operating unit group. They, especially if they are internal to the corporation, may provide:

■ Information to assist in the selection of important domain areas for expert systems.

■ Requirement specifications for the systems being developed.

■ Experts and expertise for the system development.

For the full technology transfer to be accomplished, all three groups—the transferring group, the receiving group, and the users—must devote the necessary time, effort, and technology resources to the task.

In the *COMPASS* technology transfer, GTE Laboratories acted as the advanced expert systems group, developing the expert system. GTE Data Services and later the GTE telephone companies were the units that accepted *COMPASS* and operated it. Finally GTE No. 2 EAX personnel in the telephone companies were the *COMPASS* users. In addition, GTE Data Services and other GTE organizations received the transfer of general expert system technology from GTE Laboratories and went on to produce expert systems of their own.

13.4 TRANSFERRING AI EXPERTISE

It is frequently difficult to find and hire people experienced or highly trained in the development, deployment, or maintenance of large, complex expert systems. For such systems the best available approach is often to train staff members, while continuing to look for qualified people externally. A sizable investment in time and money is required to train a novice to be a fully competent knowledge engineer or AI systems engineer. If the goal is to develop, deploy, and maintain smaller, simpler expert systems, then less background and training are required. Furthermore as expert system shells improve, even less training and skills are needed to produce such expert systems.

13.4.1 GENERAL TRAINING REQUIREMENTS

In order to operate and maintain an expert system that was developed elsewhere, a neophyte group requires training in and guidelines for the following areas:

- the application domain of the expert system
- basic expert system principles and techniques
- AI tools, environments, and hardware
- the expert system software tool's paradigm(s)
- the expert system's knowledge representation
- the expert system's implementation and system engineering

This training is in addition to any needed in the basic computer skills, such as data communications.

Beyond what is needed to operate and maintain an expert system developed by someone else, if the group's objective is to develop its own expert systems, additional training is needed in several areas, including:

- expert system domain selection
- expert system tool selection
- knowledge acquisition

■ techniques of knowledge representation

■ techniques of knowledge implementation

A company that wants to embrace AI technology should expect to make a significant investment in time and training in these areas in order to build a sufficient base of technical expertise.

> GTE Data Services personnel required training to allow them to receive and run *COMPASS* and to help them initiate an expert systems development group. The telephone company groups that received *COMPASS* required training primarily so that they could operate and maintain the *COMPASS* program.

> The GTEDS staff members selected to be trained in expert systems technology had no prior training or expertise in AI or expert systems; however, they had well-rounded backgrounds in computer software. The GTE Laboratories *COMPASS* group helped design a training program for them based on the guidelines discussed above. GTEDS personnel took GTE Laboratories-provided training in expert systems and some vendor-sponsored courses. This training, along with specific *COMPASS*-related training, enabled the GTEDS AI staff to receive, test, operate, and maintain the *COMPASS* program successfully. Later this training, plus the experience gained working with the *COMPASS* knowledge engineering team and with the *COMPASS* program, formed a good base to allow GTEDS to work on the development of other expert systems.

> GTE Laboratories developed a training course for telephone company *COMPASS* personnel that introduced expert systems in general but emphasized the *COMPASS* program and *COMPASS* operation. A *COMPASS* operator's guide was written, and it formed the basis of the training. The telephone company personnel were from the areas of information management and switching. Some had computer experience and training including one with some background in expert systems. Others had little computer background. On the other hand, all the involved telephone company personnel were generally familiar with the No. 2 EAX, and thus the need for training related to the domain was minimized.

13.4.2 AI TECHNIQUES, TOOLS, AND SYSTEMS TRAINING

Training needs related to AI techniques, tools, and systems strongly depend on the specific role a person will be filling and on the size and scope of the project. Expert system deployers and maintainers should be familiar with the software and hardware being used and should have a solid understanding of the knowledge-representation paradigms of the expert system. They should have detailed familiarity with the way the paradigms are used to implement the system's knowledge. Expert system operators require less knowledge of AI techniques although they usually need to know about the tools and computers that are the basis of the expert system program. If a group also wants to develop expert systems, personnel require broader and more detailed knowledge—the depth of knowledge needed depending on the scope and complexity of the expert system development.

Training in AI techniques, tools, and systems can range from learning what is needed from books, system documentation, and online tutorials, through a few days or weeks of short courses or vendor-provided courses, to a full university program in AI and expert systems. In small projects expert system developers and deployers might learn to use simpler software tools and hardware from the accompanying documentation. But for more complex software tools or hardware systems, they generally benefit from vendor-supplied training courses unless they are already very experienced. Note, however, that although vendor-supplied courses are often valuable, they are directed primarily at establishing technical proficiency relative to the vendor products. They are not directed toward exploring knowledge engineering or expert system development techniques in general.

> Some GTEDS personnel attended a GTE Laboratories–sponsored AI course, and GTEDS used videotapes of the course lectures as part of the training for staff members who did not attend. To learn about the expert system environments in general and the *COMPASS* environment specifically, GTEDS *COMPASS* personnel attended vendor-sponsored short courses from Xerox and IntelliCorp. They also took courses on other software tools to broaden their knowledge and to consider these tools for new expert system projects.

> The telephone company people involved with *COMPASS* intended primarily to learn to operate and maintain the system. They learned about expert system techniques and about AI hardware and software through our *COMPASS* courses for them and through using and examining the *COMPASS* system. *COMPASS* engendered their interest and their companies' interest in expert systems in general, which led them to study expert system literature and take some formal courses.

13.4.3 DOMAIN TRAINING

Expert system deployers, operators, and maintainers should be acquainted with the expert system's domain in order to understand the program's terminology, its structure, its input and output, and its underlying raison d'être. They may also need this knowledge to discuss the merits of the expert system with domain personnel and to deal with users. Maintainers of the program need a full understanding of the domain as it is reflected in the expert system so that they can discuss knowledge bugs with domain experts.

Training in the domain may be obtained from many sources—lectures, courses, books, reports, site visits, and discussions with experts and other domain practitioners. The expert system documentation itself might contain a description of pertinent parts of the domain or a glossary of domain terms related to the expert system.

> Members of GTE Laboratories' *COMPASS* staff started the project with little knowledge of telephone switching or telephony in general. We learned about the No. 2 EAX domain from several sources—primarily tutorials given by the *COMPASS* expert and extended discussions with him throughout months of knowledge acquisition. In addition, *COMPASS* staff people visited No. 2 EAX sites, read No. 2 EAX documents, and spoke to other No. 2 EAX experts.

> When GTEDS *COMPASS* personnel began the project, they already were familiar with many aspects of telephony. They arranged for switching people from GTE's telephone company near their location to provide a short training course on No. 2 EAX maintenance.

> Telephone company *COMPASS* personnel generally were familiar with switching in general and the No. 2 EAX in particular, and so domain training was not necessary for them.

13.4.4 TRAINING ON THE EXPERT SYSTEM PROGRAM

Expert system deployers and maintainers should have a detailed knowledge of the expert system program. A well-made set of expert system documents (program documentation and knowledge documentation) plus in-code documentation can provide this knowledge. But if the expert system developers are available, it might be very useful if they were to provide training on the expert system program. This training would probably save a great deal of time for the maintainers.

> The GTEDS *COMPASS* staff needed to understand the knowledge representation and implementation of the program in order to test, operate, and maintain it. Because of the large size and complexity of the *COMPASS* program, the GTE Laboratories project team put together and presented for them a detailed training course on *COMPASS*. They furthered their understanding of the *COMPASS* program by reading the documentation, examining and running the program, and consulting further with GTE Laboratories. GTEDS's need for consultation with GTE Laboratories on *COMPASS* slowly diminished to occasional telephone calls, and eventually they gained complete self-sufficiency.

> A similar scenario was followed for the GTE telephone company groups operating and maintaining *COMPASS*. We developed a detailed *COMPASS* training course that they attended. We wrote a comprehensive operator's manual and delivered it to them along with complete sets of program documentation. GTE Laboratories personnel spent time at telephone company sites working with the people operating *COMPASS*, to aid further in their training.

13.4.5 KNOWLEDGE ACQUISITION TRAINING

Although there are some formal courses in knowledge acquisition, participation in real knowledge acquisition sessions is probably the best training in this area. A great deal can be learned by working with an experienced knowledge acquisition person or team.

> In addition to accepting *COMPASS* from GTE Laboratories, GTEDS's goals included gaining skill in the full range of expert system development technology. They felt that their primary technology transfer need was in the area of knowledge acquisition skills and techniques. Therefore we arranged for a member of GTEDS's *COMPASS* project team to participate in GTE Laboratories' *COMPASS* knowledge acquisition meetings. He attended most of the *COMPASS-II* knowledge acquisition meetings, coming to our site each time the *COMPASS* expert did.

> The GTE telephone companies' *COMPASS* groups, in keeping with their present goals at the time, did not require any knowledge acquisition training.

13.5   DEPLOYMENT

A deployed expert system program not only should have the desired functionality—the domain expertise necessary to perform its function at a useful level—but, in addition, should be able to satisfy several other requirements. It should be cost-beneficial, delivering enough benefit to users to warrant their costs to obtain, operate, and maintain the system. It should be able to be integrated into the operational environment in which it will be used and to access and interact with any required external programs and data sources. It should be maintainable, and it should meet any specialized constraints that the application imposes, such as on response time or reliability.

13.5.1 DEPLOYMENT ENVIRONMENT

In Chapter 7, we discussed methods for selecting the hardware and software environment used to develop the expert system. Often it is preferable to use a different environment as the deployment vehicle for the final expert system implementation.

There are several possible alternatives that can be considered for the deployment environment. The software tool or hardware used for the development might be utilized for deployment, a delivery version of either might be utilized, or completely different systems might be used. Some of the options for the deployment environment are:

■ **The development software tool on the development computer.**
Deploying the expert system by using the development software tool on
the development computer requires no change in the expert system program due to a change in environment. (However, the expert system program may require revisions for other deployment concerns, such as
efficiency.) No time or effort need be allotted to either a software or a
hardware conversion task, allowing the expert system to be available sooner
and with no conversion expense. A major benefit is that there is no chance
that problems—possibly major problems—might occur in transferring the
expert system to another environment, and there is no chance that program
bugs will be inserted during the transfer.

■ **The development software tool on a new computer.** Under this
option, the expert system program is ported to another platform—one on
which the development software tool runs. The change of hardware might
be warranted by many considerations—cost, performance, reliability, uniformity, maintainability, integrability, and so on. One attractive approach
is to develop the expert system on the best available development computer
(which may have excellent development facilities but not be very suitable
for deployment) and then to port the program to a cheaper, more standard,
more reliable platform for deployment.

In an ideal situation, porting a program to a computer that runs the
same tool should not require extensive effort; however, the expert system
program is unlikely to be completely portable, and it probably will have
to be modified somewhat for different hardware. The extent to which such
modifications are necessary depends on the particular software tool. A good
software tool vendor should have minimized the amount of work necessary
to port the expert system. If modifications are required, it is helpful if the
vendor provides a well-written guide or consulting on how the modifications should be performed.

■ **The development software tool on the delivery version of the
computer.** If a delivery version of the development computer is available,
it might be a good choice for deployment. The delivery version of the
computer should be much more efficient than the development version,
should be less expensive, and may have other features beneficial to deployment. It should be easier to port the expert system program to this platform than to another one unrelated to the development hardware. Fewer
problems should ensue, and the porting should introduce fewer errors.
Furthermore project experience on the development hardware should facilitate the use of this delivery hardware.

■ **A delivery version of the development software tool.** If the software tool vendor makes available a delivery version of the development
software tool, it may be an excellent choice for deployment. The delivery

version should be much more efficient than the development version, should be less expensive, and may have other features beneficial to deployment. Ideally no rewriting of the expert system should be necessary. As with porting to new hardware, if modifications are required to utilize the delivery version, the vendor should provide a well-written guide or consulting on how the modifications should be performed. If the delivery version of the tool is used for deployment, probably the expert system program maintenance group will still require one or more copies of the full development version of the tool since the delivery tool will likely be missing facilities for maintenance.

■   **A new software tool.** Clearly deploying an expert system program by using a different software tool from the one with which it was developed will necessitate a rewrite of the expert system program. However, there may be major potential gains that warrant this large effort. For example, the new tool may be much more reliable than the development tool or cost much less. There may be instances when the use of a new tool is required, such as when the deployment computer is determined by external constraints and the development tool cannot be used on that computer.

There are many issues in selecting the deployment environment that should be given a different emphasis from that given during the selection of the development environment. Cost may be much more of a factor. The cost of the development hardware and software may be much less critical to the developing organization than the cost of the final system is to an internal user or an external buyer. Furthermore development typically requires no more than a few systems whose total cost may not be nearly as large as the total cost of possibly hundreds of deployment systems. Performance of the hardware and software is another factor that may be much more critical for deployment than for development. Performance acceptable in a development system may be completely unacceptable in deployment. Moreover there are additional issues such as reliability, maintainability, and integrability. These issues pertain to the whole deployed system—the hardware, the software tool, and the expert system program.

> The COMPASS deployment uses the same software tool, KEE, and the same hardware, Xerox Lisp machines, that were used in COMPASS development. The decision was made that the costs in time and effort of porting COMPASS to different hardware and software outweighed the benefits.
>
> The COMPASS software is large and complex, and a great deal of effort was put into its development. Almost all aspects of KEE's multiple paradigm system were utilized. Therefore transfer of the COMPASS program to another software tool would require a very large effort and a long delay to deployment, neither of which seemed warranted. However, we saw a major gain in offloading the communications from the Xerox computer to allow it to carry

out the main *COMPASS* processing more efficiently. Therefore an Apple Macintosh computer is used as a front end and back end for the *COMPASS* deployment system.

In a typical *COMPASS* run, the user selects the switch or group of switches to be processed. For each switch, the Macintosh computer calls the corresponding RMCS system (which has been collecting the maintenance messages from the switch) and requests the appropriate maintenance message data. The Macintosh accepts these data and sends them to an input queue on the *COMPASS* Xerox computer. They are then analyzed by the *COMPASS* core program, which runs the entire *COMPASS* analysis. When each analysis is completed on the Xerox computer, the output report is put on an output queue and is picked up by the Macintosh. The Macintosh distributes the results by sending them back to RMCS system and, optionally, prints them locally. Switch personnel access the *COMPASS* results primarily by accessing their RMCS terminals.

The deployed *COMPASS* uses the core expert system parts of *COMPASS-II* essentially unchanged but with additional input, output, and communications software developed especially for the deployment. For example, a graphical user interface was developed to allow telephone company personnel to maintain databases of site-specific data for each *COMPASS* site. Also automated communications software on the Macintosh was developed to allow *COMPASS* operators easily to customize the mix and quantity of No. 2 EAX syndromes to be analyzed.

13.5.2 RELIABILITY, MAINTAINABILITY, AND SECURITY

The reliability of a software system is often defined as the probability of the system's operating without failure for a given time period. For a deployed expert system, this definition should include failures of the knowledge, the implementation, the software tool, the hardware, and any related communications, databases, sensors, and output devices—anything that might cause the program's expertise not to be available or usable by its users when it is needed.

Reliability is usually an important feature of a fielded system; it may be less important during development. For example, if the expert system occasionally produces a software error message or it runs on a computer that occasionally goes out of service, these infrequent problems may not affect development very much. But they may be completely unacceptable to users of a fielded system. For some applications such as real-time control, reliability may be crucial. If reliability is a significant deployment issue, the standards for evaluating the expert system program should be set accordingly. Moreover the reliability of the underlying hardware and software should be a principal concern when selecting the deployment software and hardware.

Maintainability of the fielded expert system is another chief concern of deployment. Depending on the extent to which techniques for making the expert system program maintainable were used in development, it may be necessary or desirable to rewrite the expert system program when it is being deployed so as to enhance maintainability. Furthermore the full deployed system consists of the software tool and the hardware, as well as the expert system program. Thus the maintainability of the full system depends to some extent on the maintainability features of the deployment hardware and the software tool. For example, a software tool that provides poor maintenance facilities is not a good choice for deployment unless the expert system program can easily be maintained in one environment and deployed in another.

Security is another deployment issue that is often important. There may be many reasons for preventing unauthorized access to the expert system program. The program may be a valuable product that gives significant competitive advantage to the company. In such a situation, it is important to protect it from being copied or from being altered or destroyed. In some cases, the knowledge in the program may need to be protected—for example, critical knowledge of corporate expertise or corporate strategies or knowledge that would be politically embarrassing or legally threatening if disclosed. Furthermore the expert system may utilize company private data or government classified data that must be kept secure. The deployers of the expert system should determine the extent to which security is an issue. If security is important, the availability of security facilities should be taken into account when selecting the deployment hardware and software. Also security mechanisms should be included in the deployment system, and security concerns should influence the selection of locations where the system will be sited.

> Program reliability was a goal of the *COMPASS* development and deployment. For *COMPASS* to be accepted and used in the field, users at No. 2 EAX switch sites should be able to rely on it. On the other hand, there are some reasons that the reliability of *COMPASS* is not an absolutely critical concern. First, *COMPASS* is run offline, and therefore a time delay in its running caused by a program fault may not be noticed by a user. Second, work on all the recommended maintenance actions of one *COMPASS* run often is not completed by maintenance personnel by the time of the next run. In such cases, if a *COMPASS* run were to be delayed or aborted, the switchpeople would not be critically affected since they still would have *COMPASS* maintenance actions from the previous run to complete. Finally *COMPASS*'s task is background maintenance. Even if one or a few runs are not made, the switch will continue to operate, although its operation will begin to deteriorate.

> Maintainability was a prime concern in *COMPASS* implementation, as discussed in detail in Chapter 11. Security was not an important issue, although it may become more important if *COMPASS* is sold to outside companies.

13.5.3 INTEGRATION OF THE EXPERT SYSTEM

Another issue related to deployment is the ability of the expert system to be integrated into the existing operation. One aspect of integration relates to the degree of uniformity between the deployment environment and the existing operational situation. It is easier to gain user adoption if the program is run on computers that the users already have in place. In this case, the system would probably cost the users much less to deploy, and users could consider the expert system as just another application program on their own computers. If deployment using the existing user hardware cannot be done, it might be possible to deploy on another copy of a computer already in use among the potential expert system users. Although a new computer would have to be purchased, this hardware selection would make deployment more acceptable and more uniform with the existing environment. If deployment on the same type of computer that users have is not possible or desirable, there may be some gain in acceptability of the expert system if the system is deployed on a computer of a familiar vendor.

Based on all of these concerns, uniformity with existing user hardware should be a factor when selecting deployment hardware. If the users have knowledge engineering software tools in use for other expert systems, the same holds true when selecting the deployment software tool.

Another related area is the integration of the expert system program with other user systems—those that supply inputs to the expert system and those that accept outputs from it. If, for example, the expert system requires input of certain data, the deployed expert system program must be able to access these data efficiently and when needed from the user databases or other systems where they reside.

Finally consideration should be given to the integration of the expert system into the working situation of the operators and users. This integration depends on design considerations in the expert system itself. For example, the expert system will integrate better into user operations if its output is in a form familiar to or easily acceptable by users.

> *COMPASS*'s deployment hardware and software were not standard in the GTE telephone companies; however, the telephone company groups operating *COMPASS* are used to having many computer systems on many different platforms. They consider *COMPASS* just another computer system on another computer. Therefore although the possibility exists of converting *COMPASS* to an alternate platform to aid standardization, porting the program for this reason does not appear to be needed.

> *COMPASS*'s input is taken from a switch's RMCS directly. Its output is a standard text file that can be printed or transmitted as needed, giving flexibility to operators. *COMPASS*'s output format was designed to make it easier for switch personnel using the output to accept it as part of their operation.

13.6 GAINING USER ACCEPTANCE OF THE DEPLOYED EXPERT SYSTEM

A critical part of the deployment of an expert system is gaining user acceptance. Users expect a system that is technically and functionally sound and that produces an appropriate payoff. But even when this is the case, there still may be many problems, for example:

■   Users may find it hard to relate to and trust a computer program in the way they relate to and trust a human expert.

■   It may be difficult to prove to users the correctness of the expert system.

■   It may be difficult for users to understand the limits of the applicability of the system.

■   Users may not want to modify their working procedures to accommodate the expert system.

■   Users may not be able to accept a computer program that is sometimes wrong.

■   Users may have unrealistic expectations of the breadth of knowledge or the depth of knowledge in the expert system.

■   Users may (often justifiably) have fears about the expert system's affecting their job security.

■   Domain experts may dispute the expert system's results.

■   The payoff to using the system may be obscure.

■   There may be political problems related to the control of the system.

■   There may be people challenging the system if they think that its conclusions may negatively affect them.

■   The system may be unreliable relative to the needs of the users.

■   Users may find the system difficult or tedious to use.

■   Users may not understand the results of the system or how to employ them.

Other possible problems may be inherent in any specific deployment situation. Many of these problems may be eliminated or minimized by care in domain selection, knowledge representation, and implementation, thus making the expert system more likely to gain user acceptance. There are some additional steps related to educating the users, introducing the system, and the use of the system that can be taken in deployment to ameliorate or eliminate the problems.

13.6.1 EDUCATING THE USERS

Expert system users and related domain personnel and managers should be educated by the system deployers so that they have realistic expectations about the system capabilities. They should not be led to expect the expert system to produce perfect results or be surprised when it makes a mistake. System deployers should ensure that known limits of system applicability are made clear to users during training and in system documentation; notice of these limits might appear as part of the system's user interface or as part of the system output. Similarly users should be informed if there are situations or types of inputs for which the expert system produces results at a lower level of expertise than might be expected.

On the other hand, system deployers should try to get users to regard the results of the expert system as believable and expert. Users should be made to understand that the system embodies, at least to some extent, the expertise of domain experts. If the system was developed based on the expertise of top domain experts, users should be told this (as well as the names of the primary and consulting experts, if the names are recognizable.) Users should understand the level of expertise that the system has. One way to help accomplish this understanding is for the system deployers to make available to the users the results of tests evaluating system proficiency.

Users should understand how the expert system will help them. They should know the role the expert system will take—if it will act as an assistant (doing lower-level parts of the job), a coworker (doing some parts of their job), or an expert consultant (aiding them in the difficult parts of their job).

To help users accept the conclusions of the expert system more readily, they might be given access to any explanation features that the system provides. Moreover results of intermediate analyses might be made available, at least to higher-level users, to help them understand system analyses and gain more confidence in the system's correctness. When possible, deployers might demonstrate to users that the expert system was designed to fail-soft (for example, when it is unsure of its results, it leans toward minimizing bad outcomes).

Any steps that can be taken to measure system payoff or demonstrate it to users or domain area managers should be taken. For example, it might be possible to distribute the results of any field trials or cost-benefit analyses or for each system output to contain an estimate of the benefit produced by that one system usage.

> We tried to convey to all the telephone company people with whom we interacted a clear and realistic sense of what *COMPASS* could and could not do. The limits of the input domain were evident: *COMPASS* could analyze certain specific types of No. 2 EAX maintenance messages.
>
> Users in the field generally accepted initially the assertion of *COMPASS*'s high level of expertise. This acceptance was based on the recommendation of the *COMPASS* expert and the group of consulting experts from three different GTE telephone companies and was also based on the results of field trials. As users received the results of *COMPASS* runs, they were able to confirm this

assertion by examining the output of the annotated RMCS printout, which explained *COMPASS*'s analysis in a way they could understand. Some users became convinced quickly of *COMPASS*'s ability and after a short time asked that the annotated RMCS printout be suppressed and only *COMPASS*'s maintenance recommendations be produced.

13.6.2 INTRODUCING THE EXPERT SYSTEM

Expert system deployers should take care in introducing the deployed system into use. They should make every effort to introduce the system into the existing user operation without major upheavals and should try to have the system integrate smoothly with the present operational environment and procedures.

Strong measures should be taken to alleviate any unfounded user fears of the expert system's affecting job security. Users should be encouraged to think of the expert system as an assistant or an expert consultant, helping them to do a better job, and not as their rival or replacement. In cases where the expert system actually does affect user job security, this situation should be faced. Standard corporate measures taken for jobs threatened by automation should be employed to help those affected.

Potential political problems related to the organizational control of the system should be addressed openly, and a timely decision on control should be encouraged. If there are people who may challenge the system when its conclusions negatively affect them, support should be sought from higher-level managers who would not be negatively affected by the decisions and who, presumably, would want the best possible decisions made.

To aid in introducing the expert system, deployers might consider adding to the system some nonexpert features that are relatively easy to develop and may provide additional benefits to users. Because the expert system is a computer program, it may be fairly straightforward to add to the expert system some standard computer features that might increase the utility of the overall system. For example, if users have to access a database or printed data for some information or if users need to record certain data or make certain computations, these features might be added to the system even if they are only marginally related to the task of the expert system and even if these tasks require no expertise. If the expert system has these extra features, it should be easier to introduce the system into use. Users who are not overly enamored with the expert system might use it just to get access to the extra features.

COMPASS replaced one important and time-consuming task that switchpeople performed—the analysis of No. 2 EAX maintenance messages—and it accomplished that task at an expert level. The remainder of the switchperson's tasks were not affected.

There did not seem to be any fears about *COMPASS* related to job security. Instead switchpeople felt that *COMPASS* aided them in their job and gave

them more time to do other tasks. Some of them thought *COMPASS* beneficial in that it freed them to learn more about and work more with the newest
switch technology.

The question of who would control, maintain, and operate the deployed
COMPASS was a political problem; long internal negotiations slowed the pace
of deployment. *COMPASS* was not only GTE's first expert system, it also was
the first computer system for the telephone company portion of GTE that was
to be derived from work at GTE Laboratories. This combination of a new
technology and a nonstandard introduction mechanism made for unexpected
political difficulties. On the other hand, there were no problems caused by
people disputing *COMPASS*'s results, either for political or technical reasons.
Thus these possible problems did not affect deployment.

We added an extra nonexpert feature to *COMPASS* that we thought might
aid in obtaining user acceptance. Our systems programmer developed an on-
line *COMPASS* module, called the Grading Utility, which made available to
users data about switch-specific connections in a No. 2 EAX. To obtain connection information under the usual procedure, maintenance personnel must
consult two tables and a voluminous printout, in a process that may take up
to 15 minutes. But *COMPASS* must be able to determine this connection information as part of its analysis, and thus part of *COMPASS* was developed to
automate the procedure. Therefore we decided to add a user interface to this
part of *COMPASS* and make it a utility for users—usable even if they were
not running the rest of *COMPASS*. We hoped this extra feature, which took a
relatively small amount of additional effort, would help *COMPASS* gain user
acceptability. It turned out to be a good selling point for *COMPASS*, especially
for the consulting experts. However, since the mode of deployment provides
personnel at switch sites with *COMPASS*'s output but does not give them direct access to the *COMPASS* program, the grading utility is not in operational
use at present.

13.6.3 USE OF THE EXPERT SYSTEM

The deployed system should be made as easy to operate and use as possible.
Any aspects of operating the expert system that might be tedious should
be automated. Considerations of human factors should go into the design
of the deployment system's user interface. The user interface should provide the features needed by users.

The output of the deployed system should be designed to make users
feel comfortable with it. It should be concise or verbose, depending on the
domain and the level of the user. It should be easily understandable to the
user, in the language and jargon of the domain. Explanations of reasoning
might be made available to users.

Users should be able to use the system when they need it. Therefore
the deployed system—program, software tool, and hardware together—
should be made to meet the reliability requisites of the users.

During our initial discussions about deployment with telephone company personnel who were potential operators of *COMPASS*, they suggested certain improvements in *COMPASS* that they felt would make operating the system easier for them. We made many of these improvements in the *COMPASS* deployment system. For example, the prototype versions were set up to run *COMPASS* on the data for one switch at a time. Each new run required a few lines of typed input. But telephone company personnel wanted to be able to specify at one time a group of switches for which runs were desired, allowing them to run *COMPASS* unattended for long periods (such as while other work was being done or overnight). Therefore we added a facility to allow *COMPASS* to be run for a set of switches specified in advance. This included a graphical interface to make the designation of the switches to be run easier.

COMPASS's output of suggested maintenance actions was designed for low-level users. It is concise when the maintenance action recommended is a common one that all switchpeople know about, and it is verbose when infrequently performed actions are suggested. The *COMPASS* output is phrased in user terminology and jargon to make it easy to understand and use.

COMPASS's output of the annotated RMCS-printout allows higher-level users to see an explanation of analysis in a familiar form.

CHECKLIST FOR TRANSFERRING AND DEPLOYING THE SYSTEM

☐ Consider the system's technology transfer and deployment requirements when selecting an expert system domain.

☐ Consider the system's technology transfer and deployment requirements when developing the knowledge representation and implementation of the expert system.

☐ To transfer a specific expert system program from one group to another, investigate possible transfer options, including formal transfer on a specific day, gradual transfer with both groups working together over an extended period of time, and transfer with the associated transfer of personnel.

☐ To transfer general expert system technology, transfer knowledge and techniques but also software tools and utilities.

☐ Train system maintainers in the domain, the system's hardware and software environment, and the knowledge representation and implementation. This training should be in addition to any required general training on expert system and AI.

☐ Plan the training of new system developers so that the development group has competence in all expert system skill areas.

☐ Explore whether the deployment environment should be the same as the development environment, or whether it should employ different hardware (possibly a delivery version of the development hardware), a different software tool (possibly a delivery version of the development software tool), or both.

☐ Educate potential users to have realistic expectations for the expert system's capabilities.

☐ Make explanations of the expert system's reasoning available to users.

☐ Make results of intermediate analyses available to users—at least to higher-level users.

☐ Clearly state known limits of the applicability of the expert system.

☐ When possible, demonstrate to users that the system is designed to fail-soft.

☐ Measure system payoff or demonstrate it to users and domain messages if possible.

☐ Encourage users to think of the expert system as an assistant or an expert consultant—helping them to do a better job—and not as their rival or replacement.

- Make every effort to introduce the system into the existing operation without major disruption and to have the system integrate smoothly with the present operational environment and procedures.
- Take strong measures to alleviate any unfounded user fears of the expert system's affecting job security.
- In situations where the expert system actually does affect user job security, treat the expert system as any other job-affecting automation and utilize standard corporate measures for such cases.
- Address openly potential political problems related to the control of the system, and attempt to reach some definite decision on control as soon as possible.
- If there are people who may challenge the expert system when its conclusions negatively affect them, seek support for the system from higher-level managers who would not be affected negatively by the expert system. These managers should be more open to use of the expert system.
- Design the output of the deployed system to make users comfortable with it. The output should be clear, concise, and in the language and jargon of the users.
- Make the deployed system as easy to use as possible, with a good (for the situation) user interface.
- When possible, automate any aspects of using the expert system that might be tedious or laborious to the user, even if this automation has nothing to do with AI and expert systems.
- Make the output of the deployed system easily understandable.
- Consider human factors in the design of the output of the deployed system.
- Make the deployed system—program, software tool, and hardware—meet the reliability requisites of the users.
- Consider adding some nonexpert features to the deployed system that are relatively easy to develop and might provide additional benefits to users.

Prerau, Developing and Managing Expert Systems (Addison-Wesley)

CHAPTER 14

Expert System Trends and Directions

What are the major directions in which the field of expert systems is heading?

The interest in expert systems continues to grow. The numbers and types of expert system applications are expanding rapidly, as are the numbers and types of people developing and using expert systems. As the technology becomes more common, expert systems are losing their status as a new and special type of computer program. Expert system technology is coming to be, instead, an important member of the group of standard, mainstream computer technologies available to solve problems. Application areas are growing. Hardware and software for expert systems are improving and becoming more standardized. Integration with other systems is becoming more prevalent. This final chapter will survey these directions in which the field of expert systems is going. We have discussed many of these emerging directions in pertinent chapters of this book. As the field evolves, some specifics may change, but the basic concepts should remain valid.

Expert systems are being used in an expanding number of application areas in an increasing number of industries. The spectrum of expert system applications is broadening—from very large and complex to very small and simple. One important direction is toward smaller, simpler expert systems that perform limited but useful tasks. Such expert systems are often developed using an inexpensive shell on a personal computer, and they are usually developed in a relatively short time. Therefore they entail a small investment and need to return only a moderate payoff to be successful.

Another area in which expert systems are expanding is the use of the knowledge base constructs of an expert system to store and retrieve knowledge, with little or no use of the inferencing capabilities of expert systems. Thus for some applications, a rule base can be considered as a type of database allowing the retrieval of knowledge stored in rule form.

One important direction of expert systems is toward integration with or embedding into other computer systems. Increasingly, expert systems are being developed that are intended to be integrated with databases, conventional computer programs, and/or other expert systems. Expert system technology is being used as an approach to develop parts of a large system, with the goal of the seamless integration of expert systems into large systems. Users need not know or care that an expert system is part of the overall system they are using, as long as the system performs its required functions.

Another area of growth is toward expert systems that work cooperatively. Expert systems developed for specific disciplines may pool their individual talents to solve a complex multidomain problem. Also several expert systems representing distinct interests may negotiate the solution to a mutual problem.

In the area of expert system hardware, there is increasing development—and especially deployment—on conventional platforms, rather than specialized AI workstations. Conventional computers of all sizes, from PCs to mainframes, are being used. However, AI machines such as Lisp machines will continue to be valuable for developing expert systems for more complex problems—although in many cases the resulting expert systems may then be deployed on conventional platforms. Also Lisp machine boards and chips are being integrated into conventional PCs and other computers, allowing Lisp machine power inside more standard platforms.

One main current in expert system software is toward the use of conventional programming languages, both for direct development of expert systems (especially less complex expert systems) and as the base language of expert system development tools. AI research and the development of complex expert systems still generally require or are facilitated by the use of AI languages, such as Lisp and Prolog. Some tools allow development of an expert system in an AI-language-based tool and then conversion to a more conventional language.

Existing knowledge engineering software tools and shells are migrating to mainframes as well as PCs. Shells are offering more features, more paradigms, and better interfaces with external software such as graphical packages and communication packages. The portability of tools is increasing, facilitating the option of developing an expert system on one platform and deploying on others.

As expert system development tools become easier to use and understand, as specialized domain-specific tools for common domains or domain types become available, and as automated aids to knowledge acquisition appear, it is becoming easier for knowledge engineers with moderate or little training and experience—or sometimes the domain experts themselves—to develop smaller, simpler systems. Such systems may be very useful. However, for the foreseeable future, expert systems for problems of greater complexity or problems that have unique or special characteristics will require the skills of well-trained, experienced knowledge engineers.

More powerful techniques are being added to the expert system tool kit. Techniques of deep reasoning and model-based reasoning allow expert systems to use a deeper understanding of the structure and first principles of a domain to solve problems. Case-based reasoning allows the use of previous decisions in somewhat similar circumstances to guide present decisions. Learning techniques allow expert systems to improve with use.

All of these directions should allow the resulting expert systems to provide more capability and power to users and should make the development of expert systems increasingly important and beneficial.

And what of *COMPASS*—today and in the future? *COMPASS* is deployed in GTE telephone companies to aid in the maintenance of 46 No. 2 EAXs, which serve about 500,000 GTE customers. It is being operated and maintained by the GTE telephone companies with GTE Laboratories primarily in a consulting role. Interest in *COMPASS* is growing in other telephone companies that have No. 2 EAXs, nationally and internationally, both related and unrelated to GTE. Negotiations with these potential *COMPASS* users are ongoing. Thus the use of *COMPASS* may well become more widespread.

As for the *COMPASS* program, the core knowledge of *COMPASS* has been proved solid in tests and in deployment and is unlikely to change except for occasional bug fixes. But there may be some enhancements made to *COM-PASS* or modifications made to its input or output capabilities. For example, its output may be customized to new (possibly international) sites or changed based on user requests, its operational mechanisms may be improved, or it may be ported to another platform to reduce costs and improve speed. In addition, some *COMPASS* enhancements identified as desirable at GTE Laboratories during development but not included then may be implemented. For example, it is possible to incorporate a learning capability in *COMPASS*. By giving it information on the success or lack or success of each maintenance action, *COMPASS* can adjust its likelihood parameters, thus learning the actual likelihoods of each type of fault at each individual switch. The likelihoods would thus be customized to each switch site, providing some improvement on the likelihoods now in *COMPASS* (which, based on our expert's estimates, are the same for each switch).

Let us examine how the *COMPASS* project did on its four major objectives, which were discussed in Chapter 3:

■   **To encourage the use of AI within the GTE Corporation.** *COMPASS* is the first and the primary example of the practical use of AI in GTE. It is well known within the corporation and probably has been the major encouragement to the formation of other expert system groups in GTE. In particular, two expert system development groups in two different GTE companies were formed as a direct result of and with a major assist from the *COMPASS* project as were expert system operation and maintenance groups in the GTE telephone companies. Several other corporate groups or individuals were assisted by the *COMPASS* developers or were motivated to pursue expert systems by the success of *COMPASS*.

■   **To do this by developing a major expert system to solve a significant problem for the GTE telephone companies.** Based on its size and scope, *COMPASS* is clearly a major expert system. It is deployed for use at 46 telephone company sites, performing well and providing significant aid to GTE telephone company maintenance.

■   **To develop general techniques for building expert systems.** Members of the *COMPASS* team have written several technical papers (and of course this book) describing general techniques of expert system development. Some of the papers have achieved wide dissemination and use in industry and in universities.

■   **To transfer expert system technology to other GTE business units.** Techniques of expert system development were transferred to other GTE units, either directly with the transfer of *COMPASS* itself or indirectly through dissemination of internal reports and talks at internal GTE AI meetings. These techniques are widely used across the corporation in expert system developments.

We feel that the *COMPASS* project successfully fulfilled all its objectives.

The *COMPASS* developers have gone on to use the techniques described in this book to develop other expert systems. However, we all still share a pride in the *COMPASS* project and continue to keep a parental eye *on COMPASS*.

A FINAL NOTE

The field of expert systems is a vital, stimulating area. Although there are many obstacles to overcome and many pitfalls to avoid and although the technical problems can be very difficult and the nontechnical problems exasperating, I have enjoyed and continue to enjoy the challenge and the excitement of expert system development. I hope this book has conveyed some of that challenge and excitement to you and that it will aid you, the reader, in your own work in this area.

GLOSSARY

AI: *Artificial intelligence.*

AI paradigm: A mechanism that can be used to represent knowledge in an expert system program, for example: production rules, frames, and object-oriented programming techniques.

AI programming language: A programming language specifically designed for use in artificial intelligence. Such specialized languages provide mechanisms and structures that facilitate symbolic reasoning. The two most common of these languages are Lisp and Prolog. Artificial intelligence programming languages are often used for the development of expert systems or as the base language in which *software tools* for knowledge engineering are written.

Antecedent: The left-hand side-the *if* clause—of a *production rule*. This is the pattern that must be satisfied for the rule to be applicable.

Artificial intelligence (AI): The science of making machines behave in a way that would generally be accepted as requiring human intelligence. It attempts to provide ways for modeling and mechanizing intelligent processes that otherwise could not be automated. In addition to conventional computer approaches, work in artificial intelligence is often based on symbolic, nonalgorithmic methods of problem solving and the use of computers for reasoning with concepts rather than calculating with numbers. AI is related to and draws from computer science, psychology, cognitive science, computational linguistics, data processing, decision support systems, and computational modeling. Important subfields of artificial intelligence include robotics, computer vision, speech synthesis and recognition, automated reasoning and theorem-proving, natural language processing, automatic programming, automated learning, neural networks, and expert systems.

Backward chaining: A reasoning technique used in *production rule systems* when it is desired to establish which of a set of conjectures is correct. With the goal of proving

Cross-references are in italics.

a conjecture, the system searches for a rule that might prove the conjecture—a rule that has the conjecture in its *consequent*. If the *antecedents* of the rule are known to be true, the conjecture is established. If not, the system attempts to establish the rule by setting up the subgoals of proving each of the rule's antecedents. These subgoals are attacked by the same technique—finding a rule with the desired statement in its consequent and then establishing that antecedents of that rule hold. The chaining continues backwards through rules, from consequents back to antecedents. The chaining is successful if antecedents are reached that are given data or can be confirmed externally (such as by asking the system's user). The attempt fails if antecedents are reached that cannot be proved or else are known to be false. Because backward chaining starts with possible hypotheses or goals, it is called hypothesis-driven or goal-driven reasoning.

Certainty factor: A number attached to a rule or fact that denotes the degree of certainty that is assigned to it. The use of certainty factors is a common approach for representing uncertainty in *production rule systems*.

Chaining: A technique for reproducing or approximating part of an expert's reasoning processes by utilizing a sequence of rules from a set of production rules. This can involve *forward, backward,* or *mixed chaining.*

Conflict resolution: The mechanism in *forward* or *backward chaining* that determines which rule should actuate or *fire* when there is more than one rule in the *conflict set*. An example of a simple conflict-resolution technique is choosing the rule that appears earliest in the expert system's list of rules. A more sophisticated technique is selecting the rule of the conflict set most specific to the situation (thus preferring a more customized rule to a more general one).

Conflict set: In *forward* and *backward chaining* the set of rules applicable at any one time. When there is more than one rule in the conflict set, *conflict-resolution* techniques are utilized to determine which rule should *fire*.

Consequent: The right-hand side—the *then* clause—of a *production rule*. This is the result of applying the rule.

Data-driven reasoning: See *forward chaining*.

Default value: A value used when the actual value has not otherwise been specified such as for a *slot*.

Demon: In a *frame* system, a program that is triggered when a particular action related to a *slot* occurs. Actions that might trigger a demon include the initial insertion, the change, or the retrieval of a slot value. For example, an "if-needed" demon allows the calculation of a slot value to be deferred until the program actually needs the value. The slot value is "unknown" until the program tries to retrieve the value. When that happens the demon is triggered, and a procedure is run to calculate the value and fill it in the slot.

Development environment: The computer and the knowledge engineering software tool that are used during the development of an expert system.

Domain: The application area of an expert system—the problem area of interest.

Domain expert: See *expert*.

Environment: See *development environment*.

Event-driven reasoning: See *forward chaining*.

Expert (for an expert system): A person who, through training and experience, can perform a task with a degree of skill that is beneficial to capture and distribute. The person filling this role is usually a top-level task performer although sometimes capturing and automating the judgment of even an average decision maker can be beneficial.

Expert system: An advanced computer program that can, at a high level of competence, solve difficult problems requiring the use of expertise and experience. It accomplishes this by employing knowledge of the techniques, information, *heuristics,* and problem-solving processes that are used by human experts to solve such problems. Expert systems thus provide a way to store human knowledge, expertise, and experience in computers. The terms *knowledge system* or *knowledge-based system* are often used as synonyms for expert system, although some people distinguish between these terms.

Expert systems: A subfield of AI related to the theory behind and the development and application of *expert system* programs. This is the AI subfield that has evoked the most interest in industry and has resulted in the greatest number of practical applications.

Facet: A part of a *slot* that contains a piece of information related to the slot, such as the range of acceptable values for the slot, the default value, or the slot's value itself.

Fire: To actuate or trigger a rule in a *production rule system.*

Forward chaining: A reasoning technique used in *production rule systems* to determine what can be found from a set of data. The available set of known facts (data about the situation of interest), which is in working memory, is used to *fire* applicable rules. The *consequents* of these fired rules are newly derived facts about the situation and are added to working memory. The total set of facts now in working memory may fire additional rules, asserting still more derived facts. This process continues until nothing further can be discovered. Because forward chaining is triggered by the known facts or by specific events that occur, it is called *data-driven* or *event-driven reasoning.*

Frame: A structure containing information about a single entity—a concept, item, or class. It consists primarily of a set of slots, each of which contains information about the entity. Frames can be related to other frames by subclass, instance-of, and other relations.

Goal-driven reasoning: See *backward chaining.*

Hardware: The computer(s) on which an expert system (or any computer program) is developed or deployed.

Heuristic: A rule-of-thumb or strategy that aids in solving problems or making decisions. Heuristics cannot be proven formally and are not correct in all cases, but they provide an expert with a method of decision making when stronger rules do not apply. Experts develop these heuristics through long periods of task performance. The use of heuristics make expert systems capable of solving problems that are beyond the reach of conventional computer programs.

Hypothesis–driven reasoning: See *backward chaining.*

Inference engine: In the architecture of a basic expert system that part of an expert system program that provides the system control. It applies the expert domain knowledge (which is in the *knowledge base*) to what is known about the present situation (which is the information in the *working memory*) to determine new information about the domain. This process will lead, it is hoped, to the solution of the problem. The inference engine part of an expert system program often also contains the expert system's interfaces to data sources and to the user.

Inheritance: A mechanism in a *frame* or *object-oriented* system that allows all the information known in general about all members of a class to be considered true for each individual member of the class, unless express information to the contrary is known. This inherited information therefore does not have to be entered specifically for each class member. If specific information is known about a class member that contradicts an inherited value, this information overrides any inherited value. Values can be inherited through more than one level of structure. In addition, some systems allow the same entity to be a member of more than one class and thus have *multiple inheritance*.

Knowledge acquisition: The process by which expert system developers find the knowledge—facts, rules, heuristics, procedures—that domain experts use to perform the task of interest. Knowledge acquisition usually is accomplished by meetings between knowledge engineers and domain experts at which the knowledge engineers attempt to elicit the expert's knowledge. The result of knowledge acquisition is a specification, possibly in a *knowledge document,* of the knowledge that should appear in the expert system program.

Knowledge base: (1) In the architecture of a basic expert system, that part of the expert system program that stores the facts and heuristics of domain experts. It also includes expert techniques on how and when to use these facts and heuristics. As opposed to conventional computer programs, in a idealized expert system program, each nugget of knowledge in the knowledge base is essentially independent, and the sequence in which they are stored does not affect the way they are used. (2) A unit of modularity in the structure of an expert system program. A program may be made up of several knowledge bases. Each knowledge base might correspond to a partition of the expert knowledge, a particular set of related data, or a set of related support functions.

Knowledge-based system: An *expert system.*

Knowledge engineer: A person who develops expert systems, that is, who performs *knowledge engineering.*

Knowledge document: A document in which the knowledge obtained from experts during *knowledge acquisition* is recorded. The document is updated as new pieces of knowledge are found and as previously found knowledge is revised.

Knowledge elicitation: See *knowledge acquisition.*

Knowledge engineering: The process of developing an expert system. The term knowledge engineering, used broadly, indicates all the technical aspects involved with developing an expert system although sometimes the term is confined to the task of acquiring knowledge from an expert.

Knowledge-engineering software tool: See *software tool.*

Knowledge implementation: The process of taking the knowledge found during knowledge acquisition and translating it into an operational expert system program. The knowledge implementation is accomplished by employing the structures and paradigms that comprise the knowledge representation.

Knowledge representation: The process of defining the approach that will be used in an expert system program to represent the domain knowledge found during knowledge acquisition. The expert knowledge can be represented in the computer using a conventional programming language or a specialized *AI programming language,* but it is usually represented by making use of one or more *AI paradigms.*

Knowledge representational paradigm: See *AI paradigm.*
Knowledge system: An *expert system.*

Lisp: See *AI programming language.*

Message: In an *object-oriented programming* system, a communication sent from one *object* to another (or to itself). It contains information for the receiving object on which *method* to invoke and also contains any necessary parameters for the method.
Method: A procedure related to an *object* in an *object-oriented programming* system. Methods are distinguished from standard procedures in that they are stored in (or inherited by) an object's data structure and are invoked when the object receives a message from another object (or from another method in the same object). Different objects may have different methods with the same name thus allowing the same message to invoke a distinct procedure in each object. When a method runs, it may compute and return some result, make changes to its own internal data, and/or send messages to objects (thus invoking methods in those objects).
Mixed chaining: A reasoning technique used in a *production rule system* that allows both *forward* and *backward chaining* to be use for different parts of the same problem.
Multiple-inheritance: *Inheritance* from more than one source. It can be used to give an individual that is a member of more than one class the attributes of each class. It can also be a way to create an object from a set of feature-objects by "mixing in" those features that pertain to the created object.

Object: A data structure that contains all the information related to a particular entity. It might be considered a frame with additional features allowing it to contain and invoke methods and to send and receive messages.
Object-oriented programming: A set of techniques that allows programs to be built using *objects* as the basic data-items and actions on objects as the active mechanisms.

Paradigm: See *AI paradigm.*
Production rules: The knowledge representational paradigm used most often in expert systems. Each production rule represents a single nugget of knowledge. A rule is characterized by two clauses, the *antecedent* and the *consequent,* and is of the basic form: "*If* A, *Then* B.". Usually conjunctions and disjunctions are allowed in the rule clauses yielding rules such as: "*If* A or (B and C), *Then* (D or E) and F".
Prolog: See *AI programming language.*

Rule-based system: A system based on *production rules.*

Shell: An extensive package of software facilities used in the development of expert systems. See *software tool.*
Slot: A component of a frame that refers to a specific attribute of the frame entity and contains the value of the attribute if the value is known. A slot can contain fixed information probably static for the problem at hand or information that can vary during a program run. It can also act as a placeholder for information that is presently unknown but that might be filled in during the processing of the program. In some frame systems, slots can contain multiple values. Each slot can have a set of *facets,* and might have associated *demons.*

Software tool (for knowledge engineering): A software package that provides facilities to aid in expert system development. This includes full *shell* systems, knowledge engineering aids, and rule systems and broadly could include AI programming languages such as Lisp or Prolog, conventional programming languages in which expert systems might be developed, or some combination of the above.

Uncertainty: The situation in which knowledge or data in an expert system are not completely certain, for example, a rule-of-thumb that works most, but not all, of the time or a fact that is somewhat in doubt. Many *production rule systems* have ways to represent uncertainty such as by the use of *certainty factors*.

Working memory: In the architecture of a basic expert system that part of an expert system program that contains the information the system has received about the particular problem at hand. In addition, any information that the expert system derives about the present problem is stored in the working memory.

INDEX

AI, 2
  and expert systems, 2
  related disciplines, 2
  subfields, 2
AI computer language, 18 (*see also* Lisp,
    Prolog)
AI knowledge representational para-
    digms (*see* AI paradigms)
AI paradigm, 17, 18–28
  for maintainability, 286
  (*see also* Production rules, Frames,
    Object-oriented programming)
Antecedent, 19
Application area (*see* Domain)
Artificial intelligence (*see* AI)
Audiotaping, in knowledge acquisition,
    212
Availability, of hardware or software
    system, 147–148

Backward chaining, 20–22
  example, 21–22
BECAUSE clause, in knowledge docu-
    mentation, 220
Benefits, recording during knowledge
    acquisition, 231

Case-based reasoning, 343
Certainty factor, 19

Checklist
  domain expert selection, 197–198
  domain selection
    process, 96
    desired attributes, 134–137
  forming the team, 74–75
  hardware selection, 169–171
  implementing the knowledge, 296–297
  knowledge acquisition, 233–235
  planning and managing the develop-
    ment, 51–52
  representing the knowledge, 263
  software tool selection, 169–171
  testing and evaluation, 312–313
  transferring and deploying, 339–340
Common sense, use in expert systems,
    107–108
Company politics (*see* Politics,
    company)
COMPASS consulting domain experts,
    60, 196
COMPASS domain (No. 2 EAX main-
    tenance analysis), 35, 87, 89–92
  agreement of experts in, 133
  amount of knowledge required, 115
  decomposability, 124
  decomposition, 238–240
  dependency of other developments,
    130

expert (*see* COMPASS expert)
expertise in, 175
inputs, 111
outputs, 112
stability, 129
stages in analysis, 89–92, 238
  Input, 89–91
  Identify, 91
  Analyze, 91
  Suggest, 91–92
  Output, 92
steps in analysis, 238, 240–247
  Analyze Problems, 244
  Cluster Messages, 240–241
  Input RMCS, 240
  Merge Suggestions, 245, 247
  Order Suggestions, 244–245
  Output Suggestions and Annotated
    RMCS, 247
  Postclustering, 241–243
  Suggest Actions, 244
  Transform Data, 240
subtasks, 123
task definition, 110
test cases availability, 125
time to perform, 115
training for, 124
use of heuristics, 107
(*see also* No. 2 EAX)
COMPASS expert, the, 59
AI training of, 211
availability, 181
communication skills, 178
computer and AI background, 184
expectations of, 186
experience, 176, 177–178
interest in project, 181
management support for, 183
reputation, 177
selection process for, 189–190
temperament, 179–180
use of expertise for SMA 110–112, 191
working relations with, 181
(*see also* COMPASS project, domain
  expert)
COMPASS-I
development, 41–42
knowledge representation, 260–261

COMPASS-II
development, 43–44
final transfer of, 49–50
initial transfer of, 47–48
knowledge representation, 261–262
software tool selection, 147–148
COMPASS implementation (*see* COM-
  PASS program, implementation
  process)
COMPASS knowledge acquisition
assumption, 229
audiotaping in, 212
benefits, recording of, 232
expertise not experience, use of, 191
deferring details in, 228
if-then rules,
  quasi-English, 213–215
  direct use of, 227
knowledge recording conventions, 231
meetings
  access to program, 206–207
  atmosphere, 208–209
  scheduling, 204, 205, 207
procedures, quasi-English, 213, 216
reminders, 231
rules, 213–214, 215
  naming, 219
test cases in, 225–226
tutorial, 210
use of related existing rules, 226
validation and verification in, 302
COMPASS knowledge bases, 271–276
ACCESS, 273, 291–292
ANALYZE, 275
CLUSTERS, 274
COMMUNICATIONS, 271
CONTROL, 273, 293
EVENTS, 273, 294–295
MESSAGES, 272
NWR-MSG, 273
OUTPUT, 276
PATTERNS, 274
POSTCLUSTERS, 274–275
PREPROCESS, 274
SMA–41–118-MSG, 273
SMA–63–71-MSG, 273
SMA–110–112-MSG, 273
SUGGEST, 275

SWITCHES, 273
UTILITIES, 273, 289
COMPASS knowledge document, 213–217
  BECAUSE clause, 214, 215, 221
  glossary in, 221
  readability, 216
  terminology in, 217, 218–219
  updating, 227
  use by consulting experts, 303
COMPASS knowledge representation
  frames, 250–254
  likelihoods, 255–256
  object-oriented messages, 257–258
  paradigms, 248–249
  programming language code, 258–259
  rerepresentation, 260–262
  rules, 255–256
COMPASS program
  alternative for, 128
  annotated RMCS output, 93, 95
  application (*see COMPASS* domain)
  control flow, 293
  coverage, 123
  data flow, 290–292
  debugging, 279–280
  deployment, 49–50, 343–345
    hardware, 330–331
    software, 330–331
  documentation, 48, 281
  ease of use, 338
  enhancements, 344
  future, 344
  implementation,
    configuration management in, 288–289
    process, 268–269
    software engineering in, 282
    techniques, 281–286, 287–288, 289, 291–295
  input/output, 294–295
  integration of, 333
  introduction of, 337
  knowledge bases, use for modularity, 283–284
  logo, 40
  long term need for, 127–128
  maintainability, paradigms for, 287–288
  maintenance, 51, 344
  name, 40
  operation, 51
  outperforming top experts, 303
  outputs, 247
  performance requirement, 126
  programming style, 285–286
  reimplementation, 270–271
  reliability, 332
  rules, correspondence to knowledge acquisition rules, 276–277
  rulesets, 278–279
  specification, 268–269
  suggested actions, 244
  suggestion output, 92–94
  threat to users, 119
  user interface, 127
COMPASS project
  application (*see COMPASS* domain)
  champion for, 118
  consultant, 72
  consulting domain experts, 60 (*see also COMPASS* consulting domain experts)
  corporate/client interface, 67, 82
  deployers, 70
  development environment selection, 144–146
  documenters, 68
  domain expert
    number of experts, 114, 193, 194
    selection of, 189–190
    (*see also COMPASS* expert)
  domain personnel, expectation of success, 117
  domain selection, 34–35
    importance of, 35, 79
    narrowness, 116
    process of, 82–84
  domain selectors, 59, 82
  end users, 73
  environment, 37–38
    selection, 144–146
  expert (*see COMPASS* project, domain expert)
  expertise not experience, use of, 191
  feasibility prototype, 40 (*see also COMPASS-I*)

full prototype, 43 (*see also* COMPASS-
II)
goals, 103
hardware
    integration of, 333
    selection of, 37
    selectors, 61
implementers, 64
    responsibilities, 284
knowledge acquirers, 62
knowledge representers, 63
leader, 33, 57
maintainers, 72
objectives, 33
    success in, 344–345
operators, 71
payoff and benefits, 103–104
    measurability, 132
plan, 34
programmers (*see* Implementers)
project manager, 58
project technical leader, 33, 57
schedule, 34
software tool
    selection of, 37
    selectors, 61
staff, 34
systems engineer, 65
technical writers, 68, 70
technology transfer (*see* COMPASS
    technology transfer)
testers and evaluators, 69
tool developer, 65
trainers, 70
training, on domain, 327
COMPASS task (*see* COMPASS domain)
COMPASS technology transfer, 47–50,
    320–321
    of COMPASS program, 41–42, 47–50,
    320–321
    of expert system technology, 321, 344–345
    GTE Data Services and, 41–42, 47–48,
    321, 323–324
    by GTE Laboratories, 41–42, 47, 49,
    320–321, 323
    GTE telephone companies and, 49–50,
    321, 324
    organizational roles in, 323–324

COMPASS users
    cooperativeness, 120
    expectation, 335–336
    incorrect results and, 131
    introduction of system and, 120
    threat to, 119
COMPASS validation
    by consulting experts, 303
    criteria, 305
    field trials, 305, 308
    results, 305, 307, 308
    standards for, 311
COMPASS verification, 309–310
COMPASS-X (*see* COMPASS-I)
Computer (*see* Hardware)
Configuration management, 288–289
Conflict resolution, 22
Conflict set, 22
Consequent, 19
Consultant, functions and required skills,
    72
Consulting domain expert
    functions and required skills, 60
    use of, 195–196
    validation by, 302–303
Control flow, 292–293
Conventional languages, use in expert sys-
    tems, 343
Corporate/client interface, functions and
    required skills, 65–67
Correctness, agreement of experts on,
    132–133
Cost, of hardware or software system, 148
Coverage of expert system, 122–123

Data flow, 289–292
Debugging, expert systems vs. conven-
    tional programs, 279–280
Decomposability of task, 123–124
    knowledge representation and, 238–240
Default meta-rules for knowledge acquisi-
    tion, 229
Demon, 24, 250
Deployer, functions and required skills,
    69–70
Deployment, 48–50
    checklist, 339–340

considerations during development,
316–319
domain selection and, 316–318
hardware, 45–46, 328–331
implementation and, 318–319
knowledge representation and, 318–319
maintainability in, 331–332
modes, 48
operation and maintenance in, 167–168
reliability in, 331–332
security in, 331–332
software, 46, 328–331
user acceptance in, 334–338
Development environment (*see*
Environment)
Documentation,
of knowledge (*see* Knowledge
documentation)
of program, 47, 49, 280–281
Documenter/writer, functions and required
skills, 67–68
Domain expert, 5
AI training for, 211
attributes, 175–186
availability, 113–114, 181
communication skills, 178–179
computer and AI background, 183–184
cooperativeness, 180–181
domain representative, as, 184–186
existence of, 99–100
expectations of, 186
experience, 176, 177–178
functions and required skills, 59
interest in project, 180–181
level of expertise, 175–176
management support for, 182–183
none available, 190–191
number of, 192–194 (*see also* Single expert, Multiple experts)
obtaining participation of, 187–190
reputation, 176–177
selection of
checklist, 197–198
knowledge acquisition considerations,
202–203
process of, 186–190
responsibility, 175–176
step in expert system development, 12

temperament, 179–180
vs. novices, 113
working relations with, 181
Domain expertise, extent of knowledge in,
200
Domain personnel
expectation of success, 116–117
involvement of leaders, 117–118
politics (*see* Politics, company)
Domain selection, 34–35
deployment and, 316–318
desired attributes, 98–133
checklist, 134–137
importance of, 34–35, 78–79
knowledge acquisition considerations,
201–202
method for, 79–84
checklist, 96
not driven by specific technology, 108–
109
step in expert system development, 12
team, 35–36
technology transfer and, 316–318
Domain selector, functions and required
skills, 58–59
Domain task
alternative to expert system for, 128
bounds on
difficulty, 114–115
knowledge in, 115
clear definition, 110
coverage, 122–123
desired attributes, 98–133
checklist, 134–137
incomplete coverage, 122–123
long term need, 127–128
narrowness, 116
performance requirement, 125–126
previous identification of, 118
real-time requirement, 125–126
stability, 129
teachability, 124
tolerance to incorrect results, 130–131
DO-RE-MI, 219

Efficiency, of program, 287
Elicit-document-implement-test cycle,
223–225

inner loops, 267
  validation and verification in, 300–302
Elicit-document-test cycle, 221–223
  validation and verification in, 300–302
End users (*see* Users)
Environment, 17, 140
  availability, 147–148
  cost, 148
  deployment issues, 165–168
  knowledge representation paradigms,
    160–162
  legal arrangements, 148–149
  programming environment, 154–155
  security, 158
  selection
    checklist, 169–171
    criteria for, 146–168
    process of, 36–38, 141–146
    (*see also* Software tool, selection;
      Hardware, selection)
  size, 157
  software engineering facilities, 155
  system interfaces, 157–158
  uniformity with others, 149–150
  user interface, 154
  vendor, 150–152, 158–159
  (*see also* Hardware, Software tool)
Evaluation
  checklist, 312–313
  effort, 310–311
  standards for, 310–311
  (*see also* Testing and evaluation, Valida-
    tion, Verification)
Expert, 5 (*see also* Domain expert)
Expertise
  and domain selection, 112–116
  use instead of experience, 191
Expert system, 3 (*see* Expert systems)
Expert system development project
  champion for, 118
  computer (*see* Hardware)
  core development phases, 38–44
  dependency of other developments, 129–
    130
  domain expert (*see* Domain expert)
  final development and deployment
    phases, 44–51
  functions performed in, 57

hardware (*see* Hardware)
  initial phases, 30–37
  phases defined, 30
  scheduling, 32–33
  startup, 30–34
  team members, 33, 56–72
    checklist, 74–75
Expert system domain (*see* Domain task)
Expert systems, 3
  AI and, 2
  application areas, interest in, 342
  basic architecture, 17–18
  benefits, 3–4
    (*see* Expert systems, payoff)
  compared to human experts, 5
  vs. conventional programs, 7–9, 98–99
  cooperative, 342
  coverage, 122–123
  ease of use, 337–338
  fields in which developed, 7–8
  integration, 342
  introduction of, 119–120, 336–337
  limitations, 8–9, 102
  need for approach, 98–99
  payoff, 102–104
    measureability, 131–132
    vs. risk, 105–106
    (*see also* Expert systems, benefits)
  problem types applied to, 7
  roles of, 6–7
  similarity to successful systems, 112
  trends, 342–343
Expert system users (*see* Users)
Explanatory clause, in knowledge docu-
    mentation, 220–221

Facet, 23
Feasibility prototype system, 38–42
  purposes, 39
  staffing, 40
Field test/field trial (*see* Validation, by field
    testing)
Forecasting, expert system for, 108
Forming the team, checklist, 74–75
Forward chaining, 19
  example, 20–21
Frames, 23, 249–254
  relations between, 24–25

Frame systems, 23–27
Full prototype system, 42–43
  goal, 42
  staffing, 43
Glossary, in knowledge documentation,
  221
GTE Data Services (GTEDS)
  COMPASS-I and, 41,43
  COMPASS-II and, 47–48, 49
  field trials by, 310
  technology transfer role, 41–42, 47–48,
    321, 323–324
  training of personnel, 325–328
  verification by, 310
GTD–5
  expert system for, 100, 106
  stability of, 129
GTE Laboratories
  Knowledge Based Systems Applications
    Development Project, 33 (*see also*
    COMPASS project)
  role in *COMPASS* deployment, 51, 344
  transfer of *COMPASS* by, 41–42, 47,
    49, 320–321, 323
GTE telephone companies, 82
  COMPASS deployment and, 49–50
  COMPASS maintenance by, 51, 344
  COMPASS operation by, 51, 344
  technology transfer role, 321, 324
  training of personnel, 325–328
GTE-Southwest (GTESW)
  COMPASS support, 183

Hardware
  for deployment, 45–46
  file system, 164
  system software, 164
  selection, 140–159, 163–168
    checklist, 169–171
    reconsidering, 269
    step in expert system development, 16
    (*see also* Environment, selection)
  selector, functions and required skills,
    60–61
  trends, 342–343
  type, 164
  (*see also* Environment)
Help facility, 154

Heuristic, 3
  typical, 3, 15
  use of, 14–16, 107
Hybrid tool (*see* Software tool, multiple-
  paradigm)

If-then rules
  defining reasoning directly in, 227
  in knowledge documentation, 213–214
  (*see also* Production rules)
Implementation, 17, 38
  checklist, 296–297
  configuration management, 288–289
  control flow, 292–293
  coordination of programmers, 282
  data flow, 289–292
  deployment and, 318–319
  expert systems vs. conventional pro-
    grams, 266–270, 279–280
  input/output, 293–295
  management of, 281–295
  modularity, 282–283
  reimplementation, 269–270
  rules (*see* Implementation rules)
  step in expert system development, 12
  style, 284–286
  techniques, 276–281
  technology transfer and, 318–319
  without specification, 266–269
Implementation rules, 254–256
  correspondence to knowledge acquisi-
    tion rules, 254, 276–277, 286
Implementer, functions and required skills,
  63–64
Incremental development, 267
Inference engine, in expert system basic
  architecture, 17
Inheritance, 25, 250
  of methods, 28
Input/output, 293–295
Inputs, availability of, 110–111
Instance, 24
Integration, 342
  of development environment, 149
  of expert system, 333
IntelliCorp, 37, 150–151, 158–159
Introduction of expert system, 119–120

KEE
  in *COMPASS* deployment, 49, 330
  in *COMPASS-II,* 44
  frames in *COMPASS,* 240, 250–254
  Lisp use in, 162
  multiple paradigms, 249
  selection of, 37, 146, 148, 149, 154, 158–
    159, 161, 162
  training, 153
  upgraded version, 147–148, 152, 270
Knowledge Based Systems Applications
    Development Project, 33 (*see also*
    COMPASS project)
Knowledge, sensitivity of, 121–122
Knowledge acquirer functions and required
    skills, 61–62
Knowledge acquisition, 12–16, 38, 200
  audiotaping in, 212
  background knowledge, 209–210
  benefits, recording of, 231–232
  checklist, 233–235
  cycles in (*see* Elicit-document-test cycle,
    Elicit-document-implement-test
    cycle)
  debugging in, 279–280
  default meta-rules, 229
  deferring details in, 227–228
  difficulties in, 200
  documentation, 213–221
  domain selection considerations, 201–
    202
  example, 14–16
  expert selection considerations, 202–203
  initial steps, 212
  meetings
    atmosphere, 208–209
    focus, 209
    locating and scheduling, 204–207
  procedures, quasi-English, 213, 216
  recording knowledge, 230–232
  reminders, 231
  rules (*see* Knowledge acquisition rules)
  step in expert system development, 12–
    16
  test cases in, 225–226, 228–230
  tutorial, 209–211
  use of related acquired knowledge in,
    226

validation in, 300–302
verification in, 300–302, 308–310
videotaping in, 212
written materials in, 211–212
Knowledge acquisition cycle
  after implementation (*see* Elicit-docu-
    ment-implement-test cycle)
  before implementation (*see* Elicit-docu-
    ment-test cycle)
Knowledge acquisition rules, 213–214
  correspondence to implementation rules,
    254, 276–277, 286
  identifying, 219–220
  organizing, 219–220
  quasi-English, 213–214
Knowledge base
  in expert system basic architecture, 17
  multiple, for modularization, 283–284
Knowledge-based systems (*see* Expert
  systems)
Knowledge documentation, 214–215
  program specification by, 280
  quasi-English procedures in, 213, 216
  quasi-English rules in, 213–214
  readability, 216
  terminology in, 216–219
  updating, 227
Knowledge engineering, 3
Knowledge engineering software tool (*see*
  Software tool)
Knowledge engineers, 3
  in knowledge acquisition process, 12–16
  need for, 343
  talent of, 16
Knowledge implementation (*see*
  Implementation)
Knowledge implementer, functions and required skills, 63–64
Knowledge recording, 230–232
Knowledge representation, 17, 38
  checklist, 263
  deployment and, 318–319
  paradigms (*see* Knowledge representa-
    tion paradigms)
  rerepresentation, 259–262
  task decomposition and, 238–240
  technology transfer and, 318–319
  as step in expert system development, 16

Knowledge representation paradigms, 248–249
  of development environment, 160–162
  (*see also* AI paradigms, Frames, Object-oriented programming, Production rules, Programming language code)
Knowledge representer, functions and required skills, 62–63
Knowledge system (*see* Expert system)

Lisp, 18, 343
  in *COMPASS,* 258
  in KEE, 162
  (*see also* AI computer language)
Lisp machines
  in *COMPASS* deployment, 49, 331
  selection of for *COMPASS,* 37, 144–145, 154, 164
  training on in *COMPASS* project, 153

Macintosh, 50, 331
Mainframe, 164, 343
Maintainability, 281–295
  in deployment, 331–332
  paradigms for, 286–288
  style uniformity for, 284–286
Maintainer, functions and required skills, 71–72
Maintenance, of expert system, 50–51
Manager, functions and required skills, 58
Managing the development, checklist, 51–52
Marketing, for deployed expert system, 48
Messages, 27
  passing progam control using, 256–258
Method, 27–28
Mixed chaining, 23
Model-based reasoning, 343
Multiple experts
  benefits of, 194
  problems with, 192–193
Multiple inheritance, 27
Multiple-paradigm tool (*see* Software tool, multiple-paradigm)

Network Recovery (*see* NR)
Network recovery (NR), 85
No. 1 EAX, expert for, 178–179

No. 2 EAX
  description, 84
  experts, existence of, 100
  faults, 243–245
  internal testing, 85
  maintenance analysis of,
    as *COMPASS* domain, 35
    (*see also* *COMPASS* domain)
  maintenance experts, levels of, 85, 113
  maintenance messages
    analysis, 240–244
    causes, 85–87
    clusters, 240–244
    types, 85–86
  maintenance of, 84–95
    benefits of *COMPASS,* 103–104
  maintenance suggestions, 244–247
NR (Network Recovery), 85
NR20, 41
  maintenance analysis, task decomposition in, 238–240

Object, 27
Object-oriented programming, 27–28
  messages, 27
    passing program control by, 256–258
Operation, of expert system, 50
Operator, functions and required skills, 70–71
Outputs, ability to produce, 111–112

Parent-child relation, 24
  in multiple inheritance, 27
Payoff (*see* Expert systems, payoff)
PC, 164, 343
Performance requirement, of domain task, 125–126
Planning and managing the development, checklist, 51–52
Politics, company
  domain personnel and, 116–122
  system control and, 120–121
  system results and, 121
Production expert system, development, 45–48
Production rules, 18–23
  chaining in, 19–23

knowledge representation using, 254–256

uncertainty in, 19

(*see also If-then* rules)

Program implementation (*see* Implementation)

Programmers

and efficiency, 287

style modification of, 285

Programming language code, 258–259

Programming style, 284–286

conventions, 285–286

Project (*see* Expert system development project)

Project manager, functions and required skills, 58

Project technical leader, functions and required skills, 56–57

Prolog, 18, 343 (*see also* AI computer language)

Real-time requirement, of domain task, 125–126

Reimplementation, 269–271

Reliability, in deployment, 331–332

Relief device placement, expert system for, 99, 106

Reminders, 231

Remote Monitor and Control System (*see* RMCS)

Representing the knowledge, checklist, 263

Rerepresentation, 259–262

RMCS (Remote Monitor and Control System), 240, 247

in No. 2 EAX maintenance, 85

output, 85, 88

Rule (*see* Heuristic, *If-then* rules, Implementation rules, Knowledge acquisition rules, Production rules)

Rule checker, 309

Rulesets, 277–279

Scheduling, of expert system project, 32–33

Security

in deployment, 331–332

of development environment, 158

Selection

of domain expert (*see* Domain expert, selection of)

of domain (*see* Domain selection)

of hardware (*see* Hardware, selection)

of software tool (*see* Software tool, selection)

Shell (*see* Software tool)

Single expert

benefits of, 192–193

utilization of, 114

Slot, 23

SMA (System Maintenance Analysis), 85

SMA 110–112, use of expertise not experience, 191

Sofon, 219

Software

for deployment, 46

trends, 342–343

Software development tool (*see* Software tool)

Software engineering facilities in development environment, 155

Software tool, 16, 140

access to source code, 163

build or buy, 159–160

multiple-paradigm, 160–162

selection, 140–163, 165–168

checklist, 169–171

reconsidering, 270

step in expert system development, 16

(*see also* Environment, selection)

selector, functions and required skills, 60–61

single-paradigm, 160–162

use of computer language, 162

(*see also* Development environment)

Stability, of domain task, 129

Subclass, 24

Symbolic reasoning, use of in expert systems, 2, 106–107

System deployer, functions and required skills, 69–70

System introduction, 49

System maintainer, functions and required skills, 71–72

System Maintenance Analysis (*see* SMA)

System operator, functions and required skills, 70–71

Systems engineer, functions and required skills, 64–65

System tester and evaluator, functions and required skills, 68–69

Task knowledge, bounds, 115

Teachability, of domain task, 124

Technical documenter/writer, functions and required skills, 67–68

Technical leader, functions and required skills, 56–57

Technology transfer
 checklist, 339–340
 considerations during development, 316–319
 domain selection and, 316–318
 of expert system program, 319–321
 of expert system technology, 320–321
 implementation and, 318–319
 knowledge representation and, 318–319
 organizational roles, 321–324
 two aspects, 316, 319–321

Terminology, in knowledge documentation, 217, 218–219

Test cases
 availability, 125
 finding rule extents with, 229–230
 generating from other test cases, 228–229
 knowledge acquisition using, 225–226, 228–230

Tester and evaluator, functions and required skills, 68–69

Testing and evaluation
 of production expert system, 46–47
 step in expert system development, 16
 (see also Evaluation, Validation, Verification)

Tool developer, functions and required skills, 65

Trainer, functions and required skills, 70

Training, 324–328
 in AI techniques, tools, and systems, 325–326
 on development environment, 141, 153

on domain, 326–327
 on expert system program, 327–328
 in knowledge acquisition, 328
 of neophyte group, 324–325
 of users, operators, maintainers, 49

Tutorial, by domain expert, 209–211

User interface
 of development environment, 154
 domain selection and, 126–127

Users
 cooperativeness, 120
 desire for expert system, 118–119
 educating, 334–336
 expectations, 334–336
 functions and required skills, 73
 gaining acceptance of deployment by, 334–338
 threatened by expert system, 118–119

Validation, 300
 absolute, 303–305
 by consulting experts, 302–303
 against experts, 306–307
 by field testing, 307–308
 in knowledge acquisition, 300–302
 of production expert system, 46–47
 (see also Evaluation, Testing and evaluation)

Verification, 300, 308–310
 in knowledge acquisition, 300–302, 308–310
 of production expert system, 47
 (see also Evaluation, Testing and evaluation)

Videotaping, in knowledge acquisition, 212

Working memory, in expert system basic architecture, 17

Written material, use in expert system development, 124–125

Xerox, 150, 158–159 (see also Lisp machines)